For dear
Catherine —
my fellow
creative sister

this fantastic struggle

Love,
Lisa

this fantastic struggle

THE LIFE & ART OF ESTHER PHILLIPS

Lisa A. Miles

CREATIVE ARTS BOOK COMPANY

Berkeley ₰ California

For information contact:

Lisa A. Miles
35 Overlook St.
Pgh., PA 15214
mil284@aol.com

ISBN 088739-467-1

Library of Congress Catalog Number 2002110706

Printed in the United States of America

Cover illustration: Esther Phillips, *Untitled* watercolor on paper, 15" x 22"
Book and cover design: Meantimes Press, Steven Zahavi Schwartz
Artist photo: Joelle Levitt

The following who have generously given permission to use material from copyrighted works have requested the following to appear (Other information relating to permissible material can be found in the Introduction, as well as extensively in the Notes and Bibliography):

From *American Women Painters of the 1930s and 1940s: The Lives and Work of Ten Artists* 1991 Robert Henkes by permission of McFarland & Company, Inc., Box 611, Jefferson, NC 28640. *www.mcfarlandpub.com.*

THE EUGENIA HUGHES PAPERS. Permission granted by Manuscripts and Archives Division; The New York Public Library; Astor, Lenox and Tilden Foundations.

From THE FEMALE MALADY by Elaine Showalter, copyright 1985 by Elaine Showalter. Used by permission of Pantheon Books, a division of Random House, Inc.

From *I Could Be Mute: The Life and Work of Gladys Schmitt*, edited by Anita Brostoff, permission granted by Carnegie Mellon University Press, 1978.

From *Life & Architecture in Pittsburgh* by James Van Trump, permission granted by Pittsburgh History & Landmarks Foundation, 1983.

May Swenson's *"I'm One,"* taken from Rozanne R. Knudsen's *The Magic Pen of May Swenson.* Permission granted by Rozanne Knudsen; MacMillan 1993.

From NEW YORK SCHOOL: A CULTURAL RECKONING by Dore Ashton, copyright 1972 by Dore Ashton. Used by permission of Viking Penguin, a division of Penguin Putnam Inc.

From "Passion for Paint: The Life of Esther Phillips" by Meghan Shay, permission granted by *Western Pennsylvania History* magazine. Fall 1991 (vol. 74, no. 3)

From UP IN THE OLD HOTEL, AND OTHER STORIES, by Joseph Mitchell, copyright 1992 by Joseph Mitchell. Used by permission of Pantheon Books, a division of Random House, Inc.

From *Women of the Asylum: Voices From Behind The Walls, 1840–1945*, by Jeffrey L. Geller and Maxine Harris. 1994 by Jeffrey L. Geller and Maxine Harris, Anchor Books, Doubleday. Used by permission of Random House, Inc.

From *Women, the Arts & the 1920s in Paris and New York* by Kenneth W. Wheeler & Virginia Lee Lussier, reprinted by permission of Transaction Publishers: "Introduction" by Catharine R. Stimpson and "Shapes of the Feminine Experience in Art" by Sara Via Pais. Copyright 1982 Transaction Publishers.

From *Women's Madness: Misogyny or Mental Illness?* by Jane Ussher, permission granted by University of Massachusetts Press, 1991.

Early reviews from Pittsburgh Post-Gazette: Copyright/Pittsburgh Post-Gazette, 2002. All rights reserved. Reprinted with permission.

For my Mother, Father,

& 3 Brothers

Contents

Acknowledgments

I have many individuals and organizations to thank for their support and assistance in the research and writing of this book. Hopefully I will remember all. . . . As is mentioned in my Introduction, this work might not have been possible without the help and lent resources of Ken Chute, true champion of Esther's art. For the individuals I interviewed, many of them creative artists themselves: Glen Gress and Ed Evans—for opening a complete chapter of Esther's life to me, before unknown. Thanks to Sybil Barsky-Grucci, Dorothy Steinberg, Lois Monahan, Zan Knudsen, Lenore Monleon and Carole Evans. For four major artists who provided me a wealth of material and have since passed on—Milton Weiss, Mary Shaw Marohnic, Jamie Van Trump and Dr. Leon Arkus, Professor Emeritus of Carnegie Museum of Art.

It was Dr. Arkus who most substantiated for me the quality of Esther's work and the worthiness of writing about her in order to get that work recognized. Others, painters themselves, also helped by giving their positive estimation of the art—Will Barnet, who personally knew Esther, and my friends Evan Knauer, Matt Marcus and Ray Geiger, the latter who also gave much support early on in this project and who took photos of the institution.

I need to thank the New York Volunteer Lawyers for the Arts, for putting me in contact with attorney Lisa K. Eastwood. Ms. Eastwood successfully fought my case to have Esther's institution file from Harlem Valley State Hospital released to me for research and publication purpose. I appreciate her belief in my work, as well as Susan Hartman's belief, she of Hudson River Psychiatric Center (modern-day Harlem Valley Hospital).

Thanks to Sister Charlene Pavlik, former art therapist at Western Psychiatric in Pittsburgh, as well as everyone at Peoples Oakland, who taught me about the mentally ill. Thanks to Ellie Turk Barmen and Sandy Schneider of Pittsburgh's Jewish Community Center; Madelon Sheedy of the Johnstown Art Museum; Jane Scheuch of The Pittsburgh Foundation; Maureen Dawley of Carnegie Mellon University Libraries;

everyone at Pittsburgh History and Landmarks Foundation; Carolyn Schumacher and others at the Historical Society of Western Pennsylvania; the New York Public Library's Manuscript and Archives Division; and the Archives of American Art in New York City.

Thanks to Eric Seiden in Florida for converting all my old Apple floppy disks to Word. (I wrote this manuscript longhand, then put to my Apple II—which I was still using in the mid '90s) Particular thanks to Carnegie Library of Pittsburgh—the Pennsylvania Room, Art Department, and Peggy Domer of the Foundation Center. I need to credit for inspiration the authors whose work I have excerpted throughout to better detail early Greenwich Village, american art or mental illness. Special thanks for such inspiration go to Jeffrey L. Geller and Maxine Harris for their *Women of the Asylum*.

Some financial assistance for the publication came from the Pennsylvania Council on the Arts' SOS Funds—thanks to Caroline Savage for her help. And appreciation goes out to The Pittsburgh Foundation for generous late-stage help. I'd like to also thank everyone at Creative Arts Books for believing in my writing—my copyeditor Lynn Park, my publisher Don Ellis, and the Creative Arts staff. I'm also appreciative of the consideration and support given me by Maria Carpico at the Pittsburgh Post-Gazette; Marlena Davidian of Transaction Publishers; Carol Christiansen and Rebecca Heisman of Random House; and Sheila McGrath of Joseph Mitchell's Literary Estate.

Love and thanks to my family for their support of all of my creative work and their interest in this book. Special thanks to my brother Mark, who did some early editorial review of the manuscript—your comments were dear to me. And my brother Eric—who twice gave me hand-me-down computer systems from his Silicon Valley office. Thanks to Uncle Carmen for thinking of me and my work, and thanks to a special Aunt Diane in Vermont, who has always been genuinely interested in the course of my creative life.

Lastly, and very significantly, certain friends deserve mention. My dear sister Susan Spier, who lost her battle with cancer, always urged me to have faith in my work. It was also she who suggested that I talk to Glen and Ed to see if they knew of an "Esther Phillips" when they were in New York. Love and thanks to Adrienne Wehr, truly my artistic mentor and soul-sister, for all the encouragement and love and connections made for me over this and many projects. Thanks as well to Erin Snyder, who encouraged me tremendously and took such glee in reviewing the twists and turns of Esther's story as it was revealing itself to me. For Laurie Tarter here in Pittsburgh, Tina Gelfand in D.C., and Catherine Singstad in San Francisco—thanks. And to Lauren-Judith Krizner and Marcus & Larry in New York—I'm glad we got to celebrate together that afternoon when I made my find at the New York Public Library! And a final thanks to my partner Jan, for his love, support and companionship during the last stages of getting the book together.

INTRODUCTION

There's nothing quite like a discovery of something valuable long hidden from the touches of the present day. Whether it be an artifact preserved in ice, an antique or art object, or forgotten words or maxims of a past civilization, the usual feelings evoked at such a find are exhilaration, even exultation. It's especially gratifying to come upon not only the lost treasures, but a better understanding of the life of the makers, orators, creators of the objects, words, thoughts suspended in time.

Though it's possible to simply stumble across these prizes without premeditation, usually it does begin with a fascination. Something that captivates the imagination, and engages the mind and spirit. One that intellectually, emotionally and even magically draws you in, and prepares you to follow signs pointing toward a place of reward, and to make efforts sometimes difficult, yet do-able. For the author it was in becoming minimally acquainted with the background of a deceased woman artist who was behind some watercolors hung at a Pittsburgh gallery in the fall of 1991. There was something in the intriguing paintings themselves, and the story begun by a couple articles accompanying the show that pulled me in. They created an intriguing context upon which to do more researching.

In reviewing the material on Esther, one distinguishing fact perhaps unduly characterized who she was—the fact that, for a while, she had been institutionalized. At the time of viewing the show, I had been working as a vocational coordinator at Peoples Oakland, a community psychosocial rehabilitation center for those with mental illness, on the University of Pittsburgh campus in Oakland. (I essentially developed work leads for clients with manic depression, borderline personality disorders and schizophrenia.) I observed that Esther's paintings from the institution period poignantly depicted scenes from what was obviously an otherworldly existence. I believed they likely showed a creative woman struggling to understand and express the machinations that brought her to temporary dis-ease. The works vividly depicted life in the state hospital—dancing, ethereal woman-figures cornered by straight-edged, elusive doctors and nurses.

Ironically my involvement with Esther began by walking the same first steps that a friend of hers, Merle Hoyleman, would do when face-to-face with the intriguing institution paintings. With some success, I made several calls to professionals within the Pittsburgh mental health community, to market the work to people who might really appreciate it. I called fellow mental health professionals at Western Psychiatric, with hope of getting doctors and art therapists down to the now-defunct Carson Street Gallery, perhaps to make a purchase. Little did I yet know of the extent and fascinating details to which this approach had been carried out before, in a Pittsburgh of the 1950s.

I saw that not a whole lot was known about this woman artist who, now posthumously, was given some gallery space. She had been a native Pittsburgher, struggling with being an artist and artist only in a blue-collar town. Depicted as a bit sassy and free-spirited, she left for New York City while the country was still in the Depression, single-mindedly aspiring to have a better time of it in at least a more exciting surrounding. There she lived a typical artist's minimal existence, literally starving at times. There was little hint of the plenty of uniquely colorful experiences she lived out amidst her travails, in the lascivious Greenwich Village, with friends and the famous alike. It was presumed that, because she was so oft run down, her mental health gave out, and correspondence to Pittsburgh over the following years would place her in some upstate New York hospital, unknown which. It was a sketchy tale.

I was curious, definitely wanted to know more, and decided to go over to the Carnegie Library of Pittsburgh. An avid reader, but poor creative artist myself, the library was second home to me. (And even had been, I would soon learn, to Esther, Merle, and other friends in her life. . . .) I strongly desired to see if I could come up with any more on this woman who for some reason sounded to me like a real spirit to be reckoned with (in life, that is). In digging up her history, I found that all too true, and as I look back now, I can't help but humorously wonder over some of the tangled tales of loves and other various incidentals that washed ashore posthumously, during my research. Though quite entertaining, they did foil my way at times along the journey of finding the detail of Esther Phillips' life.

What I saw from the onset was a woman who painted very original works in the 1920s and '30s here in Pittsburgh, much like my very own present-day artist and musician friends. It seemed that Esther was little known or respected, and yet at that Pittsburgh gallery her beautiful art now deservedly hung, and in yellowed library artist files more words describing her originality and intensity were sitting, long-buried, a testament that she indeed produced very interesting work. After reviewing the extent of her 1930s reviews, I decided I wanted to write about her, to bring her work and her story to life, and though sidetracked at times, I've not unmade that decision since.

This Fantastic Struggle depicts a woman who endures much hardship, including institutionalization, just so that she can pursue a life of painting, and one who attempts to cope with a society that does not duly recognize artistic efforts. This book is indeed a biography, but also the tale of many forgotten artists, throughout history, and working unto this day. Woven together with letters, interviews, scholarly source material, art work, and institution documents acquired after my petition for their Court Ordered release, the book, I believe, becomes a unique cultural essay.

Esther's story is told through innumerable primary source documents and dialogues, and of course, her work, which is shown extensively throughout. There is correspondence between Esther and Merle Hoyleman, not only a dear friend, but an agent of sorts for her art. The devotion and diligence she expended as both is startlingly apparent in these letters, and also in scores of journals that reveal the intensity of her own creative life. The effects of fellow Village artist Eugenia Hughes, all nine boxes of which sit codified in storage of the New York Public

Library, illustrate another remarkable bond of friendship. They spin a tale in themselves, and testify to the strong literary tradition of earlier times. Perhaps the greatest find among them—which includes everything from actual art work of Esther and "Jerry" to diaries galore—are original copies of letters Esther wrote while institutionalized.

The voice of our main character surfaces as well out of transcriptions of visits that a niece took almost upon Esther's death bed, and especially eerily arises from the institution documents. The intact file from the 1940s provided a breathtaking glimpse into a patient's very unusual time at asylum.

Secondary source documents and dialogues, no less detailed, also tell Esther's story. Over twenty extensive interviews were conducted in Pittsburgh and New York, fourteen with individuals who personally knew Esther. Their words make vibrantly apparent the fact that they placed the same intensity and commitment that Esther did on living a creative life. In 1992, I brought Esther's art to the attention of Director Emeritus of Pittsburgh's Carnegie Museum of Art, Dr. Leon Arkus, and after looking at photos of her work, he defined her as a sophisticated independent artist with original vision, whose art, though evocative of the primitive, was "by no means naive." Ironically, senior administrators at the museum from the 1920s through the 1950s purchased many of Esther's works, but they are unaccounted for, quite possibly still sitting in storage to this day in the bowels of the cultural institution.

Excellent reviews of Esther's early work in Pittsburgh are reproduced throughout, as is information taken from the Archives of American Art in New York about the Washington Square Outdoor Shows, a mainstay for struggling Village artists. Also woven into the tapestry of an already intricately layered design of a life is scholarly material about the Federal Arts Projects, the Abstract Expressionists, and perhaps especially, women artists, and mental illness. I also visited the institution, meeting with a current-day administrator totally supportive of my research. Scores of secondary source support are carefully integrated throughout, and I tried to judiciously underscore commentary with my own perspective as a former mental health professional and especially as a working creative artist for the last ten years. (Though I have held a variety of professional positions post-college, none have been as stimulating or fulfilling as my own quest to make a living as a musician, my main artistic medium.)

The end result is hopefully a story with broad appeal and impact, informing and engaging readers at multiple levels. Because the world would not view her and her friends' work as meaningful, I write Esther's story for all the creative artists out there who know too well her fantastic struggle, but especially I write to many more, a vast audience probably unfamiliar with this challenging yet joyful existence known as the creative life, in hope to bring an artist's existence truly into view.

Before getting to Esther's story, some information about correspondence, interviews, the usage and referencing of source material, and the reproduction of the artwork:

I chose to have many letters between various parties, as well as some documents, graphically reproduced in the book. Those that are not are textually reproduced in original form or excerpted within the text. Because Esther's scrawl is less easy to comfortably read than others' writings, the graphic reproductions of her original letters are shown bordering the textually reproduced version for some choice correspondence.

As for the interviews I conducted with people who knew Esther, some surface in a real-time fashion, so that there would be an interesting give-and-take of voices throughout the book. All individuals that I spoke with, save for family, wholeheartedly consented to my using material learned from them for the publication of *This Fantastic Struggle*; as well, many interviews were tape-recorded. In many instances that seemed to warrant it, I chose to transcribe even unfinished thoughts and pauses within the conversations, indicated at times by ellipsis dots.

There are extensive Notes at end, organized by chapter, and a full Bibliography which categorizes the source material as the following: Primary Source Collections/Correspondence/Documents; Other

Collections/Documents; Interviews; Books/Periodicals/Other by Subject—Esther, Arts, Arts/Women, Arts/Village, Mental Illness, Mental Illness/Women, and Other.

My research and writing could probably not have been carried out without the material amassed by Ken Chute, a Pittsburgher who became interested in finding out about Esther's life in the early 1980s. As is noted in text and end reference section, Ken extensively conducted interviews with family and compiled his own research material. He spoke in person and via phone with family members and took notes of these conversations. Because his interest was genuine in getting Esther's art better known, he was given copies of notes and other written material about Esther that family had compiled, as well as certain photos—with the understanding that he could do with as he wished, in order to promote Esther's art.

Ken organized his information into meticulous files, he xeroxed letters and documents, and he photographed paintings that various family members showed him. Because his desire has been like my own, to bring Esther's story and art to a national public, he forwarded all this material to me in 1991. This was only after many years of his own admirable work on behalf of Esther, as detailed in the second-to-last chapter. Ken allowed me this material, on loan for the last decade, as a point upon which to embark on my own research. He gave me his permission to use this material for the publication of *This Fantastic Struggle*.

The majority of the artwork of Esther Phillips that is reproduced throughout this book and on its cover, unless specified otherwise, is held by no specific collection. Most of the paintings were at one point in Merle Hoyleman's possession, and many were found among her effects after she died. It was officially declared by the State of Pennsylvania that Merle had "no estate" because she, like Esther, had no surviving dependents. Thus, as there was no official private party owner of the works, a social worker who was assigned to Merle's case called upon Ken Chute to safekeep them.

There are some works that in recent years have migrated to the family's possession, and there are likely some works that Esther never got to send to Merle, and that went directly to family (her later life story will clarify this). At the time of Ken's photographing many of the works of Esther's that are included in this book, none had yet sold. It has been solely my choice (with the responsibility that comes with that) to show these works, and to include all written material, photos and knowledge gained via all these sources for *This Fantastic Struggle*. I believe it is what Esther would have wanted.

Lisa A. Miles, Winter 2002

Finding yourself
In so doing, finding a life,
  an identity that intensely is yours

Dear Merle:

Your recent letter reveals that you have finally lost faith in mankind and outward courtesy and promises. Such disillusionment is sometimes very helpful. In the past you no doubt counted on the seeming willingness of certain individuals in high places who showed interest in your talents and abilities but in reality were more concerned with themselves.

I have had a shocking experience this week. I happened to pass the neighborhood where I remembered (from the address you gave some time ago) Esther Phillips lived. I decided to call on her and mention you. But she was not in her room. In fact I wasn't sure she lived there at all because there was no trace of her name anywhere in the house. After inquiring of several persons I was directed to the renting office and there met the landlord, a congenial gentleman by name of Strunsky. And this man told me a story of terrible suffering endured by this artist Phillips. It was hard to believe the stark tragedy of trying to exist on nothing. I left my name and address saying I would like to see Miss Phillips and help in some way if I can. A few days later she wrote me and after a visit soon afterward I learned that it was all too sadly true. Esther Phillips is in a serious situation. She is without funds and little prospects of selling her work. And one must eat to live. I would have liked to help her but as it happens I have been sinking in debt day by day because of demands of an increase in legal support. In other words I have been borrowing my way as I go along trying to make ends meet. It is all very disheartening, I assure you. I have taken her to a place to eat and would give her whatever small sum I can afford, but that, as you know, will not solve the problem. She needs work immediately if she is to exist. I am trying to contact people who might give her a job, but she admits that her capabilities are limited and besides she is in a terribly upset condition, very high strung and that makes matters worse. I hope help comes in time, it's certainly such a pity such things are going on in a land of plenty.

By all means I advise you to stick to the Project while it lasts. As long as it gives you the necessities of life it means something. I often wish that I was earning much less than I do and be free and clear of an insufferable relationship long regretted. As it is, life is just a huge farce.

Esther Phillips asked me to convey her apologies for not answering your letter. Her nervous state of mind prevents clear concentration and the will to write. She knows you will understand.

As for myself there is little I can say, other than what I have already mentioned. Seeing others suffer causes me to believe that my misery is not intolerable. Yet my life is not what it should be.

How are things with you getting on? Any improvement?

Hope to hear from you soon.

As ever your friend,
Harold [Winters]

PITTSBURGH

Chapter One

"SHE NEEDED TO PAINT"[1]

*E*sther Phillips was born June 12, 1902, in an eastern village of the former Soviet Union. Her father, David Phillipovsky—his name shortened once in the United States—worked a farm. He was a Talmudic scholar, a Russian Jew dissatisfied with the way of life laid out for himself and his family. He was prevented from owning property, and only with the help of a village Gentile friend could he open a small inn and be licensed to sell liquor.[2] His wife, Nettie Kahn, bore three children in Russia; Esther was the third of two girls and a boy. After the family settled in Pittsburgh, Pennsylvania, it grew by an additional boy and three more girls.

At the beginning of the century, there was imminent conflict between Russia and Japan. Being drafted prompted David's his decision to bring his family to America. He evaded his government's order by emigrating in 1905 via New York City. Esther thus became a citizen of the United States by virtue of her father's naturalization. However, getting documentation to verify this caused a significant delay in her getting on the Works Progress Administration's Art Project in the late 1930s in New York City.

Nettie already had a brother in the States, and David had four; they helped the two struggling parents adjust to life outside Russia. Having visited the States a few years earlier, David decided against settling in New York City. He took his family instead to Pittsburgh, in southwestern Pennsylvania, moving into a tiny row house on Wick Street, in a section of the city known as the Hill District. Jutting impressively from the eastern end of the downtown of Pittsburgh, "The Hill" had begun to be populated en masse in the 1880s by Central and Eastern Europeans, many of Jewish descent. It was the first stop upon arrival to the city of European immigrants, and of African-Americans upon emancipation.

Due to his own striving, and with his brother's encouragement, David Phillipovsky and family no longer had to live under the oppression of the homeland. They were now settling into a life in Pittsburgh, this highly industrialized city of iron and steel. Pittsburgh had its share of problems—labor, heavy dirt and smog from the coke furnaces, and certainly a plenitude of slums—home to a large segment of the labor force. Esther's father began as a salesman. For a time, he sold clothing door-to-door with help from a loan given him by his brother-in-law, James. He was able to support his family throughout the years by being a resourceful salesman, and his hard work allowed the family to move into the middle class. Much later he invested in real estate in the historic Mexican War Streets section of Pittsburgh's North Side.[3]

FIG. 1   The Phillips family circa 1906. David and wife Nettie with children, from left, Sylvia, Barney, Dorothy, and Esther.

The Phillips family quickly became acclimated to life in the new country, and Esther's parents surely felt themselves members of the thriving Jewish community in the Hill District. On Center Avenue in the Hill was the Irene Kaufmann Settlement, an educational and social gathering point for Jewish Pittsburghers. The I.K.S., as it was commonly known, sponsored many cultural events and aimed to raise the standard of life in the community. This community center had a division known as the Neighborhood Art School, and young Esther was one of a very small number of students to make consistent use of the facility for painting and drawing. Structured classes met after school and during evening hours. The instruction was "reinforced by the desire to preserve in artistic production the student's unique imagination." A later promotional pamphlet provided a history of the philosophies and practices governing the art school: "The student, disciplined by fundamentals, is given complete freedom of expression pictorially. There is no definite course outlined, but each is watched closely and is led to a fuller realization of his ideas. The student is free to make use of the most important mediums. Instruction is given in drawing, modelling and creative painting."[4]

The Neighborhood Art School was a good place for the young Esther to spend much of her childhood time, as she was dissuaded from such activity at home, where she often drew on the backs and sides of letters she found around the house. According to her younger sister, Dorothy, the sibling who was always closest to her, "She was always making pictures and running around with them." She would also draw in the margins of her school papers—starting with the Miller Grade School in the Lower Hill. "She would scribble and doodle away anywhere she found pencils and papers, and on the walls. . . ."[5] Esther herself, towards her life's end, shared reflections with a niece, Dorothy's daughter Millie Silverstein. Esther told of feeling isolated within the family, of an unaffectionate mother with whom she didn't get along and who "chased her with a broom," and of younger brother, Barney, who constantly kicked her.[6] Likely Esther's constant picture-making antics contributed at least in small measure to some of the responses from family.

Certainly nothing stands out as much about her childhood as the influence of her time spent within the Irene Kaufmann Settlement. It was not just a retreat from what was the start of an unhappy home situation. Esther gained much technically at the Neighborhood Art School. She was given a small room at the community center, a studio also used at the time by Samuel Rosenberg, who became a beloved Pittsburgh painter. Rosenberg was both friend and teacher, peer and mentor, to Esther.

The Art School strove to "liberaliz[e] the individual who attends by giving breadth to his interests, and in [the] cultivating [of] highest emotions and noblest desires, to implant in the growing generation a yearning for beauty, and to awaken in students their particular potentialities." Then, to "cultivate these . . . in an orderly fashion to the highest degree so that students' ultimate aim in life shall be beauty in their respective fields of endeavor."[7] So it was at this Neighborhood Art School that Esther first got a taste of the liberating force of what was making itself known as her one desire—painting. She spent a good deal of her time outside of school equally outside the home, pursuing her love of art, because she felt misunderstood from mother, brothers, and sisters. She found refuge and sense of community with fellow artists at a young age. From Sam Rosenberg, whom young Pittsburgh artists much respected, Esther received superb early tutelage and motivation.

It seems Esther did care for her father, with whom she shared bits of closeness. Like her, he had an affinity for cats. He was attentive to the needs of strays, luring them with saucers of milk and food scraps. "Well, they're hungry,"[8] he remarked to family—a retort not so much plaintive as practical. These creatures surfaced throughout Esther's life in her paintings, and in the early 1940s, she lived with one whose challenged existence was curiously not unlike her own. The family never embraced any of these creatures enough to bring them indoors, but throughout Esther's growing up, cats filled the yards wherever the family lived, and this was especially the case in the small backyard and alley behind their home at 5531 Jackson Street. The family would later move to this Highland Park section of Pittsburgh around 1920, after Esther enters the Carnegie Institute of Technology.

It was in the Jackson Street house that Esther had title to one of the two attic rooms. Soon to be the bohemian, she found the garret appealing to her. She tore bed sheets to use as rags to clean her brushes, much to the ire of her mother. "Esther would say she didn't have anything else to use. Oh, my mother would raise hell about it! She would always be hemming the sheets." There was little besides art on Esther's mind. "From childhood on she was different. She wanted to draw and to paint and buy materials . . . and she ate her meals whenever she felt like it." Indeed Esther did not get too involved with family matters growing up, but the family's animosity over her art work fueled this distance. Dorothy later surmised that "she may have been a bit mad at my parents, because they didn't encourage her in her art more. But they had seven children. . . ."[9]

◊ ◊ ◊

Before Esther would have an attic studio to call her own, though, bringing her painting activities and her artist's habits closer to disapproving eyes at home, she spent her teen years getting to know a little better the world of art that existed beyond her own brush. Come 1916, though the Neighborhood Art School would stay on Center Avenue on the Hill, within the IKS, some other Jewish community activities began to be held at the YMHA, which had just relocated to a new home on the corner of Jumonville Street and Fifth Avenue.

Fourteen-year-old Esther would have been acquainted with this center, still close to her home, in a section of the city known as Soho, a neighborhood at the southern slope of the Hill District, overlooking the Monongahela River and across to Pittsburgh's Southside. A little further east of Soho was Oakland, which was fast becoming the educational and cultural center of Pittsburgh. The Carnegie Library opened in 1895, followed shortly thereafter by the Carnegie Music Hall and the Museums of Art and Natural History, and the Carnegie Institute of Technology. Groundbreaking began on the University of Pittsburgh circa 1915.

The library and the art museum were just a trolley ride through Soho, uphill and around the bend of Fifth Avenue. Esther's art education outside of the Neighborhood Art School continued at these two places, where she studied the major artists. She took particular liking to Pisan and Derain.[10] Recent changes in the American art world also awakened her senses. The real shake-up had just begun with the New York Armory Show of 1913, which brought European and new American modern art to a public still trying to get used to the many changes wrought a few years earlier by artists of the Ash Can School, and just before that the post-Impressionists.

At the start of the new century, art in America was still ruled by traditionalists—realist painters approved by that staid founding body of American art, the National Academy of Design. Membership "was essential to an artist's prestige in that era."[11] Even when Impressionism made its way into American painting, and the dark realist canvasses typical of the traditionalists turned muted, with misty tones, often "drenched in one pervasive color,"[12] the studies—often of genteel women and children, in fashionable interiors or in comfortable street corner scenes—were still conservative in nature, and backed by the Academy.

The Ash Can artists, though, were a group of painters and sculptors in New York, all believing in a freedom of expression that the National Academy just did not seem to promote, though their works still had realistic content matter. Their "raw, realistic views of lower-class city life"[13] were both emblematic of, and influenced by, this muckraking era at the end of the century's first decade. They did not seek the refined subjects chosen by impressionists, who avoided dirty urban street scenes. Because the Ash Can artists themselves "began to sponsor independent exhibitions," independent-thinking American artists could finally "begin to show their work through courageous dealers, instead of being limited to the conservative, juried salons, which frequently rejected their paintings."[14]

A major Parisian show in 1908 presented the works of Andre Derain and Matisse to a world public, which also helped the avant-garde cause. Thus until the 1913 Armory Show, the Ash Can artists and the post-Impressionists had been the avant-garde, causing controversy by their attention to social causes and "new looking" art. The 1913 Armory show introduced the country, surely as well as the young but artistically aware Esther, to the scandalously different works of Picasso, Van Gogh, Gauguin, and Marcel Duchamp, the great experimenter. A move toward abstractionism—taking the easily identifiable "subject" out of a piece of art—had begun, and a scant few American collectors now began to accumulate such work.

Always very self-directed, Esther saw to her own art education after daytime hours spent in high school. She sought out knowledge about painting techniques, as well as information about those who were charting the new artistic territory. Dorothy remembered Esther painting a great deal at this time, as well as also playing the piano a bit, an instrument she had access to at the I.K.S. Their father, who was "terribly interested in education," wanted each of his children to finish high school.[15] But though her brothers would take college preparatory classes, in 1919 Esther graduated with a concentration in business from Ralston Preparatory High School, at 15th and Penn Avenue on the Lower Hill. This would prepare her a place in the technical job market when she left school, a customary preparation at the time for many young women.

When of age, all of the Phillips children were expected to work to contribute to the household, a practice common to many American immigrant families. Often these contributions were a necessity to put food on the table, but in the Phillips family, they helped insure the boys' attendance at the University of Pittsburgh. (Later, their studies paid off, as Dorothy stated, evidently echoing family pride, "My older brother became a well-known criminal lawyer. And my younger brother was a Ph.D. chemist at Pitt. He was well-known there, a brilliant young man."[16]) As for Esther, her parents expected marriage. She, of course, had entirely different things on her mind. She had begun to study the French artists on her own and dreamed of a trip to Paris for an art education.[17] But her situation was unlike that of Mary Cassatt, the famed Pittsburgh-born artist whose family affluence and encouragement enabled her to study at that European seat of artistic liberation. Cassatt, like scores of other fortunates, didn't quite have to display symptoms of the fierce determination that drove Esther to follow her art. She and so many more less-privileged artists had to struggle to attain technical proficiency, then produce outstanding work, yet hardly be acknowledged.

Esther couldn't go to Paris, but she stubbornly resisted her family's attempts to train and domesticate her, as she enrolled in Carnegie Institute of Technology's College of Fine Arts in the autumn of 1919. She didn't have to submit a portfolio through admissions, as she was considered for the time being (and would remain so) an "unclassified" student, because of her part-time status. Her Permanent Record has the family's address still as Wick Street, on The Hill, and has as her birth date June 12, 1901.[18] She likely gave this date because it was required, for some reason, that "men candidates must not be less than seventeen and women eighteen years of age."[19]

The College's Introduction to Course Descriptions of the time put forth "Suggestions Concerning the Choice of a Course in Art":

> The man who does not enjoy the thing he must do daily, who is not engaged in work he would rather do than anything else in the world, never accomplishes the best results of which he is capable. He fails to reach his own highest development and does not render his best service. He is not happy. This is particularly true in the arts where enthusiasm counts so much and good work is not done unless the man throws his whole self into it . . . An artist is one who instinctively feels and perceives the spirit and significance of things and who expresses them in beautiful forms . . . [He] must be willing to dedicate himself to his profession and make any sacrifices of time and energy and personal comforts that may be involved.20

Esther was thus enrolled in the Painting and Illustration Department in the College of Fine Arts, where she began to study illustration and design, still life and portraiture, and a general history of art and design. She took figure drawing and composition classes, and courses in cast figures and color. Anatomy lectures were just made available to women art students in 1914, due to standards long entrenched at the National Academy of Design and the Pennsylvania Academy of Fine Art. The availability and quality of women's artistic training certainly lagged behind men's. Following a tradition set forth by the Europeans, women had not been allowed until the 1840s; they were not able to draw from the male nude at the National until 1877, and that was in a segregated class.[21] Some of Esther's classes at Carnegie Institute of Technology were still segregated in 1920.

Esther later told a confidante about this college time. He stated of her admission, "Because of the financial situation at home, it was necessary . . . to work her way through college." Esther would recall having worked hard, that "her health was not very good and that she was always a little nervous."[22] Friends and family would remember Esther working short-lived odd jobs outside her art to try to make money. At one point she took a job as a bookkeeper—but she ended up doodling in the margins and lost the position. The tuition fee for 1919 at Carnegie Institute of Technology was $25 a quarter, or $20 a quarter for evening students, which Esther was much of the time. Art supplies, always costly, added approximately $100 a quarter to the cost of tuition. Paying for those paint materials was a challenge Esther, like all artists, would constantly face throughout her life. While she was still a young woman living in her third-floor garret, she looked to supply her art before all else.

Fellow artist Mary Shaw Marohnic had known Esther since grade school, and had attended "Carnegie Tech" at about the same time. She remembered Esther's minimal way of life as a young adult, especially her poor eating habits, something attested to by many friends. Esther often visited Mary at her home in Crafton, in the South Hills of Pittsburgh. She would walk many miles to share new paintings with her friend, then stay for a meal and a hot bath. Especially after leaving her parent's Jackson Street residence later in the mid 1920s, Esther often turned up on friends' porches, "to set up her easel and paints whenever she could be assured an offer of a good meal."[23]

Esther may not have been successful in working to earn money, but Marohnic remembered her as "extremely diligent in her work—working a great deal all the time on her art." Esther's friend recollected that Carnegie Tech's art department was quite fine during the 1920s and that it included many "bold women artists as students." Students studied the

German painters, which were on exhibit at the Carnegie Art Museum. "Esther could give a good criticism. She was well-educated at Tech and other places. She had the best teachers in the world there." Mary even stressed their tutelage beyond mere academics: "I think the Fine Art Department helped almost everybody that went there to cope in the outer world, or whatever you want to call it—the outer zoo."[24]

Esther's marks in college ranged from below average in the history of costume, in French, and anatomy to very good in art composition and still-life painting courses. Her ability to do still-life paintings became evident in the interiors she did early in her career. She struggled to earn money for her tuition and art supplies, but the college likely provided some financial help. Students could offset their expenses through work on various creative projects in the art department, or by assisting instructors. It is more likely, considering that Esther's academic record left a bit to be desired, that her financial assistance came through the former, upon completion of painting projects within the department. The way Esther tells it, later in life, is that a faculty member of Carnegie Tech paid her way her third year—an unsubstantiated and unlikely, yet amusing, version of her financial aid.

Esther played hooky, sometimes cutting morning academic classes to take outside jobs, and attending only in the afternoon. She was put on probation numerous times for this, as detailed in her "Permanent Record." She told her niece that she quit school when the Carnegie Museum commissioned her to paint a mural in their cafeteria, which sits below the adjoining Carnegie Library.[25] This is quite possible, although no documentation or physical evidence survives to that effect to this day. Carnegie Tech's College of Fine Arts officially dropped Esther in June 1922, after she had attended three school years. Though extremely interested in and persistent with her painting, Esther was not quite the diligent student.

Chapter Two

"THE WHOLE TOWN WAS ON A PARTY"[1]

*E*sther was the only one in her family with an artistic drive, but she would shortly find community with plenty of others like herself. It had indeed become obvious to all within her home that "she had no inclination to do anything that would give her an income other than paint. She was so wrapped up in art nothing else mattered."[2] She had been sparked from very early on at the Irene Kaufmann Settlement to search for beauty and meaning in life, and to access this through her own unique talent. But her striving to be a painter did her little good in the eyes of family. Though she scrambled to pay for the formal art education she wanted, and desperately tried to pay for art materials on her own, Esther's parents, and even her brothers and sisters, viewed her efforts to be an artist as a selfish act. They believed that she should make money but not for her own purposes—attending to her own needs and desires.

Esther's parents would have spent any income she contributed to help send the boys off to college, the most practical investment, per-haps, for the family—or at least for the boys. The righteous sense that Esther should put back into the household in this manner was quite strong, though certainly not unusual for American families of this time. Esther would not buy into such self-sacrifice, however. She was begin-ning to run into the same impasses that many other artists, particularly women, faced. As Wendy Slatkin, author of *Women Artists in History From Antiquity to the 20th Century* states, "some cultures have de-manded that women be demure, self-effacing, docile and obedient.

These behavioral qualities, combined with socioeconomic restrictions . . . are not likely to encourage the professional excellence and independence needed for a woman to become an outstanding artist."[3]

Esther later readily acknowledged the hostility she felt toward her parents and siblings while growing up, but she dealt with this bitterness by engaging herself even further in her work. Prompted by the wise urgings set forth by the Neighborhood Art School, as well as Carnegie Tech, urgings to throw oneself thoroughly behind what one enjoys and does well, here, early in life, Esther was claiming her due. She was already acting on that growing self-knowledge, the type of wisdom and action that many people never quite attain or come to do throughout their lifetime. But what of that knowledge, what of those capabilities and actions if not rewarded by family, or more importantly, as Esther would soon see, society as a whole? She would be extremely productive her entire life—painting. But what of that productivity if it brings little money?

Frustrated that she was expected to support others' needs before her own, Esther began to detach from family at the end of her college years, and this detachment was not without consequence. It was an especially stressful time for her, marked by irritability and withdrawal into herself. Shortly after Carnegie Tech dropped her, she had a tonsillectomy and was treated for anemia, which recurred throughout her life.[4] She left her garret, her first home-studio, behind, when she moved out of her parent's home around 1923. She was twenty-one. Despite wresting herself from an oppressive home environment and moving toward a vision of a self-designed life, the lack of familial respect still bothered her tremendously.

Sybil Barsky, a sculptress, was one of the first persons Esther lived with after leaving the Highland Park home. The two women shared a third-floor attic on South Craig Street in Oakland. It was minimally furnished with a couple of cots, a card table, and a hot plate.[5] Sybil remembered Esther's repeated remarks about her unsuccessful attempts to work her way through school and her open grieving that her parents did not pay her college expenses. She especially recalled Esther's "terrible hatred of mother." She got the distinct impression that this woman strongly disapproved of Esther's lifestyle as an artist.[6] "She kept a busy social schedule, and she paint[ed] doggedly, though generally not in view of others."[7] As Esther's roommate, Sybil did witness some of Esther's painting, and she observed work in watercolors only. "Her movements were very quick," stated Sybil, who believed that Esther "couldn't sustain an oil canvas—didn't have the attention span,"[8] but a later art review repudiates this, as Esther began working in oils, and with some success, shortly after this time.

"They were struggling," said Dorothy, of both Sybil and Esther. She tried to help her sister out during the time in particular that she lived with her artist friend. "Esther never had enough money, and she was always looking for an apartment." And an apartment for Esther had to be less a living space than a working space for her art. Dorothy herself was a young woman just out of high school. "I wanted to do the best I could, but I couldn't do much but hand her a dollar or two."[9] A telling story that surprisingly surfaces by many who knew Esther, friends and family alike, communicates her lack of frugality. Sybil's version, the most detailed, was that, at a rare time when Esther held an extra $15 in her hand (or $40, as the story migrated), "She proceeded to walk all the way downtown to Kaufmann's to buy a hat for the entire amount, and then to walk all the way back."[10] Later Sybil would say that Esther actually "did this lots whenever she got her hands on some money."[11]

Dorothy, becoming the family treasurer, admirably gathered family money together to pay Esther's rent while she lived with Sybil. Dorothy was working at the Warner Theatre Building in downtown Pittsburgh at the time. On her monthly visit to Esther, she would "give the $15 directly to the landlord." She felt that if she gave the money to her sister, who was still trying her hand at an assortment of odd jobs, that she would spend it at A. B. Smith, where she had credit to buy art supplies.[12] Though in need, Esther likely felt uncomfortable accepting this money from her family, from whom she had just made a break, and who disagreed so strongly with her choice of career.

At the same time she was trying to make it on her own, Esther, no longer a student, gravitated toward the Associated Artists of Pittsburgh

(AAP), founded in 1910. Its purpose was to foster a love for the fine arts and to give the general public a better understanding and deeper appreciation of the work of Pittsburgh painters and illustrators. This certainly spoke to Esther. Fueled by frustration over familial disrespect and a real need to connect with other artists, she joined by submitting work for jury consideration. As a member, she began to enjoy and benefit from being around people with similar aspirations and frustrations.

Many Carnegie Institute of Technology fine art students were connected with the Associated Artists, elevating the professionalism of the group. Included was Mary Ballou Shaw, as Mary Shaw Marohnic (Esther's Carnegie Tech friend) was known then. (Due to several marriages and intermittent returns to her maiden name, she would be known as Mary Ballou Shaw, Mary Shaw Marohnic, and as Mary Shaw Horn, throughout her notoriety as a Pittsburgh artist.) Samuel Rosenberg, and younger teacher Bill Schulgold, both of the Neighborhood Art School, were also AAP members. Likely Esther's first involvement in a major show was in 1923, with the Associated Artists of Pittsburgh, held at the Carnegie Institute. She exhibited one work at this, their annual exhibition: *A Portrait*.[13] It seems she did not again exhibit with them until 1927. In the meantime, she was beginning to flower socially.

It was the time of Prohibition. As elsewhere across the country, speakeasies abounded in Pittsburgh, jazz was beginning to flourish, and women were asserting themselves socially en masse for the first time in American history. Mary Shaw, as she was most often referred to, was devoting time to Number 8 Center Court, a studio-gallery where she and friends Kathleen McGraw and Edith Rielly "entertained, and had a lot of people drop by."[14] (They showed and attempted to sell Pittsburgh art.)

The *Pittsburgh Post-Gazette* equated Shaw's studio to "a unique piece of Greenwich Village." And the proprietor herself—who would go on to be quite a colorful character in the Pittsburgh art scene for decades—was described throughout Associated Artists' archival material as "jocular" and "irrepressible."[15] Shaw had a wry humor not unlike Esther's, a sardonic wit still in evidence past the age of 90, peppering the conversation as this vibrant woman reflected back upon a way of artistic life. All of her memories of Esther and the times, that she would share while residing in the Marian Manor Nursing Home in the Greentree section of Pittsburgh, were emphatically meted out.[16]

"I want you to know I hadn't thought of these people for years." Shaw was sure to preface her recollections with this statement, as if to remain noncommittal as she conjured them to mind. The revelations that were to follow belied her assertion that she didn't give a damn about her past. Her commentary on Esther had actually begun, "She was sort of exotic and very interesting and very talented. She'd take something—trees and clouds—and interpret it, make it into something on paper."

Shaw's friends were a collection of underground artists, literary and theatre figures who, despite major public recognition, were leading "a very active, real life" as creative artists. "It wasn't anything fake at all. They were genuine people—not phonies. There were a lot of phonies floating around," says Shaw vehemently. She disgustedly states what most artists believe to be true, describing as 'phony' anyone who calls himself an artist, yet either is not diligently, consistently building a body of work or who creates work fit only for mass consumption, non-original, without real integrity, that simply sells out to mainstream taste.

Real artists, as Shaw is careful to explain, tended to know each other. Little matter that different artists had different individual tastes—as long as originality prevailed. The struggle to attend to one's own unique creative aspirations, yet still survive in the world, was the common bond. Though the critics would rarely reward anyone with too eclectic an artistic vision, if it was apparent that an artist was striving independently toward a personal voice, respect came from the esoteric band of peers. Artistic experimentation, in order to find one's voice, one's singular contribution, was very important. As Mary explains, her own philosophy so similar to many artists, "I never thought much about getting this or that painting done." If a work *felt* done, she proclaims, then so be it declared finished. But the creative *process-ing* itself, the experimentation, held significant meaning.

As is the case today in any city's artistic community, creative figures of Esther's time in Pittsburgh banded together at Shaw's Number 8 Center

Court and similar art spaces to intellectually stimulate, emotionally support, and, if possible, financially support each other. As Gloria Mc-Darrah explained in *The Artists World In Pictures*, "Artists themselves make an audience; they are true critics and best interpreters" of another's work.[17] With certainty, and also a bit of enjoyment, now that she is on a roll with her commentary about friends of the past, Mary Shaw includes in her recollecting that "there never was a Pittsburgh scene actually." She explains that those who frequented her gallery space were more or less underground artists with a minimal amount of Pittsburgh recognition but certainly no national attention. (She stresses that Pittsburgh was never seen as a place inhabited with valuable artists, though she and her friends of course knew differently.)

Her scene of artist peers would be differentiated, for example, from the circle of acclaimed artists from Pittsburgh and southwestern Pennsylvania that had congregated around Scalp Level in Somerset County in the mid 19th century. Their work was first brought to the public's attention through the J. J. Gillespie Art Gallery in downtown Pittsburgh. Wondrous works of realism, the paintings of this handful of artists, including George Hetzel, Aaron H. Gorson, Joseph Woodwell, and Alfred S. Wall, depicted the stark cliffs of Scalp Level, the surrounding countryside, and lush forest-scapes. The Westmoreland Museum of Art in Greensburg, just southeast of Pittsburgh, holds the exemplary work of this last Pittsburgh group that painted in the European tradition backed by the National Academy.

But Mary Shaw's gallery, and the creators and works themselves that peopled it, were quite different. The gallery itself was actually a house—"the last one on the end in the area that was in back of the Nixon Theatre" in downtown Pittsburgh. Like all underground galleries, the proprietors lived in the same minimal but amazingly resonant space as that given to friends' art. Esther was one of the many who frequented it. The taste of this sense of community was no doubt delectable to her. She had known peer artistic support from her early years at the Irene Kaufmann Settlement, but the 1920s opened up her artistic sensibility to a burgeoning social milieu at that critical time in her life when she had become very downtrodden by family dissatisfaction with her lifestyle.

"It was a hardy spot, a roaring business"—Shaw describing less the success of selling artists' work to fellow poor starving artists than the triumph of camaraderie about her gallery. With a cackle, she defines her place in back of the Nixon as "a party—the whole town was on a party." The spot was "very popular because you could pop in at any hour of the night. We did have booze and stuff there. The people used to make it after the theatre, but"—Shaw insists, "it was not *just* a speakeasy." Creativity was the main focus, and cemented the bond among all those who set forth there.

FIG. 2   Esther circa 1925
(Photo: Luke Swank)

"Our friends were very jovial and very friendly," says Shaw. "Nothing nasty about them." She fully discounts the common misconception of underground artist as dangerous punk. Though she had a reputation for poking fun at those around her, it was obvious that there was nothing harmful or offensive in the way Shaw was handling her friends and peers. There was no disdain here, in her account of her creative past. She fully embraced the characters and scenarios surfacing of a life lived with much passion, and ardently claimed the identity of artist she carried throughout her life. "I've always gotten rather involved in things . . . as well my friends. I had a great time mostly. I've lived a very busy life. . . ." This last utterance, spoke with a touch of hesitation, seems attached to a tangle of underlying feelings, and she concludes her memories with these words.

Mary Shaw described her gallery-goers as a lot of art people and theatre people, "and a lot of ordinary people who were interested in painters and pictures." It turns out, though, that a good many people who are truly interested in painters and pictures are hardly ordinary. Sometimes characters on this periphery are as colorful and flamboyant as the artists themselves. This was true of the interior decorators and designers who hung out at Number Eight Center Court. They frequented the galleries and numerous parties as much as the artists did back then, and some of these people hired artists for various work. One in particular would became a mentor of sorts for Esther—Harold Schwartz, an interior decorator with Kaufmann's Department Store in downtown Pittsburgh.

He was the first to provide ongoing meaningful work for Esther, gainful employment based on her painting abilities. He hired her as a scenic painter for his interior sets and, of most interest to Esther, she painted views of his solo design work both for promotion and posterity's sake.[18] This started to take place circa 1927, as evidenced by her titling some of her fine art of the time as *Interiors* and at least one *Department Store*. Some of her paintings possibly appeared in the showcase windows of the downtown store. Perhaps it was the visibility associated with Kaufmann's and the nature of her work with Schwartz that later helped Esther land a solo exhibit in the Warner Theatre lobby, situated right next to Kaufmann's, and participation in the Gulf Building's "Better Homes and Buildings Exhibit," also downtown. Both of these shows were to come in 1933.

Schwartz lived in the prestigious Bellefield Dwellings, an apartment complex hovering over Center Avenue near Craig Street. This was part of the artsy section of North Oakland that included the area bounded by Forbes, Craig, and Dithridge Streets, and cut through by Bellefield, just up from the Carnegie Museum. According to Sybil Barsky, Schwartz lived there along with three other men—a talented dancer, the owner of a dance studio in nearby Johnstown, and apparently the son of a Pennsylvania governor.[19] Esther drew finely rendered cityscapes and painted watercolors of the neighboring buildings, sights of North Oakland, from apartments on the higher floors of this complex, and perhaps from the rooftop. In addition, she captured the lavish interior of this structure built by architect Carlton Strong. Still standing today, but as a senior citizen center, the Bellefield Dwellings have been stripped of their former opulence. The marble floors and brass elevators remain, but there is no trace of the lush furnishings that gave the individual apartments and public spaces of the building such richness of character they had when Esther conveyed them to canvas. Many of Pittsburgh's affluent resided there, including Homer Saint-Gaudens, director of the Carnegie Museum of Art in the 1920s (and son of renowned sculptor Augustus Saint-Gaudens). Harold Schwartz may have indeed designed a great many of the living spaces. No doubt for Esther they were gorgeous images to capture in paint.

Mention of an "unhappy love affair," possibly in Pittsburgh, appeared in notations that Millie took of conversations with her aunt Esther, though Sybil Barsky would negate the possibility that this man might have been Harold Schwartz. In recalling their interactions, Sybil remembered the amusing relationship between Esther and Harold. She recalled Esther's teasing both him and his roommates with regard to her being fond of them. But as they were homosexual, nothing ever came of her friendly advances.[20] Though not with Schwartz, Esther did become intimately involved with men around 1927, and apparently had several boyfriends before leaving Pittsburgh.[21] Harold simply played a large role in her early life, and she thought dearly of him. He obviously liked her work and gave her an opportunity to profit from her talent. Esther affectionately referred to him as 'Schwartzie,' even later, when she would recall him to New York City friends of the 1950s.

Despite her new ability to earn some money from her art, the family still didn't view Esther's career choice as anything but frivolous. Reflecting family sentiment over the passing years, Dorothy would offer, "Esther never worked in any capacity on a salary basis, a skill of any sort."[22] She was indeed gaining confidence in her painting, though, come the late 1920s, due in large part to her work with Schwartz. By getting money for her art, and the respect of those who did appreciate her talent, she was finally finding affirmation as artist, and thus some measure of self-respect. She even began taking classes on and off once again at Carnegie Tech, from about 1926–1930.[23]

Esther took part in another show with the Associated Artists of Pittsburgh, held at the Carnegie Institute, February of 1927.[24] Also participating were Sam Rosenberg and Bill Schulgold. From this point on, she was no stranger to submitting works for critique. She boldly entered her paintings for consideration in the Carnegie Internationals, the celebrated biennials held at the Carnegie Museum of Art, drawing modern artists of worldwide success and recognition, as well as being open to all non-recognized artists. In 1927, she submitted the simply titled *Interior* and in 1929, *Portrait*. Come 1931, she tried for success with two: *Nude*, and *Self-Portrait*. Though never accepted into the Internationals, her submissions, records of which still exist, confirm a gutsy early belief in herself.[25]

◐ ◐ ◐

The formal name is "The Carnegie," the huge structure at Forbes Avenue in Pittsburgh, sitting along the top of Panther Hollow at the west end of Schenley Park in Oakland—the structure that houses the Carnegie Library, the Carnegie Music Hall, and the Museums of Natural History and Art. The Museum of Art, however, and the entirely separate Carnegie Institute of Technology, on its own sprawling campus a little further up Forbes Avenue, where Esther went to school, were much entwined in the early decades of the twentieth century. Andrew Carnegie himself can be held accountable for what thus became both benefit to Pittsburgh artists and a confusion to anyone trying to follow exhibitions that those various artists took part in.

Carnegie envisioned students benefiting from the close connection between the museums and the college. The collaboration that he early insured continues through the present day. Use of some of the facilities of the museum is first granted to Carnegie Mellon University (modern-day Carnegie Institute of Technology), as in the case of their School of Music presenting concerts at Carnegie Music Hall.

The Smithsonian-like building is what Andrew Carnegie christened his 'Carnegie Institute' in 1895. But when ground was broken further east, near Schenley Park, for a college (the schools of engineering and design in the early twentieth century), Carnegie christened it with the similar "Carnegie Institute of Technology." If one clipped the school's name, which many understandably did, down to "Carnegie Institute," then confusingly there were two separate entities going by the same title. People thus referred to the "Institute" to mean either the goings-on at the school or at the museums. And equally confusing nomenclature was "College of Fine Art" being used to describe one part of the technical school and "Department of Fine Art" to describe one part of the Museum. Each of these began to be used incorrectly to name activities occurring at the other.

Luckily that distinguishing reference "Carnegie Tech," though, soon came to be a Pittsburgh household reference to the school's activities. However, the behind-the-scenes of the two similarly titled yet separate entities were not completely un-entangled. They shared a common board of directors and many common benefactors, and collaborated on numerous exhibitions, most held at the Art Museum, with Carnegie Tech students and teachers, as well as independent artists, all taking part.

Programs would list such exhibitions as held at "Carnegie Institute, Department of Fine Art." This was indeed the prestigious Carnegie Art Museum, though it might appear to be the school. Thus administrators who were weighing the merit of work done by international artists often did the same in exhibits of Carnegie Tech students, as well as various other Pittsburgh artists, independent and otherwise. This certainly would have been in line with Andrew Carnegie's vision of his art museum's purpose—to bring attention not only to known great artists working internationally, but also to local creative talent. But the Museum definitely got away from this mid-century and on.

One way to reach out to as many Pittsburgh artists as possible was to allow the Associated Artists of Pittsburgh to hold their Annuals in the glamorous halls of the Carnegie Art Museum. (This practice is still in pratice to this day, though many regard it as a token effort on the part of the museum to show Pittsburgh art, for it is not the work of the numerous underground artists within the city, but the work of a few—members of that one collective organization, now being of very commercial bent.) John O'Connor and Edward Duff Balken were two administrators on staff at the museum who were especially in touch with local artists, many of whom had studied at one time at Carnegie Tech. In the late 1920s, Balken was the Acting Assistant Director under Carnegie Art Museum Director Homer St. Gaudens, and O'Connor was Business

Manager. Balken was also on the Executive Committee of the One Hundred Friends of Pittsburgh Art, an organization that made it possible for Pittsburgh Public Schools to acquire the work of local artists.

John O'Connor became personally acquainted with the local artists whose works were on show at the Museum either for Carnegie Tech, Associated Artists, or independent exhibitions. Mary Shaw remembered him as "very genuine."[26] Once he became familiar with an artist's work, he kept him or her in mind for special-invitation exhibitions jointly sponsored by Carnegie Tech and the Museum of Art. The museum even picked up any carrying charges and insurance for an artist to participate in such shows. O'Connor called upon the artists in their studios about town. As the museum's representative, he wrote collectors in attempt to market the work of young, unknown Pittsburgh artists. This personalized approach, hardly done today by major museums in search of local talent, especially suited O'Connor, who "worked hard to present local art shows," according to Pittsburgh *Sun-Telegraph* reporter Dorothy Kantner.[27]

John O'Connor's commitment and compassion are very evident in a letter dated June 1936, to Mrs. John G. Bowman, wife of the chancellor of the University of Pittsburgh. (O'Connor also knew and communicated about artistic matters with her son, John R. Bowman, and his artist wife, Melita Fils.) He wrote concerning the works of Pittsburgh artist Clarence McWilliams, whose work was on view at a late spring exhibition at the museum, where Esther would also be an invited artist: "I know the fact that his painting has been purchased is going to be great encouragement to Mr. McWilliams. I am wishing that more Pittsburghers would take a little interest in Pittsburgh artists."[28] Esther uttered this sentiment to an art reviewer in the 1930s; today scores of working artists in Pittsburgh still say it. But many talented artists are never really known far outside their circle of peers who know their work, and the process, the labors of creating that work, best. This was so for most of the Pittsburgh artists who frequented Shaw's gallery, who occasionally had their work temporarily hung, ironically, on the walls of their city's prestigious art museum. These were Esther's friends, including Mary Shaw, Bill Schulgold, and a painter named Milton Weiss.

Weiss was about fifteen years younger than Esther, and of the "second generation" of students to have studied at what was the IKS Neighborhood Art School. Close to the age of eighty, he would graciously open up his canvas-filled apartment/studio in Pittsburgh's Shadyside neighborhood to talk of Esther and art. Like Shaw, the tremendous emphasis he placed on his remembrances was a testament to both his own intensity and to his investment in the creative life.[29]

Weiss credits Esther Phillips as one of the core group of early painters who brought the fundamentals and philosophy of the early art school from its establishment in the Hill District to the latter Oakland locale. (By 1926, what had been, essentially, the Hill District's Neighborhood Art School had moved to Bellefield Street in Oakland, close to the Carnegie Museum. It became a part of the Jewish Y that would incorporate both the YM and YWHA.) Esther was still involved at the school, but no longer as a student by the late 1920s. She occasionally exhibited alongside Rosenberg, Schulgold, and other teachers there, most former alumni of the school themselves, as well as artists such as Milton Weiss, who were currently studying there.

The record of one such exhibit held at the new building survives from 1928. Esther showed seven works: *Herman Greenberg, Sketch, Portrait of a Young Man, Sketch, Sam Filner, Girl with a Striped Sweater,* and *Study.*[30] She exhibited alongside Weiss at this exhibition, but that is not where he first met her. He knew her roommate Sybil Barsky better, and it was she who introduced him to the "erratic" Esther. "One day Sybil took me up to her apartment. . . ." Buoyed by nostalgia, Weiss' voice trails off, but his face glows, unveiling a reconnection with memories of a time still vividly alive inside him. That meeting was one of the few times he would spoke with Esther. But he would recall it, for it seems she made quite an impression.

> She went her own way . . . Her art was better than a lot of people's art. Even just that one time I talked to Esther, I *sensed* what an individual she was. Somehow I wanted to paint a portrait of her. It was like a magnet—I wanted to do it. I must have known that she was fighting—painting against great odds. I must have been told that.

Milton Weiss, who like Mary Shaw would also come to be respected within the Pittsburgh art scene, continues his remembrance. "I knew her work and I admired it because by then I was starting to do much the same—creative work." Milton ended up painting a "flower piece" and indeed Esther's portrait in the apartment that day—the requisite for the latter simply being that "she was an artist and I was an artist."

Chapter Three

THE REVIEWS

*A*round 1929, things started exploding artistically for Esther. She had begun producing canvasses displaying the grandeur of the city's bridges, the odd beauty of houses rambling down hillsides in Soho, close to her first home, and perhaps what Pittsburgh will always best be known for: Mill Sites (the title of a painting or two). She was working in oil as well as watercolor, though watercolor would ever be her main medium. And though America was feeling the pain of the Depression, Esther personally started experiencing some better times. She vigorously submitted work for all possible show considerations—some Associated Artist of Pittsburgh Exhibitions, and some independent "Pittsburgh Artists" exhibitions, held at the Carnegie Institute Department of Fine Art. There were even occasional opportunities for solo shows at various odd venues.

Of the Associated Artist of Pittsburgh exhibitions, Esther would be represented at every annual but one from 1927 to 1936. In 1928, she submitted three works: *Portrait, Study,* and another *Study.* Come 1929, she submitted works entitled *Portrait* (perhaps the same one submitted for the Carnegie International of that year), *Portrait Study,* and *Landscape.* And in 1930: *Pastoral, Portrait of Girl Near Window, Head* , and *Portrait.*[1] Review after review of the shows Esther took part in of the 1930s cited her work as quite original. For the most part critics seemed to respect her for this, though she was of course scorned, as well, for doing the unusual. But she was becoming aware that artists have a hard time winning esteem not only by having chosen the path of a creative life, but also by doing work that is too far outside mainstream conceptions of art.

Esther had embraced her identity as artist from a very young age, and was slowly beginning to adjust to that identity in a healthy way. Instead of expecting empathy from others who only saw in creative ability a non-profitable talent, she was developing a sassiness that would carry her beyond all conservative judgments, color her attitude toward the public, and for the most part keep her from being negatively affected by society's rejection of artists. Scores of reviews, of either solo or group shows in which she took part in the 1930s, exist to this day in the various Art Indexes of the Carnegie Library of Pittsburgh.[2]

WATER COLORS AND LITHOS AT GULF BUILDING

POST=GAZETTE

Esther Phillips Hangs 28 Varied Works In Current Show.

NOV 30 1933

By Harvey Gaul,

Again the Better Homes and Buildings Exhibit, second floor, Gulf Building, scores of local success. Pittsburgh artists.

This time it is the virile Esther Phillips, of the Associated Artists, a name known to most of our native shows.

Hitherto the town has seen Miss Phillips "in oils," and now she drops the palette-knife for the water color box, the soft Faber No. 2 pencil, and a great number of amusing lithograph plates.

28 Works Are Shown.

Twenty-eight works in all, some transients, some fragments, some experiments, and many delightful morceaux. We might pass by the nudes, unfortunately they "don't" come off," even if they are valiant attempts at expressionism.

Miss Phillips has a vigorous mind, sees beauty in bold bits, and is not afraid to record the local scene without transposing it. One admires the sweep of her brush,

the range of her color gamut, and her understanding. She can draw when she wishes (and she doesn't wish when she is fiddling with the nude set-ups—obvious, self-conscious mats all of them) and she proves it time after time in her ramshackle buildings.

If it is an uneven show it is because Miss Phillips is fussing with several media, several schools, and hasn't quite made up her mind which way she is going—which is often a great virtue.

Around the Walls.

Miss Phillips goes rambling around our city of 70 hills and comes back with a sketch book chock full of diverting incidents. There isn't a city in America more amusing in old lean-tos, decrepid shanties, than one finds in this town, and the artists are all alive to them. In the vanguard, one finds Esther Phillips, and some of her lead pencil drawings are most entertaining, correct in perspective and accurate in mood. Sometimes it is a city square, a grass plot, a flimsy row of dwellings, a brick-house back-drop, and among the water colors one discovers many an appealing passage. It is strange, but there are rhythms and waves in the art world, and this year the whole trend seems to be toward lithography. You would think that the litho had only recently been discovered so avidly is it pursued by the local men and women. Miss Phillips has strong things to say and again the rickety buildings occupy her attention.

The show stays for the next two weeks and is worth climbing Grant's Hill to observe.

Girl's Quarrel—Provoking Paintings Exhibited Here

By DOUGLAS NAYLOR

The quarrel-provoking art of Esther Phillips, prize-winning Pittsburgh artist, was hung yesterday in a "one-man" show at the Gulf Galleries, third floor of the Gulf Building.

The public probably disagrees more violently over the work of Miss Phillips than any other local artist—unless it be John Kane. And one never hears words of politely reserved praise for Miss Phillips.

You will either say it is perfectly terrible, or that some day she will be called a genius.

Her present show is largely what might be expected, plenty of experimentation in design and color—with some of the results being swell and others left in a palpably unfinished state.

There are a couple of water-colored nudes which this irrepressible artist undoubtedly has exhibited just to irritate people who don't like her work.

There are a few watercolors in the show that reveal a sound knowledge of draftsmanship, with a few houses that look substantial and enduring—as though made by an architect.

Generally, however, this impish-spirited artist prefers to make pictures of houses that are staggering

in the last stages of collapse. She picks them out during expeditions into the slums around Soho.

Yet there is some interesting arrangements in the way old porch roofs slope, houses are falling down and telephone poles are staggering. The composition is often exhilerating to persons looking for originality.

Her critics say it isn't art. Esther Phillips says it is: that is, the "Corner of Brady Street and Fifth Avenue," above. That she sticks to a style is evinced by the self-portrait of the artist below.

The works of artist John Kane likely caught the eye of Esther Phillips long before he gained notoriety as an American primitive painter. A laborer by day, the unschooled Kane in the evening poured his leftover energy and spirit onto canvasses, giving birth to brilliant, peculiar depictions of Pittsburgh rivers, bridges, hills, and valleys. His work started to capture national attention with the inclusion in the 1927 Carnegie International of *his Scene From the Scottish Highlands*. He was 67 years old.

As does the first of the previous reviews, fellow artist Milton Weiss equally linked Kane and Phillips, showering praise on the both.[3] Certainly, both John Kane and Esther's work employed unusual composition, that arrangement of artistic components on a medium such as canvas. But Weiss' critical eye had observed beyond the scope of the paintings. "Those two were the most original artists of that period. They were the most modern, the most creative." Weiss remarked that, when he met Esther in the 1920s, "right away I saw that her work was good because by then I had been introduced, sort of, to modern art." He had been very involved with his studies at Carnegie Tech at the time and was especially interested in one professor's artistic style and philosophy—Armando del Cimmuto, Italian painter and even one-time supervisor of the Neighborhood Art School. He introduced Weiss to the new modern art, the beginnings of abstractionism, which Weiss far preferred to the realist bent of other YMHA teachers Schulgold and Rosenberg. Though he respected their abilities, he was far more interested, as was Esther, in exploring the new.

Weiss saw in Esther's early work the playings with abstractionism, and in both Kane's and hers the renegade modern spirit. It could be argued that Kane's work was not modern because he was "a primitive," a term given an unschooled artist, and as such, an artistic title of no one time period. But because he wasn't of a school, his work shared a quality of elusiveness with many of the new, emerging modernists. Kane was very much an individual, an epitome of what would be the modern artist, or at the very least the legions of those independents surrounding the modern movement, exploring their own creative voices.

A kind man, Weiss had been very generous with his compliments of Esther's art and lifestyle as he sat surrounded by walls packed with an astounding assortment of his own life's creative work. He had freely offered his feelings about schooling, after so many years behind him as a painter, including his belief that "some study is important, but there is a danger in instruction." Queried about Esther's similarity to the primitive painters—her painting style was simple in nature, with an odd play on perspective, at times charming, with a generous use of color—Weiss had been adamant in explaining the difference. "Esther was sophisticated." He ardently defined her work as showing, without a doubt, definite schooling; she made conscious use of primitive tendencies. He repeated this point three times, frustrated that someone might come across her work and not see this. "It's obvious she wasn't a naive painter. You just had to look at her work." To further iterate his point, he pronounced, "It was just in her . . . She was far ahead of her time. I don't know if she was aware of the modern movement at all. I feel that she really should be internationally known." (Weiss had actually concluded his remarks on Esther on this fiery note.)

Esther didn't mind stepping into the public debate over John Kane, who had been getting much negative press for his natural, childlike work. Finally, at least the Carnegie Art Museum and many other modern artists found it fresh and engaging. Esther had been exhibiting in many of the same shows as he since the 1920s. She fiercely defended the primitive painter much as Weiss defended her. A lover of individuality and the simple, she berated the public for their ignorance of what constitutes art. Though she herself would be driven only to paint, art alone identifying her life, she held Kane in esteem for being able to wondrously create after a hard day of laboring to support his family, as the following article—not a review but an interview with Esther—attests.

PRESS

Can't Find Any Fun Going Along With Mob

In Life

AUG 20 1933

By DOUGLAS NAYLOR

ESTHER PHILLIPS, prize-winning Pittsburgh artist, reacts like a young porcupine toward people who are smug and conservative. She is forever trying to thrust needles into a person's complacency. An interview with this young lady is hopeless. She won't talk straight ahead, but jumps around after controversial subjects.

"It is more important for art to be interesting than to be good. If a picture is interesting, it is good art." Those were two remarks by the artist that started her on a wayward line of thought.

"I find academic work boring," she remarked. "One should go with the times, and progress with life.

"A lot of Pittsburghers think that anything created in Pittsburgh cannot possibly be as good as something done outside. This shows a lack of interest in Pittsburgh art.

"I believe this is due to a lack of interest in art itself. There are not enough good exhibits in this city to stir up public interest in art.

"Personally, I think Pittsburgh is too conservative."

* * *

MISS PHILLIPS is a strong defender of John Kane. She thinks he is "one of the most delightful painters there is anywhere."

Her admiration for Mr. Kane is based on the fact that "he is able to be something after going through the modern industrial system.

"He seems to get remarkable composition out of everything and anything he sees." Miss Phillips' only criticism of the famous Pittsburgh artist was that his paintings "at times seem rather monochromatic in color."

Miss Phillips has been doing a lot of sketching around Soho during the last year, for a series of water

A water color showing a view from the top of the Bellefield Dwellings, Center and Belle nues, by Miss Phillips.

iors. She has done some interesting impressionistic work with raw colors. In many pictures the youthful artist has turned tumble-down houses into pleasing buildings.

"I think Soho has character," says Miss Phillips. "The houses all look as if they were ready to fall down. But they keep on standing up. The steps leading down to the hollow are very crooked, and patched with different colored woods, so are good for both composition and color. The roof tops are usually brilliant, in comparison to the drab gray of the houses.

"Soho, to me, represents life. The people are poor. They struggle. The place is full of energy. I am not interested in the dilettante type of person. Certainly, there are none in Soho."

Miss Phillips was born in Russia, coming to America with her parents when she was about five years old. She won a prize last year in the annual show of the Associated Artists at Carnegie Institute. Her first mural was painted recently for a "budget" room at Kaufmann's. It was called "Soho," and shows life at a street corner.

Soho was indeed representative of Esther's life, with poor people struggling, and the energy of that struggle captivating enough to call for translation in paint. Interestingly, Esther pointed out in the interview with Naylor that, in this neighborhood, there are no dilettantes, those with a superficial interest in a branch of knowledge or the arts. But Esther was referring to the common folk of Soho and their way of living, laden with struggle, as a life-knowledge. The people of Soho interested her because their lives carried the same intensity as hers, with the necessity to fully meet, from the core of one's being, the challenges presented. They had no shallow stake in surviving. They either put out great energy, or they didn't make it. Though at times they certainly took falls, these people did indeed survive, much as the neighborhood houses themselves "keep on standing up."

Artists of the Ash Can School had pronounced raw scenes of urban life as *the* vital life. Well, Esther had found the same to be true, not so much from any study of this movement as from growing up around the poor of Pittsburgh, and moving into poverty herself after she left the nest of her middle-class family. With the influence of the Ash Can movement as predecessor, many artistic movements in the 1930s centered around the poverty brought on by the Depression. Many artists consciously decided to have their art based on contemporary American life and socially responsible content matter. Esther's conveying the dynamism of poverty, setting up paints and easel on the Pittsburgh hills that afforded such a colorful view of the busy yet poor people before her, was less due to social consciousness than strict appreciation of the rich visual matter and tremendous identification with the hardships and inherent challenges of their existence. Though she could speak expressively of the inherent beauty of the lives of Soho people, it appears she was never the outspoken artist on economic political issues that some of her contemporaries would be. Esther's main focus was on images, not ideas. It is her paintings that have "strong things to say."

As the previous article mentions, and as Esther would tell her niece, Kaufmann's Department Store commissioned her to paint a mural in the early 1930s. That it was her first, as the article suggests, was not accurate if she had done the Carnegie Library cafeteria mural in the 1920s. No documentation or physical evidence (other than the mention in Naylor's article) survives to this day about this mural, as well. Certainly, Esther had a connection with Kaufmann's through Schwartz, but it is quite possible she simply vied for a commission among other artists, because the department store at the time was very supportive of the fine arts and sponsored contests for Pittsburghers to present their work. Owned by Edgar J. Kaufmann, who would in 1936 commission Frank Lloyd Wright to build for him the masterpiece home *Fallingwater* an hour southeast of Pittsburgh, the store was interested in the late 1920s and early 1930s in showing its support for the value of art in industry.

> The fact that today we are the richest of nations places on us the added responsibility of giving greater momentum to cultural development than it has ever received from any people. Business and industry must accept a share of the responsibility which opportunity imposes.[4]

Kaufmann's management commissioned nationally recognized artist Boardman Robinson to do a series of murals entitled *The History of Commerce*. In 1930 they were unveiled, along with a captivating Art Deco remodeling of the store's first floor. Shortly after that the store sponsored Art In Industry contests, in collaboration with the *Pittsburgh Press*. The contests, including calls for essays, utilized the Boardman Robinson murals as inspirational point of departure. Though most of the contests were for school children, some called for adults; it is possible that Esther completed a mini-mural for the store under this or a related competition. Under the direction of Edgar Kaufmann, who was cousin to Irene Kaufmann of the Settlement on the Hill, the store was specifically hoping to instill in the Pittsburgh public an admiration and esteem for the arts. The store even included a philosophy statement, along with the Guidelines for Submissions for the contests, making the point that, in future years, men and women unappreciative of the arts "will be as grave a social burden as the wholly money-minded citizens of the present day."

⑥ ⑥ ⑥

Other reviews of Esther's work continued to depict well the young woman artist. Marie McSwigan, a Pittsburgh art critic who would later go on to assist John Kane in his autobiography, *Skyhooks*, praised Esther's work in the early 1930s, stating that it is "certainly a departure from the 'pretty, pretty' works once considered the entire metier of women artists." This from a review that barely meets the mark of readability for posterity's sake, entitled "Bold and Original Designs Replace Pretty Pictures." McSwigan was covering an "Exhibition of Paintings by Pittsburgh Artists," Spring 1932, in which Esther had a total of three paintings— *Mellon Institute, Sybil*, and another *Marie, Beulah, and Mary*. Included in the show, held at the third floor gallery, Department of Fine Art, Carnegie Institute, were eighteen men and women, including John Kane and Malcolm Parcell, another Pittsburgher who, after some decades, would find significant acclaim as local artist.[5] Esther's *Mellon Institute* evokes painter Elizabeth Olds' *Scrap Iron* series, Olds being a student of an Ash Can School teacher and one of the early nationally recognized women independent painters. *Mellon Institute* showed the framework of the classical-design Carnegie Tech building as it was going up, "the only painting that pays the slightest heed to the tremendous construction projects around about [Pittsburgh]."[6]

"Among the most interesting paintings in the show are the three by Esther Phillips," McSwigan wrote early on in her review. She championed Esther, offering, "there are people who will add, 'if you like that sort of painting.' But they will also have to add that that sort of painting is forceful, bold and original." McSwigan comments upon, as would also reviewer Penelope Redd, the contributions that Esther undoubtedly received from her work on Schwartz's interiors. States McSwigan, "Miss Phillips unconsciously has a fondness for design. She subdues it for other values, but it crops out where least expected in *Marie, Beulah and Mary*, for instance. . . .Miss Phillips has a definite rhythm which stimulates and holds."[7]

The praise continued, from others. "Esther Phillips goes on, in her own way, painting pictures that look like nothing else yet have color, feeling and everything else a good modern picture needs. Her canvas, 'The Etcher' is enough to make you stop and say 'that's something,' and it is." So remarked critic Joseph Cloud in 1932, of the 22nd Associated Artists of Pittsburgh show,[8] in which Esther had the paintings *Back Stage, Construction* (perhaps Mellon Institute again), and *Interior*, in addition to *The Etcher*, who was likely peer Sam Filner, according to AAP records. This last painting, a prizewinner, was likely the one mentioned in Naylor's article.

Of the 21st Associated Artists exhibit, the following was written:

> Besides the prize winners there are some really fine pictures in the show about the best of which, not only for the sketch itself but for the potentialities it displays, is the larger of two nudes by Esther Phillips. This picture, quite modern in its aspect and style, is remarkably skillful and imaginative painting. Here is an artist who can put on canvas just about whatever she wants to show. She displays sensibility to beauty and considerable feeling. Her two other pictures, "Pastorale," and the smaller nude, are also quick sketches, vigorous and intelligent and a little more finished.[9]

Likely it was one of these nudes that Esther had submitted to the International this year. This critic concluded, "You can watch Esther Phillips from now on and the prophesy is better than some [that] you will someday see her in the International class."

Yet another Pittsburgh critic of the times, Penelope Redd, reviewed Esther's solo exhibit in the Warner Theatre lobby in March 1933:

Pittsburgh Sun-
Telegraph
March 31, 1933

—TWENTY-FOUR—

WATER COLORS ON DISPLAY AT THEATER

By PENELOPE REDD

An exhibition of water colors by Esther Phillips was shown today for the first time at the Warner Theater. In these water colors Miss Phillips transports those who see into a new realm of vision where a single tulip may be developed into effulgent beauty.

She has transformed a white drawing room intensely formal in arrangement into a space animated by the gay light of the sun and the moving gestures of the breezes. Plants, textiles, even the furniture participates in the general sociability engendered by Esther Phillips' instinct for design.

The series of nudes and clothed figures arranged on couches are painted with a nervous precision that sustains linear style. They are unlike any similar subjects we have seen in the neighborhood. In the portrait of an artist, she presents the same indivisibility of planes that made Pascin immune to imitators. Throughout her exhibition, the color is handled with so unerring a feeling that one is forced to conclude that intuition entered somewhat into the fabrication of these super-simulations of nature invading the urban gloom. Miss Phillips' exhibition will be on view until April 15.

Ms. Redd also wrote the forward for the show's bulletin. She compared the creativity behind Esther's watercolors to that behind two motion pictures out that week in 1933, *Private Jones* and *Christopher Strong*. Both were "born of an exploring imagination and of unconscious freedom from worn platitudes." Redd wrote that, instead of painting a "pretty tulip," Esther "paints it precisely, emphasiz-[ing] the limpid color of the flower with the means at hand. In this case, the means to her end is [setting the vase directly upon] a brown fruit wood chair with a blue cushion . . . such poetic license is permissible." She explained that Esther "takes . . . a primrose in a common earthen crock, and through her brush, imposes upon us the vision of a world in which the ordinary becomes extraordinary. . . ."[10] Years later, Esther would ironically do just the opposite—transcribing the extraordinary existence, making it seem ordinary.

Esther had 40 watercolors in the show. The list includes four *Interiors*, three *Nudes*, one *Abstraction*, a *Self-portrait*, fourteen *Still Lifes*, and a variety of other titles, including *House Pattern*, *Roof Tops*, *Museum Interior*, *Near the Mills*, and *Cathedral College*. Unlike critics Naylor and Gaul, both

Redd and Cloud praised Esther's nudes, which certainly foretell of images to come. Redd stated that to see "an exhibition of Esther Phillips' watercolors [is to see] the contemporary spirit at work in art."

The following is a further review of this same show by *The Pittsburgh Sun-Telegraph*'s art editor:

Pgh Sun-Telegraph 4/2/33

Initial Showing
Pgh Artists

An initial showing of a group of water colors by Esther Phillips at the Warner Theater is exhibited through the generous enthusiasm of another young painter, Sam Stern. Esther Phillips, although painting in Pittsburgh, is a child of no known city or land, but of the company that time occasionally gives to the world at large.

To those who have watched Miss Phillips' paintings as they appear in the exhibitions—and that includes a group far beyond the circle of her personal acquaintance, there is just one element of certainty and that is surprise. Thus, from a palette of low and rather static intensity in her oil paintings, she suddenly produces a group of water colors limpid in color filled with the sense of air enveloping and animating flowers and rooms.

Her recent water colors at the Warner are likely to surprise those familiar with her work.

In the twenty-third annual Associated Artists Show held in 1933, as in the 1932 AAP show,[11] Esther was again a prize winner. But this was to be her biggest Pittsburgh acclaim. She won the "Former Pittsburgh School of Design for Women Prize" for her *Looking Down Brady Street Bridge*, essentially a "back view of tenement houses."[12] Esther received twenty-five dollars with this award; in the same show John Kane was awarded $150 first honor for the painting *Liberty Bridge*. One of the invited jurors for the show was Ash Can artist Edward Hopper; the judgments he and two comrades made caused a stir. The AAP bulletin first quotes peeved Pittsburgh artists and critics, and then allows Hopper to have his say.

"The jury this year was looking only for naive, childish sort of work," announced a very annoyed Milan Petrovits. "It seems the jury has purposely cast aside pictures that show knowledge of painting in looking for something primitive," declared Marcella Comes. "The jury has made fools of artists before," she added. "This year's jury," decided Vincent Nesbert of the Art Institute, "went to extremes in picking radical, amateurish paintings."

Wrote Press critic Harvey Gaul, "It was wide-open field day for the John Kane School of Art, only unfortunately few members of the Scot's clan have his power. . . ."

Edward Hopper, one of America's most admired artists, defended his choice of 'naive and primitive works' by admitting that he was looking more for vigor and 'something to say' than for technical skill. "In the vast sea of technically

225. Looking Down Brady Street Bridge

ESTHER PHILLIPS

Awarded Alumnae
Former Pittsburgh School of Design for Women Prize

FIG. 3   Reproduced from
Pittsburgh Associated Artists Catalog 1933

competent mediocrity that makes up the work to be selected at most exhibitions, one grasps at anything with a sign of life and this is often found in the most unskillful things."[13]

The following is a review in its entirety of the controversial show, with its amusing depiction of Esther among the art socialites—her demeanor, like the humble Mr. and Mrs. Kane, evidently different from the majority of opening-night attendees:[14]

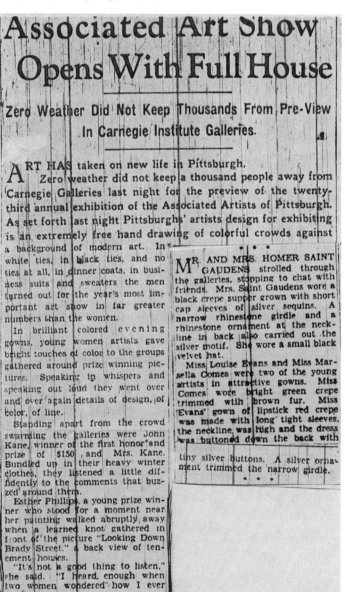

Associated Art Show Opens With Full House

Zero Weather Did Not Keep Thousands From Pre-View In Carnegie Institute Galleries.

ART HAS taken on new life in Pittsburgh.

Zero weather did not keep a thousand people away from Carnegie Galleries last night for the preview of the twenty-third annual exhibition of the Associated Artists of Pittsburgh. As set forth last night Pittsburghs' artists design for exhibiting is an extremely free hand drawing of colorful crowds against a background of modern art. In white ties, in black ties, and no ties at all, in dinner coats, in business suits and sweaters the men turned out for the year's most important art show in far greater numbers than the women.

In brilliant colored evening gowns, young women artists gave bright touches of color to the groups gathered around prize winning pictures. Speaking in whispers and speaking out loud they went over and over again details of design, of color, of line.

Standing apart from the crowd swarming the galleries were John Kane, winner of the first honor and prize of $150 , and Mrs. Kane. Bundled up in their heavy winter clothes, they listened a little diffidently to the comments that buzzed around them.

Esther Phillips, a young prize winner who stood for a moment near her painting walked abruptly away when a learned knot gathered in front of the picture "Looking Down Brady Street," a back view of tenement houses.

"It's not a good thing to listen," she said. "I heard enough when two women wondered how I ever got in."

MR. AND MRS. HOMER SAINT GAUDENS strolled through the galleries, stopping to chat with friends. Mrs. Saint Gaudens wore a black crepe supper gown with short cap sleeves of silver sequins. A narrow rhinestone girdle and a rhinestone ornament at the neck-line in back also carried out the silver motif. She wore a small black velvet hat.

Miss Louise Evans and Miss Marsella Comes were two of the young artists in attractive gowns. Miss Comes wore bright green crepe trimmed with brown fur. Miss Evans' gown of lipstick red crepe was made with long tight sleeves, the neckline was high and the dress was buttoned down the back with tiny silver buttons. A silver ornament trimmed the narrow girdle.

In addition to her prize-winning picture, Esther submitted *Puppett, Shops,* and *Study* in the 1933 AAP show. In the 1934 annual were *Two Girls on a Couch* and *Near the Mills.* And in 1936, what would be her last AAP show, she exhibited *Elizabeth* and *Old Wood.*[15] During the 1930s, Esther also showed her work in the invited exhibitions jointly sponsored by the Carnegie Museum and Carnegie Tech, such as the one McSwigan reviewed. Usually entitled "Exhibition of Paintings by Pittsburgh Artists," they were held in the third floor gallery at the Institute. It is on record that Esther was in shows in 1932, 1934, 1935, and 1936.[16] John O'Connor or Edward Duff Balken called upon the artists to attend, sometimes with written invitation; administrative archives at the Carnegie Museum of Fine Art hold some of the correspondence, or at least contain indications that such once existed.[17]

The Carnegie Institute seemed to be Esther's second home in the 1930s, not simply because she was showing her work there often. An acquaintance named Dorothy Steinberg, who along with her husband, Dr. Abram Steinberg, purchased some of Esther's work later in the 1950s, remembered how Esther frequented the library and museum halls at this earlier time, something she apparently enjoyed. Steinberg's recollection was that Esther did not relate very well to people, a different description than ones offered by close friends. But she based this on her only real observation of Esther at the time, whom she would often see at the library, usually alone, and supposedly "sticking quite close to the adjacent Women's Lounge area."[18] Likely Esther was hanging out to prompt chance meetings with O'Connor and other museum staff, who seemed to be rather accessible back then. (Not to mention meetings with famed artists. Esther later told her niece that she met Matisse in the elevator at the Carnegie—probably when he had taken first prize in the 1926 International. He was described as "a little, nondescript man with glasses."[19])

In addition to her numerous submissions to exhibitions, and being in close contact with the people who best knew fine art in Pittsburgh, in December of 1933 Esther also worked in the Public Works of Art Project of Western Pennsylvania, under Franklin Delano Roosevelt's Works Progress Administration (WPA). She registered under her parents' 5531

Jackson Street address, because she never stayed in any apartment for very long. The most visible products to come out of the WPA were the bridges and public park structures that most Americans are familiar with, so much still in evidence to this day. But the WPA had many subdivisions, one of which was the Public Works of Art Project, or Federal Art Project. Its subdivisions in most cities across the country were the Theatre Project, the Writers Project, and, for visual artists, the Mural and the Easel Projects. Only a small, though extremely descriptive, amount of documentation about the local WPA Arts Projects still exists on record in Pittsburgh, to be found at the Carnegie Museum of Fine Art administrative offices, and not within county government archives, where other WPA material resides.[20]

Like the Carnegie institutions, the WPA had a similar confusion of nomenclature for their programs, categorizing things so extensively as to seemingly rename them. The Pittsburgh art divisions were actually grouped under the title "Works Progress Administration Professional and Service Projects," and records list category names and corresponding serial numbers, with everything remotely creative included, from music to sewing projects to classification of the extensive glass industry in Pittsburgh. The *Art (Visual) #22907* division was officially headquartered out of the North Side Police Station, with sponsorship by the State Department of Public Instruction. Esther worked here under Harry Scheuch, the lone supervisor of 62 artists. The purpose of this Project was "to promote, initiate, coordinate, supervise and conduct art activities . . . creating work of art in all media in the fields of the fine and applied arts." It was extensive, with "easel paintings, lithographic prints, posters, watercolors, murals and sculpture" all included. Even Early American reproduction items were produced, to be included in both the Index of American Design and a book on Americana sponsored by the Library of Congress. Works were made and distributed for "the Public Schools, Carnegie Library, the U.S. Housing Authority and other tax-supported institutions."

As well, there were Federal Art Project exhibit locations all around Pittsburgh—at Buhl Planetarium, South Park Art Center, the City-County Building lobby, Penn-McKeesport Hotel, State Teachers College in the nearby city of California, and the Garden Market in Pittsburgh's Schenley Park. In all major cities across the U.S., similar activity was taking place. Esther created paintings at this time for the Liberman Home for the Elderly, for many grade schools, and for a public exhibition in a North Park Pavilion, all possibly sponsored by the WPA. Her involvement with the Federal Art Project in Pittsburgh lasted through June of 1934.

Associated with the Federal Art Project, for they were classified under the Professional and Service Projects, were the Museum Extension Projects across the state. Later, in the 1950s, John O'Connor expressed dismay to a friend of Esther's that Esther had not been able (unlike his own son, who was also an artist), to get on this Project in the 1930s.[21] The purpose of the Project, much like the other WPA work, was to "extend and increase museum advantages to the Public Schools of the State and to other public institutions. . . ." It employed "research-workers, draftsmen, artists, sculptors, photographers, model-makers, and other men and women from the professional and technical groups." Just a few of the materials produced: "models of historic locomotives, frontier forts, historic buildings, and of mankind's homes the world over, all built from scale drawings based on authentic research; plastic replicas . . . of fruits, vegetables, reptiles, and topographic relief maps, costume color-plates . . . dioramas; and puppets and puppet play scripts and properties."[22]

Governing bodies other than the WPA partially funded the work. The City of Pittsburgh and the Pennsylvania State College were both involved, the latter because the value of such vast creative output was deemed a realm of public education. The major uses of the products were as visual aids in the public school system, though many other public facilities also benefited, including the Fort Pitt Museum and the Historical Society of Western Pennsylvania in Pittsburgh. Though likely much of the work produced for school systems hasn't survived the touch of both youth and time, there is still output from the Art Project and Museum Extension Project in evidence today in natural history museums across the country, nostalgic mementos of a brief time when public policy at least addressed artists' dire need for work.

The inclusion of the arts in President Roosevelt's program to bring viable needed work to Americans was fateful for artists. Though the Depression was devastating to most people in the United States, ironically Esther and other artists found themselves considered for the first time. The economic downslide actually helped them. For once there was an organized means by which artists and other creative workers could earn a living by their chosen profession, their unique talent. The theory behind Roosevelt's programs was the intent to give not a handout, but an opportunity to all those needing work to do what they did best. That Roosevelt was mindful of the situation of artists, in addition to blue-collar workers, may have also enabled the general public to become more understanding of the plight of artists. If anything, the Depression reduced the common denominator of poverty—economic suffering had become more familiar to everyone. Unfortunately any extended public empathy and good will were squashed, as the program itself would be by upcoming political pressure.

For the time being, though, the WPA provided work. Artists not only earned money for their food and shelter, but gained a new sense of respect never quite possessed before. They were finally being seen and accepted as a viable part of society, at least in the government's eyes. Unlegislated individual viewpoints were much harder to change. Homer St. Gaudens, the director of Carnegie Museum of Art, published *The American Artist and His Times* in 1941, and in it delineated the significance that the WPA played in the lives of artists. He describes the 1930s as "a time when approximately 4,000 persons who called themselves artists were certainly in the submerged social strata. There was appropriated a sizable sum with which artists, 90% of whom were to be on relief rolls, were to be employed at wages of from $69 to $103 a month."[23]

Chapter Four

"FLIPPY"

*L*ike Mary Shaw, another irrepressible character of Esther's creative scene was a friend named James Van Trump. He would later be known as Pittsburgh's foremost architectural historian, and would become a beloved spokesperson on WQED public radio in the city. However, his fame came only after years of struggle as an architectural writer in the 1920s and 1930s, alongside Esther and many other underground creative figures. A collection entitled *Life and Architecture in Pittsburgh* pulled together his best-known essays in 1983. "Jamie" Van Trump, as he was affectionately known even by the public, established his reputation as a scholar-in-residence with the Pittsburgh History and Landmarks Foundation. Actually, he and Arthur P. Ziegler founded the organization in 1964, when they simply but nobly sought to stop the destruction of houses on Liverpool Street in Manchester, one of Pittsburgh's oldest North Side neighborhoods.[1]

Van Trump lived out his later years in the Wightman Nursing Home in Pittsburgh's Squirrel Hill section, a Jewish neighborhood where he spent much time as a young man. Toward his life's end in Wightman, he fondly remembered Esther, as he kindly shared a glimpse back at the late 1920s and the early 1930s. . . .[2]

In his eighties, James still looks like a marvelous creature from some liberal past, wearing a purple satin robe and sporting medallions around his neck, with flowing white shoulder-length hair and full beard. Being handed some articles written about Esther Phillips from a

1991 posthumous Pittsburgh show of her work, he was with interest now perusing the text and few photos from his bed. . . . Examining especially some professional studio shots of a young Esther so brought him back to that beloved time period that he soon begins to forge ahead, delectably verbalizing his memories. To have the opportunity to reminisce, to retell of this time long ago, of the creative way of being that he shared with Esther and others, seems intoxicating to him.

Jamie admittedly knew Esther "not well, but as part of the scene that I, myself was a part of at that time. . . . She kept turning up, you know? I never called her Esther, but "Flippy," and that's because she was rather flyaway. . . . She always seemed to be what we'd call slaphappy. All the amenities of civilized life didn't seem to mean much to her. . . ." (Van Trump next intimates that perhaps this made her difficult to live with.) "She was definitely social and often kind of silly; one could enjoy her when she was in one of her flippy moods. I thought she was funny, amusing, and so did others, our little potpourri of friends." He remembers first meeting Esther through poet/writer Merle Hoyleman—"a big, horsy woman—her *Asp of the Age* [one of the more popular of her privately published manuscripts] was one of the real triumphs I've seen." He especially admired Merle's modern use of metaphor and figure of speech, but regretted that the mass public didn't know her talent. Looking afar as he struggles to confirm his memory, Jamie states that he recalls seeing Merle and Esther together at the numerous parties that were held near the major intersection in Squirrel Hill, in houses behind the landmark church at Murray Avenue and Forbes. But Merle, Esther, and others in the scene seemed, to him, to revolve around writer Gladys Schmitt, "whose fame," was also "not what it should be." Gladys went on to become a recognized Pittsburgh novelist, getting a reputation nationally if only for a short time, with the profitable Literary Guild sales of her *David the King* in 1946.

Jamie carries on his drama with tales of the Pittsburgh artistic underground community. Gladys, Merle, Van Trump, Sybil Barsky, Mary Shaw, a friend by the name of Ernie Wright, Esther, and others would hit all the parties scattered about town and frequented by artists, musicians and the like. The friends also met at the Jewish Y on Bellefield Street, a point of convergence, where all the creative folk, especially writers, gathered for talk. Between 1933 and 1935, Esther apparently hung out much with Gladys, who, like Van Trump, was about six years younger than she was. Though "all the artistic people were drawn to Gladys," Van Trump never thought anyone was Glady's equal as much as Esther. "They were a real pair." Sybil Barsky also recalled their close friendship; she even remembered Merle Hoyleman once remarking that Gladys Schmitt was the only person to have posed nude for Esther.[3] (In Pittsburgh, that would be.)

Van Trump's wayward story continues . . . "It was true, Esther had nothing." He suggests that if Esther's family did have money (he did not know them well), it didn't show on her person or the life she was living. "Esther's lifestyle might not have been everything, but somehow or other she was a free soul." As he seemingly tries to establish exactly what he feels, Van Trump haltingly voices: "I often thought . . . it seemed to me that her looseness of life rather informed her art . . . although again, I'm not sure—when I look at some of the things she did. She had an attic room in an old Victorian mansion on Dithridge Street— the top story, it only had one dormer. She took the glass out. We said, 'Why did you take the window out?' Her response was, 'Oh, the rain can now come in. I like that.'"

He alternates from the recollections of the lighthearted, amusing "Flippy" to the more serious impressions of Esther, from her silliness to her yet almost "exotic, flowing manner—" he pausing to synch a memory with a look on Esther's face in a photograph he holds. "She was dizzy, always laughing and carrying on . . . and yet this photo, [a studio shot of Esther done by Pittsburgh photographer Luke Swank], I think, reveals the inner life of the artist. She was always rather gay, yet somehow it was forced." (Fig. 4)

While he reclines a bit further into the rocking chair that he by now has moved to with the aid of one of Wightman's nurse aides, Jamie continues talking with ease, yet definite intensity, about this period of life long behind him. He has vivid memories of friends visiting the charismatic Gladys Schmitt and her husband Simon Goldfield, both before she became semi-successful and after, when she was able to buy a big

FIG. 4   Esther, again circa 1925. (Photo: Luke Swank)

house on Wilkins Avenue in Squirrel Hill, with the down payment from the Literary Guild. In particular he recalls Esther's interaction with the many who flocked around the first Schmitt home on Shadyside's Howe Street in the early days, her sense of humor ever present. He takes delight in several times mimicking how the young Esther in conversation responded to Simon, who was quite the master of "extemporaneous limericks"[4]—

> . . . and then Esther'd exclaim, "O-oh, Simon! . . . " [ever so dramatically bending over, with huge arm gesture, slapping her knee, with a full belly laugh] . . . and we'd laugh and laugh. I can still hear her.

With only the briefest pause, Van Trump next utters, "I always liked Esther's watercolors. Watercolor was her gift." Her art reminded him of the artist Raphael Soyer, and also the French Romanticists, especially Pisan. He enjoyed her work so much that he made a point of showing some watercolors to a particular friend, and even to his own mother; both purchased a few paintings. But Jamie grows clearly frustrated now, immobilized in the conversation. He is trying unsuccessfully to remember what became of his mother's possessions—included but not limited to this painting—upon her death. Almost childlike, his balking frustration dissipates shortly, as his mind turns over new particulars. He suddenly recalls another scintillating image from the past . . . "It's just strange. I remember being some of these places . . . with Flippy. I'd be trying to get hold of Christopher Monkhouse, Curator of Architecture at Carnegie Museum [and Esther would be trying to run into art administrators there]."

Van Trump remarks, "I liked especially the interiors Esther did for Harold [Schwartz]." He recalled visiting Schwartz's apartment at the Bellefield Dwellings and there picking up one of Esther's interiors. "They were very beautifully done. Some of them were really fine, but I think at the time I also thought that she herself was so disjointed." He rambles . . . "She really in a sense wasn't my sort. . . . I don't mean to sound snobbish. . . . She did seem to know what she was doing, however."

Van Trump's family situation was quite different than Esther's. His mother lived in the East End of Pittsburgh—Point Breeze, quite close to Clayton, steel magnate Henry Clayton Frick's mansion. James came from a well-to-do family that appreciated art, despite a lack of desire to get to close to its makers. His voice crackles with amusement. "I don't know, I always thought that inviting my friends into my mother's house would have been too much for my family. . . ." Once again, with enthusiasm, he gleefully enacts repartee. This time it is a statement by his mother and—attentive to the needs of his stray friends—his own retort:

> My mother would say, "These are awful people." And I would respond, "No-o-o, they just don't have any **money!**"

Jamie Van Trump well remembers the early years of his own career, as he tried to find substantial, meaningful work, living as a young creative person, with all the struggles and pleasures. He graduated with a Master of Arts from the University of Pittsburgh in 1932. "The next 24 years were a period of intermittent job activity against a background of intensive study of Pittsburgh history and architecture, mostly in the Pennsylvania and Fine Arts rooms at the Carnegie Library in Oakland."[5] Throughout the course of his career, he published about fifty articles of Pittsburgh architectural historical significance and, he states, "never got a dime for them. I did it because I felt I had to." He offers, "At times, I'd have a job, at times I wouldn't," and recalls that the situation was about the same for Esther.

"She wasn't very good at making money, you know. I don't think she gave a damn, and I certainly didn't." He shared with Esther a sense of satisfaction at having the ability for creative output, despite the fact that it was attached to no money. He also had a desire to creatively convey, in his unique way, reflections of his hometown, as a passage from *Life and Architecture in Pittsburgh* illustrates. Not unlike Esther's paintings of Soho, here he provides the unusual and contrary perspective of looking upward at Mount Washington, that spectacular peak high above the banks of the Monongahela River, as seen from the lens of downtown Pittsburgh, that crux between three rivers and itself the usual object of view:

To the native eye there is a certain homely charm in this great hill with its low cornice of buildings—the usual late-19th-century miscellany of mansard and jigsaw curiosities, dotted with aridities of yellow brick. The whole broad scene presents another of those faintly raffish, haphazard effects in which Pittsburgh abounds. It is as if one of the wandering villages had crept up the other side of the ridge, and with one eye closed, hair all anyway, and cap pulled down, was peering over the edge with a kind of friendly slyness down at the Golden Triangle.[6]

Colleague Arthur Ziegler wrote of Van Trump and his work:

Buildings, the objects he most cherishes, are never treated in academic detachment; they are described in their human context and venerated through poetry in prose.

His writings take the form of personal essays. During most of his life, he has kept a journal in which he has recorded thoughts, ideas, events, but most often in which he has described an experience of the day. . . .

His work is an integration of a random journal among those misty corridors of our communal mind and an exacting knowledge of what was built and what happened in relation to those buildings. It is the expression of a unique sensibility as it plays over all of its becoming, and the emotional effect knowledge and experience have had. He is not lost in a romantic past; he is captivated by its existence, and by its recurrence in many forms in the present. . . .

Jamie reminds us that our buildings reflect lives; they express and symbolize those people who were involved in creating and in using them. . . .[7]

Extremely engaged by this subject of Esther Phillips' life, like the creative life that was his own, Van Trump tries to verbalize his anger and grief over a society that nary viewed creative talent as worthwhile. But he charmingly struggles to find the words, again. He is finally able to only get out that "people kind of took Esther and other artists for granted." But he, Esther, and the other artists in their circle were nevertheless generally happy. They knew that they had to exult in their talent, their core being, for they saw no one else exulting in them. Not that external regard didn't matter. "It was always something I needed to know . . . that you are being appreciated [in what work you are doing] even though you may not hold a regular job." With unsettled manner, he expresses his feeling that Esther and the others surely shared this sentiment with him. In his own case, through self-discipline and drive, he accumulated a body of knowledge about the history and environs of his home city. But only later did the people of Pittsburgh appreciate the fruits of his creative quests.

Though rapt throughout his provocative account of years past, Jamie Van Trump now is visibly weary, perhaps reminded too much by his last utterance of a very personal disillusionment. He concludes his reflections in fading voice, with another roving yet eloquent comment—an obviously favorite expression that he'd actually use in various incarnations for the third time by this point: "I am rather floating on the surface of life. . . ."

Years later, Esther remarked to friends in New York City that Gladys Schmitt's first novel, *The Gates of Aulis*, was actually about her. The novel grew out of Gladys' short story, "The House Divided." Her first published work of fiction, it appeared in the journal *Story* in 1934. Set in Pittsburgh, *The Gates of Aulis* is the story of an "ardent, intense" young woman painter, Ellie, who hangs out quite a bit at the Carnegie Museum, often mingling socially with administrators there. She is in search of happiness and fulfillment and she begins a long-distance love affair with a well-to-do older gentleman from Philadelphia who visits the museum regularly on business. He is a "wealthy, suave art collector who buys her best painting."[8] The novel relates the tale of Ellie and her brother, who try to go after what they believe in at all personal cost. But they later come to see this kind of sacrifice as impractical, and from their early idealistic ways return to more realistic paths. Ellie believed that "the success of her work depends to a large extent upon her own happiness." This was a philosophy evocative of the Carnegie Tech credo, and what the young Esther was discovering for herself. Despite similarities, though, between Ellie's and Esther's life in Pittsburgh, it appears the heroine of Gladys' novel was simply modeled a bit after Esther. There is nothing to substantiate that Esther ever had a relationship with such a gentleman, which no doubt would have made her lifestyle far more comfortable than it was. But this fictitious story of Gladys', an extrapolation perhaps on a romantic notion that the two young women shared, provided fodder for Esther's tale-telling later on, something she would be quite good at.

Though Esther and Gladys Schmitt were close in the mid 1930s, as Van Trump revealed and Sybil substantiated,[9] they would not maintain this closeness after Esther would leave Pittsburgh, unlike her friendship with Merle Hoyleman, which would continue. According to one of Merle's 1950s journals, she met Esther in the summer of 1933, shortly after arriving in Pittsburgh from Oklahoma, with her brother Rhese. Esther of course was just peaking artistically, at least as far as Pittsburgh public attention was concerned. Beginning that summer, she visited Merle often, who was living in central Oakland, on the campus of the University of Pittsburgh.

As Van Trump defined her, Merle Hoyleman was indeed a writer. For four decades, she published prose and poetry in small literary journals, some prestigious. In 1937, her work sat amidst the likes of Jean Cocteau, William Carlos Williams, and Gertrude Stein in the anthology *New Directions in Prose and Poetry*. Never would there be a larger forum for her writings, though she pursued that goal her whole life, attempting to publish her larger works in their entirety. In 1941, an opportunity to publish in book form materialized. Friend George Marion O'Donnell, of Oglethorpe University, wrote an introduction for the proposed manuscript but the project was not to be. (Merle would have both friendly and professional ties with the dashing young O'Donnell over many years; from time to time she told him about Esther's plight as an artist.) O'Donnell's Introduction is an apt reflection on Merle's "poetry of the imagination," and a learned glimpse of this abstruse woman writer and dear friend to Esther, one that can be found perhaps no where else.

> During the 1930s, the literary world was unduly preoccupied with ideas. . . . It seems significant that . . . Miss Hoyleman's

poetry has been published only in fragments, mostly in obscure magazines. In the thirties one might experiment with Marxism but not with metrics—much less with mythology. . . . For Miss Hoyleman belongs among the writers who try to make poetry with images and words, not—"my dear Degas"—with ideas. Moreover, at first sight her work appears strange.[10]

Merle saved O'Donnell's words and used them decades later when she self-published those few long poems that comprised the original ill-destined manuscript, including "Asp of the Age," which became the new collection's title. It would thus be 1966 before the Carnegie Library in Pittsburgh acquired the specially bound, primitive-looking, orange-covered oversize book, printed from the author's manuscript, with original prints by Margaret Cray Brown. It was a work obviously much labored over by yet another person so known to frequent its marble halls, making use of the wealth of cultural information there.

In another of Merle's manuscripts, *Letters to Christopher*, what O'Donnell calls "a loose novel of character," Merle has the protagonist, Phoebe, writing a series of letters to a beloved. O'Donnell comments that it is a work of "very high human-psychological and literary excitement, page by page," with the letters of Phoebe as "a kind of impressionist interior-monologue in disguise."[11] Perhaps not so oddly enough, the same could be easily said about decades of correspondence between Merle and others with whom she would feel a strong connection throughout her life, including Esther.

۞ ۞ ۞

According to records on microfilm at the art museum, John O'Connor (now the acting assistant director) personally called upon Esther in her studio/apartment on Tuesday, May 19, 1936, at 10:00 A.M., approximately seven months before she would leave Pittsburgh for New York City.[12] His visit was in preparation for the June 4–July 26 "Exhibition of Paintings by Pittsburgh Artists" to be held in the third floor gallery at the Institute. He would have walked the few blocks from the museum to her garret apartment at 415 S. Dithridge Street. Notations in museum records show that he viewed two paintings: *Colored Girls* and *Green Sweater*. However, what would end up in the show would be *Mattie*, which sold for $300, and *Portrait of Mildred,* which was not for sale.[13]

At this time Merle Hoyleman was spending her days doing what she did best—writing, and frequenting the department store and hotel cafeterias, where she drank coffee and talked literature with the passersby. Though she also spent much time at Carnegie Library, she was much more wont to interact with people in a dynamic environment, than to simply hang around the library, as Esther did. A letter written to friends years later perfectly captures what made up her days in any decade, as well her shrewd discourse.

> Planned to go to town early and sit in Wm. Penn Lobby [a prestigious downtown Pittsburgh hotel]. I enjoy surveying the crowd there—such a 'hodge-podge' of humanity. Last time I was there some old buck wanted to take me to dinner. I gave him a run for his money too. (He didn't anticipate it either.) I dressed him down. He frankly admitted he couldn't stand me for daily diet— but I HAD A MIND AND KNEW HOW TO USE IT.[14]

Esther would call upon Merle at her home in Oakland, likely taking with her a change of clothes, and laundry. While there, she surely bathed and ate well, as she did at Mary Shaw's. Esther, who seemed to Dorothy Steinberg "to have little social graces, and [was] not good at reaching out to other people," developed a strong friendship with Merle. Steinberg, who admittedly was not a close friend, said that Esther was "never a well-organized person mentally, was rather extravagant in her lifestyle, and very casual in manner."[15] Merle and Esther, like Van Trump, Shaw, and other artists, were indeed fringe characters—offbeat and unconventional in appearance and thought. With Merle and the others, Esther no doubt felt artistic and social camaraderie. Steinberg recalled that closeness between Merle and Esther, and later wondered if moving to New York did not hurt Esther simply because she broke close ties she had with people who liked and understood her, who appreciated her artistic drive. Other friends, who knew and understood Esther even better than Steinberg, expressed similar feelings.

James Van Trump remembered when Esther left town. "When she was living down on Dithridge Street, it was then that she said she was going to New York. We said, 'Oh, no, she shouldn't go. She should *not* go!' But she was determined to go—so she did." He was of the impression that she would have been better off if she had stayed in Pittsburgh, as she "seemed to need constant care." To clarify that, he said simply, "I wouldn't say that her mental state was very good." He felt that there was something a little "off" about her, the very term that a later close friend from the 1950s used to describe Esther's art. "She was under the surface. I just did not think, a person like her—[When reminiscing, Van Trump had again paused here, unsettled, arranging his impressions very meticulously]—have you ever read *Madame Bovary*? I remember that I always thought that Esther wanted something intensely, but she wasn't getting it."[16]

Esther had little contact with her family these last days in Pittsburgh—in fact, the last several years. The fiancee of Esther's younger brother Joe, who had been dating him since 1934, would never meet Esther, though they'd both view a painting of hers on display in the early 1930s at a North Park pavilion in Pittsburgh.[17] The family's opinions on her lifestyle hadn't changed, despite her bit of recent local acclaim. They conveyed to Esther the disparaging view that it was not okay to claim to be only an artist—a hint to her of something she'd better understand only with time and experience, that society little respects anyone not holding a "regular" job.

Esther's behavior was often so difficult that the family couldn't help but be exasperated with her, however. Dorothy cast the independent young woman artist, on those rare times she saw her, as "outgoing, very friendly, not particularly nervous or excitable, but someone who laughed a lot." She remembered posing for Esther in the studio she worked in at the Bellefield Y around the start of the Depression. She offered the following tale:

Esther said she'd like to do a portrait of me, but I'd have to supply the oils, the canvas. I said "o.k." and once a week I'd go to the studio and sit. Esther said she didn't want me to look at the work until it was finished. I went week after week and then Esther said she wasn't happy with it. She wasn't going to show it to me. I said I wasn't going to sit anymore! . . . She wouldn't talk about art with me; it was as if she thought I wasn't artistic enough to understand.[18]

Mary Shaw, too, remembered Esther's leaving town. "I helped her pack for New York City—she wanted to go where the real art was. Pittsburgh was sort of a side issue, you know . . . No, I didn't disagree with her decision." (Mary just didn't share Esther's strong pull toward the more stimulating professional and social whirl of the New York City art world.) "I never was particularly interested in [Greenwich Village]. I never thought very much of it because I knew of most of the kooks that were there." Though there was speculation that Esther had an unhappy love affair, possibly in Pittsburgh, Mary had sardonically discounted any theory that this was a reason Esther left. She stated definitively that nothing meant more to Esther than her painting. (Van Trump also offered that he didn't believe Esther to be very interested in romantic matters.) About Esther's having love affairs, though, Mary Shaw added, delightedly, "It's quite possible. Maybe she had two or three."

Mary Shaw recalled being surprised when she found out years later that Esther would fall upon ill health in New York. She felt Esther was "no more crazy than half a dozen others. She was a very nice person, maybe a little eccentric. . . . She had a very sound artistic sense. It may have been a bit exaggerated or under the gun, but she was a genuine artist." Of Esther's well-being in Pittsburgh, Mary said, "I don't think she was, ahh . . . overfed by any means." And of Esther's life after that point, Mary added, with a hearty yet compassionate laugh, "Every artist lives destitutely, dear, that goes to New York City."[19]

When asked if Esther seemed flighty in her desire to go to New York City, artist Milton Weiss had resolutely responded, "No. Every artist desires to go at one time or another. I also wanted to live in New York and did so for years." He continued, "Her parents and maybe some friends thought she was 'crazy,' wanting to just paint."

Any small disillusionment with the Pittsburgh art scene simply prompted Esther to move further toward an environment that might better bring her a personal vision of happiness. She was dissatisfied with the way of life laid out for her. But her dissatisfaction was not with fellow artists. Come the mid 1930s, despite the encouragement gained in having surrounded herself with like-minded and equally talented individuals, Esther was restless. She had finally found others who understood her and her lifestyle, a close circle of creative friends, and her paintings were beginning to get seen in a variety of venues around Pittsburgh, but she yearned for more. She was an artist, and a deep longing to be acknowledged for who she was, and what she did, was tugging at her.

> Out of desire, the artist creates a self which simultaneously embodies her in the world and marks her out as distinct, unassailably herself, unlike any other being. Such presence holds the encroaching world at bay, distances it, so that she occupies within an authentic self, a kind of psychic free zone in which her work can be developed. Sometimes an artist can gain access to that necessary free space by "withdrawing" to a place that gives it to her: New York, perhaps or Paris.[20]

Merle Hoyleman had moved to the Iroquois Apartments in Oakland by 1936. Though her later journals would be filled with references to Esther Phillips, only one direct notation of her friendship with her in Pittsburgh survives. Ironically, it is quite possibly the last time Merle saw her dear friend in person.

December 7, 1936–
Esther came bringing her meat and vegetables and apples. We cooked dinner together. She left around 9:30 p.m.[21]

With that, Esther left Pittsburgh for good—her art and her story eventually to resurface here, but she herself never to return. Merle received a postcard from Esther a few weeks later, postmarked Christmas Eve.

Hello—Merle
—am in N.Y.
—at 7 Morton St.—lovely apt.
—Try & come here & stay with me for awhile
Write me—love—
Esther Phillips

NEW YORK—EARLY YEARS

Chapter Five

"SHE WAS AN ARTIST & SHE STARVED"[1]

"The first month was hell! Lonely!" So Esther recalled her arrival in New York City to her niece forty-five years later. She had taken a train from Pittsburgh—$6.50 round-trip at the time—saying good-bye to no one in the family. Once in the city, she knew only that Greenwich Village was the place to go; she was intent on staking her place as soon as possible. She bought a big wheel of cheese to live on for awhile.[2] It took a few months and a few trips to Goody's Cafe to stumble upon a scene.

Goody's was "long and narrow and murky, a blind tunnel of a place, a burrow, a bat's cave, a bear's den."[3] It was apparently the cheapest eats and drink, save for the infamous "automats" that dispensed cheese sandwiches from machines, where many artists got the bulk of their sustenance. Goody's was north of Sixth Avenue, between 9th and 10th streets, and was owned by a guy named Goodman. When it came to just drinks, Minetta's was the tavern of choice among artists and writers. It was the place to go to continue, and end the night over, the creative rants and ramblings of the day.[4] Greenwich Village was a haven for those creative. In the dive bars, cafeterias, and burgeoning coffee-houses, Esther began to come into contact daily with other creative souls trying to make a go of it in the big city. These places were the principle rendezvous for Villagers, and where, more than anywhere else, Esther got to know both the artists who later would make a name for themselves, and others who would stay hidden.

Soon she fell into the routine of all artists of the Village. It consisted, usually in this order, of working at one's art; searching for cheap housing (but adequate studio space); frantic searching for means to earn money to pay for art supplies, a little food, and rent; and commiserating with everyone else attempting to do all the same. Egos clashed a bit, each arriving artist becoming competition for the other, but a sense of camaraderie overrode all. The artists came to offer each other support and encouragement, money if they had it, and a place to stay if needed. They helped each other because they knew that not a lot of others outside their circle would.

Esther had asked Merle Hoyleman to write her, and write her she did, starting a correspondence that would continue at least through the late 1950s. According to one of her journal notations, Merle got a letter off to Esther just a week after the Christmas Eve note, but there is no surviving copy of the letter itself, unlike others that Merle saved over the years.[5] Esther herself wrote again a couple of months into her adjustment to the new city. She wrote, as she painted, on whatever was available. The evident variety, in the former case, included letterhead from hotels, postcards, scrap paper. Most of the correspondence, to be written over several decades to come, was in pencil, to friends who undoubtedly got used to the semi-legible, unique scrawl.

[Feb 13, 1937] [6]

Hello Merle-

How are you?—I had written to you but lost the letter as I was on my way to mail it—I have been too worried about money etc to write to anyone—That is—I had not the inclination to do so!—

Are you working—N.Y. is very expensive—I'm dead broke—in fact if it weren't for a few friends here who bought a few water colors from me—I would have been penniless—Rent is very high here—my rent is $32.50 a month—besides electricity—food is rather cheap.

Let me know how you are getting along—etc—write soon—

Esther

Merle's brief but telling journal notations over the years would reflect the twist and turn of events in her friend's life. Merle usually noted Esther's situation rather matter-of-factly, as in the spring of 1937, when she commented on a postcard from Esther: "She is apparently happier in NYC."[7] As it happens, Esther had been making her way around the still-foreign city, catching various art exhibitions. The big one of the time was the "Fantastic Art" show at the Museum of Modern Art. It was made up of works surrealist, concerned with the subconscious and connected with automatism (automatic) drawings, and Dada, another avant-garde European movement. More importantly, Esther had just met up with a woman artist and small circle of friends, whose company she would grow to enjoy, respect, and rely on in the coming years.

⑥ ⑥ ⑥

Eugenia Hughes had been living in Greenwich Village with her father, Roy Hughes, a couple of years before Esther arrived. Both she and her father drew and painted. Unlike most Villagers, they lived a slightly more stable existence, due to his having worked as a newspaper illustrator for some years. He a widower and she an only child, Eugenia and Roy had a marvelous, unconventional friendship as father-and-daughter artists. A group of fellow artist friends—including the caricaturist Jake Spencer and humorist S.J. Perelman (famous for his writings for *The New Yorker*) congregated around the Hughes, who were strongly committed to enjoying the creative life. Like Merle, Van Trump, and many other educated people of the times, Eugenia kept journals of her activities and contacts. The first mention of Esther is May 31, 1937: "Saw Esther Phillips in Park. Does nice watercolors."[8] It seems once the worth of a fellow artist's work had been established, a Villager would recognize, and often embrace, those efforts as his own.

"Going into the Village for the first time . . . was like walking into a dream." There was a stillness about the place, almost a hush, compared to the taxi-blasting traffic, street crowds and vendors of the rest of the city. "The special quiet of the Village suggested creation rather than commerce and conveyed a tone of mystery."[9] Unlike the rest of Manhattan, the Village had a life of its own, full of creative energy. It even "looked different from New York City—small, cozy brick or frame houses on winding streets rather than looming skyscrapers. You could see the sky, you knew your next-door neighbors, and it was informal—you didn't have to get dressed up."[10]

Around any corner of the Village, one "might stumble upon a cobblestone alleyway, lined with thirty little stucco houses that look like a picture postcard from Majorca or Malaga."[11] There was definitely a quaintness associated with being there, where vendors still displayed and peddled wares in horse-drawn carts in the 1930s. "You could tell the Village was special simply by looking at the map of Manhattan, where the ordered grid of avenues and streets went suddenly crooked, twisting and turning in an unruly whorl. Small lanes looped and stuck out at angles like so many secrets in a neighborhood where the regular compass of rules went defiantly, rebelliously awry."[12]

Many artists went to Washington Square Park to draw, paint, sit, and talk of art and their world. It was set in the middle of the Village—with the notorious statue of Garibaldi at one end, and at the other, that middle of the northern side where Fifth Avenue ends, was Stanford White's Washington Arch with the inscription, "Let us raise a standard to which the wise and honest can repair." It was quite a community gathering place. Many times it became a point of departure for both painting excursions around the city and for artists' collaborative attempts to market their work. Because most artists had no phones and many also lacked consistent addresses, the park played a vital role as meeting point. When work wasn't the priority at hand, groups of friends would embark towards a beer in Minetta's Tavern, which bordered Washington Square at the corner of Minetta Lane and McDougal Street.

A lot of the Village artists in the late 1930s lived very close to Washington Square Park, many in "walk-ups," second—and third-floor apartments that bordered the southern edge of the square. Artists, of course, lived with their work; these "flats" had beautiful skylights that provided amazing illumination, making perfect studios, and they were praised by many a writer detailing the conduciveness of the Village to creative work. According to artist Lenore Monleon, later to be an acquaintance of Esther's in the 1950s, "New York University wanted to tear these studios down and they eventually did. But there was an organized protest that [she, herself] spearheaded. They didn't tear the slums in the area down, but the beautiful studios for the artists, yes."[13]

So Esther Phillips and Eugenia Hughes bumped into each other in Washington Square Park and formed a lasting friendship. It began with Esther slowly finding a place among Eugenia's circle of friends. Soon, Eugenia's journals would echo Esther's increasing involvement in her daily life. Esther's name was suddenly appearing lots, as would Esther on Eugenia's doorstep. The Hughes home was a strong focal point for the handful of friends close to them. Roy was a devoted father and faithful mentor; Eugenia kept house (actually apartment) and looked after her father's welfare and that of the friends who gathered there as well. Quite good at opening her home to others, only a few times did she express annoyance at those clamoring around her. In early summer, Eugenia notated that Esther and two other friends had come by. "Ate dinner in spite of them—finally had to offer Esther some food. . . ."[14]

Though beginning to find friendship was no doubt reinforcing for Esther, she actually missed Pittsburgh terribly in the beginning. After years of growing up and painting there, though it hadn't satisfied her, Pittsburgh had at least become a familiar artistic and social presence for her—the hills, the neighborhoods and parks she knew, her fringe friends of many years. The artistic subculture of Greenwich Village was by no means foreign to her nature, but change in general, and the new surrounding physical environment, was likely still a bit disorienting.

From Eugenia's journal:

July 25, 1937—Jake Spencer's daughter around. Esther came by— she's homesick for Pittsburgh. Sits in the park at nite and cries. Left her—and into bar for beer.

Slowly, Esther found new environments to paint, and her heartsickness for Pittsburgh diminished. She motivated Eugenia to go with her to visit all parts of the city. As in Pittsburgh, she took with her paints and easel, always ready to capture whatever visually stimulated her. In the beginning, Eugenia went along for pleasure only, but gradually became equally interested in capturing some of these images, usually in pen and ink. It seems that Esther had a positive creative influence on her. And Eugenia and friends, who were becoming more accustomed to Esther's presence, would slowly familiarize her with the partying of the Village, a bit wilder than the creative scene in Pittsburgh.

August 6, 1937—Company tonite—Ruth, Jack, Esther & [S.J.] Perelman—latter half-drunk. We went to park later—apartment hot. I sang all the songs I knew.

August 15, 1937—Esther had breakfast with me—then to park—then to aqua zoo to look at the fish. Must paint these some time. To Staten Island. Lay on grass. Sun flowing—pleasurable—open sky.

August 17, 1937—Esther came by with girl from Pittsburgh—wanted me to go to Staten Island—wish I would have.

Fig. 5 Eugenia Hughes.
Reproduced from the Manuscripts and Archives Division,
New York Public Library.

Paintings that survive of Esther's early period in New York are done in an abstract and geometric style. Their content clearly shows that Esther made her way well outside the Village, around to all parts of Manhattan, including numerous New York City playgrounds. She saw bits and pieces of the vitality of her new city and conveyed it to canvas. When not capturing the moment, Esther took mental notes on the "spirit and significance"[15] of all within her field of vision, to be later created anew from her watercolor box.

Though she enjoyed the companionship provided within Eugenia's circle, and her artistic sense was stimulated anew, Esther lived a very minimal existence that certainly threatened her good times. She tried surviving from sales here and there of her art work, but a nervousness was ever present, as she began to see that artists everywhere were suffering. So as she once again attempted, unsuccessfully, to find meaningful employment based on her talent and abilities, she began a series of moves from place to place about the Village, continually looking for affordable housing. When she couldn't pay the rent for a place she was in, she would move on before the landlord could evict her. Fellow artists, writers, and poets lived communally when necessary, "sharing each other's wealth," as Esther wryly put it.[16]

Esther's sister Dorothy recalled that at one point in the late 1930s, her brother Joe and his new wife, Bert, went to New York to attempt to visit Esther. They got directions from someone, but this wouldn't have been Merle, who did not know the family at this time. Likely it was from one of a few other friends Esther was also corresponding with. Joe and Bert came across the beautiful lofts with skylights bordering Washington Square, but there was no trace of Esther. "Looking her up," according to Dorothy, "was easier said than done. She was not there. Some young fellow was." They tried again and she was still not where they expected to find her, so they returned to Pittsburgh. The family "just couldn't understand why they hadn't been able to see Esther."[17]

Later in life Esther told Dorothy that she often tried to use ovens in her apartments to bake her ceramics. That may further explain her transience, as many landlords inevitably evicted her for such unorthodox use of a stove. And it may or may not explain one journal entry of Eugenia's from the 1930s: "Something happened to Esther's stove—got home—everything covered with soot."[18]

۵ ۵ ۵

Come the summer of 1937, just a half-year after Esther's move, Merle Hoyleman was already attempting to locate her whereabouts in New York City. This pattern became common practice over the years, as Esther moved frequently and didn't always respond in the same timely fashion to letters that Merle did. In early July, when a letter sent to her was returned, Merle then wrote John O'Connor at the Carnegie Art Museum to see if he knew Esther's New York City address. He did not. Resourceful as ever, though, Merle and Esther were back in touch in about a month's time. Esther had moved to West 3rd St. in the Village. Her landlord would be a Village legend famous for helping artists out, noted in innumerable books, stories, and other accounts detailing Greenwich Village of this time. His name was Strunsky.

Merle sometimes included notes to Esther in the letters Ann Snider, a mutual Pittsburgh friend, sent along to New York City. It seems Esther maintained a small bit of correspondence with Ann, who was likely the visiting friend from Pittsburgh that Eugenia had referred to. Merle thus found how Esther was faring through Ann and also through correspondence with a longtime friend, Harold J. Winters, who lived in New York City. Harold was business manager and co-editor of *The Handwriting Magazine* and *The Satiricon*, writing under the pen names B. M. Lawn and Arthur Spade. He and Merle had been corresponding since the early 1930s. He got to know Esther when Merle asked that he look her up. Once he did, he seriously became concerned about her situation. Harold saw only Esther's struggle to make ends meet, and overlooked the nevertheless joyous company she kept with fellow artist friends. A few letters that he sent to Merle in 1937 and 1938 vividly detail her early hard life in the city, with the most striking being that first that mentions Esther, of November 21, 1937.[19]

Harold Winters was a kind soul struggling to make his own ends meet, with a young son and an estranged wife. He was very much a businessman, but, being a writer at heart, he had an affinity towards Esther and Merle and all working artists. In that first letter, Harold spoke of "the Project"—specifically, the Writing Project of the WPA's arts division, which employed Merle. Come 1937, it was very evident that FDR would need to scale back (and soon thereafter eliminate) the Federal Art Project of the WPA, due much in part to Republican pressure in Congress. Artists, writers, and theatre people across the country felt the ax coming. Merle was feeling jaded, having not made much headway with the publishing of her writing. Like any smart artist, in addition to the WPA work, she continually marketed and sought private funding for her real work. She pursued numerous professional contacts, all potentially lucrative; few ever panned out.

Harold wrote Merle about the WPA in other letters as well. "There is much talk of the decline of the WPA Projects, reducing in number from time to time. It will bring hardship to many people, as group after group is dropped from the payrolls. . . . This is a cruel world when left without funds. I have experienced it and I know you have too." Though he wrote of pleasant things, including literary talk that no doubt stimulated Merle, sometimes Harold could not offer to his dear Pittsburgh friend much more than what, to him, were unfortunate truths. "You must learn to accept this heartless world as being the regular order of things."[20]

Upon receiving the infamous November 21, 1937 letter from Harold, Merle immediately confided in the close circle of friends that she and Esther had shared in Pittsburgh, because the information on Esther's condition upset her terribly. "She was an artist and she starved" was Jamie Van Trump's estimation of Esther's situation, based on the information passed along through Merle. [21] "She starved in the Village," offered Milton Weiss, restating what evidently became a known fact among the friends in Pittsburgh who were hearing of Esther's fate. As she would do throughout the years to come, Merle set out to inform just about everyone she trusted, personal and professional, of Esther's plight, whether they had ever met Esther or not. However, Merle did not tell everyone she knew. She was continually making notations about various people and situations. She did not want to "let information get in the wrong hands," in that it might harm certain individuals.[22] But in the case of Esther's early battle in New York, Merle felt that telling artist friends and particular arts-interested professionals could only help her friend's situation.

Merle often kept a draft of letters she sent out, a practice not uncommon in an age with strong literary tradition. She was sure to also scribble headings wherever Esther and others may have forgotten dates, and to staple together accompanying envelopes, in that romantic custom of showing time and station of departure of correspondence. Merle took time out from attending to her own important matters whenever Esther's situation so grieved her. The draft of the following correspondence, dated just five days after Harold's startling letter, reveals Merle's resourcefulness and extreme loyalty, as well her quick mind and unique correspondence style, evident in the second half's stream-of-conscious notations.

5973 Alder St
Pittsburgh, Pa
Nov. 26, 1937

Dear Mr. O'Donnell:

What have I done? I am several days late replying, and when it comes time for your letter to arrive, it won't arrive. But please, please forgive me? Since Monday, I have been so upset over Esther Phillips, a girl friend, an artist, who is starving to death that I have used every inch of my strength and strategy to call forth aid for her. Monday evening I telephoned John O'Donnor (Homer St. Gauden's assistant at Carnegie Museum) and John Bowman (Chancellor Bowman's son). That Latter's wife, xxxxxxxxxxxxxxx xxxxxxxxxxxxxxxxxxxxxxxxxxx Melita Pels, is a very good friend of Esther's. Inasmuch as Miss Melita wasn't in, I talked to John Bowman. He tells me that they had a friend, from Johnstown, who was in New York City about a month ago and that Esther was all right. However, I imagine this friend may have been pretty well fixed, and Esther preferred not discuss her personal affairs. On xxxxxx Tuesday afternoon I saw Mr. O'Connor at some length, and he said he would get in touch with Bill Schulgold (formerly of Pgh. and an artist) and look into Esther's case. I hope Mr. O'Connor will do something immediately for her--at least send her enough money so she can have a little food. (Incidentally, Mr. O'Connor's son is working under one of the artist at the Museum Extension Project, 3400 Forbes St, Pgh.) Also, on Monday night I telephoned Clara Finnegan for advice. She told me to write Mrs. Martha Colt, Supervisor in charge of Museum Extension Projects, Harrisburgh. part 1 a This, I have done this evening. I enclosed a copy of the letter from a friend who wrote me of Esther's distresses. Tuesday Tuesday evening i telephoned another friend who talked nonsense for one solid hour. I shall certainly tell Esther, if I ever see her again alive, that Ann Snider is no friend of hers. It made me heartsick--the jealousy people have for the gifted; it is wickedly cruel and despicable. The Bowmans were going to NYC over the holidays and they will look her up. If they will only understand, I shall be grateful...

Monday evening I was at Dr. Wright's again. We had
a pleasant chat...but the night was a cold one, and made it
difficult about traveling.

Sunday, Nov. 21, a friend came in the morning and took
me for a long ride over the Pittsburgh hills, and through a
xxxxxxxxx snowstorm. Can you imagine my xxxxxxxxx delight (?)
I, who loves all things in an elemental state... It was a rare
occasion, and one seldom given me.

Tuesday night I had to fulfil xx a dinner engagement
and from a promise the week before. It was Mr. & Mrs. Fitzpatrick's
whom I mentioned in early Aug. xxxx

Wednesday evening after work I was looking at the
International again. Afterwards, I stopped at Clara McVay's.
She lives at the Iroquois. I had not been there for a month, and
I feared her feelings might be hurt.

Nov. 24th

There was a brief note from James Laughlin IV. I am
posting a list of names tonight--but the conditionx of times
is bad, and against the book business. One never knows who will
and who won't buy.

Yesterday, I was in the country for Thanksgiving. I
haven't seen such a feast for a couple of years--yes, longer
than that. While I do not eat, it is nice to watch others.

Nov. 22, I received a letter from Paul Snodgrass. He
is back in New York City; and requested that I thank you, for him,
for writing the article on my poetry. I do not know what he is
doing now.

I have written Doris Levine, Lincoln Kirstein's
secretary a brief note tonight--a xxxx a reply to her letter of
Nov. 9, 1937. I have been slow, but I was waiting, hoping xxxxxxxx
I might have definite xxxxxxxxxxxxxxxxxxxxxxxxxxxxxxxxxxxxxx information about going in Dec.

The temperature jumped to 50 today, after being from
15 to 20. Perhaps it will soon be turning colder, as it is
the time of year for winter.

Nov. 20th, I saw Dr. Metzger again. He tells me my
eyes are much improved. Pxxxkxkkx Probably most that was wrong
xxxxdxxxxxxxxkxxfxfxxx had been caused by the lack of proper
nourishment.

I have rested all day, and expect to do likewise to-
morrowx.

Trust you had a splendid Thanksgiving; and will
find time to write me. .for your letters have become a part
of my existence.

                              Sincerely,

The hand-written postscript transcribed—with the especially relevant first sentence, providing documentation of possibly the most significant, yet overlooked, professional transaction of Esther's career:

> They have bought some of Esther Phillips' work (oils and watercolors) for the permanent collection in the Museum. But you know how it goes very few care . . . and fewer understand. Esther not only needs food—but love, care, and attention. They tell me she had periodic spells of starvation for the last several years in Pgh. I lent her all the change I could spare, and Miss Fitzpatrick gave me money to include with mine. I suppose after Ann Sniders rehearsal that she'll mail her a few dollars. She should!

The next letter from Harold, November 28, 1937, attests that Merle had immediately written back to him as well after his alarming letter.

November 28, 1937

Dear Merle:

I was about to reply to your first letter when your second arrived and also the two dollars in it. After receiving each letter I immediately went to see Esther . . . to encourage her by making her realize that others are concerned about her. She certainly felt grateful for the money you sent. I have been doing whatever I could, but of course it is hardly enough. If I were only clear of personal debts I would have borrowed a sum of money and given it to her, but then I have been struggling with my own personal obli-

gations. No matter how I try I cannot make ends meet. I am practically without any resources or any prospects of obtaining financial relief from other than my regular income, which is by far too insufficient for my requirements. It is a terrible feeling to be financially dispossessed and then to see someone else in so similar a predicament. . . .

All I did so far has been to give Esther small sums for carfare in order to see prospective buyers for her watercolors. I also have taken her to lunch each time I visit her. But she has been eating very sparingly and that makes me feel that I have done very little for her. The pity of it also is that she is not eligible for relief. She's here only eleven months and the requirements are 2 years. And she impresses me as being very determined to remain in New York. She claims her career demands that she stay here. A few prospects have indicated a willingness to look her work over. And it is rather hopeful because she already sold one or two canvasses.

Other friends are also doing little things for her. They have supplied her with nourishment and the landlord, a kindly old man of literary stock, is overlooking the nonpayment of the weekly rent. . . . You can be assured that I shall do everything I am capable of doing for her.

As ever friendly,
Harold

Esther got a letter off to Merle in November; the return address was "W. 3rd. St., c/o Strunsky."

[November 1937]

Dear Merle—Thanks so much for the $2.00—Came in very beautifully—but must have been an uncomfortable sacrifice for you. . . . Sometimes, I'm a little tired of it all—but so many people here are more or less in the same boat—

Mr. Winters is trying to get me on relief—He's so kind and fine—I'm very fond of him—unusual person.—Will write you a letter—darling—in a few days

—love Esther

Merle was of course always busy with her own writing, yet she continued to make time to plead Esther's cause to those in positions of power. She was in touch with one of her editors, James Laughlin IV, founder of New Directions, the avant-garde publishing house based in the Village and best known for the anthologies *New Directions in Prose and Poetry*. Merle's correspondence and journal documentation suggest that she was good friends over many decades with him and his parents. Mr. and Mrs. H.H. Laughlin maintained a residence on Pittsburgh's exclusive Woodland Road, set on the elegant campus of the woman's school Chatham College. As for James, she would later dedicate her self-published manuscript, *Asp of the Age*, to him: "For James Laughlin, entrepreneur for three decades, 1936–1966."

In addition to those people detailed in her letter to George Marion O'Donnell, Merle also wrote of Esther's situation to Emma Guffey Miller of Washington, D.C., who supposedly was a prominent sister of a 'Senator Guffey' and, specifically regarding the WPA work, to "Flo Cochrane, Supervisor of the Division of Women's Professional Projects." She continued to see John O'Connor of the Carnegie Museum on Esther's behalf, urging him to write Esther. In fact, Merle copied Harold's eloquent November 21, 1937 letter, outlining "Esther's distresses" and used that very piece of writing to plead Esther's case to all of these individuals. Merle told Harold around this time that this particular correspondence "was the only way to explain Esther's condition—and far better than I."[23] In December 1937 correspondence, Merle sent along to Harold some letters that she had collected from friends, to give to Esther. Here only ten days after Harold detailed the sorry state Esther was in, Merle had already gathered some support for her. Merle also inquired of Esther whether the Bowmans had met up with her yet, they traveling in New York, and she makes a note in her journal about asking Harold if he knows whether John O'Connor had written Esther yet.

Harold especially supported Merle's attempts to reach Emma Guffey Miller about the WPA Projects for Esther. "[Getting on the Project in New York] is the only hope for her, as her situation is very desperate. I am deeply moved each time I come to see her. She has few clothes and needs more nourishment. It's all very tragic. Have just mailed her a check which I obtained as a loan from a friend of mine in the promise that I repay very soon. So you see I couldn't do more even if I tried."[24] Harold was always encouraging Merle, as well, in her own attempts to make headway with her publishing contacts. She made a quick, spontaneous business trip to New York herself early in the winter for that purpose, but she was unable to hook up with either Harold or Esther at the time, according to her journal. Despite being glad that she was working toward publishing contacts, both friends nevertheless conveyed disappointment in subsequent letters, to hear that Merle had been in the city, yet unable to visit with them. Merle made a couple future trips, but there is no evidence to suggest that she ever actually hooked up with Esther in person there.

By January of the new year, 1938, Harold still had much the same news. "I have seen Esther a number of times and each time she gives me the impression that she feels herself sinking lower into a state of hopelessness. I try to encourage her and cheer her up and every time I give her the small sum of money I can afford, she is overwhelmed with the sense of gratitude and at the same time, a feeling of humility."[25] Esther was on the brink of giving up her fight to survive in the Village. The most remarkable letter describing her despair would come from herself, written to Merle that very January.

[January 23, 1938]

Dear Merle—

Was glad to receive your letter—am not on relief, yet—& do not know how I will make out—as yet—Dr. Leslie—a publisher of "P.M." Magazine sent for me—(maybe there's a break there—) who knows—This Dr. Leslie, being a friend of a man who bought a w. color several months ago—(the name being Herbert Matter—famous photographer on Harper's Bazaar etc) So if I get a job or some thing I won't have to go on relief—

Also—Mr. Pine of Dauber & Pine bookshop I'm to meet this week—maybe a job or some thing there!—Something must break—as I'm thoroughly disgusted, at the end of my string—my room is so depressing—& so small that you wouldn't believe your eyes if you saw it—and the building very sordid—always drunken village women—around the building—partying in some man's room—etc

Saw Norman McLeod—the other night—He does book reviews for a living—He wanted to come up and see work—but told him my room was too small to hold both me and him & my work—would have to wait until I got a larger place—He asked about you & mentioned that he read your poem in "New Directions"....Saw Winters yesterday—Gave me a dollar—

If I get too tired of this fantastic struggle, will go back to Pittsburgh and get on a Project—

I'm so tired of it all lately—that I feel completely drenched of emotion and energy—so you see what N.Y. is—It's really a cold & ugly city—utterly heartless, at most times—but sometimes it is unbelievably maudlin and warm and even though most newcomers are received by the villagers with open arms—nevertheless they are also looked upon with suspicion.

At any rate—it's some city—a city to keep away from!—though I'd like to see you, even here!—

Will write with the news.

Love Esther

Chapter Six

"THE A.M. AFTER THE NIGHT BEFORE"[1]

Soon after she sent this striking letter off, ironically, a bit of light actually shone through for Esther. Harold wrote on the last day of January that he suddenly hadn't seen much of her because she was following leads, seeing people at odd hours to present her work. "And the prospects seem good. Something may break for her yet. . . . Anyway, it is encouraging to know that there are others interested in you, and this seems to [now] be the case with Esther."

Though certainly a maddening, time-consuming effort, artists many times attempt to hook up with profitable business leaders who could, through the purchase or sponsorship of work, positively direct the course of a career. Merle certainly always worked at this, and Esther was finally finding some luck at this in New York City. It is sometimes only this extra hopefulness—that those with prominence and money (usually not found within the artistic circle) might see one's work as valuable—that can keep a creative artist sane, certainly attached to a desire, as well, to be noticed by the scant few influential figures within the art world.

"She has much better chances now than in the past," continued Harold in the same letter, as Esther sold a couple canvasses. He stated, too, that she suddenly looks and feels much better than he ever remembered. He was starting to see less and less of her. This was a good sign, for Esther contacted him only when things became intolerable and she needed a bit of cash urgently.

In a nostalgic, later letter to "Jerry"—the name Eugenia went by to friends—Esther referred to missing some of the activities that made up their life in the Village. Esther remembered calling on Jerry: "We'd paint together—then sometimes we'd go to 'Cafe Espresso' for a 'rum baba & cafe a lait '—on Bleecker Street. . . . I think of the clothes we used to sew together. I never realized before how happy I should have been."[2] Esther did have much happiness at this time, with that sense of community with other artists, but she was also unsettled, her emotions swaying on whether or not she was able to bring in money from her painting. Though she indeed recalled fond memories of the 1930s to friends she met in later decades, she was suffering economically. A nervous sense pervaded over her very unpredictable life. She lived freely and was spirited, but that still could not make up for a longing she carried with her.

Harold and Merle, the latter who was still writing professional contacts on Esther's behalf, suspected that Esther might come back to Pittsburgh at any time. Though there were now some business contacts for her, these didn't bring any sense of economic security. (Until an artist actually sees money from a potential buyer of a work, a writer from promises to be published, a musician from a possible gig, a nagging caution always tempers one's hopefulness.) From Merle's journal that spring comes the indication of the rollercoaster ride that was Esther's sense of stability: "[Esther] is unable to make any headway in New York—unless her wheel of fortune has changed [since last correspondence]."

Harold too expressed dismay over the whole situation again on April 10, 1938. Though he no longer came into contact with Esther, he wrote, "A person can't endure such hardships indefinitely. . . . She is a fine person and deserves a better fate." Esther, who had recently moved to Hudson Street, but was giving Eugenia's W. 16th St. address to Merle,[3] finally began to receive welfare payments come August, slightly earlier than the supposed two-year residency requirement. She continued to work on her art, and wasn't content being on welfare. Her desire was to get money for her painting, and a WPA Project job would allow her that, so she continued to pursue that avenue. But she wrote Merle that she was awaiting a copy of her parents' citizenship papers in order for that to take place.[4]

From Eugenia's journal:

September 13, 1938: Esther came over—to see about WPA job. She had interview. We went marketing later.

Of the two WPA visual art subdivisions, the Easel Project and the Mural Project, Esther especially desired getting on the former, even though it seemed the Mural Project was the more popular across the country. Many later-recognized artists of Esther's generation, and the subsequent generation, were on the Mural Project, which got much press for the completion of grand murals in public-sponsored spaces, often under the supervision of already acknowledged artists of the time, such as Diego Rivera, whose attraction to socialist cause directed his artistic content matter. This attention to social cause, that many artists of the 1930s embraced, diverted much American art for a while to the realist style, despite gains made in modern abstractionism since the 1913 Armory show.

Esther, however, was interested in choosing the Project which had activities that were most similar to what she had already been doing— painting smaller works on canvas and board. "Easel Project painters were required only to report back from time to time with a minimum quota of work," according to Dore Ashton in *The New York School: A Cultural Reckoning.*[5] Recalled Milton Weiss, who indeed was on that very Project in Pittsburgh, "I had a salary and they got my supplies. All I had to do was turn in one piece a month. I turned in a couple. It was wonderful. I received $80–90 a month." In New York the minimum given was $94 a month.[6] The small canvasses that the artists turned in were then used in much the same way murals were to benefit the public. When they were placed in the public schools and the like, the general population gained exposure to the arts.

Esther just missed, by a few years, when a new supervisor from Harrisburg came onto the Project in Pittsburgh. It appears there had been no set-up solely for easel painters in Pittsburgh during the small amount of time Esther was on the roster before she left. But in the late 1930s, administrators had been looking for artists for this newer aspect of the Project there, according to Weiss. He felt that Esther's getting on the Easel

Project "would have been a godsend for her." While Esther waited, though, for the Works Progress Administration to process her application in New York (upon proof of her citizenship), she in the meantime got swept away with the many wild social happenings about her.

Journals of Eugenia Hughes reveal the frolic and the lasciviousness of the Village. During that summer of 1938, she and Esther went to one party after another. Eugenia also had become acquainted with a new male friend, Annino Mariano; he too now hung out with the Hughes congregation. Over the years, Eugenia had much male attention, as scores of love letters would attest, but it seems "Anno" became a serious long-term love.[7] "The '30s were wild, wild times," Esther would tell two particularly close friends in the 1950s, Ed Evans and Glen Gress. She recalled to them the all-night parties, the nonstop comings and goings from Washington Square Park to taverns to flats. Evans got the distinct impression from Esther that the 1930s "were not so much a creative time, as a party, great-fun time," which, in the 1950s, she missed terribly. She affectionately described a Greenwich Village very bohemian, "very loose," Gress would recall.[8]

Indeed the long-standing reputation heard of the Village included not simply the strong, present creative and intellectual life but also the ardent partying. Perhaps some would say the commiserating among the creative souls there took the form of too much rollicking. But they were living intensely—soaking up all experience much as they painted or made music. In the late 1930s, there was an abundance from which Eugenia, Esther, and friends could choose their evening's entertainment—"Boogie-woogie at Cafe Society Downtown," famous singers at the Village Vanguard, "foreign movies at the Rialto on Forty-second Street," and dancing in "dance halls up in Harlem."[9] Esther and friends also frequented the 3rd street nightclubs and the numerous coffee shops in the Village, where they would meet all the famed as well as to-be-forgotten artist personalities.

Esther and Jerry did much together as two close women friends, but their circle of friendship was wide and, as photos show, representative of the diverse nationalities living in the greatest melting pot that could only be New York City. When Esther landed in Greenwich Village, she had greatly desired renegade artistic fellowship, such as she would find with Jerry, Anno Mariano, Regis Masson, portrait artist Joe Delaney, friend Fred Howard, and others. This was the close circle, according to journal notations and snapshots, its common ground the appreciation of creative and intellectual life.[10]

In the 1930s, Esther also met later-famed artists of the movement that would be termed "The New York School"—Abstract Expressionist artists Willem and Elaine deKooning. She'd bump into Lee Krasner and Jackson Pollock. She would become friends with Arshile Gorky, Franz Kline, and Hans Hofmann. And she and her friends would know writer Ben Hecht, who was extremely successful in script writing for Hollywood productions by that time, but who had gotten his beginnings with the Raven Poetry Circle held at Cooper Union in the Village. Esther later told her niece Millie about a time when she, Hecht, and a couple others were preparing for a party. "We bought some meat, in order to cook a stew. The soap fell in, and we decided to load it up with spices and put it out at the party. People raved about it . . . [it's a wonder] it tasted so good!"[11]

❦ ❦ ❦

Poet Maxwell Bodenheim was known as a real Village character. Esther thought of this writer, who always traversed the Village in dapper suit and feathered hat, as a "spiritual Poe," and considered him a very dear friend, telling Millie of making breakfast for him some mornings. Ben Hecht counted Max a friend and wrote of him, as well as his notorious exploits surfacing in other accounts of the early Village. Max had a common practice of attaching slips of his poetry to the spikes of fences, and this was sure to come up in Esther's recollecting him. He immediately asked her out to dinner after her first dictation of his impaled hallowed words, as he did with countless other women. He drank and took hashish and cocaine. Esther got to know him and Minna, one of his wives, as they hung out about the Village over the years. Esther said that Max was "nasty to many people," writing "unflattering stories of them."[12]

August 30, 1938—Sat in park with Esther. She wanted us friends to go to raise money for another woman who was unable yet to get on relief. Recited poems, then went to party. We left party about 1 a.m. and there were people partying next door.

September 2—Esther and Ruth by for breakfast. Later Anna Garcia, Gary's friends, Ronald Perry and wife. Rhea, Loretta and Jean also.

September 11—Lunch with Esther. Reg.'s birthday party in eve.

Journal entry after journal entry of Eugenia's detailed parties and gatherings from dusk on, through all hours of the night, until morning. Applicable to all, she titled one journal caption from the late 1930s "The Morning After the Night Before."

An eleven-year old Eugenia Hughes described herself in her journal, one kept along with childhood sketch pads and other artistic journals: "I have brown hair and eyes. My name is Eugenia Hughes. A quick temper is one of my possessions. I expect to be an artist or a singer."[13] Like Esther, Eugenia came from Pittsburgh. She grew up in Dormont, in the South Hills of the city. Born in 1909, she was about seven years younger than Esther. It doesn't appear that the two knew each other there at all. Eugenia was the daughter of Josephine Gosline Hughes and Roy V. Hughes, who in the 1920s was an illustrator with the *Pittsburgh Gazette-Times*. Roy may have known Esther because records indicate that he participated in the Associated Artist of Pittsburgh shows in the 1920s, up until about 1933.

After Roy's wife died, he moved to New York City to look for opportunities as an artist, and ended up settling in the Village. Eugenia, young adult by then, remained behind. She had many friends, including Kindred McLeary. He was a WPA muralist and professor in Carnegie Tech's School of Architecture. It is unclear as to whether she might have studied art at Carnegie Tech; no documentation exists along with her numerous other effects to suggest that she did. Like her father, she was an illustrator, her work being influenced by the Arts and Crafts movement and especially Art Nouveau. Her drawings captured the spirit of the Flapper, of the Jazz Age. Eventually because of her close relationship with her father (they shared similar artistic interests) and the increased stimuli of New York, Eugenia joined Roy in the Village in the mid 1930s, when she was around the age of twenty-five. Though she was quite the caretaker, at times living with her father, always looking after him and tending to her friends, she indeed led a wonderfully wild, independent, creative life.

First in Pittsburgh, and then in New York, Eugenia was by all definition a flapper. Snapshots taken with friends in the mid 1920s in Pittsburgh suggest an ease of manner—she always looked quite happy, conveying a real freedom from worry or care. They often show her surrounded by male devotees. The records that survive of Eugenia's life, the journal notations and other ephemera that she so meticulously saved for emotional and posterity's sake, vividly depict her bursting will, her spiritedness. Her artistic endeavors seemed well-provided for monetarily by her family, and that fact, combined with her own temperament—affable and outgoing—may have cultivated a predisposition toward overindulgence of some liberties.

Catharine R. Stimpson, in her introduction to Wheeler and Lussier's *Women, the Arts & the 1920s in Paris and New York,* remarked that, "Middle America was threatened by the things going on in New York." The city was "volatile and capricious enough to shelter the daring, innovative and unpredictable, which the modern woman so often was." Stimpson states that Greenwich Village and Harlem "were the places where young men and women from small towns and prairie states could forget middle-class manners and customs and create something new."[14] Though by no means a small town, Pittsburgh could only harbor the modern Esther and Eugenia for so long; they both longed to test the possibilities that New York could bring.

Sara Via Pais' essay in Wheeler and Lussier's book, entitled "Shapes of the Feminine Experience in Art," contends that "women artists of the 1920s show us what it is to let the individual self rule the shaping of the social self. They refuse to take on the protective coloration of outward conformity; they will not secrete themselves or their work behind the facade of tidy lives." Eugenia and Esther were artists; theirs was a creative work, which they did assertively, as they lived their life creatively and assertively, like all the women profiled throughout the essays in *Women, the Arts & the 1920s.* They too were "marvelously visible, audible, and they please[d] themselves."[15] Eugenia simply happened to have the ability to please others, as well—a caretaking that was a genuine part of her temperament, and not due to any social pressure to adhere to a mothering role.

Curiously, Via Pais suggests that a woman fully embodying in spirit all of the characteristics of a modern artistic woman usually "did not come to that extraordinary moment unaided." She attests that many of these women, who would "openly share a commitment to the enterprise of art" had mothers who were creative, brave, curious, and proud. In Eugenia's case, the strong creative influence seems to have been her father. Esther, of course lacked such artistic guides, and it is interesting to note how much more self-possessed Eugenia seemed because of it. Like the more secure women artists, however, Esther was still "able to demand and create [a] full and expressive life from which to generate that art." Despite lack of encouragement and the extreme poverty she knew too well, she had the necessary "intense self-awareness" and "powerful will"[16] found in all successful artists, man or woman. She knew that working creatively took commitment. But she encountered such resistance, that the ease with which Eugenia was able to live a less-stressed creative existence must have seemed a bit foreign to her.

Esther was not quite the flapper Eugenia was. Her 1920s professional photograph, she handsomely donning a beret, shows more a woman interested in seriously being taken as an artist. (Eugenia's photos are of a woman bedecked with fringes and baubles, with headband through hair.) Yet the easy gesture conveyed in Esther's portrait, not to mention her manner at least as portrayed by the Pittsburgh reviews, showed the same sense of independence and spunk that the 1920s introduced to American women. Even Esther's Pittsburgh nickname, Flippy, which did not follow her to New York, was given to her for the embodiment of the characteristics of a flapper—"flighty, flamboyant . . . and even silly."[17] Esther seemed all these things, as well a woman who absolutely knew that only that one thing could bring her real happiness, and that was her work, her art. Esther's other modeled shot, both having been taken by noted Pittsburgh photographer and friend Luke Swank, shows a beautiful, vulnerable young woman with just the slightest beginnings of worry upon the brow, the photo that moved James Van Trump to say, "reveals the inner life of the artist."

Upon leaving Pittsburgh, Esther appeared a bit more ready than Eugenia to do serious artistic work. Tired of the stale attitudes and styles in Pittsburgh, she arrived in New York ready to pursue every opportunity to translate, in her own way, image to canvas. Come 1938, the two young women—Esther age 36 and Eugenia 29—would carry with them plenty of the confidences and successes that mark the modern woman, and New York splayed itself before them in all its variety and possibility. But along with that fertile creative ground came, of course, the distractions. Eugenia and Esther, certainly drawn into the mise-en-scene of the Village, got swept up by that tumultuous tide of good times in the 1930s and the fast-approaching 1940s.

Numerous love letters document Eugenia's varied, and at times quite seamy, romantic involvements. With a wit akin to that of Mary Shaw and Esther, she describes herself at the end of an early 1940s diary entry as "the daughter of the 'lost generation,' a victim of the Prohibition and Flapper Era, the gay 20s." Because with freedoms comes the necessity to continually balance one's desires with one's course of action, Eugenia was likely reflecting, perhaps with a touch of remorse, on the impact the attitudes of the times had upon her love relationships. For it seems they occasionally suffered from her free and easy outlook. According to a later brief journal entry, Regis Masson, in particular, dear friend to both Eugenia and Esther, apparently expressed to her that he could not endure the "threesomes" and "bed sessions"[18] that were obviously coloring the late 1930s and early 1940s for many Villagers.

The tour de force that was the liberal love mentality present in those times wreaked havoc, more than once, upon Esther's personal relationships. One of Eugenia's journal entries points this out, as she comments on "talk of our menfolk" between herself and an insecure Esther. Eugenia described that her friend "feels [B.] Cooper is too decadent for her tastes. She wants to keep him at arm's length."[19] But Esther was usually well able to fend for herself when it came to intimate matters. Years later she related another tale to her niece about friend Leonard DeGrange, famous lithographer. Though he was wealthy, the Villagers considered him to be a fellow bohemian at heart. Esther told a detailed story of his marrying a woman, who possessed "a real sense of humor, once a stand-in for Joan Crawford in Hollywood." With her as his wife, he apparently bought the big house where Diamond Jim Brady had lived and settled with his family. But later leaving her and five kids sitting on the doorstep, as Esther told it, he moved back to 14th Street in the Village and asked women out, including herself. Supposedly, he even asked her to marry him. She wouldn't, and he called her a lesbian. Her response back was that she "only liked younger men."[20]

۞ ۞ ۞

Relief checks were now just beginning to sustain Esther a bit. It was at this time, September 1938, that she first began setting up for the Washington Square Outdoor Show, which took place twice a year. She, Eugenia, and other Village artists welcomed the opportunity to have their work seen by a wider public, not the least of which was simply their peers en masse. Many artists who lived in the Village their whole life exhibited every spring and fall in the show, as Esther's friend Joe Delaney did. He took part in the very first Washington Square Outdoor show and every subsequent one until he finally "retired" at a very old age.[21] Perhaps his motivation was simply the fact that Washington Square Park was ever-present to him, for he had one of the coveted "walk-ups," with skylights bordering the park, as his apartment/studio. Many artists in New York felt homage toward the Outdoor Show in its beginnings, at least, for it was the one real avenue for showing one's work, short of gallery exhibitions that were almost impossible to come by until the 1940s.

Started in 1928 under the Artists Aid Committee, the show was open to all artists and art students living in the five New York boroughs. There was no entrance fee in the early years, no judge or juries, and no charges or commissions paid if works sold. Artists sold their own work and kept the entire proceeds. A real advantage of the show was its simple nature. As an "Announcement" advertising the show in 1935 stated, there too were "no fancy programs, soft lights, or social contracts to contend with." But there was also no shelter.[22] Esther later wrote Eugenia, "When I think of the Outdoor Show I am reminded of how we used to grab our stuff in the rain. . . ."[23] The Announcement, which was a bulletin posted circa 1935 to incite artist as well as public interest, stated, "[The Washington Square Outdoor Show] enables an artist to sell his work directly to the public and to get his work before the newspaper critics, collectors, museum curators, dealers and employers of artists. . . ." In addition, many statistics were cited, including that "over 75,000 residents and tourists would see each show. 90% of artists would make some sales or have offers for their work. All would make valuable friends and contacts." Artists priced their work anywhere from 10 cents to $400, with the average being about $35.[24]

The Artist Aid Committee felt it significant to add that "more than twelve artists in the last show were represented in important museums. 20% of the work is as fine as any seen in art galleries." The committee's feeling was that "every artist and every student who has something to say in the arts and who is in need of a real market to sell his work, or would like to have the critics and collectors see his work, should enter the show." Logistics on the show's set-up followed the philosophy. A free permit to exhibit first had to be picked up. There was room for 1,000 artists to exhibit their works from noon until sundown, with each artist allotted six feet. All the streets bordering and surrounding Washington Square were used, with determination for location done through blind drawing. All the exhibitors had to remove their work at the end of each day, and set up again the next afternoon, being careful not to mar or deface any buildings, or block entrances. The only administrative obligation was for each artist to fill out a report each evening concerning the day's sales, if any. In the 1930s, the Committee accepted original pieces and sculptures in any medium. Photos, commercial reproductions, and all craft products were forbidden. And dealers, agents, or non-artists were forbidden to exhibit, unless directly and consentually representing an individual artist. The Committee also did "reserve the right of censorship if deemed necessary."[25]

Esther had been in New York almost two years come the fall of 1938, and her luck was improving. She had just begun what would be a long and rewarding relationship of exhibiting with the Washington Square Outdoor Show. Ironically, considering how long it took her to receive welfare assistance, she was on it for only a couple months, because the long-awaited citizenship papers finally came through, and she was quickly given an art teaching position with the WPA (It was easel painting she wanted, but it was a position nevertheless.) It seems most artists, not nearly earning their potential with their talent, clamored to get on one of the Projects' branches, if even for bits of time, as Esther had. There were very few exceptions; acclaimed woman artist Andree Ruellan was one of a very small number to have rejected the government sponsorship of a WPA commission.[26] But to many artists who later became recognized, and to those that never did, the Project was the single most influential element in an artist's life in the 1930s. It is rare to find negative words by artists for what the Art Project provided, except perhaps for the demeaning position of first proving need and the bureaucracy involved to get placement, as Esther experienced.

Rather than simply being handed welfare payments, unemployed artists were given an opportunity to focus on what they did best, and to be gainfully employed in that manner. Dore Ashton, in *The New York School: A Cultural Reckoning*, described how Depression years affected the group of American artists who were to become very successful in the 1940s, the Abstract Expressionists. Getting on a Project meant that "for the first time in their lives they could devote all their time to their work." An artist finally had enough temporary economic security that life was not such the mad dash for money—marketing wildly in attempt for a quick sale to buy food. "But," added Ashton, "the most compelling force that emerges is [the artists'] sense of having found each other. The decade of the thirties represented the Project, and the Project meant the establishment of a milieu for the first time in the United States."[27]

No matter if one was already the successful artist in the 1930s (like muralist Rivera) or to later achieve fame (like the Abstract Expressionists would), if one had come, as Esther did, from Pittsburgh, to join the

New York artist ranks, or if an artist was on the WPA roster in San Francisco—the Project linked everyone. Ashton suggested, and Esther's letters iterate, that even when egos surfaced and artists fought among themselves, "they were, when threatened by the philistines, a united front" for advocating public sponsorship of the arts. They "wholeheartedly defend[ed] the principle of federal aid to artists and all its wholesome, cultural by products."[28]

The flavor of the art being produced for the WPA Projects was very American. Arts Project Director Holger Cahill stated, "American art is declaring a moratorium on its debts to Europe, and returning to cultivate its own garden."[29] Ashton's *The New York School* suggests that an appreciation between artist and society for the first time in America echoed the successful European construct. Actually, the idea of government sponsorship was European, but unlike Europeans, not many Americans were motivated to pursue private collections due to any newfound love of art. Most Americans instead simply absorbed, with likely some gratification, what President Roosevelt had provided for them, the government-sponsored murals adorning post offices and county office buildings. Not until the early 1940s, when Peggy Guggenheim stirred up the art world in America, would American art collecting start to take off. Ideally, Americans would have at least appreciated art and artists more due to their exposure to it from the WPA, and looked favorably upon government support for artists to do their work, but this was not, nor continues to be, the case in an askew America, where citizens look with disdain at subsidization of the cultural, despite having little scorn for subsidies granted private enterprise.

When the ideas of the WPA were put before Congress, "it was estimated that more than half the artists in the entire U.S. lived in New York. . . . By 1934 the College Art Association estimated that there were more than 1400 artists in New York City urgently in need of relief." Because the numbers beckoned, in New York, by 1935, "78% [of WPA workers] were concentrated in New York City."[30] Actually, in 1936, the year that Esther left for New York City, all of the Arts Projects already seemed doomed, and many artists, at least in New York, were organizing to protest the imminent loss. A great deal of the problem was the public's perception that the Arts Projects and its artists had a socialist bent.

Ashton told of the "supervisor of the New York Easel Project, Rollie Crampton, recalling that The F.B.I. was always coming round to ask who was reading *The Call,* (a socialist newspaper). . . . Throughout the brief life of the federal art projects there were threats from the political right."[31] Jackson Pollock, soon to come into phenomenal fame as an Abstract Expressionist, was tagged as someone who supposedly attended communist meetings in 1929. And extreme attention was paid to Jose Orozco, who worked with Thomas Hart Benton on a mural at the very liberal New School for Social Research in New York and whose work, like Rivera's and many others', reflected leanings toward socialism.

Many artists expressed sympathies with and participated in organizations such as The National Womens Party, focusing on equal rights for all minorities; it came under suspicion for Bolshevik leanings as well.[32] Mainstream America viewed New York City as the "outpost of foreign influences . . . the mere mention of New York would call forth angry denunciations of its radical politics, art, and literature. Inflamed by the [conservative] Hearst Press, the average citizen was especially incensed by the more visible subsidized arts, the theatre above all."[33] (The public held such scorn for the risque theatre that it seems one had to be an already much-established artist to even get on that Project.)

Artistic support had gotten very controversial by 1936, and Roosevelt, pressured by the political right, decided not to make a public stand for the Federal Art Project. Many creative artists in Pittsburgh were quite aware of this imminent betrayal, as they protested when Roosevelt campaigned in their city in the fall of 1936, a fact that Merle and Harold Winters corresponded about in one of their many letters.[34] Artists everywhere were keenly watching to see what FDR would do with this very project that he had initiated. And publications behind the artists' cause ardently strived to voice their support of the Art Project. So states a December 1936 issue of *The New Republic*:

> Nothing short of the collective resources of
> our country as a whole has proved competent to
> bring the fine arts into the lives of everyday

Americans. Industry does not supply their needs; it never has and, since the motive of profit is lacking, it never will. Private philanthropy is too puny to endow them....

To dismiss the workers on the arts projects and dismantle the projects themselves will not release a large body of people for commercial or industrial employment. There has never been a place in our present industrial system for the artist, except as a flatterer of the rich and idle, or as a mere servant of business enterprise. . . . Now that the community itself has devised appropriate ways for patronizing and encouraging the arts and giving them a permanently public home, it is time that art be taken for what it is—a realm like education which requires active and constant public support.[35]

Chapter Seven

"HAVING DRIFTED"[1]

*E*sther's teaching position was, at least for her, the least desirable of those offered within the Federal Art Project, for she had to devote time to teaching others to use paints, and what she had wanted to do was of course use paint herself—like most artists on the Easel Project. But she was surely grateful, still, for any employment related to her artistic ability. Attending her class that fall were Eugenia and Regis Masson, as well as a woman named May Swenson, to-be beloved American poet, and her companion of the time, Anca Verboska. Swenson was living very minimally life at this time, like Esther and other artists. Apparently within May's diaries for the years 1938–1939 were numerous notations about Esther Phillips, revealing the fact that she was living in "acute poverty . . . always asking for money." May had noted, too, that Esther was painting Anca's portrait at this time.[2] (Swenson, like Merle Hoyleman, was occasionally published in *New Directions in Prose and Poetry* in the 1930s.) Esther's classes were held in Queens, and, according to a winter entry in Eugenia's journal, she was working on getting the location moved closer to home.

> *Dec. 19, 1938*–Called on Esther–Anca was there and they were just about to have breakfast, invited me to join . . . To Esther's class at 8:30. Must make an effort to get there on time next week. Reg set up the still life–used Baley's guitar, Esther's round brown turban, etc. . . . Walked home with Esther.

Though Esther likely was trying to maintain an apartment on her own, she used Eugenia's homes in 1938 and 1939—apartments at 7 Jones Street, then 32 Cornelia Street—as addresses where she could be found.

> *Dec. 20, 1938*–Esther and I ran into each other–lunched together–
> She did her washing here. Went to bank with Esther where she drew out
> some money and she gave me 1$. Then in cafe for beer and lots of free
> lunch of not good quality. Jake Spencer sat with us. Was expounding on
> theories of government which was going right over my head.

Many intellectual exchanges took place as Villagers sat in cafes and talked and talked endlessly of ideas, writings, and certainly politics. Esther was much a part of the mingling crowd; she later told her niece that she loved to frequent the very popular gathering spots of both Union Square and Cooper Union in the Village.[4] Naturally these spots, in fact such a scene in general, breeded eccentric characters, those few individuals even more outrageously visible in their talk and demeanor than the average Village citizen. Poet Max Bodenheim certainly was one, as was a guy by the name of Joe Gould. In Washington Square, "Professor Sea Gull," as Gould was known, sat and talked to the pigeons that gathered under Garibaldi's statue. It was here no doubt that Esther first met him. But he was also "a notable in the cafeterias, diners, barrooms and dumps of Greenwich Village," according to writer Joseph Mitchell. Like scenester Max Bodenheim was also known to do, Gould would equally brag that he, himself, was the "Last of the Bohemians," and the two, who were friends, would sometimes outrageously try to out-vie each other for the title.[5]

Mitchell, author and reporter for *The New Yorker*, befriended and began interviewing Gould in 1942, and vividly described this guy who bumped into everybody of the 1920s-1950s Village, including Esther, who was sure to later remark of him to her niece. Wrote Mitchell, "He is stooped and he moves rapidly, grumbling to himself, with his head thrust forward and held to one side. Under his left arm he usually carries a bulging, greasy, brown pasteboard portfolio, and he swings his right arm aggressively." *Joe Gould Versus the Elements* was a sketch by

Don Freeman, likely just one of many creative depictions of this Village legend by resident artists. [6]

The portfolio contained revision upon revision of Gould's "Oral History," supposedly millions of words long in its entirety. He worked with several chapters at a time that he carried with him, and he remarked that he kept others in storage in the Long Island homes of well-to-do friends he'd make over the years. But Mitchell actually revealed, after Gould's death, that the infamous "Oral History" really didn't exist except as an oral history, with Gould's well-traveled revisions being the only existing writing. But "the rest" existed in his head, as he could recite passages to Mitchell and others for hours extending into the morning as bars closed in the Village.

"The Oral History of Our Time" (Gould's preferred full title) basically consisted of "talk he had heard and had considered meaningful and had taken down. . . ."[7] His storytelling included such diversity as young medical students' retold tales of the morgue at Bellevue Hospital, to his perhaps most famous essay, "The Dread Tomato Habit," which detailed the calamitous harm of train engineers eating too many tomatoes. But Gould's most pertinent ramblings detailed Greenwich Village escapades. "Hundreds of thousands of words . . . devoted to the drunken behavior and sexual adventures of various professional Greenwich Villagers in the twenties. [Also] hundreds of reports of ginny Village parties. . . ." Gould also had a preference for how his work be defined: "the intellectual underworld of my time."[8]

Gould recited portions of the "Oral History" to Village newcomers in later decades, and "right before [Mitchell's] eyes, he changed from a bummy-looking little red-eyed wreck of a barfly into an illustrious historian." (Hoping to get one or two dollars from a tourist). Though he visited artists' studios, and attended the underground theatrical happenings of the day, Gould most enjoyed crashing meetings of the Raven Poetry Circle. He considered himself a poet, but didn't particularly care for the permeation of politic talk around writing circles of that time. As he detailed to Mitchell, "a good many people in the Village got interested in Marxism and became radicals." Then the scene became just too chic for him![9]

*January 15, 1939—*Esther, I and [Regis] Masson . . . all of us feeling bored and restless. Couldn't think of anything to do that wouldn't entail the laying out of $—tired of movies—wanted to hear some music. Decided to go to 5th Ave. Cafe for beer. Esther restless—I got somewhat vexed by her fidgeting—In cafe, musicians gone—no music except victrola. Esther ordered sandwiches for herself and me—ate too much. Admired a tall man who came in with some people Esther knew.

*January 23, 1939—*movies, movies, galleries. . . .

Many Villagers attended the various art schools, then went to the outdoor cafes afterward to talk. They mulled over the latest on the WPA from the Artists Union meetings. Art schools abounded, with the faculty of some paid through the WPA, such as the American Artists School on West 14th, and the Leonardo da Vinci Art School on 3rd & 34th, where later-famed Abstract Expressionist Elaine deKooning studied under the tutelage of WPA teachers. A very famous institution was the Hans Hofmann School of Fine Arts. Hofmann was the mentor to many artists to come out of the Village scene from the 1930s onward. With very poor English, he came to the United States in 1932, at the age of 52, after having taught at the renowned Bauhaus in Germany, home to very avant-garde creative work. At first Hofmann taught at the Art Students League in New York, where Lee Krasner, another rare woman Abstract Expressionist painter and wife of artist Jackson Pollock, studied under him. But he was ever present about the Village, and this is how Esther first became acquainted with him in the late 1930s. According to the running list of anecdotes of Village that she later supplied to her niece, Esther apparently knew both Hofmann and painter Franz Kline fairly well, better than the rest of the artists to later meet much fame. And she would meet and know Arshile Gorky, who at this time in the latter 1930s had been exhibiting a little more prestigiously at the Guild Art Gallery in New York.

Franz Kline continually exhibited, as did Esther, in the Washington

Square Shows. Equally a gregarious personality, but with "deep feelings of alienation," he had just arrived in New York in 1938, and much of his work during the 1930s and 1940s, before his Abstract Expressionist fame, was actually figurative landscapes, many of the coal country of Carbon County, Pennsylvania, where he spent his teen years.[10] Esther may have especially related to his artistic affection for landscapes, which were the backdrop of memory. Indeed, she even included in her remarks to her niece that this "good friend" came from Pennsylvania Dutch territory, a fact of Kline's life little known by the art public.

Esther was frustrated with the lack of recognition of her own painting, and merely teaching with the WPA still dissatisfied her. (Unlike a couple of the more prestigious WPA art schools, Esther likely taught somewhere in a community center setting, open to a general public curious about learning some elementary art skills.) So she continued to look to get on one of the other branches of the Project. After about a year of teaching, come September of 1939, she was still interviewing to work instead on the Easel Project, despite the fact that the Artists Projects' wheels were drawing to a halt. By this time, more ammunition had been added to the stand to end WPA assistance to artists. Ironically, "the frequently voiced criticism was that certain [Project] workers— usually actors, artists, or teachers—had never previously made a living at their purported vocations, or could not expect to do so in the future. . . . [This] contributed in no small measure to the discontinuance of the Federal Theatre Project in 1939,"[11] and no doubt the other disciplines come the start of World War II.

All artists had felt the imminent close, and had stepped up individual efforts to market their own work, as Esther and Eugenia did. They continued to take their works about town, trying to establish contacts for sales, as well as keep up to date with the exhibits in the major galleries that showed European work, much of it still Surrealist. The year 1939 brought the World's Fair to Queens, and the Museum of Modern Art mounted a monumental Picasso exhibition. Esther and Eugenia both worked hard at trying to sell their work, but as Eugenia revealed in a diary entry of this time, Esther now "lacked adequate patience and judgment," outwardly expressing frustration when their marketing didn't go so well, and she "was not so frugal with money" that she received from any painting sales. Such journal entries of Eugenia's, much in the manner of Merle Hoyleman's notations, provide insightful, and certainly not unfamiliar, commentary on Esther's lifestyle. Also, like Merle, sometimes Eugenia exhibited a gift for vivid conveyance in the briefest, most condensed manner textually possible, as with an entry of this time, "Esther with hangover."

It surely was not a good time for Esther. She lost her teaching job in April of 1940, and was then forced to go back on welfare relief. This loss saw the beginning of acute troubles for her. Regis Masson had been away for a while on military duty; Eugenia was also away, attending to health and financial matters with her father in Williamsport, Pennsylvania. Writing to Eugenia in Pennsylvania, Masson commented on matters back in the Village—"Esther is now on her own,"[12] referring probably to their friend's economic situation sans WPA help, or lack of companionship, or both. The preceding four years, Esther had been fortunate to have been surrounded by several dear friends originating within Eugenia's circle. In fact, when times were very bad for her, as they now were, Eugenia welcomed her right into her home. In Jerry, Esther always had a confidante and pal, her closest friend. Her now being away threw Esther off balance, and others close to the two could see it.

In addition, Esther and Merle completely lost touch with each other around this time. Merle still had Esther's address as "care of Jerry Hughes, 32 Cornelia St.," but that address became obsolete after Eugenia temporarily left for Pennsylvania. Merle had visited New York the year prior—actually her third visit since Esther had lived there—but the two, again, wouldn't hook up with each other. It was around this time, as well, that Gladys Schmitt and husband Simon moved to New York, but it seems Esther and her old friend also didn't connect—a shame, for Simon had been ever able to make Esther laugh. Gladys now was a busy associate editor of *Scholastic Magazine*; she was finishing *The Gates of Aulis* during these New York City years.

Esther was in an $18/month apartment at 105 McDougal Street in the Village,[13] living on scant provisions. Eugenia and Reggie tried to cheer her through correspondence. Reg Masson actually began to express serious interest in Esther's watercolors at this time, and she sent him one or two at a time. Throughout the years following, Masson strongly desired to market her work, in a layman's fashion, as it appealed greatly to him, and he certainly knew his friend badly needed sales. Esther still went out to all parts of the city to paint, as a surviving work from 1940 attests, entitled *Empire State Building*. She also likely made a point this year to see four paintings of the by-then deceased John Kane on exhibit at the Valentine Gallery in New York. It was surely dismaying to her how, only now, a larger public viewed his work as valuable. (Kane had died in 1934 in Pittsburgh, only a few years after getting Carnegie International acclaim. His was, sadly, and despite that recognition gained, a "solitary funeral," with only his wife, two daughters, and six pallbearers, one of whom was John O'Connor of the museum.[14])

The environment in New York City, with the outbreak of war in Europe, was "an even more alien environment than artists had known before."[15] "While Americans were adapting their psychology to war conditions," stated Dore Ashton, "many artists touched bottom spiritually—The natural habitat developed during the WPA years was swiftly transformed. . . ." Artist Adolph Gottlieb expressed that artists "were painting with a feeling of absolute desperation. The situation was so bad that I know I felt free to try anything no matter how absurd it seemed. Everyone was on his own."[16]

☙ ☙ ☙

PORTRAIT OF ESTHER[17]

Hung in the smoke and gloom, her face pretends
to be a sullen moon that nightly wends
its course among the drunken clouds, and sits
in acrid judgement on their shrunken wits.

Life for her is but a sad cafe,
where each check pulled is but a check to pay;
where each friend met is first a friend in need,
and thenceforth to be spurned. On that one feed
he'll harp till doomsday, and demand the price:
"Come bed with me for your bowl of soup and rice"!

And so, a somber jewel set in midst,
her broad Buddhistic countenance holds sway
above the whore, the pimp, the rabid communist
that plough the lurid fog of Life's Cafe.

May Swenson
June 9, 1940

◎ ◎ ◎

Eugenia stayed away several months, but then returned to much the same activities as before, with Esther and her other Village friends attempting to market their work, as well as continued partying. Regis, too, returned to New York in early 1941, and began working at the Gill Glass and Fixture Company, which kept him further from the Village than he'd like. He wrote Jerry of his desire to get back in touch with her, Esther, and the others. "See very little of any of the rest of the gang."[18] But a time shortly came when all the friends within Eugenia's circle would reconnect, with more endless parties and continued seamy romantic involvement for all, according to a couple descriptive notations in her journal.

Come September of 1941, Esther was still futilely trying for another WPA job. Desperation began to set in. She persisted, though war would outbreak in a few months and put an end to the matter of the WPA entirely. She had been pulling for WPA work while other artists around her concentrated on the content and style of their own work, devoting their energies to the consideration of discarding the European construct of art entirely, and moving towards complete abstractionism. Esther, though, now found herself in a hole with regard to making money. The harsh realities of the economic world were encroaching and it was becoming more and more difficult to keep the demands for rent and food at bay. She had been chasing art positions and sales, opportunities to earn respect through her art. Though her attempt to make a living solely through her painting allowed her to focus on being creative, which was all that she really desired, it was also bringing her physical and mental hardship. Because her physical being was so worn down, the "unassailable self"[19] that had marked her previously did not hold up. Anxiety was slowly undoing her.

Esther lived the artist's very minimal existence, devoted to an inner creativity that drove her to forget all else except painting. She continued to struggle with her belief that artists must devote their energy to craft, despite societal opposition and societal incredulity toward a person willing to sustain a toll on the body, to forgo adequate nutrition and housing in order to create. Though a strong woman, she had begun to hit many pitfalls as an artist trying to survive. Though gutsy, she still craved an elemental respect from the general population. Instead, what she did, what she felt, how she lived, who she was as an artist was constantly challenged, and she began to feel the blow. Her impoverished state of being, the loss of the WPA position, the unfortunate timing of inconsistency in the support system that were her friendships, and the excessive partying all brought the bottom up quicker. It was the early part of this year, in 1941, that Eugenia wrote a vague note in her journal about taking Esther to the doctor because "[Esther's] been worried about her condition for weeks. At least this will put her mind at ease." Eugenia did not clarify what Esther's complaints were. Apparently they continued throughout the next year.

⑥ ⑥ ⑥

Eugenia went away again, on extended vacation with aunts in New Jersey, during the summer of 1942. She left in early June, after having participated, along with Esther, in the Washington Square Outdoor Show that May. They had only exhibited during the second week due to getting their permits late. Esther later accounted the happenings of that spring. Some of the events as a confidante transcribes them:

```
During the first few days [of the Outdoor Show]
she was unable to sell any of her [paintings]
and developed a feeling of intense frustration.
At that time, she says her condition was very
```

bad: was unable to eat and felt tired all the time. . . .

[Shortly after this time] she went out one night. When she left her room she felt all right, went to a bar and had three beers. This made her sleepy so she went to bed. The following day she went out on a sketching tour of the east side with a friend. When she left her room she felt very "funny—numb all over—dizzy, groggy," as though she were going to faint. Instead of going home to rest, she very stupidly followed along with her friend sketching all day in various parts of the east side. She had nothing to eat, felt so badly that she thought she was going to die. Finally when she told her friend how badly she felt, he took her into a store and bought her some milk . . . thereafter, for three weeks, [she] felt very sick, thought that she might have had some stomach trouble, would stagger up and down the six flights of stairs to buy milk and oranges on which she lived for a period of time. During these three weeks she felt very fearful, had a feeling that something was going to happen to her. At the end of this three weeks' period a girl-friend took her to her home and had a doctor examine her. [He] made a diagnosis of secondary anemia and prescribed some medication as well as a diet. This friend fed her very well and took care of her so that at the end of [a little time] she felt a little stronger. However, whenever she would get out of bed and try to walk around, she became aware of palpitation of the heart. When it became necessary for this

friend to go to the home of a relative, therefore leaving the patient alone, patient found
that she was unable to take care of herself.[20]

Esther actually lived at the new Hughes residence, 44 Washington Square, all the summer of 1942, while Eugenia was away, and thus it was Eugenia's father, Roy, and the circle of visiting friends who cared for her. Before Eugenia left, she had helped Esther to get settled. The arrangement was for Esther, still on welfare, to keep house and provide companionship for Roy while his daughter was away. But it turned out that Roy needed to look out more for Esther than she did him. One evening at the onset of that summer, Roy Hughes, Reg Masson, Annino Mariano, and another friend named George Knight had all been sitting in the park, drinking. They noted that Esther did not join them. On June 9, George wrote to Jerry, who was just at the start of her time away, that Esther "saw us in park on Sunday but she ran out of sight. I guess we made her nervous."[21]

Everyone understood that Esther was staying at the Hughes residence that summer due to a nervous state. All of her friends appear to have kept a caring watch over her. Mariano, Knight, and Masson all came around that summer, "buying Esther a quart of milk a night, and ice cream," and oranges, Esther's favorites, and offered to take her to the movies.[22] Esther wrote Jerry a short note in June. "My eyes are bad . . . my depression comes and goes"—with that last part then very visibly scribbled out. She also wrote in mid-June that "Mariano was around—was very nice—wanted to buy me ice cream and take me to the movies—which I refused—as I don't think I could do it yet. . . . Mariano looks well—wants you to write—Says you haven't written but a card etc in answer to an 8-page letter. . . . I'm still dizzy [from] the walk around . . . still can do no more than 2 blocks—sometimes less—sometimes more—Uneven sort of feeling—oh well—I wondered why Doctor [R.] didn't take my blood count. . . ."

That summer, Esther did little, reading some, sleeping much, and for the most part accepting others' attending to her. Likely her reading material included Schmitt's *Gates of Aulis*, published the preceding January. As all evidence suggested, Esther painted hardly at all during this time, certainly quite a departure for her. In a July letter to Jerry, she said, "have been taking my luminal . . . iron pills . . . and watching my 3D's." Luminal was a trademark for a preparation of phenobarbital, a long-acting barbituate used as a sedative, to calm anxiety. She may have been taking this since 1941, when Eugenia first took her to a doctor. It was also a hypnotic, though, with excessive doses bringing on hallucinations, irregular pulse, and an inability to focus the eyes. A mix with alcohol could lead to tremendous difficulty in breathing. Esther did have her latest man-friend over at times during the summer. It seems his attentions to her were a bit different than Mariano and Masson's, though.

Esther and this man, who was married, had met the previous Christmas, and this would be when Esther later pinpointed her troubles beginning full-force. She described herself as "having drifted" the end of that year before, in 1941.[22] That Christmas season Esther "began feel[ing] tired and nervous." She "started drinking moderately on a social scale at the age of twenty-five [in Pittsburgh] but during the Christmas holiday [of 1941] she began to drink heavily with her boy-friend." She was, at that time, also doing "a great deal of painting and believes that she may have strained her eyes."[23] This, the first time that Esther would connect her painting activities as actually being harmful to her body, or her self in any way, was significant. Esther's relationship with this man, Frank D., had became intimate in the new year. While going out with him, she "drank rum and whiskey for two days at a time but did not seem to be able to get drunk . . . yet she was unable to eat."[25] Esther would refer to this man as her boyfriend of the time, and she would state, "I didn't realize he was a dipsomaniac and loved to drink, so I began drinking with him because I liked to be in his company. I guess I drank too much, frequently on an empty stomach. Spells when I couldn't see well, had the shakes. . . ."[24] By May 1942, her relationship with Frank had cooled down, but indeed he did visit Esther while she was ill that summer.

George Knight wrote the vacationing Eugenia in July that "[Esther] had her boyfriend Frank here till 10:30, then Mr. Masson came by. Others are getting things for her—she's nervous when they didn't (sic) come by. She doubts me. She thinks perhaps I don't want [to help her]—silly, of course, I promised I'd look after her." On July 24, Knight wrote Jerry that Regis Masson, who cared deeply for Esther as a friend, "was wild because Frank was here lying down with her." Esther also wrote to Jerry in a summer letter, stating that Frank had "moved alone to 50 Washington Square—[He and his wife] are separated—probably going to be divorced—At any rate our neighbor!—the old 'debt' liquor did it I imagine!"

Roy Hughes of course ate some meals with Esther during her stay, and George Knight also seemed to be hanging much around 44 Washington Square all that summer. Come August, Roy wrote his daughter, still at the beach, explaining that George seemed to be upsetting Esther. "He was loud, talked and moved too slowly [for Esther's tastes] and he just sends her into very bad spells. She threw up her dinner after eating with him." Also in August, George wrote Jerry that Esther "frets a lot about you . . . [she] is nervous on her own . . . but it won't be long before she's o.k," referring to Eugenia's scheduled return. Though indications from letters in August and early September point toward Esther's getting increasingly more troubled, at the same time, she had begun to enjoy a few spells of better feelings, at least getting out in the park. At one point, September 2, Knight even commented that "Esther is a whole lot better now."

Roy Hughes, though, could only tell his daughter that Esther "doesn't talk of things." Come the end of August, he had given up trying. "Of course she is too ill to talk and I do not expect it." His exasperation with Esther was evident, as he further offered, "I still find Esther a very difficult person, sick or well. I am doing my best for her, for your sake. And I realize she is very sick. Her dependance [sic] on you is complete. I gather that from her conversation to me." Around the 1st of September, Roy wrote his daughter about the love that he sees George Knight has for her (even though Eugenia's feelings were obviously for Mariano). In that letter, he stated that Esther felt George was even a bit jealous of her friendship with Eugenia. "[George] thinks there is something between [Esther] and [Eugenia] he can't share or doesn't understand."

But George gave Roy an earful as well: "I can't understand [Esther]. She is using you [Roy Hughes]. She really hates you and me too and she wants to depend on you and [Eugenia] for everything. She wouldn't work a day for her own living. She is only sick when you are around." Resentments were evidently high all around the household that summer. Roy Hughes often brought Esther breakfast, and could not help but note the new, various ill-feelings that Esther had to report daily. He wrote Eugenia that Esther's arm was paining her, or again her eyes. He remarked, in what would be the last letter, "I think it will be some time before she feels perfectly well."

As she had always liked the view from loftier spaces, come late summer, Esther found a comfortable place for her convalescence, hanging out on the roof of the Hughes home at 44 Washington Square. But the household pet Minnie, outcast, was banished there, for as George Knight wrote, "that cat drives Esther mad. She wakes her up about 2 A.M., and then [Esther] flies through your room swearing to herself . . . [Esther's] a card, but we leave Minnie on the roof now. Poor Esther—she misses you." Esther even wrote Eugenia a short note in August telling of Minnie's struggle to adjust to the precarious environment she was forced to accept. She describes the cat drying in a basket after exposure to a summer rain, with nowhere to hide. "I don't think she likes the adventure—I suppose it either develops [her] character or it helps to give an insecure feeling—I don't know."

THE INSTITUTION

Chapter Eight

"IN A HELL OF A MESS"[1]

*O*n September 5, 1942, Esther called an ambulance to 44 Washington Square. It took her to Columbus Hospital, and she was shortly thereafter transferred to Bellevue, the infamous public hospital that served the majority of the population of the city of New York. After one month's stay in the "mental wing" of Bellevue, Esther was taken to Harlem Valley Hospital, a state mental institution, about an hour-and-a-half north, in Wingdale, New York. The following letter (found within the institution records) from the superintendent of Columbus Hospital describes Esther's state when the paramedics responded to her call at Washington Square.

Columbus Hospital
227 EAST 19TH STREET
NEW YORK

October 26, 1942

H. A. LaBurt, M.D.
Superintendent
Harlem Valley State Hospital
New York

Re: Esther Phillips

Dear Doctor:

Kindly be informed that the above named was admitted to this hospital on September 5, 1942 via ambulance, complaining of general weakness and sensation of dying.

Patient states that her troubles started three months when she suddenly began to feel weak. Now she feels her "heart is giving out", spine pained her and she felt a choking sensation in her throat.

Physical examination was essentially negative.

Impression: Neurosthenia. Anxiety neurosis.

Because of patient's mental condition she was transferred to Bellevue Hospital on September 19, 1942.

Diagnosis: Neurosthenia. Anxiety neurosis.

Very truly yours,

[signature]
Superintendent

[signature]
Record Librarian

fg

Eugenia finally returned to 44 Washington Square in mid October 1942. Awaiting her was a sealed letter that had arrived via registered mail, a service notice from Bellevue.[2]

The Order of Commitment became the initial document in Esther's institution file. It would state:

> The above alleged mentally sick person is insane and a proper subject for custody and treatment in an institution for the insane within the meaning of the statute, and that she is not in confinement under a criminal charge, ORDERED: That the said Esther Phillips be and hereby is adjudged insane and that she be committed to Harlem Valley State Hospital, an institution for the treatment of mental diseases.[3]

Esther was committed to the state hospital on what was termed a Regular Order of Commitment. The doctors based their judgments on Esther's bodily, or somatic, complaints, which they found to be unsubstantiated. They decided to address what seemed to be her real problem at that time—her mental state. Hers was not an unusual commitment, as it was quite an ordinary procedure to have a petition, declaring doctors' intent, formally delivered to known family or friends. Because Esther would have stated that she had no family close by, Eugenia Hughes, who resided at the same address as the patient, would have been the natural contact. Once the obligation of notifying family or friends had been carried out, the staff at Bellevue could then proceed to bring their judgment before the State Supreme Court. Eugenia did not appear to respond to the petition sent to her house; there is nothing to suggest that she tried to contest the order.[4] It could be that there was little time to do so since Eugenia arrived back in New York just about the time the hearing was actually taking place. At that time, doctors' perceptions and recommendations in such matters largely went uncontested, certainly in cases where the patient herself had called for help.

Esther was thus committed to Harlem Valley State Hospital in Wingdale, New York, on October 16, 1942. She had been released from Bellevue and set forth on a trip by ambulance, along with a few other patients and nurse escorts, seventy-five miles upstate from New York

City, to Duchess County.[5] After their drive past innumerable farms, and then wooded, hilly countryside closer unto entrance to the town of Wingdale, which sat at the eastern edge of New York state, very close to the Connecticut border, the little aggregation in the ambulance came upon Harlem Valley. The whole town, set amidst the hills, coexisted with the institution, for indeed much of Wingdale was the Harlem Valley State Hospital. The center of town was a tiny post office set at a juncture where a railroad brought both visitors to Wingdale as well as Harlem Valley patients, escorted by guardians. Incoming packages would here be equally sorted and delivered to patients at the hospital, as would deliveries to area farmers, whose barns dotted the pleasant countryside, much of which Harlem Valley Hospital was able to claim as its own.

As with all state hospitals, state money had long set aside land to provide for those so severely ill that family environments could not provide for. Farmers living in the area worked the land that bordered, and in many cases, was part of the institution's property. These rural families lived with the institution as their neighbor. Those patients granted ground privilege thus had access to the tranquil meadows surrounding the unenclosed barnyards. Harlem Valley State Hospital was a typical, if perhaps not more scenic, institution for the mentally ill. All across the country, the massive, foreboding brick structures that were mental institutions were set on lovely, spacious countryside. Each construction was assigned a number, even more important than a distinguishing name, and of course served a different function within institution life—some as dormitory buildings, with men living separate from women, some buildings strictly for recreation and entertainment purposes, and others as vocational arenas for the patients. There were also separate administration buildings and dormitories for staff, and facilities' maintenance structures. There were approximately 2,000 patients at this institution in 1942. Harlem Valley Hospital took the overload of patients from New York City, but also from other areas from across the state instead of receiving patients solely from its own directly adjacent "catchman area." [6]

Upon arrival, Esther and the other patients were ushered into the

hospital. "A bath and shampoo" was followed by a physical exam. At 5'4"
Esther weighed in at 138 pounds. It was noted that she was "well nour-
ished," certainly not reflective of her nutritional habits prior to going to
Columbus Hospital, but perhaps a reflection her weight was considered
at the far end of the norm for someone her height. On a Statistical Data
Sheet compiled that first day, Esther was classified under the category
Unstable, a selection of one from among many other choices: Schizoid,
Cycloid, Paranoid, Epileptoid, Hysteroid, Neurasthenoid-Hypochondri-
acal, Anxiety Character, Compulsive-Obsessional, Psychopathic,
Apparently Normal. [7] She was then taken to the ward that she would be
residing on, and several days later went for her admission interview
with two institution doctors. The Abstract of Commitment for her
written up after that interview includes a description of her meeting
with Bellevue doctors. It is fascinating in its elaboration of Esther's story,
much of it based on her own testimony, at times verbatim. The Abstract
is as follows, and shown in actual form where readable:

NOTES

Hospital No. 10547

Name ESTHER PHILLIPS   Identification No. _____

ABSTRACT OF COMMITMENT

DMITTED: - October 23, 1942 from Bellevue on a regular order of commit-
          ment signed by the Hon. Julius Miller, Justice of the Supreme
ourt of the State of New York, Oct. 16, 1942.

ETITION OF: - Nathan Mandel, Lay Superintendent, Bellevue Hospital, NY

ROPERTY: - None.

ISTORY OBTAINED BY PHYSICIANS: - Nativity: Russia. Date of birth: 1905.
                        Is a legal resident of N.Y.City and
as resided in New York State 7 yrs. Address of patient: 44 Washington
q., N.Y.C. Female; white. Religion: Hebrew. Birthplace of father:
ussia. Unknown if patient had any mentally sick relatives. Apparently,
es, patient has been considered as of normal mental standard. Treatment
or syphilis denied. Characterized by: 9/19/42. Patient brought to
olumbus Hospital via Ambulance Sept. 5, 1942, complaining of general
eakness, that spine could not support her weight, throat sore and
ulling, choking sensation at her neck, physical exam. was essentially
egative. Continues to think that her health is failing that her heart
is pulling out of her body and she was uncooperative and irrational at
times. No known relatives in N.Y.City.

PHYSICAL CONDITION: - Patient sweats considerably, but is in no distres
                    Eyes, pupils equal and reactive. Mouth, negative
Neck, no thyroid palpable; chest, clear to P.A. Heart, sounds very
distant, no murmurs, not enlarged to percussion; regular rate. Lungs,
B. S. Vesicular, no rales; abdomen, negative; reflexes, all present, an
hyperactive; no Babinski; Extremeties, no edema.

MENTAL CONDITION: - Well oriented and intelligent. Speech over-product
                ' relevant and coherent. Patient appears under tensi
and frequently breathes deeply. Slightly depressed and stable, somatic
complaints. Hypochondriacal. Unhappy love affair. Impression-anxiety
nervous. Overtalkative and restless; mood is not appropriate to conten
of thoughts, smiling when she related about her sickness; (throbbing
weakness, choking sensation; no evidence of visual or auditory hallucin
ations; nervous breakdown over 10 years ago.

PATIENT SAID: - (Trouble?) It's a long story. In June I began to feel
              terribly tired and nervous. I've had terrific sinous
trouble. My head got funny- I couldn't catch my breath. My childhood
wasn't happy.- a feeling of insecurity. They did not want me to go to
. school. felt I should contribute. My mother didn't like me- father
all right. Got along better when I left- felt completely relieved.
(When?) In 1932. (Not married?) I've had lots of opportunities. It's
probably part of a pattern- my lack of security as a child- lack of
interest and real feeling. (Date?) 22- Monday, September 1942. (Place?)

Bellevue Psycho. (People stare, make remarks?) No. (People against you
No. (Voices?) No. (Visions?) No. (Depressed?) I'm not happy. (Suicida
No. (CTA) Perfect- regular- I'm menstruating now.

TENDENCIES: - None.

                                              Mashe Syrkin, M.D.
                                              Sidney Rubin, M.D.

The Abstract continues, describing the Harlem Valley interview and
early observations:

MENTAL STATUS

ATTITUDE AND GENERAL BEHAVIOR: This patient is
a well-developed and well-nourished white woman
of 37 [Esther likely made herself younger upon
admission] who has been ambulatory since admission. She is generally quiet and cooperative,
appears to be depressed and when any members of
the ward personnel talk with her she becomes

agitated, wrings her hands and, in an overtalkative manner, describes many somatic difficulties. She eats fairly well and except for the
first two nights following admission, she has
slept without sedation. She is clean in habits
and personal appearance.

STREAM OF MENTAL ACTIVITY: Patient speaks rapidly and goes into great detail in response to
all questions. She shows definite pressure of
speech but does not exhibit a flight of ideas.
Throughout the interview patient frequently interjected remarks to the effect: "Oh God—how
can I go on? Oh, I'm in a hell of a mess . . .
I feel like I'm dying . . . I feel like I'm
going into a coma . . . I can hardly keep my
eyes open . . . I'm so tired. . . ." etc.

EMOTIONAL REACTIONS: Patient's emotional expression varied considerably throughout the
interview. At times she became quite agitated
as she spoke about her troubles. At other
times, without any alteration in content of
thought, she appeared to be quite apathetic and
indifferent. She explained this by saying that
she was resigned to her fate, knew that she was
hopeless and that nothing could be done for
her. At other times during the interview she
appeared to resent efforts of the examiner to
make her keep to the point.

MENTAL TREND: CONTENT OF THOUGHT: Patient expresses numerous hypochondriacal ideas to the
effect that her heart, head and throat feel terrible. She suffers from a generalized feeling

of "tightening all over her body." She believes that her eyes are in terrible condition, are getting worse all the time, and that she will soon lose her vision. Expresses nihilistic delusions to the effect that she is "all gone," that her body is dead, that she is going into a coma, that she is helpless and hopeless and that only a "medical miracle" can help her. Patient acknowledges overindulgence in alcoholic beverages for periods of two or three days at a time between Christmas of 1941 and the end of May 1942. Says she drank upon the insistence of her boyfriend who, incidentally, is a married man with whose wife the patient was acquainted, but states that in spite of the amount she drank, she could not become drunk. During this same period of time patient acknowledges having smoked marijuana cigarettes in an effort to relax. Denies the use of other drugs. Patient acknowledges heterosexual affairs with eight or nine different men since the age of 25 or 26 and says that several years ago she submitted to the practice of cunnilinguism upon the insistence of her boyfriend. Patient says that during the Christmas season of 1941 she began to feel tired and nervous. . . .

[This feeling continued through the spring]. About the beginning of June, she went out one night . . . When it became necessary for [Eugenia] to go to the home of a relative, therefore leaving the patient alone, patient found that she was unable to take care of herself. She lost her appetite, became weak and began gradually to become worse and worse. . . .

During 1941 she was doing a great deal of painting and believes that she may have strained her eyes. She had been on relief for the preceding two or two and a half years and had made unsuccessful attempts to find any kind of a job in order to support herself. Says that she started drinking moderately on a social scale at the age of 25 but during the Christmas holiday she began to drink heavily with her boy-friend . . . Her relationship with the boy-friend was an intimate one. She had met him shortly before Christmas and became intimate with him in February. Before him there were eight other men. Her first experience occurred at the age of 26. Says that she would become intimate with these men because she would believe herself in love with them. Prior to the age of 26 she had boy friends but did not go beyond petting. At this point patient spontaneously expressed her belief that, in spite of her intimacies, she has always been a repressed individual. She attributes this to her early childhood which, she says, was a very unhappy one. She recalls that when she was eight years old her mother did not seem to want her. She recalls that as a child she always liked her father better but she says she believes this to have been normal for a girl. She believes that she resented her brothers and sisters when she lived at home because they seemed to get more attention than she did. However, she was a healthy child, played the piano, drew, and had many friends.

At the age of seventeen she entered Carnegie Tech., taking an academic course and art courses. Because of the financial situation at home, it was necessary for her to work her way through college. She recalls that she worked hard, that her health was not very good and that she was always a little nervous. Says that while working in her art classes she can recall always feeling elated—very high and excited—very happy—almost in an ecstasy. She says that she has felt this way throughout her life whenever she has done a good piece of work. She believes that these spells have occurred frequently since the age of seventeen and have lasted sometimes a few hours and at other times for a day or two at a time. In recent years these feelings of elation have been followed by a period of tiredness. This tiredness was characterized by being irritable and not wanting anyone to talk to her . . .

After Christmas of 1941 and after she had begun to drink, she began to have strange feelings around her heart. She was aware of palpitation, noted that when she climbed stairs she would become short of breath. She remained in this state, feeling tired, irritable and aware of palpitation of the heart until about May. . . . During the first few days [of the Outdoor Show] she was unable to sell any of her [paintings] and developed a feeling of intense frustration. At that time, she says, her condition was very bad: was unable to eat and felt tired all the time. Along about the fourth day, she sold four of her paintings and became very excited and elated. She recalls having gone to Hearn's Department Store to buy a dress one evening and being in such an excited state that she was almost in a daze, felt very excited, "funny and groggy." During the show she sold nine or ten pictures for a little over fifty dollars.

The Abstract of Commitment also included comments about Esther's reading and writing abilities, her remote memory, and a description of previous illness. Interestingly, no mention is made of the luminal Esther had been taking over the summer. Dr. Barasch concluded the Abstract by stating that she had "partial insight and judgment" into her condition. "Patient says that she knows that she is not normal mentally and recognizes the need for state hospital care and treatment. Says that she is very sick physically as well as mentally." As noted, and emphatically underlined by one of the doctors, Esther mentioned that she had a "nervous breakdown over ten years ago." But of course no one in Pittsburgh had made such a strict statement of her mental health. Merle had indeed mentioned, though, of hearing of Esther's "periodic spells of starvation for the last several years in Pittsburgh" in the 1937 letter to George Marion O'Donnell.[8] Likely, Esther knew that she had often been in a nervous state since the mid 1920s, and thus affirmed for her interviewers, when they asked if she ever had a breakdown, that she felt she did in Pittsburgh. (Sybil Barsky-Grucci, old Pittsburgh friend, said, upon hearing about this comment, that Esther was likely just referring to when she was stressed as she tried to find work to pay for school costs.)[9]

Esther was indeed intelligent enough to sort out just what the doctors at Harlem Valley were treating her for. Though she complained about physical problems and the doctors treated her for mental, it doesn't appear that she spoke out too loudly against being placed at the institution. Upon admission, she may have accepted the institution as a place of rest, feeling that she needed comfort and security while she was unwell. Indeed it did provide respite. According to the doctors, Esther "[did] not recognize her somatic complaints as evidences of mental illness," or at least admit to the connection between the two.

Immediately upon Esther's admission at Harlem Valley, administrators called upon Eugenia, she being the closest stated friend. The hospital wrote her on October 23, Esther's admission day, requesting that she visit the hospital so that Esther's physician might talk with her concerning her friend's condition. They felt that Eugenia's "cooperation may be of considerable assistance in the intelligent understanding of

[Esther's] case."[10] Eugenia again chose not to respond to hospital administrators. She likely felt useless to help, and couldn't stand to see Esther in such a predicament. So requests for information from the hospital went ignored, even over more trivial matters such as a laundry ticket bearing Eugenia's name being among Esther's possessions. Numerous attempts to confirm if Eugenia desired this returned to her went unanswered.[11]

All the time that Esther remained institutionalized, it appears that Eugenia never once visited. She was apparently too uncomfortable with seeing her friend in the setting of a state mental hospital. Instead she chose only to write to Esther, often in spurts of months at a time, and then no contact for a while, when apparently she grew frustrated that her friend was still being confined. And Eugenia no doubt felt the burden of Esther's sickness upon her own shoulders with the well-intended yet weighty requests by friends for her to help remedy Esther's situation. A more recent friend within her circle, Michael Duner, wrote her that fall of an early phone contact Eugenia did have with someone from Bellevue, regarding the time that Esther was there: "I worry about you, dear, and Esther. Take care of Esther's plight. Please send me the name and address of Esther's social worker who spoke to you."[12]

Though Eugenia had the caretaker in her, she could only do so much in this, what must have seemed a very delicate, situation. Unable to bring herself to visit the hospital, she nevertheless encouraged others to go to see Esther, sending clothes along that Esther often asked for. Annino Mariano would be who responded to that initial request for information that Harlem Valley had originally asked of Eugenia. A separate page in Esther's institution file stands as a testament to his account, though much of his reflections echo what the hospital gathered already from Esther herself. Some details gathered from him:

> During the past two years [Esther] has been very much concerned about her economic situation. Although on relief, she continued to paint and she would frequently go without food in order to buy materials to work with...

During the past two years she has been very irritable and difficult to get along with. Her social life was considered normal. She would have an occasional date, went to bars occasionally for a few beers. About last Christmas, she seemed to start drinking a little more than formerly but was never seen in an intoxicated state by this informant . . .[14]

Chapter Nine

"GREETINGS FROM WINGDALE, N.Y."[1]

Ward Notes, as well as Doctor Visit Notes, were transcribed periodically at the institution, almost daily in the beginning. Both, in addition to Esther's letters to Eugenia, tell much of Esther's story early on at Harlem Valley. The first Ward Note is a description of Esther's first day, October 23, 1942: "Pt. quiet and cooperative. Says she has no feeling in her body. Oriented as to time and place—says she is an Artist and worked very hard. Became nervous and then started to drink and smoke marijuana cigarettes."

Dr. Barasch expanded on the original entry. (Unless a visiting doctor is specified, nurses or attendants who interacted with Esther on a daily basis documented Ward Notes that follow from this point on.)

> October 23, 1942—
>
> [Patient] states that she was taken to Bellevue Hospital after two weeks at Columbus Hospital where she went because she was "on the verge of becoming unconscious" . . . states that she attended Carnegie Tech for three years and is a painter by occupation . . . She denies hallucinations. Delusional ideas, except for the foregoing, are not in evidence. Patient is markedly overtalkative in a rambling manner. Has no insight.
>
> Dr. Barasch

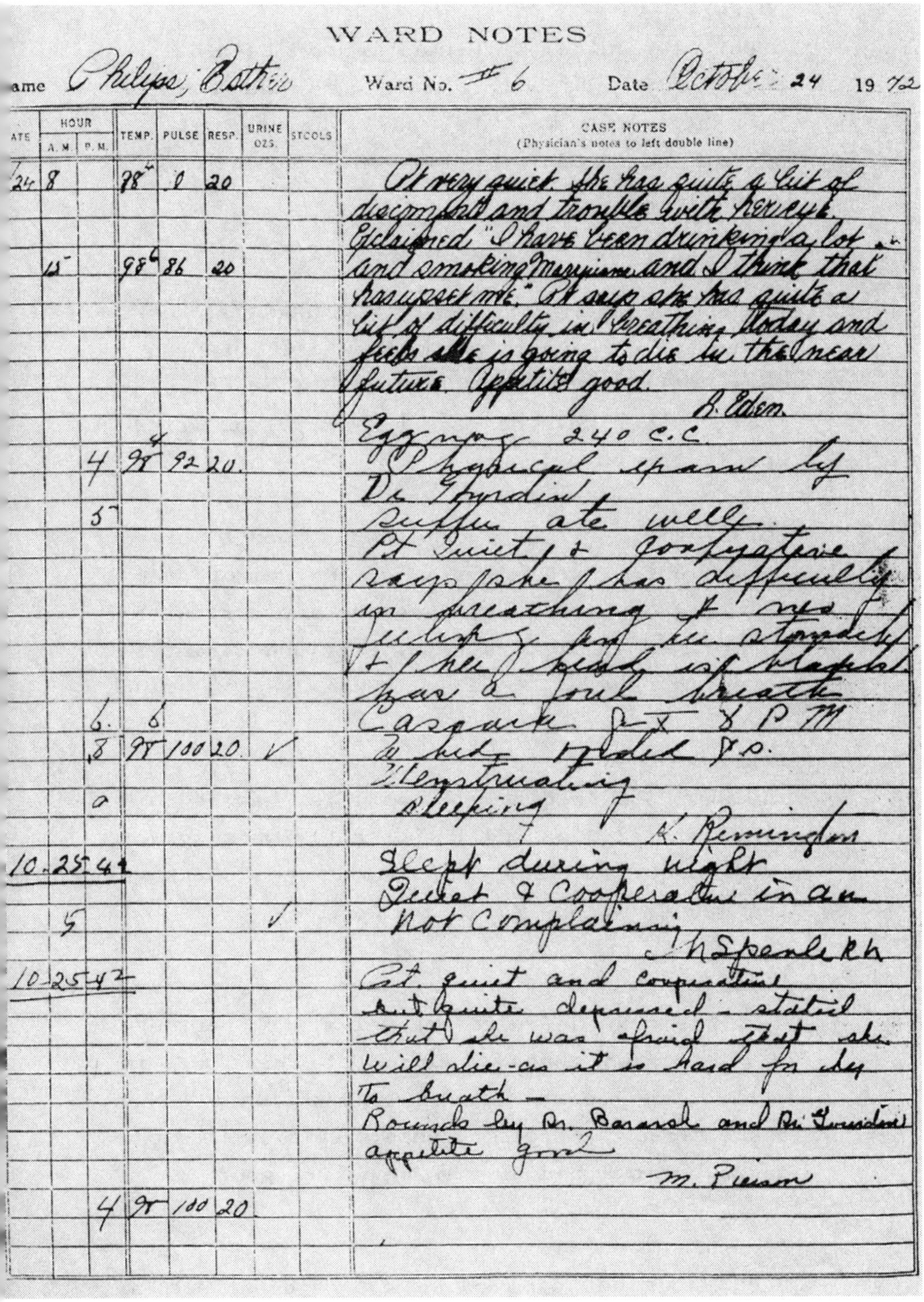

WARD NOTES

Name *Phelps, Bettie*   Ward No. #6   Date *October* 24   19 72

DATE	HOUR A.M.	HOUR P.M.	TEMP.	PULSE	RESP.	URINE OZS.	STOOLS	CASE NOTES (Physician's notes to left double line)
24	8		98°	0	20			Pt very quiet. She has quite a bit of discomfort and trouble with kidney. Explained "I have been drinking a lot and smoking marijuana and I think that has upset me." Pt says she has quite a bit of difficulty in breathing today and feels she is going to die in the near future. Appetite good. *B. Odem*
	15		98°	86	20			
		4	98°	92	20			Eggnog 240 c.c. Physical exam by Dr. Gordon. Supper ate well. Pt quiet & cooperative, says she has difficulty in breathing ... stomach ... foul breath
		5						
		6	6					Cascara ... 8 P M
		8	98°	100	20	✓		... Menstruating. Sleeping. *K. Remington*
		9						
10-25	4							Slept during night. Quiet & cooperative in a.m. Not complaining. *M. Spenle R.N.*
		5				✓		
10-25	4							Pt quiet and cooperative. Pt quite depressed — stated that she was afraid that she will die — as it is hard for her to breath — Rounds by Dr. Barach and Dr. Gordon. Appetite good. *M. Pierson*
		4	98°	100	20			.

FIG. 6

10/24/42—

Pt. very quiet. Exclaimed 'I have been drinking a lot and smoking marijuana and I think
that has upset me.' Pt. says she has quite a
bit of difficulty in breathing today . . .
Appetite good.

10/26/42—

Pt. talking a great deal. Talks about her work
as an artist. Says her most recent paintings
were brilliant and that a friend is displaying
them for her and that she had marvelous write-
ups in the paper.

10/31/42—

Restless during night . . . Pt. never stops
thinking of herself and has the impression she
is in a critical condition. Lazy and disinterested in others.

11/1/42—

Claims she is disgusted at life, has had all
kinds of maladies and is patiently waiting for
the end to come. Says all this in a very cheerful manner with a smile on her face.

11/4/42—

Pt. is neat and pleasant—talks with patients
. . . states that she does not think she is
well enough to be down on [Recreation 4]. Was
transferred too soon, because she is still sick.
Makes her own bed in a.m. Appetite good.

11/5/42—

Pt. does not dare to walk outside—afraid to
trust to being on the grounds . . . does not
seem sick in any way.

11/9/42—

Pt. says doctor does not pay any attention to her—only wished she could die—as she is getting worse every day . . . talks continually about her condition, annoys other patients talking about it . . . [states] that she is too weak to do any work or make her bed. Untidy about her appearance. Idle on ward.

November 9, 1942—

. . . [Patient] believes that she has been getting worse all the time since her admission here . . . She has repeatedly stated that she is patiently waiting for the end to come. On the ward she is generally idle and seclusive; claims that she is too weak to do any work. Remains without insight into her condition. Dr. Barasch

Three weeks after being admitted to Harlem Valley, Esther wrote to Eugenia:

[11/12/42]

Dear Jerry—

I feel very sick—my eyes are getting worse—I do not know what is wrong—but I do know that the Bellevue experience (1 month)—has played havoc with what's left of my health—I honestly feel I am dying— my eyes are glassy & I have terrific difficulty in breathing—& my head gets tighter & tighter. The doctor says that the extreme exertion of having climbed six flights & not having eaten right & drank was very bad—He

wants me to hope for the best—If I had been here this spring things would have been different—
because it was then that I was so very tired—& strangely I did my best work then. How come?—
I can't draw anymore—I forced or rather I did with what little vitality I had—did some lovely
drawings at Bellevue—which I dedicated to you—tho I don't suppose you can get them—

If you come please bring several of my good w. colors—"Lady of Pompeii Church" & the
scene from So & So's window on Third St—I can't remember his name—[turns out be painter
Jack Small, according to Eugenia's journal] "The 3 Little Girls in the Park" & a few others—
perhaps—The view here is very beautiful—but am too ill to do anything about it—

lots of love, Esther

Then, scribbled along the sides of the notepaper—

I am really trying my best to get well—but I am frightened. I feel I painted too much
when I was so ill—but it's too late to think of it now.

November 16, 1942—
. . . it is not possible to discuss [patient's] situation with her to any appreciable extent because she . . . expresses herself to the effect that it is a waste of time to talk about the same things all the time. All efforts to get her to participate in some of the activities are futile. She remains without insight.

Dr. Barasch

11/18/42—
Pt. just sits all day. Takes no interest in anything. Urged to go out walking.

[11/21/42]

Dear Jerry—
Thank you & Louise for the package—I appreciate it lots—but have no
feeling for anything anymore—I am still very miserable—feel numb—& weak
all over—You'll never recognize me anymore—my eyes have changed. They've
become very weak . . .

I can't draw anymore let alone paint—I can't believe I ever actually lived in an apt., made my own breakfast—cleaned—dressed myself in the most becoming manner I knew. …Also I think of the clothes we used to sew together. Sometimes I think I should have been like Ruth Thompson—live in a furnished room—not have had housework to contend with, or my own sewing or cooking—just painting and sleeping and eating in restaurants as she always did—That's why she was so strong.

Well it's too late now—I feel as if I shall never have another chance—This last spring if I could have relaxed completely—and eaten with you or someone things would have been different—But of course George was so hard on my nerves & practically took over your establishment—I am very bitter against him but there's no use in thinking about it now. I should simply have gotten a more comfortable place that wasn't so difficult to climb to—& simply not to have seen you as long as George was around as he undoubtedly irritated me to the breaking point—or at least made me terrifically hyper-tense—I feel he was as harmful to me as Frank was with his drinking—You could tell this to George—it doesn't matter—now—but I had to express my bitterness—He knew all along I was not too well—but used to insist upon upsetting me all the time. He even went as far as to tell Charles [G.] that he enjoyed irritating me—Well you can tell him he's <u>partly</u> responsible for a wonderful job on me—

I know I sound like a paranoic [sic] blaming my troubles on other people—but other people are quite often responsible—I don't even feel as bitter toward Frank as he meant to be kind and after all I did not have to drink—he didn't force me—

Well—that's enough of that!—At least, Jerry, whatever happens I still love you very much & hold no grievance against you—but when you come <u>do not</u> bring George—as I will insult him if you do.

love Esther

Before I forget—if you could bring some of my clothes…[if] you could let me have the peasant skirt I made—the red one with blue rick-rack … we're forced to take walks here & it's getting cold—please try to get my coat.

11/24/42—

    Pt. crying this a.m. when attendant was try-
    ing to show her how to make her bed. She said
    she was stupid and couldn't learn anything; the
    reason why she was this way was some wise guy
    made her drink and then ruined her.

11/26/42—

Pt. cursed this a.m. because of getting up
early—5 a.m.—says, 'I didn't sleep all night.'
Pt. slept soundly all night.

[11/29/42] *Tues. Nite*

Dear Jerry,

This will be a short one as I still have difficulty—etc. etc.— . . . My visitors to date have been 1 visit from Masson—& Frank Dunlevy—Sunday nite—Jack Small—Tuesday aft.—w/a parcel of fruit—& cake—I get very depressed—I realize I must have human companionship—I sure do miss you—& Mr. Hughes . . . I still have trouble with my back—it seems so weak—well—that's all—

love Esther

Regards to Roy & Mrs. Herbert

Esther usually didn't date her letters; at most she might write "Tues. Nite," as above. Eugenia often placed the date in brackets herself.

On December 7, 1942, a postcard embossed with "Greetings from Wingdale, N.Y.," arrives in Eugenia's mailbox. It showed a colorized sunset over a tree-lined stream. Esther writes the following:

Dear Jerry—Thanks for sending my clothes & Mariano—I would love to see you, tho—more than anyone—Try to come—incidentally please send me some of my <u>underwear</u>—<u>sweater</u>—skirts &—also try to get my wintercoat from the cleaners.

—Esther

Along the sides and top of this postcard, Esther scribbles,

I still feel like nothing! I hope Frank suffers for me.

12/10/42

Dear Jerry—

I supposed you got my card—but to make sure I'm writing this letter—Perhaps I feel a tiny bit better—It's hard to tell—My eyes are still very bad, nevertheless—2 pinpoints for eyes—etc etc. . .

*Are you in good health? And your father?—Do you see Masson ?—Does he still go
to George's?—That place seems so hazy and far away from me now—I just can't believe
I'm the way I am...*

*I may ask you to try to sell one of my water colors—for some change I need around
here, perhaps for glasses—$10.00—would be acceptable for the sale, if any.*

*Also—please Jerry—keep my w. colors in your place, not Louise's—I incidentally
give her my love—Remember me to everybody—Your father—Masson—even Edith
[C.]—Herbie—etc—God, but I'd like to see you—Jerry—bring Masson or somebody
with you—*

> love
>
> Esther

*I am enclosing 2 drawings. Have been drawing some—can work with very little
effort—almost subconscious—feel like Renoir—practically have to prop my eyes
open—to see—*

Esther sent two small sketches with this letter, one of *Harlem Valley*,
showing the Facilities Maintenance Building with the rolling hills in the
background, and another sketch of the same size—perhaps a self-portrait—was a prototype of watercolors to come.

Another December letter to Eugenia includes the following:

*I know I don't sound very logical, but that is to be expected, feeling as I do—don't send me
my [watercolor] box—as I really see badly and have almost no equilibrium—line drawing
is easy for me ... it is an advantage in a way to do sensitive lines,—I am still frightened—
do not know whether I'll live or not—to be truthful, but have decided to do the best I can ...
I know there's no justice in this world—I know [Frank Dunlevy] will never suffer—you see
I'm not lamenting the love—but the slow poison, liquor—in other words, that was forced
down my throat—Send clothes, underwear—Try to visit—Maybe you'll never see me
again, so make an attempt.*

In the first couple months of Esther's admittance, Harlem Valley
Hospital tried to ascertain financial liability of their patient. Both
Harlem Valley and the State Department of Mental Hygiene write
Esther's parents at the address given by Esther—5531 Jackson Street in
Pittsburgh, indeed where they were still living.[2]

December 1, 1942

RE: ESTHER PHILLIPS

Mr. David Phillips
5531 Jackson Street
Pittsburgh, Pa.

Dear Sir:

I am taking this opportunity to inform
you that your daughter has been a patient at this
hospital since October 23, 1942, suffering from a
mental illness.

It would be desirable for some member of
the family to call at the hospital so that the
physician who is taking care of Miss Phillips
can obtain information concerning her past life.
In the event that it is not immediately possible
for some member of the family to come here, I am
enclosing herewith a history blank which is to be
filled out and returned to us as soon as possible.

Yours truly,

H. A. LaBURT, M.D.
Superintendent

JB:ms
Encl.

m 26-0, M. H.

M. J. TIFFANY, M. D.
COMMISSIONER

TATE OFFICE BLDG.,
McKINLEY SQUARE
BUFFALO

H. BECKETT LANG, M. D.
ASST. COMMISSIONER

204 873
STATE OFFICE BLDG.,
50 CENTRE STREET
NEW YORK CITY

STATE OF NEW YORK
DEPARTMENT OF MENTAL HYGIENE
STATE OFFICE BUILDING
ALBANY

New York City
December 7, 1942

Re: Esther Phillips

Dr. H. A. LaBurt, Superintendent
Harlem Valley State Hospital
Wingdale, New York

Dear Dr. LaBurt:

      In accordance with your letter of October 29, 1942, in which you furnish the names and address of the parents of the above patient, I have written to the parents but have not received a reply. Will you kindly keep this case in mind, and notify the writer of any visits of correspondents living within New York State.

                Very truly yours,
                W. J. TIFFANY, M. D.
                Commissioner

            BY: Geo. D. Mattice
                Special Agent

GRMattice:RY

DEC 1942
RECEIVED
HARLEM VALLEY
STATE HOSPITAL

But in the entire time that Esther would be at Harlem Valley, there was no recorded visit from the family. Her file also contains no evidence of written communication from her parents. Only in June of 1943 and eight months after her admittance, would a brother write the hospital.

Barney Phillips
Attorney at Law
614 Bakewell Building
Pittsburgh, Pa

June 28, 1943

Dr. H.A. LaBurt
Harlem Valley State Hospital
Wingdale, N.Y.
Re. Esther Phillips

Dear Sir:

I am a brother of Esther Phillips and a rumor has come to me that she died some months ago. I last heard that she was a patient at the Harlem Valley Hospital. Please advise me.

Very Respectfully Yours
Barney Phillips

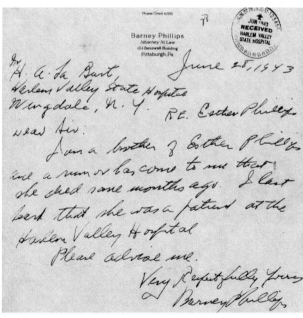

FIG.7   Original of Barney's letter

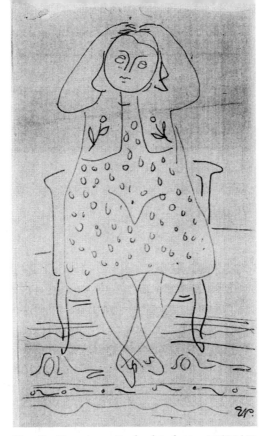

FIG. 8   Drawing attached to letter 12/10/42

FIG. 9   Attached to letter 12/10/42

The hospital replies immediately, as this inquiry was be the first (and only) from family. They "happily informed" him that his sister was "alive and well, and continues to reside at this institution. She is enjoying satisfactory physical health. We regret, however, that there has been little improvement in her mental condition, but everything possible is being done for her care and welfare."[3]

Esther's parents would have been the only ones to know and disclose the name and whereabouts of the hospital to their son. No friends in Pittsburgh at the time of Barney's writing in 1943 knew what was going on with Esther; there could only be speculation. Though right after she moved to New York she wrote a couple of other Pittsburgh friends, Merle was the only person she would have confided in about her institutionalization, but the two hadn't communicated for a while. Thus any rumors (as opposed to guilt feelings on the part of parents or son) would likely have originated with the few friends she had written to, or other Pittsburgh artists that knew her—as they wondered why they hadn't heard from her or about how she was faring in "the big city." If there was speculation early on from anyone that knew Esther in Pittsburgh, it is unlikely that Merle took any part in it. Her concern for Esther was genuine and she understood her friend's transient lifestyle. Most significantly, even after finally corresponding with the institution and finding out information on Esther, neither Barney nor his parents passed along any information to her friends. They provided no corroboration of mental illness, no institution's name, no statement on her very existence.

Chapter Ten

DIAGNOSIS

Prior to Esther's first Christmas at Harlem Valley, in December of 1942, the hospital, as at the start of every holiday season, sent out word to patients' friends and family of the importance of thoughtfulness at the holiday season. "Suitable gifts include articles of clothing, smoking material, toilet articles, (except files or other sharp instruments), non-perishable foods that do not need cooking, games, puzzles, cards, checkers, chess games and books. If you wish to send money with which the patient may purchase luxuries...mark it 'to be deposited to the patient's Luxury Account.'"[1] Esther was remembered this holiday with a package from former art student and friend May Swenson.[2]

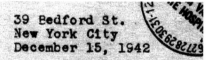

```
                              39 Bedford St.
                              New York City
                              December 15, 1942


Harlem Valley State Hospital
Wingdale, New York

Gentlemen:

     Under separate cover I am forwarding a

Christmas package for ESTHER PHILLIPS, a patient

at Harlem Valley.
```

The package contains a box of hard candies, and a pair of woolen gloves.

It will be very much appreciated if you will arrange for this gift to be brought to Esther on Christmas Day. She is a friend of my room mate and myself, and we would like to express our good wishes with this little surprise.

Thanking you for your cooperation, I am

Sincerely yours,

M. Swenson

M. Swenson

Please keep contents of package in confidence until Christmas Day.

Ward and Doctor Visit Notes and letters to Jerry continue to document Esther's early days at the institution, a time when both her irritability over the routine of hospital life and her spunk in attempting to deal with it, is quite evident.

December 16, 1942—
Patient has shown some improvement during the past month: She is more cheerful, helps a little with the ward work, goes on walks, converses with some of the other patients, has been doing some drawing. Numerous somatic complaints persist, particularly her complaint that her eyes are bad and that she cannot use them very well; however, she is not nearly as agitated as for-

merly when she relates her complaints. She appears to derive some satisfaction from the examiner's frequent assurance that she is better and that she will continue to improve.

Dr. Barasch

12/31/42—

Pt. complaining of Pt. Minnie L. States that patient L. annoys and upsets her and that if she was herself, pt. would take a 'poke' at her.

1/3/43—

Pt. says she does not get fruits or salads enough—too much starchy foods—says fruit juice and green salads make her feel better. This patient is a very nervous person and any kind of noise bothers her—Wakes at the first sound of wind or any noise—aside from noise sleeps well—is always pleasant.

1/10/43—

Pt. stated, 'I think I'll die, or go blind tonight. I feel awful.'

1/12/43—

Pt. states that she has a cold but [doesn't] want doctors to know about it. Pt. stated on ward that Pt. Dabelstein, who was transferred, was dead! Upset patients on ward! When questioned about it, stated 'I just imagined it.'

1/13/43—

Says she won't tell the doctor [of her cold] for fear he would send her upstairs. Also says

she wants to die—she wants to sleep all the time—
hard to get out [of bed] in a.m. Have to call
her 3 or 4 times—then pull covers off.

January 16, 1943—

[Patient] continues to make many somatic complaints which vary in intensity from day to
day. Remains without insight.

Dr. Barasch

1/17/43—

When told by Attendant Mrs. C. Hall to try
and do some work and forget about her trouble,
Pt. became impudent and told attendant to mind
her own business and to shut up.

1/18/43—

Pt. always telling her troubles to Pt. J.
Hueser. States she has to tell someone who will
listen. When told not to bother her troubles to
other patients, became very angry. When attendant told her patients can't be bothered with
her troubles, [she] stated 'this God Damn place
is enough to make patients sick.' Pt. [also]
sarcastic to other patients on ward.

[2/5/43]

Dear Jerry—

Was very pleased to receive your letter—& the ten bucks—Thanks for making the sales—tho, I wish you would use the rest of the money—for yourself...I still feel like something that doesn't even remotely resemble a human being—I do wish you could come out here to see me...

I keep wishing it were 1942—and could do things differently—but since life & health is a gift, it could never be retracted...

love Esther

2/12/43—

When giving out store supplies [pt.] became impatient, started to cry, using profane language, calling attendant names. When asked to come and get her things, became very sarcastic in her remarks.

2/15/43—

Pt. was asked why she didn't go in dining room to work this a.m. and pt. replied 'I go in whenever I can and that's that.' Very sarcastic . . . [pt.] always very moody, inclined to be cross.

3/3/43—

Pt. very irritable this a.m., trying to quarrel with Pt. R. Rubin.

3/9/43—

Pt. was very quarrelsome; when woke up this a.m., wanted to know '[what] sort of a school was being run here, that [she] had to be told when to go to bed, and when to get up . . . and all you attendants can go to Hell!'

March 16, 1943—

Patient says she feels dopey all the time, her head feels light, feels as though it "cracks" all the time . . . [and] she still fears that she will become blind. Her backbone feels weak and she has trouble holding herself erect. When she went for a walk the other day, she had a feeling as though she could not get enough air into her lungs. On the ward she makes a fairly satisfactory adjustment, helps with the work in the patients' diningroom occasionally. Believes that there is something "physically wrong" with her mind.

Dr. B

3/17/43—

Pt. is more noticeably disagreeable, when attendant tries to reason with her, states she is tired of living, and realizes she is good for nothing.

3/26/43—

Pt. states that she is getting worse, and that she is getting a desire to throw things at anyone. Also states, 'while Dr. Barasch passed through the dining room yesterday, I wanted so much to throw the plates at him. I wish . . . I could do that!'

March 29, 1943—

Patient is TODAY TRANSFERRED TO BUILDING 28 for further care and treatment. It is felt that perhaps working in the [Occupational Therapy] shop may be beneficial. Her somatic complaints persist.
Dr. B

April 13, 1943—

Patient is fairly neat and clean and quiet and friendly during interview. She stated that she had become sick and gone to Columbus Hospital because she felt she was losing her mind. She told an incoherent story. "I had a boyfriend—Christmas before last. I didn't realize he was a dipsomaniac and loved to drink, so I began

drinking with him because I liked to be in his
company. I guess I drank too much, frequently
on an empty stomach. Spells when I couldn't see
well, had the shakes and on one occasion at
least I saw mice running around the room. Began
to have imaginations—visual hallucinations.
There were mice in my place, but I did see them
with my imagination too, but no voices. I was
fidgety, I could not paint, could not sleep."
Patient admitted smoking marijuana cigarettes.

Dr. A. F. Rizzolo

Dr. J. Barasch had begun compiling a case summary for Esther
Phillips' six-month evaluation on February 22, 1943. In it he first reiterated Esther's family history, recent personal history, and current illness
symptoms, including the observations taken at Columbus and
Bellevue Hospitals (all exactly transcribed, or generalized, from her
Abstract of Commitment four months prior). As for the subsequent
course of her condition, from the date of admission on, and based on
attendants' Ward Notes and on doctor visits, Dr. Barasch wrote,
"Despite the persistence of her hypochondriacal complaints, the
patient has at all times made a satisfactory adjustment to the hospital
routine." He comments upon the fact that Esther's adjustments were,
as expected, happening in a steady fashion, and that past December,
she had even become interested in doing some free-hand sketching.
However, "she has remained without insight into the nature of her
somatic complaints."

Dr. Barasch concluded his preliminary diagnostic discussion:

In this case we have a mental illness in a
thirty-seven-year-old white woman in whom personality changes were first noted about two
years prior to admission. . . . Emotionally, at
times, she has been quite agitated insofar as
her somatic complaints have been concerned but

at other times she has been rather apathetic and has explained her apparent apathy by saying that she knew that she was a hopeless case. While there are some psychopathic features in evidence, it is felt that for statistical purposes, the diagnosis should be PSYCHONEUROSIS, HYPOCHONDRIASIS.

Come April 22, 1943, six months after Esther's admission, Dr. Barasch, Dr. Rizzolo, and the Clinical Director of the hospital, Dr. B. B. Young, in conference, agreed upon the diagnosis, PSYCHONEUROSIS, MIXED TYPE. A photo taken of Esther in the hospital was attached to the case summary.[3] (Fig. 10)

FIG. 10   Photo of patient Esther Phillips, attached to her Case Summary in the institution file.

A hypochondriac, the most lay of the terms that would be used to describe Esther's condition, is one who believes he has physical ailments, with no physical basis to support that belief, or who is simply sick with various ailments much of the time, always interfering with one's life. (This condition is commonly recalled by the expression that one's problems are "all in one's head," an expression, of course, that suggests mental problems in general, but that really epitomizes this one specific mental condition defined as hypochondriasis.) The doctors found no substantiation of Esther's physical claims, but that doesn't mean that she wasn't feeling some of the physical distress that she was complaining about. Hypochondriasis is characterized by the ability to create physical discomfort from mental distress, i.e., "mind over matter." Thus Esther may have complained at times about non-existent physical discomfort, and at other times ill state of mind may have indeed created bodily discomfort that the doctors could not, or would not, corroborate. Most importantly, she became convinced of a marked change in her own physical health. This conviction epitomizes hypochondriasm, even when no such change was actually taking place.

Esther's diagnosis incorporated both the Neurasthenia and Anxiety Neurosis that was noted at Columbus and Bellevue Hospitals. Neurasthenia, a "psychophysiologic nervous system reaction," is closely tied to hypochondriasm. According to Drs. O. Spurgeon English and Stewart M. Finch, in their *Introduction to Psychiatry*, it is characterized, by "fatigue, lassitude, multiple vague somatic complaints, and a general lack of adequate emotional participation in everyday activities."[4] This was exemplified all too well by Esther's early admittance behavior, certainly different from her usual extreme emotional participation in the artistic activities that were her life. Geller and Harris in *Women of the Asylum: Voices From Behind The Walls, 1840–1945* describe neurasthenia as "a general state of malaise, depression, impaired intellect and irritability, accompanied by neuralgia [intense pain that occurs along a nerve] and muscle weakness" and say that it "was thought to be caused by excessive mental labor, anxiety, or deficient nutrition,"[5] and also "overwork . . . and worry resulting from the stresses of modern life."[6]

Anxiety neurosis also is intrinsically linked with hypochondriacal complaints. English and Finch stated that those with any neurosis "will exaggerate the slightest hint that they suffer from any organic ailment" and that "the patient with anxiety reaction usually believes that his condition is comparatively hopeless as well as serious." They also say that anxiety neurosis proper is actually "the presence of a chronic, diffuse anxiety . . . [that] never entirely disappears." Over time, it "decreases working ability and efficiency."[7]

Hypomania, too, can be considered another facet of Esther's diagnosis of mixed type psychoneurosis. In its latter stages, "the individual becomes more grandiose in his ideas and jumps rapidly from one thought to another. He may become involved in large but unrealistic schemes."[8] It indeed is one phase of the manic depressive-like cycle that Esther seemed no stranger to, along with her other symptoms. For, as her Abstract of Commitment revealed, Esther was up at times in her life when she was doing her art, and down at others; she was elated while in art class or after having sold a work, but down when her artistic abilities were overlooked.

There remains no doubt that Esther was suffering from mental dis-ease when she landed in the institution in 1942. Her emotional problems were manifesting themselves in nervous reactions and hypochondriacal complaints. She had come to believe that she had definite physical ailments, though she was in "good general physical condition, "[9] according to the doctors. "The belief that our suffering has a physical cause is always persuasive, because it relieves us of all responsibility,"[10] If Esther's body bothered her, she didn't have to think about her state of mind. "A result of a change in ego stability" is one way English and Finch described the cause of neurasthenia, who saw the entirety of a psychoneurosis as "an attempt on the part of the individual's ego to find some solution to its unconscious problems."[11] How stable was Esther's sense of self? Why the emotional pain, the cyclical depression, the chronic anxiety, the bodily complaints?

The precipitating factors that led Esther headlong to the mental institution—the extremely poor eating habits; the loss of her position with the WPA, which had been an important recognition of the worthiness of her artistic talent; the acute bouts of drinking that were a bit excessive for her constitution; the unusual, and likely emotionally hurtful love relationship; and quite possibly the taking of luminal, which, if it didn't produce harmful side-effects at least sufficiently depressed her enough to curtail her painting—all these incidents pushed her over an edge already arrived at. Because she was making no money at her art and was overcome with depressed thoughts, she simply felt she could no longer function. Her calling the ambulance was but a plea for help for a breakdown that had been long in building, over years. Esther had deep-seated anxiety as an artist all her life, chronically living in poverty; she willingly chose a path that, though far from profitable, allowed her to tap her creativity. She rebelled both by being an artist and by being a woman breaking from traditional roles. Ostracized for both by her family and much of society, she felt an outsider, though her self-concept as artist was sufficiently strong enough to guide her courageously through much of her life experiences.

Esther suffered with uneasiness about the way that she lived and worked, so different from mainstream Americans, even though it brought her much personal satisfaction. She had community but that alone was not enough. Even her perceptions while institutionalized seemed unconscious statements about her lifelong way of artistic being. "[She is] tired of living and realizes she is good for nothing," says a doctor in the Abstract of Committment. She wrote Jerry that she was "frightened—don't know whether I will survive or not—know there's no justice in this world." Esther got "apathetic and indifferent," because she became "resigned to her fate, knew that she was hopeless and that nothing could be done for her."[12] She looked, not unnaturally, for esteem and respect from a circle larger than her own, despite her own knowledge that her work and the work of her friends was indeed important. To create that beauty for her own eyes was not enough, though. An immense longing to be acknowledged for what she did was never fulfilled. Her falling ill was a way to say that something was wrong, a subconscious attempt to bring attention to herself, for her strength was not enduring. But she was not consciously in touch with this quite natural vulnerability within herself. The denial and the lack of insight caused her unbalance. She was out of touch with the emotional pain, so she got physically sick.

After her Case Summary was completed, it being a necessary evaluation set up to most properly identify, after a relegated observatory period, a patient's condition, hospital staff simply continued monitoring a patient's behavior and administering whatever treatments deemed necessary by attending physicians. Documentation continued, through ward notes and the like, until change, if any, over time and circumstance of residing in the hospital, was noted.

```
June 2, 1943—
    . . . [Pt.] was inclined to be somewhat silly
in her behavior. Pressing her eyes she stated
she is unable to see properly; that she gets
dizzy spells and feels that she has pulmonary
tuberculosis. General physical condition is
satisfactory. Patient is being placed on [vita-
min] B-1 and nicotinic acid.
                        Dr. A.F. Rizzolo
```

Dear Jerry,

I am just writing a short note—feel too numb and weak for more than that … What I want is this—Could you possibly darling send me my summer clothes … Another thing— I need $15 for glasses … My eyes weren't examined yet … but now I'm so much weaker … they're going to see if that will help any. I hope everybody is well— love Esther

P.S. You can sell any one of the w.colors—for the money—
Esther

July 26, 1943—

This patient has shown considerable improvement in her physical condition. Probably as a result of medication. However—she continues idle and to express innumerable somatic complaints without apparent physical basis.

Dr. A. F. Rizzolo

The only "medication" Esther received, according to all Notes and the doctors' Order Sheet, were the B-vitamins, nicotinic acid (niacin), liver tablets, occasionally mineral oil, and Cascara GRX [Cascara Sagrada]—an herbal laxative considered emotionally purgative. Dr. Rizzolo obviously felt Esther to be specifically deficient in the B-vitamins and niacin, and the liver tablets would have provided iron to attend to her periodic anemia. Interestingly, a major source of niacin is milk, which Esther craved in the summer of 1942. Extreme niacin deficiency leads to a condition known as Pellagra, whose symptoms are dermatitis, diarrhea and dementia (the "3 D's"). Major niacin deficiency causes loss of strength, headache, and incidence of mental symptoms, everything from insomnia to mania to mild psychoneurosis. Niacin supplement therapy is known to rapidly bring alertness and vigor back to patients.[13]

Esther's poverty had certainly leveled her to a point metabolically that, hand-in-hand with the very insecurity she experienced as artist, brought about her demise. The two factors were undeniably related— both ugly, constant demons that had rendered her unstable by mid-life. English and Finch had described neurasthenia as a "complicated interrelationship between . . . endocrine and emotional forces,"[14] as they tried to address both the psychological and chemical/nutritional standpoints of the mental disease.

[July 28, 1943]

Dear Jerry,

Please excuse me for not having answered your letter before this—and especially for not having thanked you sooner for the clothes—but I am not of this earth anymore—I feel too woozy for anything rash. Although the doctor here has been very nice—giving me vi. B—& other pills—but I really feel as if I've burned out my flame forever-

I happened to glance at a book of short stories—and noticed so many women—that is, creative women, in their biographies, that so many have passed out at around 40 or a little under—at least around that age. Emily Bronte—Elinor Wylie etc. that I sort of wonder— By that—don't think I'm comparing myself to those women—but since I have been creative in my own little way—perhaps that's my fate, too!—

I really wish I could write you humorous and witty things—but my mind does not comprehend that sort of thing yet—Perhaps the only way I get that now are in my very bad drawings—There are, as a matter of fact humorous incidents here, emerging once in a while from an otherwise tragic atmosphere. And there are lovable unfortunates here clinging to each other for support, courage and general friendship when not involved completely in their own suffering or perhaps dream world.

Well at any rate—I'm here, you're in N.Y.—the world's at war—and that's that! I can't say any more—so goodbye—

love

Esther—

Will send you a few drawings next time—too tired to pick any out—

love, Esther

This would be the last letter between Esther and Jerry for awhile. Come December of 1943, a little over a year after Esther's admittance, Eugenia and her father become anxious to learn what would become of their friend. Michael Duner again tries to help both Esther and Eugenia; he writes the hospital to inform the administrators of Eugenia and Roy's concern over Esther's case. And Duner also writes the Hughes', revealing his feelings about Esther's situation.[15]

December 10, 1943

Supt.
Harlem Valley Hospital
Wingdale, New York

Dear Sir:

I am a friend of Miss Esther Philips, a patient at
your Hospital for some time.

Miss Eugenia Hughes and her father, Mr. Roy Hughes
of 44 Washington Square South, New York City, are
very much interested to learn how Miss Philips is
getting along and if there has been any notable
improvement in her condition. I have known Miss
Philips for some time and shall be very glad to
help her in whatever manner you might suggest.

If there is anything she needs, please let me know
and it will be sent her.

We all hope that her mental condition has improved
sufficiently to enable her to assume her place again
in society, and should it be so, I feel reasonably
sure that a number of Miss Philips' friends would
be only too glad to be assitance.

Please express our best wishes and regards to Miss
Philips. If she is able, we should be pleased to
hear from her.

Thank you.   *Does Miss Philips need any money?*

                              Very sincerely yours,
                              Michael Duner
                              Michael Duner

Post Office Box 584
General Post Office
New York-1, N.Y.

December 10, 1943

Dear Eugenia:

I have just written to the Supt. of the Hospital where
Esther Philips is a patient. Be most assured that I
shall be very glad to do my share in making her present
situation in some manner more cheerful.

I think that Esther is as much a victim of an unfortunate and vicous cycle of circumstances as she is is
also a victim of a desolate society. If we can by some
individual act do something about it we in some measure
redeem that situation which is indelibly in our memory,
the knowledge of some person's agonizing defeat, sorrow,
wistful, empty, memory of grief.

I shall be extremely happy to have you and your father
and Mariano over at my place sometime this coming Tuesday
night. Will you please let me know. I have some new prints
I want to show you. The place is very nicely arranged now
and I haven't heard another person's voice here in many weeks.
Won't you please try and come over? Thanks.

My very Kindest Regards for your father, Mariano and yourself.

Affectionately,

Michael Duner

336 West 11-th St.
New York, N.Y.

CHelsea 3-6193

Always timely in their response to inquiries of patient conditions, Dr. I. M. Rossman, acting director of Harlem Valley at the time, writes Duner of Esther's continued bodily complaints and feelings of inadequacy. He expresses that Esther had at times shown an interest in her drawings and paintings, but that "her efforts have not been well sustained for any length of time." He did add what would be the first hint of true hospital encouragement of her artistic endeavors: "Attempts are being made to arouse her interest constantly." As was standard, the hospital also provided a list of needed clothing articles for the patient to anyone writing on her behalf. Dr. Rossman also includes that Esther "was glad to hear of your regards and acknowledges that she did not write as she feels somewhat depressed."[16]

Esther was terribly out of her element still, within, and with regard to her new surroundings. Eugenia, too, still felt her own inadequacy, not knowing what to do of Esther's situation. So though there had been a flurry of correspondence between Esther and Eugenia right after Esther was admitted to Harlem Valley in October 1942, it had definitely tapered off mid-year 1943, with the last substantiated correspondence between them being Esther's July 1943 letter. It would not pick up again until the fall of 1944. Though the institution provided respite from poverty, the troubled Esther would experience some solitary, dark days ahead at Harlem Valley. Even the Ward Notes would be few and far between from mid 1943 through 1944.

> 6/44—
>
> [Pt.] sits in chairs all day long with hands over her face; when spoken to will say 'Don't bother me.' Idle on ward, complains of not being well. Eats and sleeps well.

> 9/44—
>
> Idle on ward, cooperative, does not leave ward, only for meals.

"Day after day passes. Nothing but the same routine. My life is a hardship as much as it is a blank." So spoke Margaret Starr, institutionalized from 1901–1902 at the Mount Hope Retreat in Baltimore.[17] Her experience, and the experiences of many other institutionalized women are detailed in *Women of the Asylum: Voices from Behind the Walls, 1840–1945.* By publishing their written accounts, Jeffrey L. Geller and Maxine Harris ensure that the voices of these women will not be forgotten. And the myriad provoking reflections so parallel Esther's existence.

Esther hadn't yet moved back toward the only thing that would bring her peace in this strange new home—her art. Though in her first letter to Eugenia she had asked to have some of her old paintings sent to cheer her, she halted her request of them. And most importantly, though she certainly used her artistic talent a bit in the hospital thus far, it would be some time before she would truly rediscover it as her balm. In the meantime, dreary month after month passed for over a year of this woman's life in the early 1940s.

(nine women)
And love, in a garment of oblivion's guards,
Swabbed by timelessness
Cerates hate with a pungent, heavy skin.
Boneless belligerence netted in human sound
Hurls itself against the fertile minds of spheres.
And, nine women of these regions ground
The tines of their forks upon the howling emery wheel.
Beautiful, bulging vigor bent close to the hungry white.
White, lean points of metal
Stung hot by the shrill whistling wheel
Moved ominously into vacuity
Where volatile minds follow this element
Returning to a less troubled state.

nine women)
It is they who have saved the ore rock.
To sift in shallow-circled trays.
Wooden trays, soft in powdered stone and iron,
Are oozing, hissing with body moisture,
While nine women follow each in line
Stand in thin trays, grinding their forks away.
Eighteen horny feet, deadened to sensitivity,
Tamped vibrantly before they began to ossify.   18

Chapter Eleven

THE VIEW FROM BEHIND BARS

We become mad . . . "if we stay inside our prescribed roles and routes . . . or if we speak out, or move outside our designated paths."[1]

"In order to come to some understanding of what causes women to be mad, or to be labelled as mad, we need to deconstruct the very concept of madness itself." So stated Jane Ussher, echoing the libertarian psychiatrists Thomas Szasz and R. D. Laing, as she sifted through psychiatric, sociological, and feminist perspectives of madness in her *Women's Madness: Misogyny or Mental Illness?*[2] Szasz and Laing both radically argued for a different perspective on the mentally ill. In the 1960s and ˋ70s they boldly put forth the idea that the very "diagnosis of madness [is] a moral judgment based on value-laden conceptualizations of health and illness."[3] One man's conception of unhealthy behavior, in other words, is not all men's. But there is an accepted norm, a mass moral value judgment established by those in power, in the majority, in the mainstream of a society, defining just what is healthy and unhealthy. According to Szasz and Laing, madness of any degree is more a label than anything else, one that is all too easily given to those who behave too differently from the mainstream. These deviants are seen as dangerous and stigmatized, called crazy for simply challenging conventional thought. (As even Szasz and Laing had been condemned for attacking the modern medical model which, pathologizing distress, focuses on looking for physiological causes of, and using drug treatments for, mental illness).

Attention has always been focused on the "crazy" person, instead of an examination of the society in which that person, and all persons, are trying to exist. Szasz and Laing were the first to swerve most prominently from that path, seeing society, ever unwilling to celebrate diversity, as that which is unhealthy, or crazy. The two psychiatrists, in addition to some feminist and sociological theorists, agree that the symptoms of madness are better seen as "a reflection of the inequalities and conflicts within society."[4] For man or woman, mental illness is about "problems in living," as Szasz outlined throughout *The Myth of Mental Illness: Foundations of a Theory of Personal Conduct.*[5] Those having difficulty conforming to the mores and manners of a society would not be ill in the eyes of the "anti-psychiatrists" (as Szasz and Laing were known) but demonstrating a healthy response, "a perfectly rational adjustment to an insane world,"[6] if they were to move toward arenas where they felt most healthy.

Esther's move to Greenwich Village to be with others who valued art and creativity was such a movement. Perhaps not only, then, "out of desire" but also out of **necessity** does the artist create "a self which simultaneously embodies her in the world and marks her out as distinct, unassailably herself, unlike any other being. . . ."[7] Because withdrawing to a place that gives such access might be more than outwardly locational, it might be within. For in trying to develop one's work, the artist finds himself also pulling in toward a world of morals and manners that make sense to him—an exclusionary inner life. In order to not be assaulted by the crazed machinations of society, artists stay sane by sticking to each other, keeping to themselves. Esther moved toward a psychic space that would nurture her, and away from one where she ironically was taught early to follow her talent, then was ultimately punished for it. There were no positive social outcomes for her choosing to be an artist.

We are all confronted with the fact that our social roles need to be confirmed by society if we are to be considered healthy. Szasz noted that artists, creative people, the poor and displaced, fringe characters—all dealing with rejection by society—are usually labelled "crazy" by western culture. "The typical American mental patient today is usually a poor person in trouble or accused of making trouble, who is declared mentally ill against his will."[8] Szasz pointed out, as did other scholars from the 1970s on, that women who rebelled through the ages have been treated for mental illness and have found themselves institutionalized more often than any other demographic subgroup in western culture. Esther healthily recognized who she was, quite aware and knowledgeable of her ability, and mindful of her life, though it was different from her family and society's conception of what it should be. But she was stigmatized both as artist and unconventional woman. Her needs were far different than what family, and ultimately society, needed or wanted—a person producing steady income from a "regular" job, and a woman steadfastly devoted to home, husband, and family.

Behaving and living inherently different, then, from the mass of society, is enough to provoke severe denunciations from those in the dominant, homogeneous majority. As Szasz and now others directly contend, such "different" behavior has contributed to landing individuals in state mental hospitals. Because of "the conflicts inherent in the tensions between individual needs and the needs of society,"[9] further symptoms of what is commonly accepted as mental illness manifest in these people who live and act differently from the norm. What becomes slowly visible, upon contemplating the vast scholarly literature now available on madness, is that in the deviant's struggle to fit either the mold of one who is working at a "good job" or one who is the "right type of woman" to marry, for example, or even to choose to try to coexist in a society that only esteems such individuals, the deviant can go mad. It was of course the latter that so wore on Esther, making her feel as if she wasn't measuring up.

Libertarian psychiatrists, feminist counselors and humanists see the person who has been labelled crazy as having legitimate suffering, indeed—much of which stems from societal pressures to conform, to deny one's innate, unique nature. These very scholars and social workers do not deny the presence of unusual traits of behavior in such suffering individuals, just as it can not be denied that Esther began exhibiting odd behaviors and mannerisms. But they argue that these traits are cultivated as basic coping mechanisms, "a way of being in the world" that protects the individual to a certain extent. Elaine Showalter also documented similar patterns in those who developed mental illness, and reflected that madness is in actuality "the desperate communication of the powerless,"[10] as they attempt to stay afloat. Extreme manifestations—crippling paranoia, bizarre personality disorders, and the like—that truly get in the way of living, might be viewed as examples of coping mechanisms gone awry, tested too rigorously, perhaps, in the external world or within the asylum walls.

Szasz, Laing, and numerous other writers in the fields of mental health, and sociological and cultural studies, including Phyllis Chesler, Kate Millett and Shere Hite, have spoken of the rash and overwhelming labeling of women as "crazy."[11] Phyllis Chesler offers that "madness and asylums generally function as mirror images of the female experience . . . as penalties for **being** `female,' as well as for desiring or daring **not** to be."[12] According to Adeline T. P. Lunt, one of the institutionalized women in Geller and Harris' *Women of the Asylum*, "a close, careful study and intimacy with [many female institutionalized patients] affords no stronger development of irregularity, eccentricity, or idiosyncrasy, either in language, deportment, or manner, than might be met with in any society of women thrown together, endeavoring to make the most of life under the most adverse and opposing circumstances."[13] Margaret Aikins McGarr, also represented in Geller and Harris, and who lived a life in poverty, reflected on her thoughts before being sent to an asylum: "I could not believe then that I was not right. I was as sane as any of them; perhaps a little high-strung; my nerves a bit frayed, due to overwork and too much to think about. . . ."[14]

Many women who rebelled against standards of "proper womanhood" throughout history found themselves truly chastised. Charlotte Perkins Gilman was institutionalized in the late 1800s due to a breakdown that came shortly into her marriage and after the arrival of her daughter. She felt inadequate as a wife and mother; family life seemed a prison to her. She felt no sense of purpose there, just "distraught and unable to manage her life," according to Geller and Harris.[15] She had things to say as a writer, and was compelled to claim that, to go toward that life instead. She faced tremendous scorn because she had a child and tragically felt inadequate to raise it, yet she could no longer repress her desire to fashion her own life. Many of her writings, including the short story "The Yellow Wallpaper," depict her sorrow and bring to life the manifestations of her misery. She aptly described the mental disease that occurred for her as she first tried to live out a role unsuited for her nature, then tried to break from that role. Gilman saw mental illness, at least for a women (but certainly applicable to all in equally displacing situations) as "often a form of logical resistance to a 'kind and benevolent enemy' they are not permitted to openly fight. . . ." Gilman had even suggested in her own writings, like Szasz and Laing, that "in a sick society, women who have had difficulty fitting in are not ill but demonstrating a healthy positive response."[16]

Interestingly, Sara Via Pais asserted that, especially before the liberating 1920s came around, the label of madness easily befell any woman attempting to break free of oppressive roles. She expanded on her statement of the individual and social selves, stating, "An artist lives and works out of the individual self, but growing up female has traditionally meant learning to repress the one in favor of the other. Women artists of earlier times had to bury the individual self under the social self, showing its passive-impassive face to the world. Those who could not quite manage the juggling act could still be neatly confined within the verdict of insanity."[17] Phyllis Chesler, too, describes in her Forward to Harris and Geller's *Women of the Asylum* that "adjustment to the `feminine' role throughout history **was** the measure of female morality, mental health, and psychological progress."[18] Symptoms of mental disease, like the neurasthenia that Esther developed, are representations of the unconscious feelings of a person attempting to protest such things unjust. Elaine Showalter, who found in her own studies that the mass of American neurasthenic patients are female and often educated, analyzed the work of Dr. Margaret Cleaves, neurasthenic sufferer and author of "Neurasthenia and Its Relation To Diseases of Women" and *Autobiography of a Neurasthene*. Showalter described Cleaves' attributing female neurasthenia "not simply to overwork but to women's ambitions for intellectual, social, and financial success, ambitions that could not be accommodated within the structures of late-nineteenth-century society."[19] Shere Hite has asserted (with the polled responses of over 3,000 women of all social strata to back her) that this still continues to some extent, along with the societal chastisement that goes with those efforts, even in the last decade of the twentieth century.

Indeed women who don't want to adapt to establishment mores rebel as Esther did, having to aggressively defend their creative drives, because they are often directly, hostilely attacked. Later-to-be acknowledged artist Alice Neel experienced this as well, when she was institutionalized around the start of the Depression. She looked for help, and a psychiatrist said to her, "Well, it seems you had a rather bohemian life. But you see it hasn't gotten you anywhere." (But Neel acknowledged that her breakdowns actually came about due to the repression she felt in her puritanical family.) Upon her release, she joined the ranks of other "bohemians" boosted spiritually and financially by the WPA, and then she later went on to become an acclaimed American artist.[20]

What is admired as assertive in a man is often maliciously attacked as aggressive in a woman. Looking out for oneself in the male sex garners the prize of money, success, power. The too-rare woman who exhibits it often sees scorn and roadblocks in her way. Interestingly, Jane Ussher states, "Labelling us mad silences [women's] voices. We can be ignored. The rantings of a mad woman are irrelevant."[21] Not being allowed the equal expression of anger as men in western society, women who do show this sometimes necessary, natural human emotion are called "bad," instead of the equivalent `strong' and `assertive' in a man. (Granted, the extreme exhibition of anger in men, and equal societal disregard for the cause of it, lands men not so much in asylums but in jails.) Women's cries often go either neglected or are quickly dismissed, even though it is a commonly accepted fact in psychological theory that depression is often, in actuality, repressed anger.

Various documentation and women's voices themselves provide uncanny testament that it is women pondering their status as domestic servants, questioning their roles as nurturers of men and children before their very selves, wondering over the ability to have their voices truly heard and respected, fighting to have equal opportunity and income, desiring simply to show their true selves to the world, and angrily speaking up about all such repression that most have bouts with mental illness. These women are called either "mad," in their repression of anger (depression), or "bad," in their rebellious spirit. This "dismissing women's anger as illness" and "dismissing women's misery as an internal flaw"[22] is very wrong, and yet it is present still in this modern day.

At the heart of much anger and depression that both men and women feel is the experience of having one's individuality dismissed. This could be any small uniqueness about an individual, fundamental differences in moral outlook, or sexual differences. Thomas Szasz included homosexuals and sexual "deviants" in his discussion of the stigmatized subgroups of society that, like assertive women, creative artists, and the poor, have been rashly labeled mentally unhealthy. "[There is] psychiatric preoccupation with the disease concept of homosexuality. . . . [This] conceals the fact that homosexuals are a group of medically stigmatized and socially persecuted individuals."[23] By the same token, women too comfortable with their own sexuality, who might even celebrate sexuality, have been called aggressive, treated as deviants, labeled mentally unwell, documents Szasz and others. Certainly Freudian theory in the twentieth century did little to help society properly understand the many facets of woman's nature, especially the wrong-headed declarations that women comfortable with and assertive about their sexuality were really uncomfortable with their own sex, and desired to be men.

Being a homosexual, being associated with homosexuals, or simply being what some consider very sexual all brought the label of "mentally ill" (and the scorn that goes with it) at the time that Esther found herself institutionalized. That stigma still persists today, despite a society slightly more tolerant than in days past. Esther's institution records contain denigrating comments by various hospital officials, speculation that Esther had homosexual tendencies. Friends Gress and Evans—who would know her, as well as her "lustiness" for men all too well in the 1950s—state that they *never* took her to be homosexual. But the institution file includes doctors' belief that she was, as they also state that the more "decadent" details of her life largely factor into her mental unhealth. But as Elaine Showalter, Geller and Harris, and others have documented, doctors certainly invited discussion of, and prevalently attached diagnosis to, mental health patients' sexual life. In Esther's case, her candor about the lascivious Greenwich Village atmosphere of the time was only fodder for curious doctors. They likely, too, attached homosexuality to Esther due to her close relationship with Eugenia Hughes. Elaine Showalter's research attests to this. She wrote of Martha Vicinus' work (author of *Independent Women: Work and Community For Single Women, 1850–1920*), which tells of "loving friendships between single women [being] attacked as deviant and perverse."[24]

All reflected in that common yet shattered looking glass of the female experience that is the institution, Adeline Lunt, Margaret Aikins McGarr, Charlotte Perkins Gilman, and Alice Neel have added to the chorus of voices that call for a different understanding of the suffering of all those who fall mentally ill—to see the symptoms exhibited in a different light, and to seriously consider the cause of the pain. For Esther Phillips did become mentally unhealthy, as did all of these women and the scores of others who found themselves wanting help for towering depression and fatigue, or who were smashing the stereotype of how a woman's life in this society is defined. For Gilman it was the dreariness of domestic life, and thus the desire to break away to an independent one. For Esther, it was of course living an independent life of her own choosing, with all the challenges, ill effects, fears, insecurity, and especially economic inequality that a life of nonconformity and freedom can bring.

Esther, like her very own father, was dissatisfied with the way of life laid out for her. Also like him, she exercised her free will in making the choice to move away from an "oppressive homeland" (not her family's household as much as the mores of establishment America). Unfortunately, she was condemned for choosing liberties she felt necessary. Artists and others who indeed are happy as they break from the mainstream and go toward a way of life that speaks to them are still confined by the definitions of that larger society in which they inevitably still live. But the mainstream world around Esther was indeed desolate and at least as sick as she ever found herself to be. For if she had stayed inside the roles her family and society thought appropriate for her, she surely would have gone mad. Yet Esther may well have been deemed mad simply by speaking out against and living against convention. Indeed evident, though, as substantiated by the tremendous wealth of primary source material documenting her illness, her attempting to coexist, to adjust to familial and societal rejection caused her to indeed heartily feel and display mad symptoms. Hence her at times crippling hypochondriasm.

❻ ❻ ❻

Esther's inner fog of despair slowly started to lift in the fall of 1944. She decides to get back in touch with Eugenia, and writes a couple of letters at this time.

> Dear Jerry,
>
> I'm so sorry that I couldn't write to you before this, but I felt more like the other world than this. I still feel quite vague and dazed most of the time, but suddenly now, I felt a vague, strange, and then real impulse to write you—knowing or rather remembering that you and your father had written to the doctor. I still feel almost no hope for myself—but I won't go into it— What I want Jerry, is this—my water color box & 2 good brushes—& some colored pencils—an assortment... & also 1 or 2 large pads—
>
> Strangely, when I write this letter I'm wondering if you're well—as I have some weird feelings about people now—esp you—your father. You're well—I hope—

Jerry. Also I wonder if you still live in the same address—I feel since I've changed, everything and everybody else are also changed—I've read a little—Thomas Wolfe's Web and the Rock and You Can't Go Home Again. I still feel he's wonderful. . . Remember me sometimes.

love Esther

Dear Jerry

    I remember writing to you about a month or so ago, but since I don't know whether or not you received [it]. . . I thank you for [your book]—I read it completely—I liked every one of the essays—and the commentary at the end by his publisher describing his methods is very interesting—he seemed to work the way a painter does—saving all his notes—at any rate, it was amazing the way they were compiled and edited finally by this publisher—It seemed to me that love as well as patience was required in a task like that. . . If you have made any decent sale or sales for me I could use a little cash—& if I could have some more supplies like <u>paper</u> & 3 tubes—green, white, blue [of paint]. . . It's just awful being like this the way I am now. I don't want to talk about it—at any rate, you are in my mind as far as anyone can be in it—Jerry—

love Esther

P.S.—*I'd love more books.*

Come March of 1945, Esther sends Eugenia two small sketches of the rolling hills and train going through Harlem Valley. She scribbles the caption, "This is the landscape up here seen from behind bars." (Figs. 11, 12 & 13) Eugenia was getting impatient once again to know if Esther

FIG. 11   Esther to Eugenia 3/17/45

FIG. 12   Esther to Eugenia 3/17/45

was making any progress. Gaps in her responding to Esther's letters are likely due to her ongoing discomfort over the situation, for most all such gaps are followed by pressing inquiries on the part of Eugenia, her father, and friends, action that forces the institution administrators to inform them of their current plans for Esther.[25] Though the institution very kindly responds to all inquiries, Eugenia was never content with the fact that her friend was residing in a mental hospital.

It had been a year-and-a-half since Michael Duner inquired of the situation for Eugenia and her father, and over two years now that

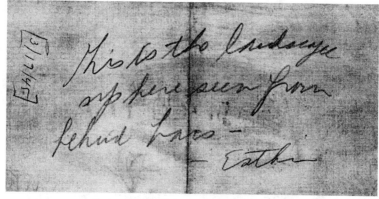

FIG. 13   Esther to Eugenia 3/17/45

Esther had been gone from the Village. This time, in the spring of 1945, Eugenia, her father and friends seek assistance from a New York City congressman to better learn of Esther's fate. For a letter is on file in the institution record from Vito Marcantonio, Representative from the 20th District, New York, a congressman famous for fighting social injustices in New York City. "Still a legend in his old neighborhood" of East Harlem, he stirred the under-represented to vote, and was especially a champion of the Puerto Ricans and the Italians. Five thousand people "who spoke all the languages he did, and several others," would later attend his funeral, expressing gratitude for his possessing devotion and diligence unlike that found in any politician.[26] Marcantonio addresses Murray Rossman, Acting Director of Harlem Valley, April 13, 1945.

VITO MARCANTONIO
20th Dist. New York

ase reply to
4 First Avenue
York 21, New York

Congress of the United States
House of Representatives
Washington, D. C.

APR 1945
RECEIVED
HARLEM VALLEY
STATE HOSPITAL

April 13, 1945

Dr. Murray Rossman, Acting Director
Harlem Valley State Hospital
Wingdale, N. Y.

My dear Dr. Rossman:

I am writing you in behalf of friends of Miss Esther Phillips who has been confined in your institution for quite sometime.

If it is at all proper and possible will you please inform me what the present physical and mental condition of this patient it and whether it is likely that she will be released in the near future.

Sincerely yours,

Because the letter was addressed to Murray Rossman, no longer Acting Director, there was some delay in responding to the inquiry. Marcantonio writes again the following month, and then it is Dr. Alfred M. Stanley, newly appointed director at Harlem Valley, who replies: "I am pleased to inform you that the above named patient has shown a definite trend toward improvement. Mentally, she has lost many of her previous noted somatic complaints and is able to answer simple questions relevantly and coherently." (Eugenia, of course, would have been more than aware of this from the two letters the preceding fall where Esther displayed intelligence and lucidity in interpreting the essays she had been reading.) The doctor continues, "At a recent interview it was noted that [patient] has also lost her previous delusional ideas . . . Her physical condition is satisfactory . . . If this improvement remains permanent, we will be able, in the near future, to consider her for home convalescent care. Be assured that everything possible is being done for our patient."[27]

> 4/27/45
>
> Dear Jerry,
>
> Received your package & thanks very much—You mentioned something about sending some magazines and the Wolfe short stories—I'll be glad to have it—I find it very difficult to read—but make a great effort and manage somehow between the noise and my own condition to somehow complete a book—
>
> Look, Jerry—if you have made the sale or sales to Margaret S. & if there's any cash left over from the expenditure of the material you sent, could I possibly have some cash—There's a sort of store here where one could order candy or cigarettes etc. Only, Jerry, if there's something left over—Don't put out anything otherwise—And of course you're free to sell any of my stuff, at any time—whenever opportune—
>
> I will have a batch of w. colors to send you soon—Could I have some stamps? Take good care of yourself—and of Roy—
>
> love Esther

Ward and Doctor Visit Notes also detail the change in Esther in 1945.

May 26, 1945—
This pt. continues to show improvement and at the present time is neat, cooperative and has

been assisting for the past two weeks with the
ward work . . . She is well-oriented for time
and place. No delusional ideas or hallucinations are elicited. She eats and sleeps well
and has no physical complaints.

Dr. M.M. Bandler

5/45

   Pt. has lately taken an interest in painting,
also helps with light ward work which she never
did before. . . .

Painting was the one thing that Esther could call her own her whole life, but in her recent despair of the last three years, she had all but abandoned it, if only momentarily. Her spirits really began to pick up once she started painting again full-force at the institution in 1945. Esther began writing fervently to Jerry, asking her to send art supplies, and she even began talking art sales again, as when she was living in the Village. Esther would shortly write over and over again, "I'll have a batch of watercolors to send you soon. . . ." This course of Esther's resuming her work in the hospital, after some time, is very typical of any professional artist fallen so ill. Though understandably out of their normal element at first, as any hospital patient, artists generally find their way once again toward their work. The work of Edward Adamson, in *Art As Healing*, provides some insight into such a progression. Adamson practiced art therapy at an institution for the mentally ill in England, and he came into contact with patients picking up paintbrush for the first time, as well as professional artists who passed through the institution's doors. *Art As Healing* presents the work of, and Adamson's reflections on the both. But of the professional artists, he provides:

> When [a trained artist] is first admitted into hospital, he seldom
> wishes to paint. It is only when he feels in control once again
> that he can recommence his work . . . Great artists who have
> experienced periods of illness have often used their altered
> state of mind in the service of their art. The artist can journey

within, explore and return . . . Art obliges us to communicate with the inner self, and in so doing, to engage in a dialogue with both our destructive and creative forces. The destructive powers have precipitated the problem, so that the symptoms of illness we observe are merely the acting out of an unresolved, inward struggle.[28]

Likely the stability of the institution's roof over her head, with the adequate meals and medical attention that went along with that, enabled Esther to slowly feel a type of security about her environment. Though it was certainly not a pleasant place to call home, Esther nevertheless was having bodily, basic needs met. At this point in her adjustment to the hospital, she began to realize that she might here focus on her art. She of course had also found out and reflected on the fact that Eugenia and her father had written to the doctor on her behalf; that surely helped to jar her static state, to move her to write her friend again. There was a small desire to go forward, toward the people she cared about, toward the creative process, the life she understood—painting, reading, thinking, corresponding with like-minded individuals—toward her essential self. Her creativity helped her construct herself again. She started to pull herself through.

◎ ◎ ◎

The summer of 1945, Esther was reading much from the institution library, and writing now even more detailed letters to Eugenia, who, unfortunately, was not returning all correspondence. Eugenia indeed received every letter, though, carefully tucking each away with the rest of her sacred personal belongings. Esther also began to paint numerous scenes inside the institution, of whatever she came across, wherever she was allowed. She did watercolors done of women on the indoor basketball court of the recreation building, Smith Hall, of women bowling in an alley that was, unusually, located in Esther's dormitory building, and women dancing in various stages of nudity around the sitting rooms (called "dayrooms") of her dormitory, Building 28.

COLOR PLATE 1

COLOR PLATE 2

Color Plate 3

Color Plate 4

COLOR PLATE 5

COLOR PLATE 6

Color Plate 7

Color Plate 8

COLOR PLATE 9

COLOR PLATE 10

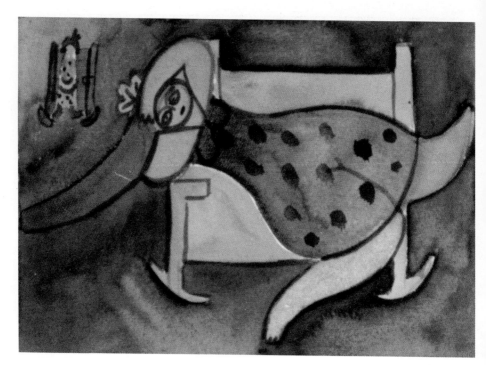

Color Plate 11

Color Plate 12

Color Plate 13

Color Plate 14

COLOR PLATE 15

COLOR PLATE 16

Color Plate 17

Color Plate 18

COLOR PLATE 19

COLOR PLATE 20

COLOR PLATE 21: View of "whole countryside,"
looking back all the way toward railroad tracks and tower.

COLOR PLATE 22

COLOR PLATE 23

COLOR PLATE 24

COLOR PLATE 25

COLOR PLATE 26

COLOR PLATE 27

COLOR PLATE 28: "*Hickey Cement Mixer at Gowanus Canal,*
by Esther Phillips 1957"

COLOR PLATE 29
(Owner: Carol Evans, New York City)

COLOR PLATE 30
(Owner: Carol Evans, New York City)

COLOR PLATE 31

COLOR PLATE 32

Building 28 was a typical institutional dormitory. Each floor had long rooms, or "galleries," as they were sometimes known, that housed the bedrooms off to each side—really just small sections separated by half-walls. Privacy at the institution went no further than this.[29]

> We learned to jump up briskly at the sound of the rising bell, and to dress speedily without answering back . . . Some had to be forced, and others were not able to clothe themselves, for they could not think. The rest of the incapables were conducted to the toilet en masse, while we, the more capable ones, would voluntarily make our hasty toilets. . . .
>
> —Margaret Isabel Wilson[30]

With the routine of morning activities behind them, Esther and the others were ushered downstairs to spend most of their days in the day-rooms, located on floors other than those with gallerie-rooms.

> I remember there was this huge room. The day room. And all these people. Hundreds of people. Some of them were leaping around the room and doing all kinds of weird things. . . .
>
> —"Joyce"[34]

There were times when the patients were escorted around to various other buildings, usually for recreation and entertainment. Smith Hall also held a bowling alley and an auditorium, in addition to the gymnasium where Esther would set up easel to record the women playing basketball. Within the various buildings, Esther captured all the "Activities of Daily Living" (or "ADL," as institution staff would refer to it) that comprised her life, and the life of every woman at Harlem Valley State Hospital.[32]

Many of Esther's interior institution scenes are of the baths adjacent to the gallerie-rooms. But adjoining the dayrooms, as well, were baths. Like the sleep chambers, only half-walls on each side separated these, and, as evidenced by Esther's paintings, they had no visible front curtains.

There were four washbowls and you waited in line to brush your teeth and wash your face. . . .

—Mary Jane Ward[33]

I wish you could see the bath; presumably it still goes on. Each Wednesday would be devoted to a half day for the weekly group bath. At 9 A.M., the nurse would call in about eight persons in relays; they would undress (some couldn't) then they stood in line and were bathed two by two in a shower, where the other inmates rubbed the patients vigorously, scrubbed the feet and hair, rinsed them and turned them out, while another inmate brought towels, hustled them to the other end of the toilet, while the nurses handed them their clean clothes, made them dress themselves, if they were able, and rushed them into the sitting room.

—Margaret Isabel Wilson[34]

Once a week was fine-comb night. You squatted at Miss Hart's feet and she went through your hair with a fine comb. Beside her on a stool was an enameled pan of some clear fluid that you hoped was a strong antiseptic. She dipped the comb in that pan. The same comb was used on everyone. She combed you quickly and efficiently, if roughly, and that was that.

—Mary Jane Ward[35]

Esther's `women series'—these paintings done inside the institution's buildings—are vital and compelling, and later commanded more attention than any of her other work. Esther was perhaps struggling to understand the machinations that brought her to temporary mental illness; definitely, she was getting back in touch with herself. Essentially, she was creating, this force pushing her despair from the forefront of her vision. Just the process of painting again, the doing, the experiencing, slowly, steadily, certainly lifted her. Whether or not she was finding answers to or peace over the troubles that had plagued her, the environment of the mental institution and its inhabitants captivated her artistic sense, just as past environments had.

Much later at a posthumous show of Esther's work, in Pittsburgh, 1991, the women series paintings drew remarks. Art reviewer Megan Shay wrote of these works:

> The women cavort in various stages of nudity while stiff doctors and nurses appear sullen and clothed in distant doorways or overwhelmed by the bright activity of the inmates. Graceful, Matisse-like forms meld with bright background colors and startling accents of red, green or yellow hairdos, exotic jewelry, picnics and bowling lanes, and a general sense of frolic and camaraderie fills the paper. The overall simplicity of form is strong. Her feeling of color is consistent with the rest of her known work, as is the humor, impudence and sense of character location.[36]

Esther's ardent creations, many back-to-back and some angrily crossed out, like others done at various times throughout her life, were a bit different from her early Pittsburgh and New York landscapes in that the surrounding environment was so peopled. For the first time, Esther's field of vision included so much humanity, the "lovable unfortunates" who were so much like herself. This enabled her paintings to speak so clearly of her very existence then. In some ways, like recognized artist Mabel Dwight's paintings of "ugly, obese strippers," Esther's women series are a wry commentary on one segment of life. Candor prevailed in the paintings of both, a willingness to accept the inevitable. The same "clinging to survival that captures the hearts and minds of the viewer"[37] of Dwight's strippers catches the eye of those seeing Esther's depictions of naked women roaming the dayrooms and halls of the institution At least every bit as instinctual, powerful, and distinct as her earlier works, they do so again with a "definite rhythm which stimulates and holds."[38]

Esther's mindset at the time may have in some ways contributed to differences found between her earlier work and her institution work. In many of the institution paintings, for example, similar elliptical shapes appear in far corners of the paintings, be they clouds or lights. Uncannily, they suggest eyes in either background. Edward Adamson in fact noticed in the art work of his psychiatric patients that the eye motif is "by far the most frequently used symbol in psychiatric art."[39] Its presence can suggest a range of meanings, from its very symbolism of the ego, as well to the fact that the mentally ill and certainly institutionalized people are constantly watched, which is capable of creating a paranoia in and of itself.

The paintings of the bowling alley in Building 28 are but one example where lights take on a strange presence within the picture Esther provides of institution life. They provide an eerie, yet somehow appropriate luminescence over the droll scene of what seems women's heads, lined up along benches like the bowling balls themselves, looking out at the game before them. Esther captured the picturesque scene—beautifully carved wooden ball returns, odd punching bag–like light fixtures, and glowing green walls. It seems many of the institution's observation rooms were also painted in this actually calming green. (*Trapped in Silence*, a 1980s movie starring Marsha Mason and Kiefer Sutherland, was shot at Harlem Valley Hospital, including footage of this bowling alley.) Clinicians sitting on raised seating, auditorium-style, in an adjacent room to the alley, studied patients through a small window. What isn't evident, unless one visits the institution, is that Esther's charming green bowling alley is set deep in the bowels of Building 28. One arrives there only after passing a series of underground tunnels that not only connected many of the institution buildings, but that provided a tour of the basement "therapy" and "isolation" rooms along the way. The latter small cells, with chained windows looking out only onto the tunnels, were where disruptive patients spent dark days. Patients placed in isolation were spectators to the lines of women escorted to the recreation of the bowling alley, as were patients like Esther, making their way among the underground passages, met with the gaze of those experiencing a darker side of institution life.

Esther's interior institution scenes are fairly pleasant, her institution polka-dot-garbed women accented with semi-smiling faces. She never conveyed what she likely witnessed as she traversed the basement of her dormitory. Only hints of the grim realities of the asylum appear in some of her works—women with hands and arms strapped as they sit upon a bench, in a room full of much other activity, as in the bottom right corner of one of her paintings. (Color Plate 13)

> Beside me, sitting, or rather crouching on the same bench, were a few silent and very filthy women, with their one garment indecently torn . . . One very fat old woman who could not speak in English, was sitting on the floor . . . one pale girl sat weeping bitterly, and shivering upon a bench with very thin clothing. Several were silent and appeared to take no notice of anything. These were melancholics in nearly the last stages of despair. One, in quite the last stage, I inferred, was tied to her hard bench with her arms and chest tightly confined by a straight jacket, and attempting to commit suicide by fiercely beating her head against the wall . . . Some were lying on the floor, exhibiting the most indescribably indecent appearances.
>
> —Sophie Olsen [40]

The straight jacket described above, or "full-body jacket," as it was sometimes called at Harlem Valley, was common at all institutions for the mentally ill—perhaps the most common method of restraint for an unruly patient. It would in fact be used after verbal warnings failed to send the message that there were ground rules to abide by. These temporary restraints were used in full view of others in the dayroom and at recreation time. Strangely, they were also called "camisoles" at Harlem Valley or "corsets" at other institutions, when used on female patients, for they echoed, however ironically, the wrap of lingerie.[41] "A close-fitting garment made of strong linen . . . [with sleeves] of sufficient length to cover the entire hand, and [sewn] up as mitts, or a bag," the camisole could render a patient helpless, "by means of lacing down the front, and strapping the arms across the body. . . ."[42] "Muffs," often described in the writings of institutionalized women, also appear a bit in Esther's paintings—"a contrivance something like a pair of leather mittens with steel attached, so buckled as to hold the hands together."[43]

Chapter Twelve:

THE LIBRARIAN

[September 10, 1945]

Dear Jerry,

I've had the sudden impulse to write to you again—and for fear the impulse would leave—I acted upon it—I know you must be busy—or I should have heard from you— Every now and then my mind visualizes our past friendship and I feel that if I could write a few words it's as if we were having a conversation together—It's needless for me to men- tion anything about myself as I think you could understand—Remember, Jerry, when I have any consciousness, I think of you always—and my work—and yours, too, of course. I loved looking at your things—and your father's. Are you exhibiting?—I suppose most of our friends are.

Has Masson come back from war—what's happened, tell me something, anyways about the people you bump into—

If you could sell any of my watercolors that you have—I could use the money ... Also if I could get a few more tubes of w.c. paints—green, blue & white—I would like it—some paper—I don't suppose I have any of my old clothes still around—I'm in rags, or any of my shoes—if you find them or rather still have them please—

I have been reading a little—with a great deal of difficulty, however, the newspaper, day by day—& some books—Ernest Hemingway's For Whom the Bell Tolls, *and I've just noticed in fact that he invariably writes or rather injects a bull fight into everything he's written—[so I judge he's a lover of them]. The Spanish call it something I forget now— For a while I thought there was going to be a Chinese revolution—but it seems alright now,*

though I don't exactly trust Chang Koi-Chek—I suppose its temporarily checked—this
hatred of the communists is very great—however—I'm so tired—now so goodbye Jerry
dear—also to your father—

                    love Esther

        (*Please Write*)

                                        October 17, 1945

Dear Jerry,

   Was glad to hear from you—hearing from you is almost like seeing you—I sometimes
look across the porch into the next building—and when I see someone who resembles you—
a little—I immediately visualize you—sitting in Washington Square Park—waiting for
me—and it makes me feel as if my life had been lived so long ago...

                    love Esther

Esther finishs the letter by again requesting art supplies of Eugenia,
inquiring of any painting sales, and mentioning all that she was currently reading.

                                        November 27, 1945

Dear Jerry,

   I received your clothes and letter—thanks so much—Also Sal—for his nice present
and you—for having gone to the trouble of getting it—I suppose Sal and Edith are still
happy with each other—They're both very nice people—She is very lovely and intelligent
and of course so is he. Your description of the "dump" on Park Avenue is very graphic
indeed—It seems a strange place for the Russian-American Institute. I could almost smell its
coldness—a little different from the Whitney, isn't it? How we used to love to imagine how
we'd take over the Whitney—'come the revolution'...

Esther continues here, as in each letter, to inquire of Masson's "shipping out," of Anno, and others.

                                        [March 1946]

Dear Jerry,

   I am writing again, not being certain that you received my other letter—Are things
going about the same with you?—And how do you feel,? etc. I feel so long and far suspended

from time that it's unthinkable or talkable—I become very frightened sometimes—Who do
you see—tell me something about our acquaintances—what they're up to etc...

Esther here requests a photo of her friend, again inquires of Masson, and questions whether or not Eugenia still has the cat, Minnie—her old ally.

Dear Jerry, I've written several times—and am puzzled about you—whether you are
ill—or something—You're the only person I hear from, when I do, and look forward to some
news occasionally—Can't you write, just a little about yourself? ...I know it's hard—selling
anything without exhibiting—but just 1 or 2 would bring me just a little, enough for some
cigarettes or chocolate occasionally—There's a store here, in the hospital...It's awful, really,
not having a penny occasionally—It's like being completely dead—Are you well? Please
write me and tell me about yourself. And how is your father? Of course I realize that time
wroughts changes not only in one—but all—So—nothing surprises me anymore—I am
now attempting to read <u>War and Peace</u>*—The librarian here has asked me to write a review*
of it, for her—She seems to be short of reviews—I wrote one for her on one of Brom-
field's—a book on the German occupation in Paris—before the freedom...At any rate—
it's about the same with me—and with the ravages of time—you can judge for yourself—
So—Jerry, please try to get me a little $—
>   *love Esther*

At this time, Esther had been granted the privilege of sitting out on the veranda that connected building 28 to the others. Here she set up easel, contemplating the railroad tracks immediately before her, and farms beyond, as additional painting content. (Color Plate 14) She continues to write letter upon letter with little or no response from Jerry, who was attending to some personal matters she would write about in later letters. Esther was bursting with a growing, renewed energy for more outside contact, though, which prompted the institution's director, Dr. Stanley, to write once again this May to Congressman Vito Marcantonio, who had requested information on Eugenia's behalf the year before. Notably, Dr. Stanley mentions Esther's desire for oil paints, certainly an indication that she was growing confident in exploring the range of her painting ability once again.

> I am writing to you at the request of the patient [Esther Phillips]. I take this occa-sion to thank you and request that if you can find time to do so, to have some of her friends either visit her, write to her, or in any case send the patient's oils and canvas to the institution, as the patient has requested these supplies in order that she may keep her-self occupied....

But a year had passed since the initial correspondence and the over-worked congressman, sought after by the masses, had already gone on to a million other projects. He could only write back that "a thorough search of my files has failed to reveal any information concerning [Esther Phillips]. Will you be good enough to send me a copy of whatever you have in your file concerning Miss Phillips as I am anxious to help her in any way that I possibly can. . . ." The surely (and so unusually) sincere politician concludes, "You may be sure of my interest in Miss Phillips case and that I shall continue to make every effort to find the missing communication which has been so unfortunately misplaced."[1]

The most important thing to come out of Esther's evident restless-ness was that she had caught the attention of the Senior Director of Harlem Valley Hospital with her urgings not simply for visitors, but, uniquely, paint materials. Needless to say, the correspondence from New York City's most colorful politician also helped. Dr. Stanley indeed knew who Esther Phillips was, and that she wanted to paint. This would prove instrumental to the remaining time she would spend at Harlem Valley.

Some of Esther's despondency remained as she heard less frequently from Eugenia than she desired and as she still found herself in a restrictive environment, despite the new recognition from some at the institution that she was indeed an artist. But her painting soon brought her to a better place.

> May 28, 1946—
>
> This patient['s] appetite is good and she sleeps well. Weight 137 lbs. She is well oriented in all spheres. Patient offers several somatic complaints, complained that her head feels broken and that she is unable to sleep. She states that she does not desire to return home.
>
> Dr. D.J. Lacovara
>
> 7/46—
>
> Pt. somewhat seclusive on the ward. Plays the piano frequently, but music is somber and moody in type. Untidy in dress. Takes no interest in personal appearance.
>
> Of late patient has been going to the library with librarian and writing anecdotal accounts of some of the people she knew in Greenwich Village. Other patients seem to categorize her very readily. Fairly cooperative to suggestions—eats and sleeps well.

Esther got one more letter off to Eugenia this summer, another impassioned attempt to maintain the bond between them. The letter was more unusual in appearance; as others, it was written in pencil, but in a frantic scrawl, on a wide-ruled tablet.

Dear Jerry,

    My water color box and tubes of color, (most of them unused) together with all the watercolors I did, and meant to send you, Jerry, were confiscated by the nurse and attendant indiscriminately, probably never having seen a paint box before, I imagine—So you see, I am without a brush, tubes or paper or box. So could you collect an old w. color box, some paint—and a brush and paper—(Does not necessarily have to be the best). It helps me from feeling completely dead, as you would understand, especially since I have no money either. I am writing little stories about people I know—we know—at Mrs. Sheldon's suggestion, who is the librarian here, and the only human I've met here, in this desert of misery. I am not willing to say anymore, as the letters are left unsealed, and censored in the doctor's office, before they are mailed out— That's simply the procedure here—I imagine the rule is the same in all the Insane Asylums.

                  love Esther

   think of me sometimes, Jerry, as you are constantly in my thoughts.

The problem that Esther had with the nurses' understanding her need of art supplies was short-lived, like the many ups and downs she had been experiencing. The problem being quickly corrected, as Esther explains in an upcoming letter, she would then have excursions into the nearby countryside. She was granted this privilege to paint about the grounds under the jurisdiction of the librarian who had befriended her.

9/46—

Pt. has been painting since residing on this ward, will sit on porch and paint landscapes and etc. . . Goes out with librarian at lunchtime and does some painting. [Has] shown some improvement. Seems more friendly with patients and is usually pleasant when spoken to—Eats well. Fairly neat and clean.

Eugenia finally did write Esther back, after a long period of not responding to letters, at the end of the year in 1946, as can be surmised by the following return correspondence of Esther's. In it she tells of the interesting activities that filled the remainder of her summer and fall.

Dear Jerry,

Thank you for your lovely gift and letter. It was really good to hear from you—after an absence of so long—(and wondering what's happened to you)—I am glad that your arrangement with Mariano and R. are working out! [R. may be Roy; this is perhaps referring to a living arrangement between Jerry and Mariano] And what you've mentioned about Reggie surprises me—and yet—people change a little with the ravages of time—(And I suspect "time" was a great factor in making Reggie do what he did!—But, all in all, he seems (from what you say) to have changed not so much!—

You mentioned about sending me a paint box—you won't need to—Jerry—I've had one sent to me by Elenor Rosendahl... through the efforts of Mrs. Sheldon (the librarian here) who coincidentally is a friend of hers, too!) It seems Elenor has a summer home near Mrs. Sheldon—who lives around this part of the country—and how it came to the notice of Mrs. Sheldon that I knew Elenor was this way—I had been writing some stories about the Village—and one particular one was about Strunsky. The story got in the hands of Elenor—and of course she was surprised that I was here and that Mrs. Sheldon and she and I were acquainted. So Mrs. Sheldon explained about [me] needing a box—and Elenor sent me a beautiful one. Some things of mine have been sent on to N.Y.—they are supposed to be exhibited—When I get any definite information about it—I'll let you know. The doctor here made it possible for me to paint and then a friend of his—to possibly show them. Mrs.

Sheldon took me out on her lunch hour (in her car) [this] summer and I did the country around here (limited of course to the grounds) which are almost as large as a country village …Also when you have time, look up Elenor Rosendahl—she's somewhere on 48th St—She tried to get in touch with you…

love Esther

The main road in Wingdale runs between the institution proper, with dormitories and other buildings, and the surrounding country-side. Immediately across the street from the official entrance, one is met first with its facilities' management buildings, as they are cut through by the crossing of the railroad tracks. Beyond these buildings lie the farms. Looking out upon the steam rising from the mainte-nance buildings, Esther created her first paintings of the institution's "exterior." It was this view she had drawn from her window and then painted from the porch of Dormitory Building 28. Once allowed to set forth across that main road, Esther lunged forward to capture the scenic yet still-unfamiliar outdoors. Interestingly, she chose never to paint the dormitory and other buildings of the institution behind her. The few canvasses that do show the view looking back toward the rear of the maintenance buildings have as their background muted green, obscuring the reality of the institution's presence further beyond— though she provided intricate detail of the presence of other build-ings in the foreground, perspective notwithstanding. She would not reveal the harsh red brick structures in the distance that were the place of repository for her and so many others the preceding four years. (Color Plate 16)

FIG. 14   Railroad crossing and facilities' maintenanance buildings, Harlem Valley Hospital

FIG. 15   View back upon Building 28, Harlem Valley Hospital (As seen from railroad tracks)

FIG. 16   The view upon crossing the railroad tracks, going toward
the farmland, and looking at tower from behind.
Compare to Esther's painting, Color Plate 16.

The sky was blue and bright, flecked with small clouds, soft and downy; the air was filled with a moist blue haze that crept into the shadows to deepen them and clung like a garment about any little hidden distance. I looked up and filled my eyes with the blueness, breathed it in, absorbed it through every hungry pore. I started to move; it was the first time I had been out alone for three years. . . .

My powers of observation became very acute, more acute than they had been before—or have been since. This was partly because I had unlimited leisure to look. There was absolutely nothing to interfere. I had all the days of summer to keep filled. . . .

—Jane Hillyer [2]

Attention to Esther was no doubt fueled by the librarian's kind regard for this interesting and talented woman patient. Mrs. Sheldon surely urged the hospital to facilitate Esther's intense desire to paint. But fortune would have it that many in the hospital became interested in Esther as painter, from Senior Director Dr. Stanley on down to two attending doctors, Dr. Rizzolo and Dr. Reese. Many beneficial connections could then be made by those coming across Esther's work, for both Reese and Rizzolo happened to be friends with an artist in the New York City area, a well-known teacher at the prestigious Arts Students League, a Mr. William Barnet, who often visited the country homes of the two doctors just outside Wingdale. They also visited him in Manhattan. The two doctors, along with Dr. Reese's wife, Beatrice, "saw talent in Esther . . ." as Barnet would recall, adding, "and I verified it."[3]

Barnet was a painter and printmaker. He in fact became the official lithographer for the Arts Students League beginning in 1934, making prints for Orozco, and many other later-to-be-famed artists.[4] He forged new ground in lithography with his unique addition of vivid color. Barnet was considered, and considered himself, an Independent painter, one who, among much else, liked satire. Above all else, as is evidenced by his life's work, he was, as defined by Dore Ashton, "a tender humanist, deeply concerned with the experiences of the perceptive-active individual."[5]

Esther's paintings caught Barnet's eye. As she worked on the institution grounds, he occasionally began to pay her visits, along with Dr. Rizzolo and his wife. (After having gone out several times with the librarian as chaperone, Esther was granted free ground privileges to paint the countryside of Harlem Valley.) Barnet, recollecting Esther almost fifty years later, would state that she was "quite a vital artist." [6] He distinctly remembered her and her work of that period, when it was first brought to his attention the fall of 1946. "She was a lovely woman, very nice . . . wide open in her feelings about life. A very talented artist, no question about it." He defined Esther's painting style as "not expressionistic. Very loose—the paint flowed (she used the brush in a flowing way). It was still guided, controlled. But there was no attempt to make [the image] gestural . . . not tight." He added that she "played with space. She would make [content matter] large or small not according reality, but to her feelings," and her style was only "*seemingly* naive—childlike."

Clearly, Will Barnet even remembered Esther as she looked back then, for he felt she was "built like the women in the institution paintings." He, too, commented that the works of her women series were her strongest. Barnet felt that "she had just lost touch. . . unfortunately landed in the institution. It was a tragedy that the family was so negligent. I don't think they really understood what it meant to be an artist."

Dear Jerry,

I enjoyed your snapshot. You don't seem to have changed much—physically. It's really a marvelous snapshot—It makes me think of the times, (and many times they were) when we took such horrible pictures together. . .You mentioned about wanting one of me—You wouldn't want to see one of me now!—I'm much heavier etc.—and besides no one here has a camera—But I'll see what I can do! . . . About 40 wc's are supposed to be exhibited some-time or other perhaps at the Levitt Galleries. They're in NY but nothing has happened yet—will let you know when anything definite happens. I could use some _mat_ boards for some things I've finished recently. So if you could send about 4 or 5—will appreciate it. Send it care of Mrs. Helen Sheldon, librarian, Harlem Valley State Hospital, Wingdale, NY. Mrs. Sheldon is going to NY for a day and will look you up—at your business address—She is a lovely person and I know you will like her—she is a good friend of Elenor Rosendahl's, too. At any rate I'm anxious for you two to meet—and she is very anxious to meet you!

I enjoyed hearing from Masson. He mentioned his coming marriage to your cousin, etc—maybe she'll do the bossing now, instead of he. It certainly is a most peculiar turn of events. . .

love Esther

Esther had written another letter to Eugenia in February 1947—a very short one. As if the preceding few months hadn't been active enough for her, Esther's attention would be yet directed upon another development at this time.

Dear Jerry—

I could use some _matboards_ for some things I've finished recently. So if you could send about 4 or 5—will appreciate it. Send it c/o

Mrs. Helen Sheldon

Librarian,, Harlem Valley State Hospital

Wingdale—NY

Could you possibly send me my oil paint box if it is still in existence. I hope you are all well—

love Esther—

P.S. Will write a longer letter later.[13]

Esther had really come into her own at the institution by the beginning of 1947. She was getting much attention from fellow patients for both her amusing stories of Greenwich Village and her prolific painting activities, she had privilege to go about the grounds by herself to paint, and she had caught the eye of many who appreciated and respected her as an artist, all making the rest of her time at Harlem Valley more comfortable. Certainly unusual for the senior director of an institution, Dr. Stanley was very familiar with the case of this artist patient, due in no small part to all the efforts being made on her behalf by others around him. But those numerous efforts would not be the only reason why Dr. Stanley was taking a personal interest in the patient Esther Phillips. Ironically enough, in the midst of this vitalizing time for Esther, when the hospital began granting her truly special privilege in order to conduct her artistic affairs, Merle Hoyleman popped up once again in the story of Esther's life, contacting the hospital via letter. It is easy to imagine what transpired after Merle's initial inquiry.

Chapter Thirteen

"ABOUT ESTHER PHILLIPS"[1]

*A*s it appears in her journal, Merle Hoyleman had actually made a flurry of attempts to locate Esther starting back in March of 1945.

March 5, 1945–
Called Beatrice Lewis—to see if knew anything about EP. She said J. Van Trump had picked up 1 of E's works at Keystone Picture Frames [in Pittsburgh]. They let him have it for $3 w/ piece of frame. She thought Anna Stein would know Esther's brother's name and address.

March 8, 1945–
On to Barney Phil.'s office in Bakewell Building. Dorothy could not ascertain any info. re: EP [Apparently this is Esther's sister Dorothy, perhaps also present that day in the office, or whom Merle later questioned about Esther].

March 10, 1945–
Mailed letters to G.M. O'Donnell & Dir. of Mus. of Mod. Art [This is the director of the Museum of Modern Art in New York. Merle wrote them to see if they had "any knowledge of the artist Esther Phillips."]

March 28, 1945–
Letter from Dorothy C. Miller—curator of Mus. of Mod. Art re: EP [Nothing else is notated, but Merle likely read that they never heard of Esther]

Snippets of information came back to Merle over the next year and a half. Various friends brought photos of Esther along to her, but they all dated from years prior, shortly after Esther had arrived in New York City. Come the fall of 1946, Merle was getting anxious to find out what had happened to her dear friend. Perhaps she suspected that Esther might not have been doing well emotionally; she may have felt that Barney and Dorothy were not telling the truth when they said they knew nothing of Esther. Either way, Merle put out word to friends that Esther might have fallen into ill health or trouble. And she decided to contact places in New York City where she felt she might get some information on her friend.

Merle knew that, for most of the general and certainly the poor population who fell into ill health in New York, Bellevue Hospital was the infamous clearinghouse. So she contacted the hospital sometime this year; she might have been working on this angle for a while. Her even

Fig. 17　Merle Hoyleman circa 1945

getting a reply from their bureaucracy was remarkable. For come the fall of 1946, she would learn that her friend had been indeed admitted there back in 1942. This information was enough for Merle, who had suspected something strange with Esther, to take further action. So while investigating further with Bellevue administrators, Merle took out a personal ad in the *Bulletin Index*, a Pittsburgh social weekly, on October 26, 1946.

> *Help! Artists, collectors, and those of your ilk—for reasons which I don't want to shout from the house tops now, I am interested in collecting any available information regarding the paintings of Esther Phillips. If all those who own any of her work will jot down a brief description, eg. is it a painting, watercolor, sketch; state approx. date of purchase, etc. I will appreciate it enormously. I am anxious to list her work according to subject material and chronology. Thank you, M.H. Box 301-M3*

Merle did not note in her journals if a response came from the ad, but she received further correspondence from Bellevue that would chart Esther's course. An envelope dated November 13, 1946, arrived in her mailbox, with Bellevue Hospital as the return address. Devoid of contents, it survives to this day, with the words "About Esther Phillips," scrawled across the front in Merle's hand.[4] (Fig. 18) She decidedly disposed of the contents herself, being very careful, as always, about

FIG. 18

information that, if gotten into the wrong hands, could damage a person's reputation. "You know me . . . my middle name is caution," she would once write a friend.[5] But the contents surely revealed to her the mysterious place where her friend was residing, for on record in Esther's file at Harlem Valley Hospital is the following:

Merle Hoyleman
Rear 4920 Centre Avenue
Pittsburgh 13. Penna.

Jan. 18, 1947

Superintendent
Harlem Valley State Hospital
Wingdale, N.Y.

Dear Sir,

George A. Greene, Assistant Superintendent of Bellevue Hospital, Psychiatric Division, advised me to write you. Several friends are endeavoring to learn of the whereabouts of Esther Phillips, the distinguished Pittsburgh artist. We are interested in listing her completed oils, watercolors, etc, and if she is physically able, she could be of great assistance in this compilation.

Also old friends to write her, and remember her with gifts if she is physically able to receive them.

Any information you can give us to enlighten us regarding Esther Phillips, will be greatly appreciated.

Sincerely yours,
Merle Hoyleman
(Miss)

Always professional, Merle was sure to invoke Bellevue's Superintendent's name. She was shrewd and knew just how to go after what she needed, for, as is likely obvious, her primary concern both in the *Bulletin Index* ad and this letter was not necessarily in listing any watercolors, but in finding out what had happened to Esther. She realized that Esther would surely get the message that the intent of her writing had less to do with business than friendship. Merle was keenly aware that she needed to get on best possible terms with hospital officials; her plan was likely to impress them with the fact that Esther was an important, prolific artist whose works were in the hands of many collectors. Merle, however, had no idea that Esther had of late made an artist's name for herself, ironically, at this mental hospital. (And that any incoming gifts were a moot point unless they were related to art).

This letter, via hospital notation along the top margin, made its way to Dr. Greenberg, one of Esther's attending physicians, in Building 28. Upon receipt of this correspondence he had Esther sign the following on the bottom of the very letter itself, to stand in her institution file:

Scant, like much of Merle's journal documentation would be, was one such dated January 27, 1947, and minimally noted as "Letter from Wingdale, NY about Esther Phillips (Dr. Stanley)." Merle destroyed the actual letter, which was, of course, the hospital's reply to her inquiry, the first of many pieces of correspondence between the two parties. Again only Esther's institution file would reveal the contents of that significant note:

Jan. 24, 1947.

iss Merle Hoyleman
ear 4920 Centre Avenue
ittsburgh 13, Pa.

Re: Esther Phillips

ear Madam:

In response to your request for information, we wish to say
hat Miss Phillips is getting along quite well at present. She has
round privileges and is quite interested in her painting. She has
one many landscapes in water colors and has expressed the wish that
o gifts be sent to her but that she is quite anxious to sell these
aintings. I believe her price, at present, is $10 per picture and
f any of her friends wish to buy and would trust to her taste, she
ould gladly send some to them. When questioned about her ability to
ist her complete oils and water colors, she stated she had sold so
any in the past that she could not remember them all.

We trust this answers your request. It is being given to
ou with the express permission of Miss Phillips.

Very truly yours

Alfred M. Stanley, M.D.
Senior Director.

g:ngj

Merle grabbed the ball and went running. She began an all-out cam-
paign to try to assist her friend. Rather than slowly try to find more
information on Esther, then take on the institution by challenging her
friend's commitment and insisting on her release, she chose instead to
act by attempting to get Esther's art sold in Pittsburgh. That was what
both Esther and Dr. Stanley would be all for. All of Merle's official correspondence with the institution went through the senior administrator.
He personally chose to monitor the progress of any sales Merle made for
Esther, rather than delegate it to someone else. He of course received
important feedback from attending doctors, especially including Dr.
Rizzolo and Dr. Reese on the circumstances surrounding her behavior
as she conducted her painting about the institution. Once the institution received monies from any sales of Esther's paintings, they would

deposit that into an account of her name, some for use while at the hospital, the rest to be given upon full release.[6] Though she saved none of these letters either, Merle surely also directly communicated with Esther, despite the fact that her letters to administrators were written in a tone as if she were communicating to her friend only through word passed along to her; any questions, for example, that she wanted to ask of Esther she respectfully brought up with Dr. Stanley first.

Merle Hoyleman's first action in Pittsburgh was to visit John O'Connor, assistant director at the Carnegie Art Museum in Pittsburgh, to show him, according to a journal entry dated Jan. 30, 1947, this "letter from Wingdale." So now became Merle an agent for Esther's art, in addition to friend. In very frequent letters to the hospital, some even arriving before she received a reply to the previous letter, she detailed her actions taken on behalf of Esther, who by then was certainly going down in the records as one of Harlem Valley's most unusual patients.

MERLE HOYLEMAN

Rear 4920 Centre Avenue, Pittsburgh 13, Penna.
Feb. 12, 1947

Dear Dr. Stanley:

Thank you very much for your letter of Jan. 24, 1947.

All of Esther Phillips' friends are glad to know she is making progress, and are happy that she is physically able to paint.

I have consulted a number of people regarding the sale of her landscapes at ten dollars each. All these friends to whom I spoke, wish to make their own selection. If she is willing, and the hospital is also willing, and will trust me; I shall attempt to sell ten for her. The paintings would have to be packed with either pieces of wood (such as veneer) or beaver board between them, and sent to me by express. I will take excellent care of them, and those I cannot sell for Esther, I shall return. I shall send the money to her or to you, as per your instructions.

Hoping that something can be worked out whereby we can assist Esther, I shall look forward to hearing from you at your

Dr. Alfred M. Stanley
page

MERLE HOYLEMAN

Res. 4920 Centre Avenue, Pittsburgh 13, Penna.

Feb. 12, 1947

convenience. If you have any other suggestions which might excel my ideas, as well
as her friends in Pittsburgh, I shall
appreciate if you would let me know. I
have arrived at my conclusion after con-
sulting a number of persons. Some are
in a much better position to know about
art matters than I, and this method of
trying to help Esther, is their concensus.
With kindest regards and best wishes,
I am

Sincerely yours,

Merle Hoyleman

Dr. Alfred M. Stanley
Senior Director
Harlem Valley Hospital
Wingdale, N. Y.

Feb 15 1947

Dear Dr. Stanley:

Find enclosed a money order for twenty dollars ($20.00), for
two of Esther Phillips' landscapes.

We hope she continues to improve mentally and physically.
Such a gift as hers should have an opportunity for development.

I will continue to send amounts as I can sell the landscapes.

Please let me know if there are any other ways in which I can
be of service or regards to her.

With the kindest regards and best wishes to you personally, I am
Sincerely yours,
Merle Hoyleman

Am hoping this money order won't inconvenience whoever must
cash it for Esther Phillips. We hope this which she has earned, may
bring a moment of cheer to her heart. We are all very proud of her.

February 27, 1947

Dear Dr. Stanley,

Thank you very much for your letter of February 18, 1947.[7]

I shall look forward to receiving the ten landscapes of Esther Phillips, and will do my utmost to sell all ten at ten dollars each. I can appreciate how much Esther needs this kind of assistance. It will help to give her support to want to continue her art.

Sincerely yours,

Merle Hoyleman

Merle surely felt that if enough people bought Esther's work, it would help toward her release—whether it cheer her sufficiently or the hospital view the success as measure of health, or both. Surely, too, Merle could see that Harlem Valley was far from mistreating Esther. She continued to promote Esther's paintings to professional contacts and friends in Pittsburgh. While so doing, she even ran into Esther's young adult nephew Milton Salamon, a bit of a bohemian himself in the late 1940s. (Dorothy later revealed that she and her sisters only learned of Esther's fate through Milton, who learned it through Merle.[8] If true, then it would seem that Esther's parents only shared the letter from the institution with their sons.)

Merle's vast networking on behalf of her friend—by now presenting Esther's art work and not simply pleading for monies to be collected, as in the late 1930s, was recounted by numerous letters and journal notations.

March 12, 1947

Dear Dr. Stanley,

Esther Phillips' landscapes arrived safely on March 4, 1947. Thank you very much.

Would you please be so kind as to inform me whether Esther can have company? It may be that she is not well enough; and, of course, we would not want to do anything that would delay her complete recovery.

On the other hand, she might not care to see either of the following persons—(1) Gladys Schmitt (2) Her nephew, Milton Salamon. Miss Schmitt, the distinguished Pittsburgh novelist, has known Esther for years, and, I think, this nephew was a favorite of hers. If Miss Phillips would care to see either, or both, I'd appreciate you letting me know. I do not care to give anyone her address without your permission and knowledge....

> *Sincerely, yours,*
> *Merle Hoyleman*

The hospital replied to Merle's inquiry that, "when interviewed, [patient] stated that she would be very pleased to see Miss Gladys Schmitt but feels rather sensitive at this time about seeing any members of her family or other relatives. We would encourage visits as we feel that this would be of considerable benefit to Miss Phillips. NO restrictions are placed on correspondence or visitors."[9]

Friends Dorothy Steinberg and Gladys Schmitt, the latter now returned to Pittsburgh, had learned of Esther's institutionalization through Merle. "She painted her way back to health," is what Steinberg understood from Merle's descriptions of Esther. She would recall, years later from her home in New York City, that Merle told the story of how some librarian discovered Esther as a painter and "got her pencil and papers . . . and with that her recovery began." Steinberg, who always felt that Esther had an "excellence in watercolors," remembered that Merle would show paintings that had been sent—ones that seemed autobiographical, depicting "women in a bathroom" or of various institution landscapes. Steinberg back then was still working and living "on the [artistic] scene" in Pittsburgh and arranged gatherings for Merle to come bearing Esther's work, both while she was still institutionalized and then later, in the 1950s. Though a few who attended these gatherings were artists and creative individuals, it seems "mostly professionals in the field of psychiatry and social work bought [Esther's] work," being that many of her and her husband Abram's friends were doctors, as he was.[10]

Steinberg and husband, who live on Riverside Drive in the upper west side of the city, have always been avid art collectors. Their apartment displays artifacts from around the world and a vast, valuable collection of work by the most renowned modern artists—as well as five pieces by Esther Phillips. Typical of many of Esther's works, one of the five is actually two—a panel painted on both sides.

From Merle's journal:

March 15, 1947–

Drew out the $20 Milton S. had given me for 2 of Esther's landscapes. Saw O'Connor. He said he was too busy to see E.'s watercolors. Took landscapes to Alice M. and Rose D. . . . saw them . . . up to Von Fuhrer's office. . . .

Merle at this time also began talking to a Miss Marin from the Outline Gallery in Pittsburgh about Esther's work. Run by Elizabeth Rockwell, of Rockwell International fortune, the gallery sponsored modern art, movies, and lectures. Merle also contacted Esther's old mentor, artist Sam Rosenberg, who was then gaining much fame in Pittsburgh. In addition, she "brought landscapes to Mrs. E. E. Moore, wife of the president of U.S. Steel," the company above all others in Pittsburgh.[11]

Likely in an attempt to better understand the environment in which Esther found herself, Merle set out in early spring to talk to friends about state hospitals and psychiatric facilities in general. Though it doesn't appear that she in any way ever questioned or challenged Harlem Valley Hospital administrators' judgment on Esther's condition, she never went uninformed about relevant matters. (Her investigative skill, coupled with her writing abilities, had in fact led to various engagements—by the WPA and The Historical Society of Western Pennsylvania— as a researcher and writer of Pittsburgh folk art, poetry, and black history.) About psychiatric facilities, Merle acquired valuable information from a nurse-friend that she would personally make use of later. She wrote in her journal that spring that Western Psychiatric Hospital in Pittsburgh "takes 150 patients from various state institutions. . . . 70% of the cases are purely functional . . . 75% of the people who go to the hospital are there [simply] because of 'bad mental habits.'"[12]

Mar 26, 1947

Dear Dr. Stanley:

Find enclosed is a money order for twenty dollars ($20.00) for two more of Esther Phillips' landscapes.

Thank you very much for your letter of March 18, 1947. I have contacted Miss Gladys Schmitt and explained that Esther would enjoy seeing her.

I will continue to send amounts of money as I sell the watercolors.

With kindest regards and best wishes to you personally, I am

Sincerely yours,

Merle Hoyleman

In April, Merle marketed to a Mr. Dickson of First National Bank in Pittsburgh, *Post-Gazette* art reviewer Douglas Naylor and wife, who purchased some paintings,[13] and various other friends. She also received correspondence from Gladys Schmitt,[14] who with husband Simon Goldfield had just the year before bought a big house on Wilkins Avenue in Pittsburgh's Squirrel Hill, from the Literary Guild's down payment for her novel *David the King*. As revealed by one of Merle's journal entries only of years later, Gladys' husband, Simon Goldfield, apparently didn't appreciate Merle's encouraging Gladys to visit Esther, even though the desire very likely originated with Gladys herself.[15] Simon often was upset over the fact that people would call upon Gladys' wealth and influence[16]—in this case, he apparently thought, to remedy Esther's situation.

James Van Trump commented that their circle of friends knew that Simon "had words" with Merle in 1947 regarding this situation.[17] Gladys, the successful authoress, as well as busy professor of English at Carnegie Tech, was stressed, easily pulled in many directions personal and professional. "Gladys had difficulty keeping her commitments in proportion to her energies," according to her niece, Elizabeth Schmitt Culley. Gladys and Simon formally adopted Culley, and she shared her reflections of them in an essay in *I Could Be Mute*, an anthology of essays regarding Gladys' life and work. "Simon frequently interjected a word of caution."[18] Van Trump and other friends, though, apparently felt he went a bit far, fencing his wife in. Actually, in wondering over what Simon likely said back then when Esther's name might have come up in conversation, Van Trump had stated, "I believe [Simon] would have simply injected that `Esther was crazy.'"[19]

```
Ward Note from 4/47—
    Pt. continues improving in appearance. Takes
more interest in herself. Has an unattended
parole card. When on ward reads—seclusive. Gets
along better with other patients.
```

Merle continued to see John O'Connor at the museum to consult him about getting Esther's art recognized. The art and the letters Merle proffered made him aware that Esther was doing much painting while at the institution and that she desired greatly to sell her works. Once Merle had started to receive Esther's watercolors, she obviously pursued many leads to promote the work, but none more important than the Carnegie Art Museum in Pittsburgh. As Merle would document, it was John O'Connor who was "collecting Esther's work for years,"[20] and likely who most prompted the purchasing of her works for the permanent collection in the museum[21] back in the late 1930s.

Thus Merle made sure to keep O'Connor and art museum officials informed of Esther's current situation. It appears that Miss Hoyleman made a veritable pest of herself at the museum, often appearing unannounced. There are quite a few notations in Merle's journal that O'Connor and other administrators, Homer St. Gaudens and Wallace Richards, were too busy to see her. But Merle's persistence paid off. She managed to squeeze past angry secretaries enough times to show Esther's paintings, many of the institution, and for them to make an impression at least upon O'Connor. Her journal entries hint at what must have been lively exchanges between herself and those who worked to screen the public from the museum's top officials. Wallace Richards' secretary was always shooting Merle "cursory glances."[22]

Merle left as many as three to four watercolors at a time with O'Connor. He apparently considered them for museum (or personal) purchase, with Merle to retrieve them later. As her journals also indicate, she took care, most of the time, not to leave paintings for too long with any one prospective buyer, even if that buyer happened to be on staff of a prestigious American museum. At one point, however, she noted that she had let too many—thirty watercolors—amass at O'Connor's office. It seems that Merle continually dropped off additional ones that she felt of great value, as they were quickly coming in to her. As difficult as it is to get past the door of senior administrators at any museum, Merle, a non-visual artist and a layman, by definition, as an agent in the art profession, managed to do so—making sure the curators of this prestigious museum were constantly reminded that Esther Phillips (and certainly also Merle Hoyleman) existed. Merle did appear to overstep her bounds just a bit with O'Connor in the spring of 1947, though. She remarkably had secured a fairly big show for Esther in Pittsburgh, and in a letter to Dr. Stanley, she would referred to O'Connor in a curatorial fashion for it.

May 15, 1947

Dear Dr. Stanley:

Find enclosed Mary Adeline McKibbin's letter.

We are hoping this proposed show for Esther Phillips' *work in Pittsburgh will meet with your approval and that there is no conflict with any forthcoming show in NYC.*

I have raised funds from her friends for mats and sign. The latter is to be placed at Arts & Crafts Center during show.

Will appreciate it if the man in New York City [Barnet] who has the forty pieces will select the best and forward them to me. If the ones in New York City have mats on them, he can send me with or without mats.

We wish to have 20 for the gallery, and I am certain John O'Connor, Assistant Director, Fine Arts Dept., Carnegie Museum, will be pleased to make a selection from the Pittsburgh and New York City groups for display at the gallery. Persons, who have bought them in Pittsburgh, are willing that they be used at the gallery.

We all are hopeful that this event will give Esther renewed support and revive her spiritually. I am also hoping we can sell more of her work to assist financially. If there are any questions which you wish to ask I shall be glad to do my best with answers.

It seems I have been long getting this matter "going" but my time is quite limited. My chief concern is to help Esther recover, and be well again. That is all that is important now.

With kindest regards and best wishes, I shall look forward to hearing from you.

Sincerely yours,

Merle Hoyleman

Upon receiving this letter and a subsequent one that provided O'Connor's museum address,[23] Dr. Stanley, ever agreeable to having Esther's work promoted, directly shipped thirty watercolors to John O'Connor at the Carnegie Museum of Art in Pittsburgh.[24] Though Merle's intent was certainly honorable, she would have done better to involve O'Connor, already quite busy with museum duties, less directly. He instead was forced into the uncomfortable position of replying to the institution. He responds, still cordially, to Dr. Stanley, as he writes, "the watercolors should not have been shipped to me as I really do not have anything to do with the exhibition. I have turned the watercolors over today to Miss Merle Hoyleman . . . a friend of Esther's [who is] making plans for the exhibition."[25]

Also in accordance with Merle's initial requests, Dr. Stanley had begun tracking down as many of Esther's works as possible in order to have them sent to Pittsburgh for the show.[26] This request, granted, would actually turn out to be another unfortunate mistake in the long run. For despite Will Barnet's efforts, there would be no gallery show for Esther within the New York art scene, which was seeing intense change at this time. Barnet sent some paintings along to Pittsburgh at this time, in 1947, and again in 1948–49[27] as per Dr. Stanley and Merle's request. (Merle brought those later works in to O'Connor as well.) Thus it appears that none of perhaps Esther's best work—the institution paintings that Barnett originally held onto—remained in New York City for potential future shows. Barnet recollected, as best he could, close to fifty years later, having eventually forwarded all of those he had to Pittsburgh, likely including one of 1949 curiously entitled *Barnet Show*.

Dr. Stanley writes Merle at this time that Esther, again, "has shown definite improvement, is much more cheerful and has gained in self-confidence during the past few months. . . . We appreciate your interest and active work in her behalf." He adds, in this May 21 letter, that "Miss Phillips has done many paintings since then which, in her opinion, are superior to much of her earlier work and has asked that we permit her to send these to you so that you will have a rather extensive selection to pick from. This is being done."

Because of the recent changes in Esther's outlook, the hospital first started to seriously consider her for Convalescent Care in June of 1947, and pursued this option with her. Convalescent Care was a trial period before final discharging of a patient. Often it took place within the homes of cooperating families of the patients, or in boarding homes, where money was given to those overseeing a patient's adjustment to the environment outside the hospital. Sometimes high-functioning patients would be released "unto their own care," still temporarily, and their adjustment would be monitored through periodic visits to a clinic connected with the hospital. According to current-day administrators at the Hudson River Psychiatric Center, which in later years oversaw Harlem Valley Hospital, 90 percent of the patients, during the time Esther was at Harlem Valley, were released contingent on some form of convalescent care before being fully discharged from hospital supervision. The majority of these would go on family care or boarding home care. But it would be different for Esther.

Surely word that she was being considered for eventual release brought intense feelings for Esther. After residing at Harlem Valley approximately as long as the average length of stay for an institutionalized woman during this timeperiod (4.7 years),[28] come the summer of 1947, Esther was no doubt in many ways ready to leave. But the institution roof over her head oddly brought a security, a stability that was lacking in her life prior. In her own time she had become not only adjusted to the institution, but even come to truly depend on the steady meals and the valuable time to paint, rather than constantly searching for adequate housing and grappling for an income.

June 2, 1947—

[Patient] says she does not want to go on family care. Does not feel secure enough. She eats well and sleeps only fair but says noise bothers her . . . She wants to stay and paint around the premises here. She is quite pleasant and at times somewhat facetious. She smoked marijuana at one time and describes her sensations in a graphic manner. She is most cooperative and her paintings are being sold at a profit.

Dr. F.L. Wright

June 2, 1947—

Patient today seen by Dr. Greenberg. It was decided she was not suitable for family care.

Dr. F.L. Wright

Summer '47—

[Pt.] has ground parole and she is out every day [and still reading lots in ward].

Excerpts from two of Merle's letters this summer:

Dear Dr. Stanley,
    Find enclosed is a check for twenty dollars for two of Esther Phillips' watercolors. . . .

Dear Dr. Stanley,
    Find enclosed is another check for twenty dollars ($20.00) for two more of Esther Phillips' watercolors. . . .

June 9, 1947—

Patient is described as pleasant, friendly, clean and neat. In interviewing her she is some-

what overactive and impresses one as emotionally poor integrated and labile. Patient is
well-informed but reasoning seems affected and
in discussion appears somewhat superficial. Patient feels that she can control herself from
alcohol and drugs, but this writer believes
these are rather promises which she is evidently unable to keep. There would of course be
no objection if this woman were permitted out
for a short while in the company of an intelligent and reliable person on whom she could
lean. Otherwise this observer believes she is
more rather to relapse. She is already 42 years
old and therefore not a good subject for more
psychotherapy.

                                    Dr. E. Kaufmann

It is a speculation as to exactly how much psychotherapy Esther had
while in the hospital, for it was still a new practice come the second
quarter of the twentieth century. Though there was certainly abundant
documentation in the hospital records of Esther's stated troubles, and
the physicians' understanding of those troubles, it doesn't appear that
much forwarding on of that knowledge to Esther occurred. Or, at least,
it was not documented—save for the one reference above. The intensive working-through of a patient's troubles, with a therapist's help—
essentially what constitutes psychotherapy, or psychoanalysis—has
been primitively tagged "the talking cure." This didn't seem to have
occurred in any great frequency, or to have contributed in a major way
toward Esther's eventual release. Instead, at Harlem Valley, as at most
institutions in the 1940s, there was a push for vocational development,
or socialization skills, or, in Esther's case, freedom to return to a hobby
or skill one was good at.

Perhaps had she the opportunity, Esther's response to psychotherapy might have been one similar to Jane Hillyer's, an institutionalized patient in the 1920s, a response not unlike many who, through

therapy, come into touch with the neglected facets of themselves that have significant impact on self-understanding. "For three years I talked, unburdened every fear, every horror, every despair, that I had been conscious of and many that I did not know, save as they **affected me emotionally**. A certain concrete terror of early childhood was 'excavated.' In itself it proved to be unfamiliar, but the emotion of which it was the hidden center was as old as I, as new as yesterday. . . . I and all things connected with me had been so discussed. . . . It was all commonplace and human. . . . The relief was indescribable. . . ."[29] Ironically, Esther's physicians constantly noted that "she remains without insight into her condition," but it doesn't appear that they tried all that extensively to provide her with that insight, to guide her to self-understanding. What Esther likely needed most while in the hospital—work with a therapist to understand the underlying causes of her anxiety—she probably did not get.

Geller and Harris, in their introduction to *Women of the Asylum*, observe that, rather than therapy being discussed, institutionalized women "talk of the meals, the crowding, the lack of privacy, and the often brutal and inhumane treatment by the ward attendants."[30] Esther's experience in the institution appears far less traumatic than that, certainly less traumatic than most. Being allowed to paint, to exercise her unique gift, surely allowed her to sort through her own feelings, a personal therapy. Actually, with the extensive range of outpatient psychotherapeutic services offered today in this country, especially since de-institutionalization that occurred in the 1970s, "what hospitalized Esther in the 1940s would not have today," according to Susan Hartman, administrator with Hudson River Psychiatric. The acute problems that overtook her in the early 1940s could surely have been properly addressed if community mental health services, like the ones set up to monitor Convalescent Care patients, were available en masse when Esther was admitted to Harlem Valley.[31]

Both good and bad have come with the advancements made in dealing with mental dis-ease, however. Now Esther would likely be treated pharmacologically, as well, with medicines often too rashly given out to simply curb those symptoms. (In 1952, tranquilizers were introduced in psychiatry, and the psychopharmacology movement began, with mental illness being treated within the medical construct of disease.) Indeed even Esther had been prescribed the barbiturate luminal prior to institutionalization—certainly a harsh first step to curb anxiety. Esther's treatment, if she had sought help today, and at a community mental health center as opposed to a private medical doctor, would definitely have been of a psychotherapeutic bent, to initially help her understand her behaviors and actions, where they sprang from in her psyche, and to work toward eliminating those that were most troublesome.

The best system would allow for the person seeking help to have a voice in the choosing of that help. And that is precisely what Geller and Harris' work points toward—listening to the person with dis-ease, himself, for the variety of actual treatment options is far-reaching, ranging from behavioral work, feminist therapy, self-help groups, medication, examination of repression within the family or feelings of oppression from society. A woman might simply need child care—or a man the permission to safely, fully feel his emotions—for "symptoms" to go away. According to Jane Ussher, "madness is more than a hormonal imbalance, a set of negative cognitions, a reaction to a difficult social situation or the reflection of underlying unconscious conflict. Madness is more than a label. It is more than a protest. It is more than a representation of women's secondary status within a phallocentric discourse, a reaction to misogyny and patriarchal oppression." Actually it can be all or any of those things, in addition to much more.[32]

Chapter Fourteen:

"THAT MAD SCAMPERING ABOUT"[1]

Just seven short months after Merle reunited with her longtime friend, via correspondence and Esther's paintings, there was a one-woman show of Esther's work at the Pittsburgh Arts and Crafts Center. It opened on August 23, 1947, with Esther's name spelled out in big letters out front, all while the artist herself was still institutionalized in eastern New York state. No records seem to exist to this day marking the show, though it indeed took place, according to journal notations of Merle's and remembrances by the Steinbergs and other Pittsburgh friends.[2] Remarkably, since it wasn't that long ago, no internal records exist of any of the shows prior to 1970 at the Center itself, today known as Pittsburgh Center for the Arts. It can only be concluded from the vague remembrances of friends that both institution landscapes and Esther's women series comprised it. Reviewed it must have been at the time, though, for, as noted in her journal that summer, Merle "sent Esther clippings of the show." Surely Esther's family would have been aware of the show and would find that it was organized by this woman friend of Esther's named Merle Hoyleman.

```
Summer '47—
    Patient has ground parole and she is out
every day [and still reading lots in ward].
```

Even while assembling Esther's work in preparation for that show, with help from the Steinbergs and Doug and Lois Naylor,[3] Merle had still been pursuing other sales leads. She had brought many of the works sent by the institution to Sybil Barsky-Grucci, Esther's old roommate from two decades earlier. Being an artist herself, Sybil helped Merle price the work; Sybil even found buyers for two of the works that summer, and for one later that fall. She purchased four herself, of the women series, that she has kept unto this day, feeling they are "outstanding," and (as VanTrump had also mentioned), reminiscent of Pisan. [4] Since Merle was in her life again, Esther apparently did not correspond regularly with Eugenia, according to a gap in the sequence of Eugenia's saved letters. Interestingly, from around this same time onward, Esther's handwriting is remarkably more legible.

Merle marketed Esther's work this fall by visiting Margaret Frye, a woman associated with Carnegie Steel, and Merle's own doctor, Myer Rubenstein, who would purchase three paintings.[7] Doctor Rubenstein, a well-known dermatologist, was married to Sibyl's sister, Belle, and according to an article in the *Pittsburgh Press*, both he and his wife were true patrons of the arts in that city.[6]

FIG. 19   Compare to Esther's painting, Color Plate 18.
This is what remains standing today, one silo only,
next to the unique hillside-hidden structure.

Sept. 2, 1947

Dear Dr. Stanley,

   Find enclosed another check for twenty dollars ($20.00) for two more of Esther Phillips' watercolors. . . .

Oct. 22, 1947

Dear Dr. Stanley,

   Find enclosed Claire Warmen's check for ten dollars and for one of Esther Phillips' watercolors. . . .

Nov. 17, 1947

Dear Dr. Stanley,

   Find enclosed a check for ten dollars ($10.00) from Myer Rubenstein for one of Esther Phillips' watercolors. . . .

This fall, Merle ran more often than before into Esther's nephew Milton Salamon, she noting their brief encounters in her journal. Both Milton and his Aunt Dorothy must have wanted to find out more about Esther's friend. Though their earlier meetings seemed friendly, apparently Milton Salamon and Merle did not get along very well by this time. Merle noted on one occasion that he picked up watercolors from her and was "very livid," but she did not elaborate further in her journal.[7] Meanwhile, Esther continued to be busy working on her art at the end of the year and beginning of 1948. She sent Merle yet another shipment of watercolors, though she was also concurrently working on oils. As organized as ever, Merle was sure to notate that Mrs. Naylor purchased one of the watercolors from a batch that came at this time.[8]

```
March 11, 1948—
    This patient was interviewed with the object
to find out how she feels about a possible
change of her status. She stated that she is a
little afraid of the venture and somewhat eva-
sive. She also admits that she could not make up
her mind and that she was full of anxiety and
```

fears. When this matter was discussed with her she was not too hot about it. She was sighing and somewhat tearful. She has absolutely no interest in her relatives, never writes and is completely indifferent towards them, which she frankly admits. Apparently for a long time the patient has shown absolutely no attachment. She is an extremely narcissistic individual, apparently likes the hospital and the security and comfort. She gives truthful discussion of her past difficulties such as drinking and smoking marijuana with out revealing any motivations. Though she has strong homosexual lines she became involved with a married man. She admits that she is not very discriminating and also brings out some conflict with her mother who has died in the mean time [Merle likely sent notice]. Emotionally she is somewhat flat and there is some ambivalence and ambiguity in her way of discussion.

                                        Dr. E. Kaufmann

From Merle's journal:
March 15, 1948—
Letter from Caresse Crosby saying she couldn't use any of Esther's work in *Portfolio X* and she no longer had her gallery. [Crosby, whose name shows up from time to time in the journals as another of Merle's correspondents, was editor of Black Sun Press in Washington, D.C. and a part of the literary scene of which Anais Nin was at this time on the East Coast. Both Crosby, Nin, Henry Miller, and others were collaboratively writing erotic short stories for "bread and butter" money in the late '40s].[9]

"It is a recognized fact that when an individual has been in a neuro-psychiatric institution for a long period of time, and has become so well adjusted to the hospital milieu that he knows or cares to know of no other way of life, he is said to have become 'institutionalized.'"[10] Sure enough, dependency occurs, as it did with Esther. Regardless of the quality of care provided, placing a mentally ill person in an institution is going to be antithetical to an individual's gaining self-reliance, which must eventually happen, to get well enough to function in society. Except for patients with extreme diagnoses, the move toward self-reliance can only occur through the process of working through *with* a therapist those problems presented—the informing, analyzing together, and coming up with workable solutions to difficult, obstructing behaviorisms and mental processes (psychotherapy). Also socialization skills must be gained—learning how to find housing and a job, participate in self-help groups, gather for social functions first within the mental health community and outside of it, even organize to rally politically for the rights of the mentally ill. These are all empowering and necessary components of recovery, to be found within any good psychosocial rehabilitation community center that works hand-in-hand with institutions. Such centers now exist offering those very things; they once did not.[11]

Just as self-control cannot truly come when drugs are prescribed to quell symptoms of dis-ease, self-reliance unfortunately doesn't happen when one is expected to conform to the living norm of an overseeing body, the hospital. But by housing patients together—the extreme cases (smaller in number than generally realized) and those just having difficulty coping with life at a particular time—the institution unfortunately works against an individual's truly getting well, well enough to cope in the real world. By serving as the functionary body for the individual, the patient then doesn't have to address ways of coping with real life.

It can be argued, and has been, that institutions should acknowledge their part in the dependence. Harris and Geller, reflecting on the women's writings in *Women of the Asylum*, note that "a 'prison stupor' [would develop] in patients whose [real life] social contacts diminished and who became passive and unmotivated."[12] Geller and Harris, and Byron G. Wales, in his discussion of the "Adjustment to the Total Institution," all mention that most practitioners convey to their patients the attitude that they are not trying hard enough to get better as they cling to the hospital, an attitude that some of Esther's doctors conveyed to her. Dependency surely occurs, suggests Wales, and it is indeed often expressed by doctors that this is the patient's fault, that he "really enjoys being taken care of by others."[13] Though an element of truth certainly is present in that statement, it is surely recognizable that mental hospitals do their part to foster dependencies. For clinging to something that provides the necessities of life, especially when those necessities are so hard to come by in the "external world," is anything but unnatural. One could argue such an action is a necessity, a will toward survival. Suggesting that a patient's dependency is bad, symptomatic of his illness, an unnatural attitude and unnecessary behavior to hold, is at least a bit misleading, at worst severely wrong.

Hospitals, as in the case with Esther's, whose treatment at Harlem Valley was mild compared to the norm, in fact *look* for an adjustment to hospital routine once a patient is admitted and throughout the course of his stay; the official record uses such exact language. If "satisfactory adjustments" happen, as Dr. Barasch commented about Esther in the Abstract of Commitment, the patient is considered more healthy. According to Byron G. Wales, mental hospitals are "notorious for inhibiting an individual's liberty and substituting security for freedom."[14] In her Forward to *Women of the Asylum*, Phyllis Chesler refers to Adeline T. P. Lunt's reflections. "[She] notes that within the asylum the female patient must cease thinking or uttering any original expression." Quoting Lunt directly, she added, a woman must "study the art of doffing [her] true character . . . until you cut yourself to [the institutional] pattern, abandon hope."[15] Lunt also remarked that in order to be considered sane, one must "suppress a natural characteristic flow of spirits or talk. . . ."[16] Geller and Harris state that doctors started to consider the fact that perhaps "institutions promoted conformity and actually worked against the free expression of an individual's healthy personality." Fortunately, but slowly, during the second quarter of the twentieth century, some doctors slowly became aware that "long-term institutional care was in itself detrimental to the mental health of patients," notes Harris.[17]

Thankfully, Esther was allowed to paint, for doing so moved her further away from the downward spiral central to institutionalization—rejecting one's own abilities because they are "impaired," and trusting only in the "parent" hospital. Esther's trust was intrinsically in her work, however. She came back to that, and it delivered her from the manifestations of illness and the syndrome of institutionalization. "Each woman's pain has its own history, its own roots—and its own solution."[18] For Esther, the final solution was to embrace who she was again, not shy from it. Like the women writing of their institutionalization experiences in *Women of the Asylum*, Esther, too, was not quieted, her spirit not broken, for she had utterance that also survives to this day—her letters to Merle and Eugenia, and especially her paintings. Nothing speaks more for Esther than these, which were representations of her core being. They tell a story of her experience in the world—for a time at least, a strange world in which she felt very out of place. For whatever mystery still remains regarding Esther's institution stay, very evident are her determined depictions—institution life unusually and brilliantly captured. The story of her life during this critical timeperiod could not have been spoken more eloquently or intensely than here, through her paintings, which were her therapy.

Because she was at least industrious at her art, grounds for Esther's dismissal at Harlem Valley were more seriously considered in 1948. Even after she began the therapeutic process of returning to her work, which got her well again, the tremendous force of security that she had come to feel while in the hospital weighed on her, and she still fearfully rejected the thought of self-sufficiency. But this also would soon change, as her confidences, once strong in her life, returned.

◈ ◈ ◈

Throughout much of 1948, Merle continues to make real progress in getting Esther's works seen and purchased by even more individuals. She took new paintings to Mr. Dickson of First National Bank in early June; he bought from this batch. And she notes that he even gave her money in order to "send Esther more paper."

July 23, 1948

Dear Dr. Stanley:

Find enclosed a money order for forty dollars ($40.00) for four of Esther Phillips' watercolors—Saul Boharas. M.D. purchased them.

Also enclosed is a check for forty dollars from Abram Steinberg, M.D. for four watercolors.

If you can send me two or three wood carvings I may be able to sell some. Mrs. Steinberg is interested.

Thanking you again. . . .

Sincerely,

Merle Hoyleman

The hospital may have provided wood for Esther, or the acquisition of such possibly came out of her art sale savings. Will Barnet did remember the hospital's providing Esther with space in one of the buildings to work on her watercolors and oils, as well as her woodcarvings, by this point.

MERLE HOYLEMAN

4535 FORBES STREET

PITTSBURGH 13

July 28, 1948

Dear Dr. Stanley:

If you care to include a new group of Esther Phillips' watercolors I shall try to sell some of them. Both the Steinbergs and Boharases are enthusiastic and would like to examine more of her work in lieu of purchasing—I am sorry I failed to note this in my last letter. I did mention about sending me two or three of her best wood carvings. Mrs. Steinberg is still interested. . . .

Sincerely yours,

Merle Hoyleman

They find dressing room scenes, also those with surrealistic effects more engaging. . . .

Dr. Stanley, who certainly had become quite an agent in his own right for Esther's art, responds to Merle that Esther is "sending thirty of her latest paintings. She has completed some wood carvings, but does not believe she has a sufficient number to send for a display. If she wishes, she, of course, is free to forward them to you."[19] Merle, though, was beginning to have her own problems. As noted often in her journals over the years, she "took treatment" for thyroid problems. New, heavy medication was prescribed for a thyroid growth in April of this year, and come late summer, this ailment really began plaguing her. In her last bit of correspondence with the hospital for awhile, Merle notes in an August letter that "Esther wrote she is sending four cherry wood carvings and six oils. I am waiting for these to come and I shall show one at a time. . . . I shall continue to send money as I sell them."

The hospital was obviously helping Esther to ship these larger works back to Pittsburgh, and any monies collected from Merle they deposited into Esther's account. Because they realized that Esther was gaining self-sufficiency rapidly, and they would soon be able to release her, the institution allowed the door to slowly open to the world that she was apparently now becoming anxious to return to. Though it seems a bit incredible, Harlem Valley Hospital allowed her to make trips on her own to New York City in search of housing and work. It wasn't uncommon to grant to any patient who already had an unattended parole card about institution grounds to attend to these matters in this way. The institution was showing its trust in her, that she would indeed conduct such a search and return by night train to Wingdale. Obviously, there would have been dire consequences to contend with if she didn't comply with the institution guidelines. But Esther did comply, as she had become excited by the idea of release, as substantiated by an upcoming note by Dr. Greenberg. What is unbelievable is that some patients, however high-functioning, were expected to suddenly go out in the real world again to look for housing and work and be successful at it. Thankfully, Esther survived the rigors of this undue test, the components of which, today, social workers provide, working hand-in-hand with patients to help them make a reentry into society.

Come the late summer of 1948, Esther shares the news with Eugenia. They here resumed correspondence, after that period with only a few very brief letters, while Eugenia attended to some strained personal affairs and Esther happily met Merle's continual requests for paintings. The first letter Esther sent that made the disclosure of imminent release evidently was lost, because in the following, they're already discussing apartments:

[August 1948]

Dear Jerry

Received your letter and was very sorry to hear about your father's being ill at St. Vincent's. I hope he will be alright—I suppose it's his high blood pressure. It certainly must be trying for you, too, to be at his side—and on your job etc—And I certainly do appreciate your looking up and telephoning about places for me—A cold water flat is about the most reasonable to get for me—I don't care what sort of "dump" it is—I'll manage very well in it—It's just that I must have a place in order to leave—Has Reggie Masson come back to N.Y. yet?—Perhaps he can "agent" some things for me—Will attempt to get in touch with him when I get to N.Y. I hope you, Mariano & Reg & family are now on better terms.-

love Esther—

P.S. I do hope Roy feels better—give him my sincerest regards.

9/4/48—

Pt. has lone parole about grounds. Does a lot of painting. Goes to NY occasionally seeking a position and room for she may go on her own— Fairly neat and clean in appearance. Enjoys eating. Weight 165 lbs.

September 3, 1948—

Patient is ambulatory on the ward, clean and neat in dress and appearance, sleeping and eating well. Physical condition is satisfactory. Patient pants and coughs. During the interview, she appeared tense, anxious, fearful and

restless. Her productions were profuse, interrupted by silly giggling, extremely vague and
circumstantial. As soon as patient made a
statement, she turned and twisted it and
finally retracted the sentence. She appeared
narcissistic and bears a grudge against her
family. Her emotional affect is flat. She could
not name her admission date, not even approximately, but otherwise was fairly well oriented
and her insight is defective.

Dr. H. Lederer

Despite the above, five days later, on September 8, 1948, Dr. Greenberg entered the following in Esther's file:

Sept. 8, 1948: CONVALESCENT CARE APPROVED. This
patient, when seen, shows the same poor judgment and lack of clear thinking which has characterized her since her admission. She rejects
the hospital completely, insisted on being fully
discharged and not placed on convalescent care,
although she had been one of the few female patients who had ground privileges although she
had not yet reached the menopause, is not working, has had the personnel of the hospital run
her errands for her so that she could continue
to get the things to paint with and often send
away and help arrange for the sale of her paintings. Her attitude is that she could go to New
York City and would within two days find an
apartment. Her judgment is poor. She is uncooperative. However in view of the diagnosis of
Psychoneurosis and the fact that she probably
has never been a clear thinker, she is approved

to leave as soon as some provision is made for her to have a place to sleep for a short time to give her a chance to find something for herself. She was informed that we would not allow her to have the $200 which she has here and which is only about 25% of what she has collected for her paintings, but would be given $100. Social worker is to contact the Salvation Army.

Dr. C. Greenberg

Esther now writes Jerry weekly about the preparations that must be made in order for her living situation outside the institution to be seen as a stable one. In light of the other letters to (rapidly) follow, this first was a bit premature:

9/9/48

Dear Jerry—

Am expecting to leave the hospital within the next 10 days—or so—and wonder if you could find me an apt—or lookout for one—a room would do—temporarily—If unsuccessful—the hospital will arrange for the Salvation army to rent me a room for a little while, until I find a place—Will see you in N.Y. soon—Will write you a day before I arrive—so we can meet—& will tell you my plans—

Am anxious to see Anno & Masson—

love

Esther

xxx

Could hardly wait to see you—

9/20/48

Dear Jerry—

Just received your letter—and am just as anxious to see you! Yes, I do know the apartment situation is quite serious—but I will try my best when I get to N.Y. to get some sort of place—I will stay at the Salvation Army for a few days or so—then I will look around—

Mr. Barnett, (sic) a friend of Dr. Rizzollo's (sic)—a teacher at the League etc etc—has some plans for me—Will try to get me some sort of commercial work—too—Will tell you all about my plans—

Am sorry to hear about your argument with Reg—As a matter of fact—you mentioned when I am in N.Y. that Masson wanted to talk over some plans with me—So, of course, I shall see him. Will probably see you in N.Y.—in about 3 weeks the latest—as I'm a little held up in account of my teeth—I am getting a partial denture—& my gums aren't quite ready for the impression—In a week or so—they will be—I will then leave & come back for the teeth, which will be ready & waiting for me—

If I do find an apt—I'm wondering about the state of my furniture—or if any of it could be salvaged—Well—there's time enough to think about that—

So, for the present, Jerry—goodbye—

Love
   Esther—
Regards to Anno—

[Sept. 25, 1948]

Dear Jerry—

Received your letter and check—for $100.00 and had to look _twice_ and _thrice_ to make sure it was so—What were the things that Reggie bought? I suspect _some_ or _one_ of the subjects were one of my nude comps—(bathroom scenes). Please thank him for the sale— & when I go to N.Y. for the day before I finally leave the hospital, I'll surely look him up as he requested—

There are several contacts I must make when I get there—I must see a Mr. Will Barnett, a friend of Dr. Rizzolo's (sic) here—who teaches at the league & who has some stuff of mine—I want to get his advice about who to see about a show—

There's a gallery, a new one, I understand in the village that I shall contact—and several on 57th St.—I simply want Mr. Barnett's advice on whom to see first, for my type of stuff—etc—

I will write you before I go, & suppose I should inform Reggie—too—or he could know from you when I come to N.Y.—

How is Anno—? Is he still without a job?—How is the outdoor show coming *along?—Remember to tell him, that if he sells any there—he can take half of what he takes in—Tell him not to be in a beer joint when it rains or the things will be ruined—Remember how we raced against the rain?—with never a mishap—if I remember clearly—Those were the days—I suppose Raynor Olson is still plunked in the middle of the arch with his marinery marines etc—*

Well—give my love to one and all you see—and especially to yourself———Esther xxx

Sept. 28, 1948—

Writer interviewed Miss Phillips this morning. She is in good contact. She apparently has resolved some of her problems. At the present time, she has a couple of hundred dollars which she feels she should be able to use for her living in New York City for several months. During this period she feels that she will have an opportunity to make some contacts so that she will be able to support herself. She realizes that it may be difficult and that if she is unable to do this, she might have to return to the hospital. The big problem is finding her living accommodations. However, the writer has agreed that she be allowed to go to New York on our ambulance to be given the opportunity to see if she can find herself a room, and return by train that evening. If necessary, she may have to do this on one or two occasions. As soon as she has found a room, the writer will agree to her being placed on convalescent care to her own custody under the supervision of the social service department.

Dr. A.M. Stanley

Esther and Eugenia continue to correspond a lot this fall as Esther got her accounts in order at the institution.

Oct 2/48

Dear Jerry—

Will be in N.Y.C.—Wednesday—to search for a room—and if I find one, will be able to move in the next day—but in any case *must be back in the hospital Wed. eve*—Plan to leave by hospital bus—early Wed. morning—(The bus makes weekly trips to Bellevue to pick up patients)—Will probably arrive in N.Y.C. by 11—or so—

Will call you up—then & perhaps if you are free we can have lunch together. Then I shall be on my way to look for a room———Around 4 oclock thereabouts (the actual time schedule will be given me). I will have to get the train to Wingdale—from the Grand Central—

So, you see that will leave me not much time to look around—however—I shall do the best I can—and at any rate—I do want to see you—even if only for a half an hr. or so— It will still leave me a reasonable time to look around—Well at any rate—I shall call you up—when I land—

love

Esther

Oct 20/48

Dear Jerry—

Have decided to postpone going down to N.Y.C. again until Wed. The hospital bus didn't make their usual trip this week so thought it advisable then to wait.

There are 2 cold water flats advertised in the N.Y.Times which I should like you, if you will, to call up about, for me—One is on McDougal St—Tel—Al—5-0326—Call from 9 to 12.

The Other—

Tel—Gr—5-8609—

(call Sat or Sunday)

or

T.E. 8-6272—

(call Monday)

I will appreciate you calling about these very much—

Do you know whether Reggie is back yet?

I hope everything is alright with you—

love

Esther

The majority of cold-water flats were located in old warehouse space around the Hudson and East River waterfronts. These were infamous living and working spaces that artists rented during the late 1940s and 1950s. Three-quarters of the area was devoted to the studio proper, usually with a corner furnished with a cot and a hot plate.

```
11/48—
Patient has ground parole card. Does quite a
bit of painting on her own. Goes to New York
occasionally seeking an apartment and a posi-
tion. Off ward most of the time.
```

Nov 23/48

Dear Jerry—

I know you are quite busy, what with taking care of your father & your job etc, but I wondered if you could, or have Anno call the Endicott Hotel *or* Broadway Central *on* Broadway & 3rd St *for rates—(weekly rates)—*

I simply must have some place to stay for a week in order to give myself adequate time to look around for a place … Please do call the two above mentioned hotels—& let me know immediately.

I will try to make it up to you for all the effort you are putting in, on my behalf—believe me. Jerry—

> *love*
> *Esther*

P.S.… Do you know if Reggie Masson is back yet?—Are you still on unfriendly terms? I hope you've made up your differences—

> *love Esther*

[early winter]

Dear Jerry,

Was just able to go to the 22nd St. address after I left you. And it had just been taken, said the super., whose head barely emerged from the basement—I see now that I must have an early start—say about six o'clock in the morning to find anything—At any rate, upon walking up [W.22nd St.] I must have seen no less than about 50 or more houses with furnished rooms—no vacancy signs—It was very discouraging. By the time I was through—

I discovered I had 20 minutes to make for Grand Central—I was on 57th St. at the time—so dashed in and out of two exhibits—a sculpture show and painting—and stayed exactly one-half a minute in each place . . . I'm sure the proprietors of these galleries must have thought me 'nuts'—It was as if I were on roller skates—In retrospect—it is funny—but I was ready to drop from fatigue. . . It's amazing how I could laugh so at all that mad scampering about—and nothing accomplished yet—I have not only to have my sense of humor—but cash coming in to continue this—But I'm not really discouraged entirely—I don't dare allow myself to be— When I was on my way to Greenwich House—I saw none other than Anca [Verboska] sitting on the same bench in Washington Square Park—(she didn't see me—thank goodness). I would have made myself known to her—but had no time—& besides was not on very friendly terms with her, so didn't want to waste any time there! And her hair is dyed red—I do not think it attractive—. . . Sorry I couldn't contact Reggie—He is so practical and always knows of some thing—

love Esther-

Really enjoyed seeing you, Jerry-

also Anno

Another exhibit Esther saw while on her quest for housing was the Elie Nadelman exhibit at the Museum of Modern Art. She describes to Jerry, in January: "It was very beautiful and exciting . . . and a great many people dressed to teeth—who seemed more interested in each other—than in the various exhibits—but who, if asked, could blab an earful about what they saw. You know precisely what I mean." Esther continued visiting the city, in attempt to locate an apartment, throughout the winter. She even took some of her work along and marketed it to galleries, while she was out and about in search of an apartment. Also according to the letters, it seems that Eugenia and Reg were doing the same with both Eugenia's and Esther's art as they concurrently searched for apartments for their dear friend. Esther and Eugenia, like many artists, could be very diligent in marketing themselves and their work, though their success at getting sales was not directly proportional to their perseverance.

After five months of scrambling to find housing, Esther was finally successful in early February. She booked a room at the Hotel Marlton in the Village. She had met the requirement that the institution set for her release. So after residing there six and a half years, Esther Phillips finally left Harlem Valley State Hospital.

CONVALESCENT CARE: February 3, 1949:

The patient was today placed on convalescent care into the custody of herself. She is staying at the Hotel Marlton, 31 West 8th St., NYC, and then at her friend's house, Eugenia Hughes, 68 Bedford St. until she finds an apartment for herself. She is to report at the Psychiatric Institute, 722 West 68th St., NYC on March 18, 1949 at 10:30 a.m. DIAGNOSIS: PSYCHONEUROSIS, MIXED CONDITION. MUCH IMPROVED.

Dr. Kaufmann

NEW YORK: LATER YEARS

Chapter Fifteen

Looking Forward . . . with Much Enthusiasm[1]

While Esther had been institutionalized, a lot had happened in the art world. Certain village artists had started to capture the attention of the world, as the focus on art shifted from Europe to America, namely New York City. Mass America, too, had slowly begun taking new notice of the American artist. Despite the imminent fame of some, artists still had the common link of bonding in response to society's ongoing disregard for their lives' work and little understanding of the freedoms associated with pursuing creative work of an independent nature. Artists knew that despite the strange new attention on artists in general, the mass of society still cared little of the artist's fate or would ever truly accept him as a viable part of society.

As Esther had, many American artists looked toward Paris at the beginning of the twentieth century as the place to experience a creative existence. Most did not have the resources to study there; Greenwich Village came to be a congregation for like-minded souls. Other artist colonies scattered throughout the United States originated in the same way, for artists understood artists and wanted to be in communities that nurtured their creativity and its accompanying way of life. "Until the Depression . . . there [had been] little support for the artist's view of himself as a necessary functionary in a sound society," wrote Dore Ashton.[2] A few select artists before that time had found themselves at the beck and call of a few wealthy patrons. "For Americans, an artist had always been valued . . . as historian of manners and morals, flatterer of social status, or glorifier of national aspiration. . . ."[3]

During the 1930s artists had taken on a functional role, but still at the calling of a nation. Despite the socialist themes of much of their work, artists were nevertheless ever mindful of the American democracy that was their employer. Their audience was that American society who saw their government-sponsored works in the very public domain of post office and town hall. Despite the exposure, artists were now valued strictly in this national perfunctory sense, "and very rarely for his imaginative spirituality," or any individual experimentation in work content and style. "The history of American painters who digressed from the motifs established by their patrons is a record of repeated cries of loneliness and despair, a story of flinty, determinedly reclusive eccentricity," commented Ashton. "If [the artist] were neither reporter nor flatterer, America had little use for him; yet a longing to be acknowledged was never overcome."[4] Of course, the patrons could be private or the U.S. Government. The same statement could apply to any who had the National Academy on their backs, or who had no patrons at all. Basically, an artist was never made to feel good about simply cultivating his or her own creative vision. Unique voices in the arts, creators exploring and refining their artistic contributions, were stuck, because anything too unique, done simply for aesthetic sake, was not seen as a contribution to the cultural heritage.

The advent of the WPA brought at least some financial security and some measure of respect and peace of mind to artists. But indeed, "until the myth of the artist as inspired soothsayer [would take] root . . . the American painter was almost always caught in his own conflicting desires to be wholly individualistic and, at the same time, a member of his society.[5] Once the Arts Projects collapsed entirely due to eventual disregard from the American public and politicians, artists found themselves scrambling once again for both sustenance and integrity. But the time had finally come for the American artist to make a name for himself in his own right in the early 1940s, just the time when Esther had landed in the institution. Rejection of European ideal, theory, and practice was rampant, and drove the change. Greenwich Village wasn't Paris, and over passing decades American artists realized they didn't want it to be. Something new was on the verge of creation, forged by the artists' continual toil and sense of community and the financial reward they began to receive starting with the WPA work of the 1930s.

Poet W. H. Auden, attracted by what he termed the "openness" of America and in particular the New York City art scene in 1939, was led to even comment, "There is no past. No tradition. No roots."[6] A "communal infrastructure" formed in the days of the Depression carried into the 1940s.[7] This bond among artists led to a collective security to finally experiment with a new American style and to revel in the illusory respect that was about to come with it. The way for at least a bit more fame, if not more dignity, was paved for the art scene as a whole. The "imaginative spirituality" that eternally characterizes all artists anywhere around the world, but was not yet acknowledged by an American public, finally gained ground as the decade of the 1940s progressed, to peak, perhaps, in 1950. Though Esther wasn't there first-hand to witness the awakening in the early 1940s, she knew well the atmosphere that forged it, and she would equally be at home in that very atmosphere upon her return there.

> "A shrink would describe the Village as a psychotic community
> . . . a favorite Village bar like the admissions ward at Bellevue."
> —Seymour Krim[8]

Though there was no more WPA, activities of most Village artists in the early to mid 1940s remained essentially the same as before—creative work by day and a still-vibrant night life. There were the all-night cafeteria gatherings, with talk and arguing through all hours until morning, and dive bars so popular that you could telephone an artist at his favorite drinking establishment. The decadent after-hours parties continued to occur, in the age-old tradition of the creative life, but they seemed to dwindle in number and frequency at the outbreak of the war. "Nighttime roundtable discussions," in the cafeterias, particularly the Waldorf on 6th Avenue and 8th Street, "drew together a post-World War II band of artists who were in the process of discarding traditional European and American concepts of art and seeking a more personal idiom."[9] Some artists began banding together in groups that suited their personal styles. There was the Federation of American Painters and Sculptors, whose members included Milton Avery, Balcomb Greene, and Mark Rothko, and the American Abstract Artists group, actually established in 1936, in part to counterweight the realist bent of the WPA work. Other artists chose to remain even more independent.

Certainly, the one figure on the scene whose appreciation for individual style no doubt helped to guide many of the Village artists to consider a new, American "school" of painting was Hans Hofmann, due to his work in the progressive European art construct that was the Bauhaus. Hofmann, who was twenty years older than Esther, was very approachable, a respected artist and teacher, though he himself had never formally studied and even commented, "I never believed in an academic training." Woman student Nell Blaine said of Hofmann, "He treated everyone as an individual, saw your needs and really had the insight to know what you were trying to do and help you do it."[10] Though an important figure within the art scene in New York, Hofmann didn't get major recognition for his own art in America until 1941, when Peggy Guggenheim independently started representing him. And this representation foreshadowed what was to come in the New York scene in general. What had formerly been underground was about to go big. The lucky few were about to have dealer representations and one-man shows.

As the Nazis took France, Guggenheim brought her impressive, growing collection, including many of the surrealist works of the time, back to her home New York turf. The Museum of Modern Art had opened in New York in the late 1930s, but it primarily showed European artists, much of the works cubist and surrealist. The only museum showing modern American art since 1931 was "The Whitney," fortuned artist Gertrude Whitney's ever-growing collection of the work of Village artists around her. Actually in 1939, Peggy's uncle opened his Solomon R. Guggenheim Museum of Nonobjective Painting (known also as Art of Tomorrow) on 54th Street. Piet Mondrian and the Bauhaus artists were among those first showcased.[11] Esther and Eugenia, who kept abreast of developments in the art world, would have known of all of these happenings. This small museum came about due to the influence of Baroness Hilla Rebay von Ehrenweisen, an artist herself, who persuaded Solomon Guggenheim to move to collect the nontraditional. Come the late 1940s her dream, with the tapping of his fortune, began to fully crystallize with the commissioning of Frank Lloyd Wright to build the signature structure that would house the collection thereafter known as "The Guggenheim" (as in museum).

When Peggy Guggenheim and husband-to-be, artist Max Ernst, arrived in 1941, their Beekman Place home in New York City soon "became the scene of huge parties where she introduced the surrealists and other artists-in-exile to the Americans."[12] Suddenly, money was mingling among poverty at wild parties some of the luckier Village artists caught wind of. Guggenheim was trying to get to know who was out there; she was interested in creating a showplace of American painters, as she began to sense the growing intensity of the Americans' desires to stake a place of their own within the art world. Famous European artists frequented her gallery, and the no-name (except amongst their own circle) New York artists, quite aware of this fact, tried for chance meetings,[13] much as Esther had done back in the gallerie-rooms of The Carnegie Museum in Pittsburgh.

In 1942, Peggy Guggenheim opened a New York gallery-museum, christening it "Art of This Century," quite similar to the title of Rebay and her uncle's space. The work of the leading European modernists and modern American artists who had a bit of following, including Clifford Still, Mark Rothko, Robert Motherwell, and William Baziotes, were all shown. Guggenheim soon opened her gallery to new artists, not yet recognized, who were working in New York, in the same manner as she had independently represented Hofmann. Soon thereafter, other gallery owners followed her lead.

Guggenheim specifically catapulted the career of a man she had taken a special liking to. He was to become a symbol of success for his fellow artists in the New York scene, a radical young hero to an up-and-coming generation of artists. He was the first American artist to truly capture the imagination of the mainstream American, who embraced his mystique as a culture renegade. His name was Jackson Pollock, and Guggenheim commissioned him to do a mural for her home. In 1943 she gave him his first New York exhibition. Esther remembered this artist ten years younger than she as "handsome and cocky."[14] If Hans Hofmann was the father-figure to Village artists, Jackson Pollock was the young, glamorous son.

Pollock was creating in a unique style, one that would propel American art into international realms of attention. His style of work would come to be called Action Painting, due to his infamous "Splatter Paintings," well meditated upon yet still spontaneous drips onto canvas. They came to symbolize the American radical artistic attitude, the needed break from the European, and perhaps the momentum artists needed to rebel and feel good for the first time about doing creative work in America. Pollock, like gestural painting comrades Franz Kline and Willem deKooning, among others, began to find ways to merge surrealism and abstractionism in an expressionistic mode that greatly appealed to the New York art world elite. They were about to make names for themselves, with the help of Guggenheim and others with money and influence, as the founding "Abstract Expressionists." Some others within this "New York School" (yet another label for the movement that included the Abstract Expressionists and other newly distinguished modern independents) were soon to find their measure of success, but Pollock would ever be the most celebrated.

The year 1944 brought larger recognition to Arshile Gorky, and Guggenheim gave Hans Hofmann, who was then 64, a one-man show. All artists had now become ever hopeful to be recognized in the spotlight that was beginning to shine on the New York artist scene—always watching for an opening, a "break" that could push them out of their poverty and perhaps define a career, as artistic lives were now thought in terms of by a steadily increasing watchful public. At this time in the institution, Esther would have just been coming out of her early dark period. Back home in the Village, dealers and critics were passing over her artist peers, who were on equally uneven ground with their work overlooked. "Pressure grew among artists not enjoying patronage from the Establishment but bonded by their work for the WPA and their common psychic situation."[15]

The Abstract Expressionists would soon be congregating in living and working spaces around 10th Street. Artists Willem and Elaine deKooning found at this time that they "couldn't go out at any hour of the day or night without bumping into someone and getting involved in a discussion."[16] The 8th Street Club was founded in the mid-to-latter 1940s because the Waldorf Cafeteria was getting too crowded. It seemed that the more newly successful, artists in their own clique now and who perhaps no longer had to eat at the Waldorf, were looking for other meeting grounds to discuss their art. The Club, as well as the area around 10th Street, became a center for the New York artist elite. Some of the artists saw their abrupt success not as good fortune married with talent but truly came to believe that their gifts were far above the other New York City artists, which was not necessarily the case. Certainly some exceptional talent was present, but some egos far exaggerated their individual abilities and overlooked the scope of artistic endowment that was the Village.

It was at the Club, and the Cedar Tavern—"workingmen of the neighborhood [were] as comfortable in the plain, well-lit room [of the latter] in the afternoons as [were] the artists at night"[17]—where one could expect to find those of the New York School. Though they banded differently now, due to a glimmer of light focusing on them and though success went to the heads of some, the majority knew just the same where their public was truly coming from. "The Club represented the solidarity of vanguard artists banded together [still] in defiance of an uncaring mass society."[18] Yet also at the cafeterias, those predecessors of the new art meeting place, the underground artists still banded just the same.

"At their 10th St. headquarters, [which became synonymous with the New York School] noisy round table discussions and panels on art were followed by dancing and socializing."[19] The publicized reverie of the New York School started to attract the attention of those outside the Village. More of the American public was slowly becoming better acquainted with an artist's life in New York City. This favorable, albeit voyeuristic, new attention to artists likely didn't hurt Esther's treatment in the institution on two counts. First, she would have been granted great privilege to carry on her artistic endeavors there. Secondly, Merle Hoyleman back in Pittsburgh was spurred on to locate where the best artist she knew personally had disappeared to.

In 1945, Jackson Pollock and wife Lee Krasner bought a house away from the city and the Club, which was still at its fruitful beginnings. It would be their needed creative retreat. All must have realized that good work needed focus, some sanctuary space in which to flourish. These two, as well as Balcomb Greene and wife Gertrude Glass, who built a summer home on Long Island, were perhaps the first New York artists to signal a trend away from the more generalized "party times"[20] of the 1930s and a move toward more creative space—despite the fact that there still was much partying, celebrating the successful, and outside crazy attention given to the artist coterie of the city. At their farmhouse, Pollock worked in the spacious barn, and Krasner made a studio in one of the rooms of the house proper. Esther, working away fervently at her own retreat, painting barnyards and countryside, was likely aware of the dynamic happenings back home, for she had become the avid reader. Yet she did not inquire of those events when she wrote Eugenia towards the end of her institution stay.

Jackson Pollock didn't relinquish the good times with his close friends just because he moved away from the city. A heavy drinker, he returned for after-work gatherings often, with Kline and deKooning, who had lofts in the Bowery section of town and who were also now getting their share of the limelight. The Club was flourishing. It was dominated by men, but some women were included—Elaine deKooning, Mercedes Matter, Helen Frankenthaler, Jeanne Miles, Nell Blaine, and Joan Mitchell were some of those included.[21] Artist Miriam Shapiro spoke of segregation within the Club where she and her husband went on Friday nights. "I had no sense of camaraderie with the men." Louise Bourgeois said, as well, "I had the feeling the art scene belonged to the men, and that I was in some way invading their domain."[22]

In fact, the men in the Club had begun to see an opening—a light beginning to shine on American painters—and they were clamoring to the forefront. Wives who were also painters—Shapiro, Krasner and deKooning—managed to get a foot in the door, but much less so than their husbands. Unlike during the 1930s, when the laws governing the WPA staunchly set forth equity for both sexes, women now began to be left behind by the men becoming known as the Abstract Expressionists and others of the New York School. Jackson Pollock, Franz Kline, and Willem deKooning are all names that became synonymous with the first generation of Abstract Expressionists (There later to be second and subsequent waves). The women of the first generation, though, came to be known considerably later.

The 1930s had been a good decade for women artists, due to the non-discriminatory policies of the WPA. "Never had women in such large numbers undertaken and completed projects of such magnitude."[23] The head of the New York Project had been, in fact, a woman, Audrey McMahon. Lee Krasner worked as an assistant to muralist Max Spirok in the WPA; she also became a leader in the Artists Union, due to the heated-up political scrutinizing of the Projects by the HUAC (House Un-American Activities Committee). And she was a member of the exploratory American Abstract Group, as was Alice Trumbull Mason and sculptress Gertrude Glass Greene, well before some male Abstract Expressionists even considered the concept.

"These programs [of the Project] were notably free of sex bias." A 1930 census has "40% of all practicing American art professionals as women."[24] Increased educational opportunities for women, beginning with the mid-19th century, had finally culminated in this. But according to Charlotte Streifer Rubinstein, author of the very definitive reference text, *American Women Artists,*

> after the giant leap forward taken by women artists under the Federal Art Project in the 1930s, one might reasonably have expected them to come into their own in the 1940s and 1950s, as American art moved toward world leadership. But just the opposite proved to be the case. The forties, fifties, and sixties turned out to be a period of increased discrimination. The leading galleries carried few works by women, and very few women had solo shows in major museums in this period. When the famous exhibition, "The New American Painting," [would go] abroad to tour the capitals of Europe in 1959, only one woman out of seventeen artists [6%]—Grace Hartigan—was included.[25]

What happened to the 40 percent from 1930? Why did women who showed their work prominently in the 1930s seemingly not have staying power in the 1940s and beyond? It seems artists themselves defined and monitored the 1940s movement in art in America, with no governing body such as the WPA to ensure equity, so opportunity indeed became slanted. As Rubinstein explained, "Male artists, beginning to smell high stakes in the offing as American collections and museums began to come of age, formed an unofficial old boy's club in which the work of their female colleagues was not taken seriously."[26] Artists scrambled to the top of the pile to make a name for themselves. Longing for artistic power and control of the art scene, and in a better position socially-politically to announce anything with authority, men competitively pushed their work out there. Women nevertheless worked within these same movements for some time. The WPA had helped accelerate women's catching up for the historical neglect of their artistic contributions. Yet despite the strides made in finally getting similar training to men and similar access to possibilities of becoming technically excellent, theoretically informed and sufficiently inspired, women's struggle for acceptance in the 1940s was still so great.

Krasner, who had encountered sexism from early on as a student , said, "I couldn't run out and do a one-woman job on the sexist aspects of the art world. . . . I was able to work and other things would have to take their turn."[27] Eleanor Munro, in *Originals*, recounted the example of "Krasner paint[ing] in light bright colors and a [male] teacher at the National Academy of Design told her to 'take a mental bath.' Painting light when convention and the males ordained dark had landed both Mary Cassatt and Georgia O'Keefe in trouble before her."[28] Krasner, who had known many within the art scene before the Abstract Expressionist movement gained force, lost her footing, as all the connections being made seemed to be between males or benefiting mainly male artists. This type of behavior was similar of course to the tradition of exclusivity established by the National Academy. Now the male artist's position was just cast as sexier. "Machismo was part and parcel of a psycho-esthetic that cast male artists as sublime-tongued-and-fingered prophets in touch with the `chaos of ecstasy.'"[29] Eleanor Munro added that, "[women] did not take the podium as prophets to define schools or movements."[30]

Men got one-man shows that broke open their careers. Women were usually given shows in groups, such as Guggenheim's "Thirty-One Women" in 1945, which included mostly already recognized artists such as Frida Kahlo. An exception was Guggenheim's sponsoring a solo show of Irene Pereira's work in 1943. But even here, as before, the same names of women artists always come up. "The range and vitality (and existence) of the 100s of competent women artists in America is completely overlooked."[31] Those artists "left out," actually many male and female both, would have a response by the end of the decade, though, to the evident separatist attitude cultivated by both the gallery-owners and a few of the artists themselves. Vanguard work went well beyond the not-so tidy lines painted by the Abstract Expressionists. Other artists of both sexes were doing all kinds of inventive, individual, original work in the Village. So, as explained Rubinstein,

> Because few commercial galleries were willing to show their avante-garde work, a certain number of artists decided to create cooperatives. The Jane Street, Tanager, Hansa, March and other artist-run galleries began to cluster around East 10th St., near the Club, making this a lively district where people mixed and met. A third of the artists in those galleries were women, a much higher percentage than in the prestigious commercial galleries.[32]

⑥ ⑥ ⑥

Esther had been released on Convalescent Care February 1949. The details of her life back in New York City come from the records the institution kept of her time on convalescent care, as overseen by the Psychiatric Institute, the outpatient clinic located in New York City.

```
March 18, 1949: PSYCHIATRIC INSTITUTE: Patient
came into clinic alone. She is now living at 44
Downing Street and has been doing some paint-
ing. She has made over $500 in the short time
```

she has been out of the hospital through the
sales of some paintings. She has put over $300
in the bank and with the rest of it she has
bought some clothing and is using some for expenses. She has not started to teach art as yet
but this is mainly because she has no apartment
of her own. She hopes to be able to rent a studio
for herself. The telephone number at the above
apartment was given as Chelsea 35578. Patient
was given an appointment for April 15th.

LB

March 18, 1949: PSYCHIATRIC INSTITUTE: The patient came to the clinic alone. She looked well
physically but was still dressed in a blowsy
fashion. Mentally she seemed to be alert, appropriate emotionally and displayed no particular overt symptoms or signs. She has been making good progress with her painting, having
sold a number of pictures and also having begun
to teach. She is sponsored by a fairly well-
known artist who is sending her pupils whom he
does not have the time to teach. So far the
patient seems to be making an excellent adjustment, maintains a good drive and goal and has
no complaints....

Dr. A Gorfinkel

For the late 1940s, $500 in painting sales within a month's time was
not too shabby an accomplishment, especially right after coming out
of an institution. In fact, it was exceptional. (Equally remarkable was
that by the end of her institution stay Esther had amassed $800 from
the sales of her paintings.)[33] Reg Masson may have been the purchaser
at this time of a few of Esther's works, though surely not all. For she was
already starting to maneuver within the circles of those more suc-

cessful. The "famous artist" Dr. Gorfinkel referred to would turn out to be Milton Resnick; he indeed knew Esther and would buy some of her work. At the time, Resnick was himself studying under Hans Hofmann. Meanwhile, back in Pittsburgh, Merle, though chronically sick now due to her thyroid ailment and subsequent heavy medication, was once again attempting to pin down Esther's New York City address. Because she had no luck getting correspondence and a package containing one of Esther's watercolors to Esther via Eugenia's address, in early March she again wrote her faithful correspondent and Esther's champion, Dr. Stanley. "I am expecting to show a group of her pictures around March 20, 1949, and to a N.Y. official. . . ." Merle also writes to him of Mrs. A. Steinberg, who "has been very generous in arranging earlier gatherings to show Esther's work. . . ."[34]

Dr. Stanley writes Merle back, telling her that Dr. Rizzolo's wife would forward the package to Esther, who had left some things with her when she was placed on Convalescent Care.[35] After this correspondence between Merle and Esther, the two apparently lost touch again, this time because of Merle's serious ill health.

April 15, 1949: Patient is still living at 44 Downing Street but she expects to move from there within the near future. She is quite busy, having been commissioned recently to make four woodcarvings at $100 a piece and she says in general that her business is very good. She expects to have a show of her work soon and within the near future she may be able to have time to take on some pupils whom another artist plans to refer. At the present time she displays adequate insight and her hypomanic behavior and ideation are very much in evidence with only a light veneer of control. She speaks under pressure, is suspicious in her productions and is emotionally labile. Of course, this is probably her prepyschotic behavior and if she gets no worse she will probably get along quite well. She understands her own dynamisms in a fairly satisfactory manner and is certainly adult both in her thinking and plans for the future. She shows very little immaturity. She has some money in the bank totalling $190 and feels quite well over it. So far, she impresses the examiner as getting along but however it would be well to keep her under continued supervision. She was given another appointment for May 27th.

Dr. A. Gorfinkel

April 28, 1949: Visited 44 Downing St. and found the patient in the apartment with the dog she is taking care of....Patient appears to be in very good spirits, and she has been busy at work on her wood carving, all of which is in good order. She apparently is living quite simple, is able to get out every day because of the dog and is quite pleased with the neighbors who are very friendly toward her....

FIG. 20 One of Esther's woodcarvings from this period. (Owner: Carole Evans, NYC)

Esther did not jump back wholeheartedly into the decadent scene she left in 1942; she centered herself a bit more around her creative work. The times, too, had changed with the war and its aftermath, with the wildest experiences being had by the successful Abstract Expressionists and their followers. The focus of parties seemed to be around the success of an artist or artists, and did not have the more proletarian feel of earlier decades. Though she no doubt was still quite close with Eugenia and her old friends, life didn't seem

FIG. 21 & FIG 22   Esther, Jerry, and Masson's dog, Murphy, circa 1950.

so closely tied with them as before. Like others, it seems, she was in a rebirth, truly focusing on work, something perhaps never fully achieved in the 1930s. Because it was a retreat from the pressures to make money to sustain herself, the hospital seemed to get Esther in touch with this focus. Back in the city, though she still got about the Village, she stayed in a bit more with her dog companion, "Murphy," and she continued, as in the mid-to-latter stages of the institution, to be extremely productive putting out work.

The April 28th entry continues:

> . . . She still has not heard anything from the Shaffer Galleries but is hopeful that her paintings will be on exhibit sometime in the future. She is planning to exhibit at the Washington Square [Outdoor Show] during the next month. She asked about different people at the hospital and wished to be remembered to them. She will be living in this apartment until the end of May and then she must look for something

else. She does not seem to worry about the future and in fact she is quite hopeful. She
still has about $185 in the bank and is trying
not to use any of this money. She hopes to be
able to obtain a loft of her own in the village where she can have students and do her
work. It is felt that patient is making a fair
adjustment at this time.

LB

In trying to survive as an artist, Esther again went toward teaching, as many creative artists often do. Though it didn't satisfy her early on, and rarely truly satisfies others who often do so only in order to make ends meet, Esther embraced it again as the only visible outlet beyond painting to help her survive.

In May 1949, Esther exhibited once again at the Washington Square Outdoor Show. The show changed slightly since the 1930s. With the 1942 spring show, the overseeing committee began charging a small entrance fee, in that year, one dollar, part of which was devoted to the Russian War Relief. Around 1947, newcomers to the Village comprised half the artists represented, whereas shows prior had artists that for the most part had been exhibiting year after year, with little percentage of newcomers.[36] But with the fever around Abstract Expressionism, record numbers of artists soon flocked to the Village to stake their territory. Participating in the Washington Square Outdoor Show was simply a part of that. The nature of the show soon changed, due to the fact that not all people trying to become successful in art were true artists. Many to be in the shows from now on lacked genuine talent, or simply tried to emulate what was a hit with the art market or the mainstream public.

֍ ֍ ֍

It was around this summer of 1949 that Esther met Edward Kinchley Evans, a fellow Villager and former art student at Columbia. The two became close friends. Esther was now temporarily out of touch with Merle. As previously in Esther's life, as one close friend drifted away, another drifted in. Ed would recall working in his studio while Esther stopped by one day. "I'd started casting very thin layers of clay, which I'd then break into shards . . . and make necklaces and the like." Esther visited his studio and got an interest in doing the same. However, she did not have the resources he did, to use plaster of Paris to achieve thinness. "Esther didn't understand how I'd been able to do them so thin; she started making little clay 'patties'—plaques which she did her marvelous little women on."[37] (She began painting views based on her institution women-series on them.) Later some turned up adorned by cats, "winsome still lifes," and other single-figure portraits. She also "mold[ed] quickly-formed figurines, also based on the asylum forms."[38] Both Ed and Esther then put underglaze painting on their ceramics and, like Esther did with Eugenia, would pal around together to market their work.

Ed Evans' comments confirm that Esther was doing some painting from memory of the institution. Though there would years later be misunderstanding about exactly when Esther painted some canvasses and tiles depicting content like the women series—still during her institutionalization or after—it is only now clear after reviewing all documentation of her life that the ceramics akin to the women series were done later. Likely they were completed from memory and inspired both by Ed and those canvasses no doubt scattered about her places of residence.

June 16, 1949: Worker telephoned patient and was invited to come right down to the apartment at 44 Downing St, New York City. Patient was waiting for the worker when worker arrived. She is staying in this apartment for another week, during which time she hopes to find an apartment of her own . . . She has finished most of her wood carvings and is now thinking about making a ceramic block print of some of her 'nudes' and sending them to some companies. She appeared to be a little worried about financial matters although she still has $170 in the bank. Her main concern was that none of her paintings have been sold recently . . . However, she insisted that she is not too worried as she feels that things will work out . . . Her exhibit at the Shaffer Galleries may come up in the fall. She is looking forward to this with much enthusiasm . . . She is still doing her own cooking but occasionally eats out. She has grown to love the dog "Murphy" with whom she is taking care of . . . She has been getting out and seeing friends and has been getting some relaxation . . . No problems could be elicited at this time other than the housing problem which the patient seems capable of solving for herself.

LB

July 8, 1949: The patient came to the clinic alone. She looks well and says that she is feeling well. She was quite talkative, animated as usual but shows no overt signs of any pathology at the present time. She has plans for the future, expecting to open a class in instruction and expects to get some clients through an acquaintance of hers, another artist, engaged in the same field. She has made some money and some more money is coming in for contracts which she has fulfilled. . . .

Dr. A. Gorfinkel

On August 8, 1949, Life magazine ran an article entitled "Is Jackson Pollock the Greatest Living Painter in the United States?" It described

Pollock with artistic techniques, and especially manners, "incomprehensible."[39] The editors were goading the public, "virtually invit[ing] the readers to respond indignantly in the negative," according to Dore Ashton.

> September 2, 1949: This patient came to the clinic alone. She remains neat, clean and pleasant. At this time she states she has $105 in the bank and is not worrying financially. She continues to look for a part-time teaching job. Patient is selling a substantial number of small wooden carvings, from which she is supporting herself. She is doing some larger carvings but has not been able to sell these. Patient continues to have an active social life.
>
> Dr. M.M. Bandler

> October 28, 1949: [Patient] is her usual cheerful self and states that she now has a new apartment which she has sublet. She is residing at 62 St. Luke's Place, NYC, Apt. 3B. Our patient states that this is a nice apartment and then goes on to explain that it is nice but too expensive. Patient has some money in the bank and is apparently doing satisfactorily. She states that she is selling some of her work. She has one customer who buys every month at least one thing from her and he is doing this not only because he likes her work but because he is helping her financially. Patient has started a nude class of art work which she holds in her apartment one night a week. She has eight pupils for this. Our patient is very optimistic, even euphoric.
>
> Dr. M.M. Bandler

November 17, 1949: Patient is subletting a very pleasant apartment. In fact it is a one-room studio. She had her wood carvings out on the table and apparently was doing some work on them. She has had some difficulty selling her works lately but does not seem to be too discouraged about this. She is asking higher prices for her wood carvings and this may be one of the reasons why she has not been able to sell as quickly as before. Mr. [Milton] Resnick from whom the patient sublets the apartment is a friend who apparently has bought a good many of patient's paintings because some of them were on display about the room.[40]

Patient is still making some of her own clothes, doing her sewing all by hand. She still has some money in the bank but not as much as before because it is costing her a good deal more to live now. . . .

Patient is now interested in ceramics and has been doing some clay modelling with this idea in mind. She has been seeing friends occasionally and has been going out to the movies. She still has the dog, Murphy, which has been given to her now and who apparently is a companion for her.

It is felt that patient is getting along as well as can be expected.

LB

December 22, 1949: Worker called at 62 St. Luke's Place but was told the patient was not at this residence at the present time. Mr. Resnick who rents the apartment allows the patient to stay here when he is out of town. He is now

returned and will stay in the city until February. He could not tell worker patient's exact
address but believed she now has a furnished
room on Houston Street. Worker left her name
saying she would get in touch with the patient
by letter.

LB

January 6, 1950: PSYCHIATRIC INSTITUTE CLINIC:
This patient came to the clinic alone. She is
now living once again at 62 St. Luke's Place in
the Village. She is apparently getting along
well. She has friends but states that she feels
that her work is more important than socializing. Patient is still selling some of her paintings, gives lessons and apparently is doing
satisfactorily. Patient is anxious to be discharged and the undersigned feels that there is
no reason to hold this patient on Convalescent
Care any further. Condition, Improved.

Dr. M.M. Bandler

January 20, 1950: Worker telephoned patient's
residence at 62. St. Luke's Place, New York
City and again spoke to Mr. Resnick, from whom
the patient is subletting the apartment. Mr. R.
is still in town and therefore patient will not
pick up residence here for another few weeks.
Patient stops in daily to pick up her mail but
he is never sure when to expect her. He feels
she is getting along well and seems to be
happy. Not too much information was obtained
since it is not certain how much Mr. R. knows
about patient.

LB

It was probably a bit maddening for the social worker attempting to neatly document Esther's place of residence. There is in fact a contradiction with the residences given for Esther. She in actuality probably lived with Eugenia when Milton Resnick was in town, and was just telling the Psychiatric Institute that she had her own place. It was surely evident to the social workers and doctors that her life as an artist was a bit more unusual than most. Thankfully for Esther's sake, they seemed accepting. Even too, if she did not entirely believe her comment to them, that her work was "more important than socializing," she at least knew what to say to representatives from the Institute, and she seemingly convinced them.

Likely America's increased fascination with artists didn't hurt Esther's situation, as the Psychiatric Institute, working as an arm of Harlem Valley State Hospital, considered her recovery. She was fully released as a patient approximately a year after being placed on Convalescent Care; her seven and a half years under the watchful eye of the institution had come to an end. Her discharge papers, interestingly, were mailed to the address where she was subletting, the residence of the famous artist Milton Resnick.

February 3, 1950: DISCHARGED: Patient is today discharged from the hospital records to the custody of herself. Certificate of Discharge mailed to patient.
  Diagnosis: Psychoneurosis, Mixed Type.
                Condition: Much improved.
                    Dr. C. Greenberg

Chapter Sixteen

"THE FLIGHT OF ESTHER PHILLIPS' FINGERTIPS"[1]

Thus come the beginning of 1950, Esther was completely out from under the gaze of the institution, living an independent life once more. While she was making her way back into the Village, *Life* had begun to run articles about the New York School. After the sensational 1949 piece on Jackson Pollock was the May of 1950 spread of a select group of artists, the Abstract Expressionists. *Life* dubbed them the "Irascible Eighteen," as they were protesting the Metropolitan Museum of Art's conservative jury policies, and demanding more attention in general from American museums. It seemed that the American art world finally paused to consider the cries of all the artists in the Village, those forward-thinking creators who were trying to bust through, once and for all, the conservative wall still in place within the art establishment. The time was right. Though the article featured only a select group, their outcry was a common plea for mainstream America to simply take notice of their working lives. With this, all artists finally won some recognition, if only momentarily.

What before fully hadn't come to fruition with Pollock's individual success and others' later emergence now became abstractly realized for all working within the Village, but of course only those artists who fit a particular progressive mold were fully embraced, media darlings. More success would soon follow the few artists spotlighted in this *Life* spread, as the mainstream of America was bombarded with media images defining just what the Village artist was—someone modelled after the Abstract Expressionists. Popular culture adopted these eighteen figures. In-fighting began to get worse among the Village artists, for the eighteen represented excluded many more, and the sensationalism of the media wasn't entirely to blame. Only one among the celebrated group of eighteen was a woman, artist Hedda Sterne. Lee Krasner was in fact "deeply hurt" when the Irascible Eighteen organized their protest and "invited [her husband] Pollock to join them, but left her out."[2] So though the mainstream attention to an artist's cause was a victory for all artists, it nevertheless was a pinnacle for only a few. As Raphael Soyer, realist artist, teacher at the Arts Students League, and friend of Esther's, put it, "Overnight, all these people became geniuses and the other artists were neglected. You heard only about these Abstract Expressionists all the time."[3]

The glamorized tales of decadent Village life captured by American writers and mythologized orally for decades became much more a reality with photographs and of course television depicting the partying for an American public more than curious to know intimately of the goings-on of the Village. In 1950, Jackson Pollock had $6,000 sales.[4] The 1949 *Life* spread had thrust him very much into the limelight, pushing him to produce more quality work, and his drinking stepped up. "Art openings [of the more successful artists] were jammed and so was the Cedar Bar . . . where deKooning, Franz Kline and Pollock congregated and engaged in aesthetic debates and even occasional physical brawls."[5] Esther saw less of Franz Kline, deKooning, and the "cocky" Pollock because the so evident rowdiness of the streets of the 1930s had moved to within the more elite clubs. And neither she nor the guys ran into their mutual old friend Arshile Gorky; severely depressed, he had taken his life in 1948.

The lives of many, many Village artists—most, in fact—were not transformed by the fate that bestowed such grand recognition on some. Esther and her friends were of that larger group. Their daily artistic life was still that of typical Village artist who gathered at the all-night cafeterias, talking and arguing until morning, just as the successful did at the Club. No doubt conversations were polarized at the two distinct hangouts—one lamenting the selective praise for a few, the other wondering what to do with their newfound fame. In addition to the diners that Esther frequented from the 1930s, there were now others, serving up the same fare. The Jefferson was "one of those big, roomy, jukeboxy diners. It was on the west side of 6th Avenue . . . open all day and night." There was Stewart's Cafeteria and Hubert's Cafeteria, and "many saloons and dives on the west side of the Village."[6]

FIG. 23   Jerry (far left), friends, and Esther (far right).

The times were still fun, despite the fragmentation within the Village artistic scene. By the mid-1950s the newly famous and the not-so-famous alike still found themselves mingling together at bars around Sheridan Square and especially at the Five Spot nightclub, to watch Charlie Mingus play. The Village Vanguard, the artists' dive bar located in a cellar near 7th Avenue South, now teemed with tourists who flocked to the Village to catch artists at work and play. Esther and others like her found, come the 1950s, that it had suddenly become "hip" to be an artist. Esther still would have found her familiar Goody's Cafe and Minetta's Tavern post-institution. Even though it was in the Italian section of the Village, with many old-fashioned neighborhood bars and restaurants, Minetta's had begun attracting tourists, like the other bohemian spots in the Village.[7] By this, she was surely disgusted.

Mitchell, interviewing the infamous Joe Gould at Minetta's on a regular basis in the 1940s and 1950s, wrote, "I learned later that many of the men and women who frequented [the dives] had been bohemians in the early days of the Village and had been renowned for their rollicking exploits. . . ."[8] He continues, playfully stating that many, at the point he met them, were "in advanced stages of alcoholism." After Esther left the institution, though, there is nothing to suggest that she ever excessively drank again like her unfortunate momentary episode with liquor in 1941. In fact, Ed Evans and friend Glen Gress would say they never saw her touch a drink, that she "seemed a teetotaler" to them. In the 1950s, Esther "may have visited the taverns [only] to meet the various sundry artists," according to Evans.[9]

The area around the 10th St. Gallery was symbolic of the success of the New York School and the Abstract Expressionists. It was clamorous and bustling, as was the mindset of all brushing up against each other there. Ed Evans would reflect:

> The 10th St. Gallery—that was the beginning of that school, and you have to understand back then, particularly in the Village, and all around, everybody was out to make a school, and I'm sure Esther would have also wanted to be a part of that. There were people who had been around since the '30s and they knew her. We were all friends—Larry Rivers, Milton Resnick. . . .[10]

Ed commented on the crossings of the famed and the not so fortunate at the new coffeehouses. "Generally in the East Village, coffeehouses started springing up and around Cooper Union and all. That's where most of us, successes or not, spent the afternoon drinking coffee, talking about art. . . ." (Esther met the refugee Chagall one day in the 1950s at one of the coffee shops; she later in life told her niece that he "used color indiscriminately."[11]) "And just as the writers seemingly went to the White Horse and other taverns, artists seemingly went to the coffeehouses. All of us who could afford a cup of coffee would go. It was a wonderful way to spend the afternoon—especially in the summer."[13]

Art critic John Gruen echoed Ed Evans' reflections in *The Party's Over*. Rubinstein would summarize from his book that most artists nevertheless still relied on each other during the changed atmosphere: "In the lean forties, as artists struggled to forge new styles, they were a fellowship. They visited one another's studios, drank tea at one another's homes, and brought out their works one at a time for their peers to discuss and criticize."[13] Esther, Eugenia, Ed, and other artists were *of* the same scene that spawned the New York School. They were simply a few of the forgotten many. "Great art," stated Gloria McDarrah, "lives off lesser artists."[14]

                                                 ◉ ◉ ◉

In both spring and fall of 1950, Esther was exhibiting watercolors at the Washington Square Outdoor Show. Likely these were both her institution paintings and new paintings. The spring show's catalog listed her 193 Houston Street address and specified that she was assigned to set up her exhibit at Sullivan Street, one block down from McDougal. Pittsburgh reviewer Megan Shay years later remarked of the watercolors of this timeperiod. Her comments would be relevant with regard to the art content. It must be noted, however, that she believed, according to all known information at the time of her research, that Esther was at the end of her institution stay at this time, in the early 1950s. It is interesting to speculate on the context of Shay's remarks considering that Esther had just been released and was on her own now for a couple of years.

> . . . a dramatic change took place in Phillips' paintings [in 1951]. The backgrounds become dark and brooding. The detail in facial expression increases, and the expressions themselves become moodier, glowering or hollow. More clothing is depicted and a sense of constriction and discontent is pervasive. The paintings present a curious sequence, from light [when first institutionalized] to dark. Ordinarily, one would associate such darkness with a relapse or a disenchantment. . . . The change, however, is so dramatic and mournful that one has to wonder if, in fact, she knew she would soon be released. . . .[15] [Of course, she had just been released of a few years, and was back on the streets of New York].

Come the fall of 1950, Esther's registration with the Outdoor Show gives Eugenia's new address, 68 Bedford Street, as her home. Eugenia, and thus at times Esther, lived in this brownstone house—still well-preserved to this day—for a good many years in the 1950s.[16] It was catty-corner from a three-and-a-half story Victorian once owned by Edna St. Vincent Millay and husband at 75 1/2 Bedford Street. Though Esther likely never met Millay, who was no longer living in the States by the late 1920s, Esther much later told her niece that Millay was a "pain in the ass," that she would see Millay at her mailbox, and that Esther was irritated because "they'd rope off the street to take pictures of her house."[17] Likely the street was roped off when Millay died in the early 1950s, and reporters in New York City would have flocked to what Esther referred to as the infamous Village "dollhouse."

Sometime in 1951, the minimal financial security that Esther had upon release from the institution came to an end—the savings that she had built up, and the money from sales to Milton Resnick and others immediately after her release. She found herself once again looking for welfare assistance. The New York Department of Welfare wrote to the institution to inquire of Esther as applicant.[18] New Harlem Valley director Leo P. O'Donnell wrote back, giving a one-page background report taken almost verbatim from summaries in Esther's file, with this additional comment at the end: "Temperamentally she was not suited to work as a commercial artist, looking upon this as much beneath a person with her creative possibilities." Typed across the top of this correspondence: 'Privileged and Confidential—for professional purposes only—not to be used against the patient's interests.'"[19]

An undated short note arrived at the institution just before this welfare correspondence. In it, Esther unleashes her sarcasm on Dr. Greenberg, her old denigrator.[20]

> Dear Dr. Greenberg
>
> I am money-mad. In fact I am like Hetty Green [miserly woman who wouldn't allow her sick son to spend money visiting a doctor]—I wondered if you could send me my balance of $50.00 (or so)—to add to my acct at the Corn Exchange Bank—or should I keep it at Harlem Valley Hospital at 2% interest?—
>
> My regards to your family—
> Sincerely
> Esther Phillips

Merle and Esther hadn't communicated since shortly after Esther was placed on Convalescent Care. Merle didn't get to hear of the new joys and familiar struggle that Esther was experiencing as a free woman and artist once again trying to make it in the Village. Ironically, Merle herself now plunged into that hole of darkness, admittance to a mental hospital, just a few years after Esther's release from Harlem Valley. She was committed for a short time to Mayview State Hospital, just outside Pittsburgh. Like Elizabeth T. Stone, whose writing is included in *Women of the Asylum*,[21] Merle was committed by a brother. Though it can not be discerned what his motivations were, his stepping into her life seemed to cause her much misery. His actions replicate vast, documented, wrongful commitments throughout history of women by male family members. Susan B. Anthony and Elizabeth Cady Stanton wrote passionately in 1861 about the record number of rebellious wives, daughters, and sisters institutionalized for views and behaviors that angered family.[22]

Merle Hoyleman's experience in Mayview, even though very short, was a much more cruel experience than Esther's stay at Harlem Valley. Just as Margaret Aikins McGarr wrote of an institution too often being "a living hell instead of the rest and relaxation and cure it should be and is declared to be,"[23] Merle detailed an experience anything but therapeutic in an open plea to various friends and professional contacts after her incarceration. She laid out by letter the circumstances of her tragic commitment and institutionalization in the spring of 1951.[24] "You will see that I am in a mental hospital. My Oklahoma brother, Rhese, signed me in here in early March and now does nothing about getting me out. . . ." Merle relates her story, that she started taking prescribed heavy medication for a thyroid growth in April 1948. By November of that year, she had taken quite ill; she believed that she "was allergic to some source from which this new type of medication was made, or to the carrier in the medication." Her physician took her off the medicine and soon put her on other medications, also in heavy doses, to treat the ever-enlarging gland. She was also given megadoses of radioactive iodine, which finally reduced and arrested the growth, but which Merle felt caused other physical and emotional problems.

In February of 1951, Merle took violently ill again, with no one being able to diagnose the cause. She wrote that, "Rhese, my Oklahoma brother, flew to Pittsburgh, broke into my apartment at 4524 Forbes St. He arrived at night." Merle commented on her brother's known sadistic behavior and her own debilitating weakness. "I had been too ill to permit any stranger to come into my apartment. I had not seen my brother for fifteen years (nor had my brother done anything for me for fifteen years) and how did I know who he was? (Personally, I think I was just getting over an attack of intermittent fever or typhoid fever when Rhese arrived.)" She insisted that Rhese first have the police come to properly aid in identifying him before she let him in (she had family pictures on her dressing table), but he refused and forced his way into her apartment. "I suffering from shock and delirium, my brother took me to Shadyside Hospital where my case was diagnosed as insanity in one weeks' time." Her penchant for research, including her inquiry into practices at Western Psychiatric of a few years prior, could not help her. Merle told the reader of her letter that Shadyside Hospital overlooked the fact that "Pennsylvania law requires a ten-day observation period to declare one insane."

"The next morning my brother brought me to Mayview State Hospital—fourteen miles from Pittsburgh . . . [Merle believed he placed her at a state hospital, as opposed to private, to avoid any financial liability for her care]. Dr. Schirer, (my personal physician for twenty years) was not on the staff at Shadyside Hospital, therefore could not enter the case." Via this letter, Merle was trying to win support for her case, in order to be released from what she termed "unfair illegal incarceration." She sent it as a plea to many friends, and equally dropped names of all her friends, and their status in the community, throughout the letter. She wrote of friends having always worked on her behalf, and included hopeful language that they would do so again. She writes of, and to, Caresse Crosby, Lincoln Kirstein, George Marion O'Donnell, Paul Mellon, and Mr. and Mrs. H.H. Laughlin—all loyal friends and influential figures in the world of publishing.

The incompetence of Mayview State Hospital, in diagnosing and treating her, Merle then outlines in detail. She first describes the hospital routine at Mayview. "There is no provision made here for diet. The chief sources of food are starch, because it is cheapest. I am succumbing to starvation," which Merle felt "leads first to insanity, then death." She went on, "The patients yell around and curse night and day. Such vulgarity of tongue, no one has ever heard and no one can find any peace or quiet with all this. Patients constantly talking to selves, coupled with incoherence, is unbelievably overwhelming. The attendants allow patients to wash their pubic and rectal regions in the toilets (insanity, of course) as well as to wash hands and face in toilet, plus occasional sudsing of garment, as well as playing in bowel movement in toilet bowl without correcting them. There is incompetence and neglect on every side—no actual aid to correct patients' insane habits."

Merle continues her letter by referring to Rhese's selling off all her furniture, much of it having been gifts from supporters like the Laughlins, who obviously believed in her as a writer, and who tried to aid her in her poor economic situation over a fourteen-year period. Merle also believed, at the time she wrote this letter, that Rhese might have disposed of all of her writings. (Friends told her they feared he burned them.)

Only after three months did hospital officials properly attend to her case. They deemed Merle sane enough and sent release papers to her brother, back in Oklahoma. He did not respond, and she therefore could not leave. Disgusted with the legality and bureaucracy of the situation, Merle writes of "not being able to find out anything when one is considered a lunatic—it is as if being behind bars. . . . They do as they please and you are helpless. . . . [The institution] is run in a lazy fashion with overseers to taunt and lie to you." She concludes, "I am hoping my friends will band together and see that I am released promptly."

Obviously, treatment of the mentally ill at Mayview, like at many institutions, continued the downward spiral it had been following from the century prior. During the time that she fervently waited, needing "rest and quiet and exercise outdoors," the hospital instead crazily administered, mid-summer, one of the most severe treatments practiced upon mental patients. "Whatever nervousness I now possess is due to shock treatment. . . . I now pay the price of wrong diagnosis and indifference."

Merle concludes her letter:

> There is vast festering in this place; racial and religious intoler-
> ance, intimidation, sadism, masochism, eviction, favoritism,
> tyranny, etc. . . the qualities that do not belong in a democracy.
> The Federal Government will have to pass, as the Child Labor
> Act, a law to protect the mentally ill who are defenseless; and
> stop these corrupt practices. Further, the federal authorities
> should houseclean this institution and investigate where the
> taxpayers' money actually goes. Should maintain federal inves-
> tigators here all the time.
>
> The information in this letter is confidential . . . please con-
> sider it so.

◎ ◎ ◎

Esther did not know what had happened to her dear correspondent
in Pittsburgh. She herself was preoccupied, though, with staking a renewed place in the Village, again working hard at her art, searching for
cheap housing, scrambling to earn money, and commingling with all
others still doing the same. When Merle was released from Mayview in
October 1951, she evidently wrote Esther about her own recent foray
into a mental institution. A responding letter, from Esther to Merle, on
October 15, attests to this.

> *Dear Merle—*
>
> *I am so happy to hear from you—Ernie Wright and I tried to find out where you
> were—I called him up as soon as I heard from you—as he was in the midst of writing to
> people about your whereabouts. It was awful of your brother to do what he did to your fur-
> niture and manuscripts. And I feel almost guilty about my portfolio being safe—Don't
> send it back—*
>
> > *Esther*

Esther had hooked up once again with her old Pittsburgh friend
Ernie Wright. He was a writer, and part of the circle of friends who had

congregated around the Jewish Y on Pittsburgh's Bellefield Street. He now lived in New York, having begun teaching at the liberal New School for Social Research in the Village. The University of Pittsburgh had let him go due to his communist leanings.[25]

An autumn letter from Esther described to Merle the place she was maintaining at this time, on West 23rd St. As primitive as the infamous cold water flats that most artists lived in, it had a coal stove even in the 1950s:

Dear Merle

Thanks for the card—& so glad you're getting settled—Everything takes time. I am writing this from a cafeteria—My place (that is the place I share with my landlady—is cold—so I parked myself in this cafeteria for a few hours—

Am also waiting for a friend to break some _wood_ for me to start my coal fire (for my coal stove). I am working on a few carvings—am anxious to get back & work on them, also to start my supper cooking—I will appreciate very much what could be done for my w. colors—Maybe _Art Rental Gallery_ could sell one or two. _Mel Evans_, now Editor of Doubleday Pub. Co. (of cheaper novels) bought _3 w. colors_ recently—(several months ago)...

love

Esther

In early 1952, Roy Hughes, Eugenia's father, died after an illness of some time.[26] Though her address was still listed as 159 W. 23rd St., Esther no doubt spent a lot of time at 68 Bedford Street, visiting with Eugenia at the time of his death. Esther continues to be in close contact with Merle, who was about to pick right up where she had left off many times before, marketing Esther's work in Pittsburgh. Esther wrote on average of once a month. She did so at the end of January, thanking Merle for a sale—a woman in Pittsburgh had bought a work. Esther began to keep a list of her contacts, her buyers, compiling addresses and phone numbers, and asked Merle to note such information for any future sales she would make.[27]

Feeling much more herself in February 1952, Merle aggressively again set out to market not only Esther's work, but also the work of a couple other Pittsburgh artists she took a liking to. She took her work to several prominent Pittsburghers—including E. E. Moore of U.S. Steel.

She took to his office: "[Esther's watercolors] large size 24 in #, smaller 19, smallest 3. Drawings counted = 91. These are in large pasteboard container."[28] She continuously took new work to him, as he had an obvious interest in Esther's paintings.

June 1952

Dear Merle,

    I'm writing for me and Esther. Esther feels guilty, about not writing to you lately, but she certainly hasn't been feeling well lately. . . [She] has been working pretty hard, and will probably have a show next year. She is in the Washington Square Outdoor Show now. . . Esther wants to know if you have sales lined up for her? She needs $. Esther will write to you as soon as she begins to feel better. . .

as always, Ernie Wright

Beginning in 1952, a $2 admissions fee was charged for the Washington Square Outdoor Show, as well as yet another change—the admittance of crafts. This factor changed the quality and quantity of fine art represented, for even though quality craft is an art in itself, many less than quality crafts were entered into the shows from this point on. And many artists only had less than quality material as their representative works of art. Esther, Ed Evans, and others took advantage of this policy to sell their less-fine work in order to make a minimal living and continue to practice their fine art. "We placed [our ceramics] in a couple of the shops around the Village, and we did the Outdoor Show—our paintings and our ceramics." They had both become mindful of the changes taking place surrounding the show. They had soon found that "nine times out of ten, the ceramics sold but not the paintings." They sold each piece for one dollar.

[June 18, 1952]

Dear Merle,

    Thanks for the card—I'll have to reread it as it was a little difficult for me to decipher some of the handwriting, as I suspect I have a little eye-strain. I have been ill for awhile, owing to the terrific cold lived in, in my horrible place, this winter, whom I share with my landlady, a paranoid in a fairly advances stage if I judge correctly—I became sick too, just being in that atmosphere—and besides she is taking advantage of me (monetarily)—overcharges . . . I moved there out of desperation—hoping to get out very soon—and I've been there almost a year . . . I may find something, (*a place of my own*) no *sharing,* if I could accumulate a few months advance rent—So if you could sell a few paintings—at any price. . . I have some very interesting paintings—street scenes, still lifes and interiors—nudes. I'll appreciate anything, Merle, dear, you could do for me—as my health depends on getting out of the unbearable rut I'm in. . . I do ceramics now—but too hazardous to send at great distance—

love, Esther

In Pittsburgh the preceding month, Merle had begun a routine of having friends over to her apartment to see Esther's latest work—be it watercolors, or drawings.[29] At her apartment on July 19, Merle noted that she showed Esther's drawings to Harry Golden, a Pittsburgh artist, and to Rich Davis and John Bolton, also likely artists. She received some information from Esther, at this time, about pricing. "I should get more for large ones-$25—but use your judgment as I need to raise at least $100. . . ." Obviously, the fact that Esther's work was met with good regard in Pittsburgh bolstered her self-esteem, working back in New York. Esther writes on August 2:

Dear Merle,

Thanks for all the compliments—I sure could use them—Seriously—am very happy my work meets with such approval. I presume you will see J. O'Connor soon—and I will leave to yours and Mr. O'Connor's judgment about exhibiting where and when. I am terribly in need of $—so the sooner things break for me the better—You may have to use your own judgment about prices—as I must sell...

love Esther—

—I hope O'Connor likes these things

Merle continued corresponding with others to generate interest in Esther's work, her assertiveness and loyalty never waning.

August 27, 1952

Carl Jones-

There is a group of Esther Phillips' drawings currently being shown in Diana Kaplan's window at Studio Shop in the 100 block of Oliver Avenue [Pgh]. Stop and glance at them. They are paintings Esther did in past two years (not from new shipment I took to E.E. Moore on August 14, 1952). Diana will display more recent drawings later on. . . .

We might, [perhaps], catch a glimpse of each other some Sunday noon at Webster Hall. I go there every Sunday . . . in order to exchange hellos and perhaps a few words with old comrades and occasional new acquaintances. There are many interesting folk who tarry there over their excellent coffee and famous coffee cake. . . .

June 4, 1952

Carl Jones-

. . .The drawings are still at my place—3322 Ward St. Stop when you can. Bring whomever you wish with you when you stop to see the drawings. There are many and varied persons and friends who call on me and I shall enjoy anyone whom you bring along. . . .

> *Faithfully,*
> *Merle Hoyleman*

The drawings are very fine and I know you appreciate [such] things. I continue to prod you about seeing the drawings.

Merle also wrote a similar letter to Mrs. H. H. Laughlin at the end of summer. She mentioned her time in Mayview and her physician, Dr. Shirer, who supported her in her belief that "dirty tricks are frequently played on innocent women by ill-begotten [people]." On August 13, 1952, she again held a gathering at her apartment for interested parties to view the new shipment of Esther's watercolors. A letter to Earl E. Moore provides details:

Dear Earl Moore,

For fear your secretary will fail maybe to give you the pertinent details regarding the new group of watercolors which I left at your office August 21, 1952, I write,

Esther Phillips is generally considered by Pittsburghers whose opinion is respected: Pittsburgh's most sophisticated woman artist in the past twenty years. [This statement echoes Pittsburgh artist Milton Weiss and may well have come verbatim from him as he likely visited Merle's apartment to see Esther's works in the '50s]. I have been trying to help her return to normal life after a severe breakdown in New York several years ago. (I have known her since summer of 1933.) She has recovered though and by painting—and this new group are definitely the brightest in mental outlook and shows signs she may return eventually to her former level. At the moment her environment is not conducive to bring about the final upward step in her work. Therefore I am only trying to dispose of a few of the drawings in an effort to lift her from her present surroundings. A man with whom I worked on the Federal Writer's Project (now teaching creative writing at the New School for Social Research, NYC) wrote me this summer that Esther's appeal was genuine. Would I please help her.

This new shipment arrived July 14, 1952. I had several people to my place and as a result—around August 13, 1952 I sold four (John O'Connor Jr. of Carnegie Museum—Fine Arts Dept. has been collecting Esther's work for years—bought two from her new shipment). I, however have been greatly handicapped by a hemorrhage I had in my right eye [Merle began having eye hemorrhages around this time, and they continued at least through 1957 sporadically]. . . . Since there are several people waiting to see the watercolors in lieu of purchasing—I would appreciate obtaining them at your earliest convenience . . . also I am to see a man early in October about a proposed show of her work. . . ."

Merle had visited O'Connor in his office that day of August 13; she sold two of Esther's works there. From Merle's journal: "[O'Connor took the line drawing of a nude (back rendition) and the harbor scene (New York harbor at dawn). He was grieved because Esther [had been unable to be a part of] the Museum Extension Project [WPA—1930s, Pgh]. He also said her drawings are very different from her early work—but she is getting back to herself. This I felt also. I rushed down to Museum Post Office Station and sent Esther $18.50 for the two drawings. Kept out $1.50 for cab fare."[30] Though Merle and O'Connor butted heads at times over the subject of helping Esther, they genuinely had the same interest in Esther's art. He probably made the purchase for the museum, but it may have been personal. His statement about Esther's "getting back to herself" suggests that he perhaps liked her institution works less than her earlier ones. Esther surely asked Merle to take only her fine art—her oils and watercolors—to John O'Connor and later Edward Duff Balken. Though she sent Merle tiles, they were mainly for Merle's pleasure, as tokens of gratitude for the marketing. However they, too, began to sell to friends in Pittsburgh, who were taken with the tiny paintings on ceramic.

September 17, 1952—

Dear Merle,

…I've been very busy turning out work—ceramics, tiles, paintings, carvings—must run around this week with tiles—for some new outlets—what a hassle! But I'm always happy when I make sales or contacts…I've been having trouble with my teeth—one is on the verge of falling out of my mouth. The clinics here are lousy!—And the ones that are pretty good— charge too much—I will have to figure out what to do … Will hustle around for the sake of getting my teeth attended to …I hope you are well—and getting somewhere with your man- uscripts. Do you plan to come to NYC? I would love to see you—Merle—New York is some- times a "mad house"—the way one has to live here—exorbitant rents, etc…Last week sold twelve tiles to shop (frame store in Village)—but broke again. Owe week's rent—but am to see someone tomorrow—about consignment—also will be in group show soon

Remember … keep for yourself—as many tiles and ashtrays as you would like—also when you sell anything take some money out for yourself—please do—take at least one- quarter. I insist.

love Esther

On October 3, 1952, Merle began her day by visiting Wallace Richards, new Director at the art museum; she took in Esther's work and the work of another woman artist named Sara. Merle wrote in her journal that Richards, preoccupied while talking with her, "never sat down all the time." She then wrote Esther:

Oct 3, 1952

Esther—

A line to let you know at 2 pm today I saw Wallace Richards [at] Dept. of Museum. Have waited one solid month to do so. He was busy with [Allegheny County Authority] arranging for a Parking Garage. . . .

Well the thing was this—I saved from all the drawings you sent what I considered your finest. I wanted to get you into 1952 International (this year's) but simply could not manage to see Richards—So he asked me to write a letter to him giving a description of painting . . . name of artist etc and mail it to him. I shall attend to this matter early next week. This is formal procedure for presenting material for International—You have worked hard and long for such a break and I have watched everything you have done. . . . I hope for bigger and better things for you from here on out.

Hastily written,
Merle.

On October 21, Esther responds with a letter, and also sends ashtrays and tiles, which now depict content other than simply her women figures. Esther writes of selling a dozen tiles to a shop on 4th Street, and a gallery. "[The woman owner] buys them once a month from me— (Children's subjects) mostly—for investment. She likes artists. So I was able to get up my weekly rent! Made a few other small sales, but need money desperately."

Merle continuously saw O'Connor "in the hallway"[31] at the museum that fall, showing him Esther's paintings. She tried to make the same headway with Wallace Richards that she had with O'Connor, continuously setting up appointments with his secretary. Gordon

Bailey Washburn, curator of fine arts, caught wind of Merle's agent-ing and would wrote her.[32] Merle noted that she also then went to the museum, but his secretary was out, and she apparently couldn't speak with him.[33] The other artist for whom Merle was marketing, Sara, got some details of the fascinating discourse between Merle and the museum officials:

> . . . [Washburn relayed] that your drawing must be in oil. All paintings must be in oils. He did not say whether the next International would be two or three years from now—The secretary failed to acknowledge letter on Esther's drawings so I'll make it point to go out to Museum, & see Richards—some noon at cafeteria. Must see O'Connor anyhow so I'll kill two birds with one stone. . . . His stupid secretary misread my letter which always infuriates me. Had CB check both my letters to Richards—as I always do. . . . You know me, don't you. My middle name is caution. . . .[34]

Hopefully Merle's persistence in this matter played no part in the stroke Wallace Richards suffered in January 1953, after which he was no longer a target for Merle's insistent marketing. Merle never gave up. To her credit, she made Esther's name and story known to many in Pittsburgh who cared about art. In the process, she became known as quite a character herself. Merle's journal entries probably reflected her creative take on the events in the lives of those around her, being metaphors for consideration, notations likely for future writing possibilities:

> A split-second whim: Woman
> Tuesday singing, harp—Flight of
> Esther Phillips' fingertips—
>
> Oct 3, 1952   Merle Hoyleman[35]

F<small>IG</small>. 24

Chapter Seventeen

"Every Inch of Strength & Strategy
to Call Forth Aid"[1]

Joe Gould, or "Professor Seagull," was still in circulation when Esther was released from the institution. She no doubt ran into him at Goody's or in Washington Square, where he was still extemporizing about various activities that made up his and other Villagers' lives, the fodder for his supposed manuscripts. He had begun to proclaim, "I do more living in one year . . . than ordinary humans do in ten."[2] Unfortunately this was less a statement of diligence and accomplishment than a predilection. It was also an unwanted reality, ironically, of his, and many artists,' fate. Despite that, he was still feisty come the 1950s, sparring with the "nasty"[3] Max Bodenheim—commenting about the lack of a name Max had made for himself as poet. Joe Gould turned up in Eugenia's journals over the years; she referenced him as a colorful writer/bohemian figure. Like she did for so many, she would note his death, when it made its advance.[4]

Like Esther at various times in her life, Joe Gould's friends gave him money regularly—a dollar or two—when they saw him. Esther surely related to his trying desperately to get teeth or eyeglasses. All that the majority of the mainstream working public had access to, the bohemians found out of reach. Like Merle and Eugenia did for Esther, Gould's friends would write each other to tell of his status. One particular piece of correspondence contained: "Joe Gould is in bad shape. He is using up time and energy . . . running all over town getting together enough dimes and quarters for the bare necessities, and it is killing him."[5]

In the early 1950s, Joe Gould would collapse on the Bowery and an ambulance picked him up and delivered him to Columbus Hospital. Because Columbus didn't provide psychiatric services, he was transferred on to Bellevue, as Esther was. He would then be sent to Pilgrim State Hospital for the Mentally Ill on Long Island. There, apparently, his bohemian friends would visit and tell "how much they knew about psychiatry—a subject about which they were fantastically ill-informed," detailed a nurse. (Perhaps they should have endeavored to tell her about bohemianism, instead.) Gould would die at Pilgrim State Hospital a short time later.[6]

December 4, 1952—

Dear Merle

...I am very happy that you are trying to get a book ready (You should and deserve to be published)...I was carving today and am tired. It is a nude twenty inches high—very nice—Think I have a customer. (The frame shop that buys my tiles—is interested in it for their personal use at home). [Esther would later tell her niece that some of her carvings— the nudes—would actually be modeled as lamp bases].7

love, Esther

[Dec. 15, 1952]

Dear Merle,

Received your air mail letter—The story is this-

I was forced to get on relief for a while—a few months and they wanted to check up on the current sales I made—I am getting off—this week—so simply disregard any mail you get from them—that's all—Just don't answer them. I have been selling quite a lot of tiles and ashtrays lately—one shop—keeps ordering them form me—wish I had more such outlets. And today—sold large ashtray and tiles to a friend—for gifts—I am spreading out in my contacts and hope in a month or so to be getting along better—I am doing a series of new paintings of N.Y. scenes—the best I've ever done—rich and strong—and I will go back to oils—soon—too...

How is your book coming? Let me know more about it. You know I am very much inter-
ested in your writing. You have great creative ability—movement and rhythm—Do all
you can to publish your letters—Ernie is not doing so well—Has only one class at New
School...

love Esther

I always appreciate any sales you make—and want you to take some commission.

Esther writes Merle throughout 1953 and uses Eugenia's Bedford Street address. She was then doing oils, which she described as "very engrossing." In a February 10 letter she tells Merle to pass along her regards to O'Connor and Balken. She was doing some marketing of her own in New York, and teaching part-time again—this time, finger-painting to old people. "Just a little money earned to pay my rent and a little food."[8] She writes of expecting to sell an oil or two to Mel Evans, editor of Doubleday Publishing, and mentions that she'd like to grant Edward Duff Balken's request for oils, but needed to be sure they were perfectly dry before shipping to Pittsburgh. (Doubleday had a Perma-books division that put out a "New Voices" anthology; Ernie Wright looked into this as a publishing contact.) She would again state in several other letters that oils would be too sticky to send if not completely dry. Because the materials for oils were more expensive, and the labor more involved, she affixed a price of $50, up to $100. "I am doing some exciting and entertaining ones—think you might agree."[9]

Edward Duff Balken, now retired from the Carnegie Art Museum, apparently desired to further his private collection of art. Through Merle, he first saw Esther's watercolors and then wanted to see oils.[10] In addition to her fine art and tiles, Esther started doing ceramic jewelry, a practice continued throughout the 1950s and 1960s. A Village frame shop that helped Esther immediately bought some. She wrote of selling earring sets, pins, and medallions. Spring of 1953, as to be expected, Esther sent plenty to Merle to keep for herself, as recompense for all the work done on her behalf. At the end of May, Esther poignantly writes to Merle, imploring her to keep some of the money from sales. "I keep thinking of those years at the hospital and if it hadn't been for your tireless efforts in my behalf I'd probably be God knows where. I sure would like one of these days to see you. . . ." She also includes that, due to being sick with many colds this spring, she did not get around quite as much as she would have liked to sell her new jewelry. Also, oils done in January were "still not dry . . . and now the humidity must be contended with!"

Come the start of summer, Esther was transient again. The return address on her envelope is Eugenia's Bedford St. address, but she wrote Merle that she was "living in a horrible room in Harlem temporarily . . . all my things are at Ernie's—some life!" In August, Ernie wrote Merle, "Esther Phillips is here, working at some sculpture." Years later Esther told her sister Dorothy about her good friend Ernie Wright. She surmised that "Esther could always go [to see him] for a meal."[11]

"Still doing some ceramic jewelry," Esther informs Merle in summer. "Sold eight pieces in one day at the shop where they are on consignment. Half of money, however, goes to shop—very small profit for me—but expect more outlets and everyone raves about my jewelry." Esther wishes Merle well, including the hope that Merle's eyes would improve. And Esther, as she would often do, asked Merle to tell more of herself when she corresponds.[12]

July 8, 1953—

Dearest Merle

I suppose you thought I had forgotten you— You know that will never happen—as long as there is breath in my body—& some vibration in my noodle! . . . [Esther goes on to explain that she is still teaching] . . . barely manage enough to pay rent—and eat a little . . . [Esther was painting regularly in oils at this time] . . . Some exciting ones!"

love Esther

In Pittsburgh at the end of August 1953, Merle telephoned Gladys Schmitt and husband Simon Goldfield to ask if they'd buy any of Esther's watercolors. But as noted in Merle's journal, "Si curtly said 'No.'" Merle then told him she had been "disappointed with his attitude" in 1947, when Merle called to inform Gladys of Esther's situation at Harlem Valley. She added that she thought it "unkind of him" to speak of Esther's situation the way that he had and to look unkindly on Merle's communication with Gladys, who had been such a longtime friend of Esther and Merle.[13]

On August 26, Esther writes that she is "painting ferociously . . . doing some beautiful oils" and doing jewelry. She also had several orders for ceramic belts, at $20 a piece—"a lot of work." All told, Esther found herself "as busy as a one-armed paper-hanger!" Ernie Wright was equally busy, as he was being published by Permabooks. He even suggested, via Esther, that Merle should send her writings to him, and he would see what he could do for her through his publishing contact.[14]

◎ ◎ ◎

"For your letters have become a part of my existence. . . ."
—Merle Hoyleman

Both Merle Hoyleman and Eugenia Hughes provide a testament to the tradition of letters that survived until approximately the mid-twentieth century. Both women played enormously important roles in Esther's life, their friendships with her to each span approximately twenty-five years, from the mid 1930s at least until the early 1960s. The vehicle sustaining the tie for Merle and Esther, once she left Pittsburgh, would be only correspondence—personal letters between the two, and formal letters to institution officials. (Certainly it was only letters that kept alive the bond between Eugenia and Esther during the time that Esther was in the institution). Unlike Eugenia, Merle saved nothing of the notes from Esther that period that she was institutionalized—not even envelopes. Her own standards of confidentiality about such "delicate issues," however, took her astray from her usual routine, which, like Eugenia, was to save anything written to or from someone. In the literary tradition, this act was about as sacred as the actual writing of letters. (Indeed once Esther was released from Harlem Valley, Merle saved many letters from her friend.)

Equally important to letter writers was to save newspaper clippings mentioning friends and business contacts, as well as various memorabilia documenting the life of friends and of oneself. Both Eugenia and Merle were expert at this. To be found among Eugenia's varied ephemera, for example, was a clipping commenting on the risque marriage of her Pittsburgh friend Melita Fils to John R. Bowman. Though Eugenia and Esther had not known each other in Pittsburgh, they both knew, ironically, Melita and her husband, a well-connected collector of art in Pittsburgh. Melita was about Esther's age and had been an art student at Carnegie Tech around the time that Esther had been there. Though traveling in other artistic circles around Pittsburgh, Eugenia knew Melita from this time as well. Surely Eugenia and Esther discovered, perhaps via the perusing of this very news clipping, that they had a mutual Pittsburgh acquaintance in her. (It had been a bit scandalous when the University of Pittsburgh Chancellor's son married Miss Fils, a woman eleven years his senior. The two later split and today the surviving Bowman family hardly remembers John's first wife, except to recall that she was somewhat "exotic and bohemian," and soon after left Pittsburgh.)[15]

Both Merle and Eugenia wrote on a near-daily basis to a variety of people in their lives—friends, parents, aunts, business contacts. Though weighty intellectual and serious emotional conveyances certainly had their place in correspondence, the majority of the letters, very common, simply transcribed daily comings and goings, friends run into, assorted contacts made, and schedules clarified. In addition, both women kept extensive journals or diaries. These were often simply filled with transcriptions of quite regular activities, new friends met, professional advancements made, even weather conditions described, unlike the more contemplative use of journals today. Eugenia gave little directives to herself in her entries: "Must paint these sometime," or "must make an effort to get there on time."[16]

Writer that she was, Merle's entries often became drafts of larger pieces (as did James Van Trump's "recorded thoughts, ideas, events . . . [and] experience[s] of the day" transforming into his unique essays[17]). Most writers used journal notations as inspiration, even if they did not provide direct content material. And such viable literary material was taken into consideration when writers of that era developed characters.

An editorial comment on Gladys Schmitt's *Gates of Aulis* stated that Gladys writes of "the dreams, the letters, the casual thoughts of [all] her characters."[18]

Though Esther likely wasn't a journal-keeper, both Eugenia and Merle would recognize familiar utterings in Esther's letters—details of what she was working on, what was ready to be shown to potential buyers, what she needed in terms of supplies and certainly money, and insistent conveyance to her friends that they take a cut of her sales. Both Eugenia and Merle had acted as agents of Esther's art; of course it was correspondence that allowed for that to occur. Both friends knew firsthand the importance of marketing one's work as writer or artist. Helping to market anyone else whose work they respected came naturally to them. As creative artists, they had learned to not expect to be sought out, so it was necessary to reach out to a small public that apparently desired and appreciated original art. Because Esther often found herself in situations not exactly conducive to the self-promotion of her work, her friends stepped in to pick up the slack. Letter writing provided the means and method for that, especially for Merle.

While institutionalized, Esther was comforted both by receiving and being able to write letters first to Jerry and then to Merle. Merle's greatest assistance was marketing Esther's work, representing Esther where Esther could not represent herself. Eugenia's was providing vitally essential companionship over more than two decades. Esther came to see that Merle was doing everything in her power to get her art around, and Jerry was there for her, again and again, to provide a temporary roof over her head, before and after she left the institution. Both women were constantly there for Esther throughout her adult life. Writing made that possible. Surviving writing attests to the fact that, in these two friends, Esther undoubtedly saw a purpose of life common to her own—devotion to freedom within an artistic "way of being." It is the letters and journal entries that paint the pictures here—of Eugenia, undoubtedly Esther's closest friend, and Merle, her dear principal agent.

⑥ ⑥ ⑥

Come September of 1953, Esther began listing 20 E. 14th Street as a primary address, though Jerry's Bedford Street address still showed up from time to time. Merle was trying hard to get another Pittsburgh show together for Esther, in particular at the Carlton House, but apparently this never panned out.[19] Esther continually wrote that she "need[ed] money badly." She was working on finalizing the preparation of her oils for shipment to Merle, in order for possible sale to Balken.

As Esther suspected they would, the New York Department of Welfare wrote to Merle,[20] inquiring about her situation.

Dear Miss Hoyleman,

We are writing in the interest of Miss Esther Phillips whom we have been assisting through this welfare center. She advised us . . . that it will be possible for her paintings to be exhibited in Pittsburgh through your efforts provided that transportation for them can be arranged. Her hope is that they will be sold.

Through our facilities, we have been able to offer Miss Phillips a few days work at a local Recreation Center. However, this does not utilize the maximum of Miss Philips' abilities. Are you able to assist her in securing the kind of employment she desires? What prospects of the profitable sale of these paintings exist?

Finally, should this plan be fully realized, please inform us of the sales which are made and of all monies permitted to Miss Phillips. Perhaps the favorable disposition of these paintings on which she is placing so much emphasis, will enable her to be completely self-supporting. . . .

Merle would not give them any information without first contacting Esther. "They wrote as though they would pay the express charges on them," writes Merle on November 1, and she added that she "[doesn't] want to get mixed up with those Welfare people." Esther, too, preferred to have a sale of a painting itself pay for such charges. She wrote back two days later, agreeing, telling Merle to "just disregard the letter . . . or, later write them and say you are trying to get me a show—but do not know when or where."

At the end of the month, Esther also writes a very long letter detailing a change in Ernie Wright's behavior. She begins, "I've been awfully busy teaching part-time (ceramics) at a center for 'oldsters.' It is connected with welfare. And am busy making jewelry, belts, ashtrays, tiles, (ceramics). . . . "Ernie has become *very viscious* [sic]—I think his mind is getting bad—He has become a frantic homosexual and has tried to break up my friendship with the fellow who lives with him—He has maligned me and always identifies me with viscious remarks he makes in criticism of him—He is a problem—and I want no part of his friendship anymore." Esther went on to say that his recent behavior had lost him several classes, also, "because of his possessive interest in young men. He will try to grab your boyfriend. . . . He likes to align himself with creative people—but in vengeance try[s] to put one in a subservient position. . . . I feel he has a real jealousy for any talented person. . . . If you have a friend (male) he will do everything in his homosexual power to ridicule or malign you to your friend." Esther includes in this letter that she was trying to get hold of Mel Evans for the sake of Merle's writing, but that "he has become unapproachable—He was supposed to buy some more paintings of mine—but never gets down [to the Village]. He married again—Clifton Fadiman's ex-wife!" Esther inquired again about Balken and the oils, and she ends her letter, "am doing exciting oils and carvings. Will try to have a show here next year."

In 1953, Esther lost her most significant patron, John O'Connor. After retiring from the museum, he left the Pittsburgh area entirely. Edward Duff Balken had taken an interest in Esther's oil paintings this year, as the letters attest; he also held onto several of her recent drawings for a short time. Probably because O'Connor was no longer with the museum, Merle's journal notations of marketing the works there would cease. The last notation was a December note regarding Balken and some of the drawings.[21]

Esther taught at the center for the elderly through February of the next year. Immediately after that employment ended, she wrote Merle, "I have no income now but what I have to get from selling my ceramic jewelry." She does write of some good news, though, in that she "expect[ed] to get a break from an exclusive shop (American House)"[22] for her ceramics, which were popular around the Village. She had even added ceramic beads to her repertoire this year. "Sold a nice little amount—mostly through friends! Esther also implored Merle to sell "at any price" whatever she sent her.[23]

The New York Dept. of Welfare wrote again to Harlem Valley Hospital in May 1954, the second time in a three-year period. They were "interested in securing the names and addresses of all relatives listed on [the hospital's] records." They asked, too, if, Esther had "any visits and may we please have their names (sic) and addresses?"[24] Dr. O'Donnell could only respond that, "as [Esther] was discharged from our records on February 3, 1950, it will be necessary for us to receive her signed and witnessed authorization to furnish such information. Upon receipt of this, I shall be pleased to comply with your request."[25] Also in May, Esther exhibited her ceramic jewelry and new beads at the Washington Square Outdoor Show. The Archives of American Art in New York has both a picturesque description of the Show at this time and, with it, an explanation of the show's origins.

> Every spring the sidewalks, stoops, fence posts, and fire escapes surrounding Washington Square blossom forth with brilliant canvasses, wild watercolors, still lifes and sculptures. . . It's the Washington Square Outdoor Art Exhibit, a perennial favorite with Greenwich Village pedestrians. To this colorful clothesline exhibition come multitudes of art lovers in search of a masterpiece hiding in a doorway or hanging on a garden gate. . . .
>
> One spring day during the Depression, a penniless artist picked up his palette and began to paint a picture in one of the streets off the Square. As his canvas took shape, a passerby stopped, admired the work, and offered to buy it on the spot. Afterward, the painter, his pockets lined with silver, together with a group of artist friends, decided to exhibit their work in Washington Square. Later, with the assistance of Gertrude Whitney, the Washington Square Outdoor Art Exhibit opened. . . .[26]

In October of 1954, Esther was of course in the Outdoor Show once again. Ceramics were paying her living, according to what she told Merle, who sent a letter via registered mail to Bedford Street in early October.

She writes Esther, "Will you please let me know if you are well and safe. It has been so long since I heard from you." A few days later, Esther does respond. And she even writes Merle a little later this month, "I've been sick, more or less, all summer with the added strain of getting up more rent (moved downstairs) $50/month. . . . Have own kiln—but work awfully hard. (No more welfare).

November 30, 1954—

Dear Merle,

. . . so busy knocking out my ceramic jewelry and putting them on consignment. . . Have been having the usual financial struggle—only in some sense—worse—some better. Am completely on my own now. Have been for a year—no part-time teaching. Depending entirely upon my ceramic crafts—One important gallery sells my stuff—along with some very famous craftsmen—The gallery is "Talents Unlimited." There are other shops—however—but as yet they don't do the business for me. Am back a whole month in my rent. (medium-sized room).

love, Esther

About this time, many of the cooperatives and minor galleries started to centralize around 4th Street, in addition to 10th Street. Many of the artists were now in a sense truly thrown up against each other, scrambling to be picked up by one of the major galleries as "the successful artist." Jasper Johns and Robert Rauschenberg teamed up to produce the American "Flag" series. Though surely it was refreshing for artists to see peers still striving for other independent work amidst all the Abstract Expressionist commotion, the camaraderie of previous years was not as present. Even those artists who were cashing in on the new attention to American art were beginning to worry about the effects of a rapidly growing art market, created anew on the tails of the Abstract Expressionist success, on their lifestyle and, more importantly, on the quality of their work. With the footing of the artistic community buckling under around her, Esther, like other overlooked artists, surely felt a new insecurity as this closest support system seemed less available. "The increasingly public nature of the activities surrounding the New York School became unendurable," stated Dore Ashton. "Despite the deep-seated suspicion of success on the part of the New York School [rooted in the 1930s], success was [now] insidiously attacking their unity. . . ."[27]

The 1955 flyer for the Washington Square Outdoor Show had advertisements for the multitude of more underground "spaces" for and about artists. Among them was one for "Evans Studio"—that specialized in "handcrafted jewelry in ceramic, enamel and silver." This was actually just one of four spaces that Edward Evans and his new friend Glen Gress were involved in at the time. Evans Studio was on 4th Street; Ed's wife Carol ran it by night and he by day. In addition, Gress and Evans were involved in their Focus Gallery on Greenwich Avenue, a "4th St. Gallery," and a small shop on Patchen Place. And now a shop owner of the Village House on 10th Street, artist and activist Lenore Monleon represented works similar to Glen and Ed's; she was friends with both. Come this time she also met Esther. Her Washington Square Outdoor Show bulletin advertisement, shown right above the one for Evans Studio, described her shop specializing in the "unusual in jewelry/ceramics/painting/sculpture."[28]

Esther's nephew Milton Salomon moved to New York City in January 1955, and he looked his aunt up. Milton was the first family member to actually see Esther since her move from Pittsburgh almost twenty years earlier. He remembered passing on his Aunt Esther's address and circumstance to his Aunt Dorothy and possibly, as well, to his Aunt Molly, Esther's other sister.[29] According to Dorothy, he uttered to them, "If you are able to send some money. . . ."[30] Actually Milton and then Dorothy may have started to get the family to consider helping Esther at this point, in 1955. But Glen Gress would say that, from what they learned from Esther, the family didn't want to help at first, which would have been at this time, when Milton connected with her and informed the family about her. Glen would add with certainty that help indeed *did not come* at this time for her, in 1955.

Years later, Milton reflected on his memories of meeting up with Esther in New York, in a way interestingly akin to both Van Trump's description of Esther—"flippy," but also "exotic . . . with a flowing manner"—and Dorothy Steinberg's—"casual in manner" yet "extravagant."

Milton Salamon recalled her as possessing both "humor and grace." He added that when he saw her, Esther seemed pretty cheerful for the most part. She had friends, "a very tight little group."[31] Esther's circle would have more likely been Ed, Glen, and newer friends, rather than Eugenia and the old crowd. Esther was still in touch with Eugenia and Regis Masson, and likely others from the old circle, just to a lesser extent, as they were more dispersed about the city.

On encountering Esther's "great sense of humor," Milton, who knew of Esther's being institutionalized through Merle, believed that any "old tensions" Esther might have had were apparently gone. Milton said, "Naturally I was distressed by her [economic] situation. I did what I could about it, but it was a way of life for her. She had a grip on life. It was a day-to-day battle, but I got the definite impression that she was out to survive. Life was exciting to her, and New York was a wonderful place to be at that time. There was so much to do that was free—so much entertainment available." Esther introduced Milton to "distinguished poets, writers and artists," giving him a taste of the exciting life she led. She also entertained him with stories of her past, including her life in Pittsburgh. Salomon expressed his sure belief that Esther had a "quite deep friendship" with the head of the art department at Carnegie Tech when she attended there.[32] Likely she was referring to John O'Connor of Carnegie Art Museum, but Esther liked to keep everyone guessing. She enjoyed adding fuel to the fire of speculation over the commingling of lovers and mentors in her life. Because she always threw additional pieces into the mix, she may have been less than clear with Milton on this subject.

Upon coming across his aunt in the Village, Milton Salamon tried to help by selling some paintings, even attempting to arrange a show for her with some connections he had, including his friends Larry Rivers (who was a famous artist), and Charles Egan,[33] who ran an important gallery in the early to mid-1950s and who was very close with the Abstract Expressionists, even a part of their weekly softball games.[34] In the first letter mentioning her nephew's arrival in the city, dated January 5, 1955, Esther tells Merle that she found him "very interesting and sweet." She adds, "I am having a show here—and need whatever watercolors you can send me—Package them and let me know the express charges and Milton will reimburse you." Now, of course, Merle had known Milton Salomon in Pittsburgh, and her last interaction with him was less than pleasant.[35] So Merle responds to Esther's request for watercolors with an emphatic letter on January 14, one that shows, sadly, the mentality of a person who has faced much adversity in her life. Though a paranoiac streak is clearly evident, many eloquent truths are equally expressed in this letter, with its whole range of emotions.

> *. . . This message is to warn you again. When people become* *TOO NICE BEWARE OF THEM. When people tiptoe and slip* *around, YOU WATCH THEM. Honest people are always straightforward and natural. Only cowards and crooks slip around. Don't let any of the subterranean forces fasten barnacles on you . . . All people need to do is drop a tablet in your coffee and you will never know what happened to you. Then they can ram you back in the hospital . . .Watch out that someone—especially if you have a show which will make the price of your work go up . . . It's the money the riff-raff want—They don't care anything about the person who created it—they want the money that's in it. . . .*
>
> *When I was working to get you out of the hospital everyone was a coward. People are scared to death of a (m)-hospital. Afraid the doctors will slam them right in if they even visit patients. It has been done a lot of times. No one I know could go near a m. hospital—or have anything to do with it. Please remember I worked alone on your behalf. I DON'T WANT ANYTHING TO HAPPEN TO YOU NOW. I'm horribly poor. But I am a woman of principle. I stand for what is right.*
>
> *Not one will buy me a typewriter so I can type the book on. It is generally jealousy, carelessness and bold indifference. . . .*
>
> *Artistic people are always gullible and can be made the target for anything. Crooks are aware of this fact.*
>
> *I've been holding on to your drawings so when the price goes up you will have something to fall back on. In short to protect you against the gangsters and crooks. I know what danger is. When will your show be?*
>
> *I will wrap drawings up soon as I can. . . .*

Esther's reply January 19, 1955:

Dearest Merle-

Read your letter—and was very happy to hear from you agree with you wholly on your ideas—but one __must__ find some consolation in this life under this miserable system—I pay $50—a month rent—am always behind—so naturally try every and sundry means of earning a living—So—naturally I want to have as much of my paintings to choose from as possible—and after I choose what I want I could always send back to you what I don't choose immediately—so dear if you could send matted and unmatted ones C.O.D....

It is unknown exactly what potential show Esther was even referring to, as Milton could not recall, (Perhaps one relating to his knowing Charles Egan) but it, too, unfortunately never seemed to happen. On February 1, Esther writes Merle that she could keep the watercolors, after all, for a fall show that Merle was apparently trying to get together somewhere in Pittsburgh.

In the spring of 1955, Esther once again exhibited in the Washington Square Outdoor Show. Works of that year may have included *Waterfront from the Brooklyn Bridge, Williamsburg Bridge*, and *Hickey Cement Company*. In the late summer, she started looking for a loft/studio apartment. But these of course would have demanded more money, as real estate moguls, too, cashed in on the art world boom. They continue to do so unto this day in any area of the city that has become known as particularly artsy (in the 1990s it would be Soho). They would buy the abandoned warehouses that artists had always used to do their work because that work was now getting attention, and then scalp those very same artists by dramatically raising the rents.

On August 6, 1955, Esther writes Merle:

...Did a sample order for [ceramics] Steiner jewelry—They discovered my work in 1 of the stores—asked me to do their sample order—Did it—figured out that I made very little profit—quit—Left them in the lurch—And they are mad!...Had signed a contract with them and broke it. They are trying to tie up my stuff—that resembles the order—But there is nothing they can do—as they didn't entirely hold to their bargain—which was to have supplied me with a loft and large additional kiln.

Am looking for a new place—my place is awful and too expensive. $50—month for a
miserable room. Need a loft—lots more space—etc.…. I see my nephew—wonderful young
man.…

Come September, Esther moved, not to a loft, but to a new apartment at 24 Cornelia Street, right off 4th Street, the hub of the underground. Only two doors down from Glen Gress, it was three rooms—a "place for my kiln and me."[36] Glen would remember it as "very rundown." In a letter to Merle at this time, Esther writes about "lots of money troubles." A small entry that appears in Eugenia's journal for this September (those entries mentioning Esther now appearing very few and far between): "Took Esther to Waldorf Cafeteria for tea and donut. Gave her her skirt." [37]

Colorful people trying to make a creative living were still the composition of the Village, though ever-changing from its earlier days. Passersby would see "women with long hair and no make-up, men wearing sandals or boots and sometimes a beard."[38] Esther's "blowsy look" (Glen's description) was a little less chic than the now-successful artists perhaps, but of the same "scrappy" look that has always defined underground, resourceful bohemians. "Her mode of dress was very European—peasant-like, unintentionally. She'd wear three or four skirts at one time, several blouses and a couple sweaters because sometimes she didn't have coats. She originated the layered look for warmth—a very distinctive way of dressing." (She, or all artists) Glen also remembered Esther as "a plump woman, not obese or heavy—softik."

During that fascinating interview where James Van Trump had, with his reflections, brought to life a young Esther Phillips, he particularly remarked on the way she was dressed in a photo from her New York years in an article he was skimming. It was a photo of Esther and two unidentified men on a Village street corner. Brought up with an evident fondness in his own heart for that kind of look, and of course lifestyle, Jamie remarked, "That would be [her type of dress]. I think that was the way she really liked to live. And that would be her type of crowd—the guy with the beret and scarf. . . ."

Chapter Eighteen

"THAT SITUATION INDELIBLY IN OUR MEMORY"[1]

"We're raking up a lot of memories that I had buried."[2] Sitting in the office of the Laurel Highlands Regional Theatre, situated in an old church off Butler Street in Pittsburgh's Lawrenceville neighborhood, Edward Kinchley Evans is recalling the days when he and his partner Glen Gress lived and worked in New York City, creating alongside Esther Phillips and others. The two men were not from Pittsburgh; they moved first to north central Pennsylvania in 1969, when they decided to leave New York for a quieter environment. There Glen focused on theatre work and the men stayed about nine years, before moving to Savannah, Ed's hometown, then back to New York City for a bit. In the early 1980s, they moved to Pittsburgh to live and work in the arts; about ten years later they decided to purchase a beautiful old home once owned by the Sonny Von Bulew family, in Emlenton, sixty miles north of Pittsburgh. They still commuted to their work in the city, having come upon this church years back. They thought it was the ideal spot upon which to build a theatre company. It was the focus of their work life, with Glen as director and Ed as screenplay writer.

Glen is rehearsing in the other room with his company, a core group of devoted, mostly underground theatre artists, acting pupils of Glen and friends of both his and Ed's. Evans is leafing through pictures of Esther's watercolors, and in his southern drawl, he answers questions and pours forth information about "dear 'Estha.'"

We knew her in the years from about 1950 to 1969. The three of us painted. Esther was a wonderful free spirit, very loving. Life was always an adventure for her. We painted a lot—the Ships's Graveyard in Staten Island. We'd three trek over early in the morning, and paint and come home or we'd go to Coney Island and paint there. We'd go down in the south part of the Village, over toward the Hudson River where there's a lot of warehouses and on Saturdays, of course, [they were] all empty. [These would be the spaces semi-converted into living spaces, cold-water flats, and rented out by slumlords capitalizing on the art boom]. We'd paint a lot there and in Central Park, and if possible if we could loop somebody in to buying a painting we'd do it 'cause it was very desperate [in those] days. The subway was 5 cents. It was very bad times money wise for everyone. . . .

Eddie, as he is known to friends, sits intent at a table in this office, where he also manages the business end of the theatre while Glen holds acting classes and directs productions. Here theatre-goers, men and women alike, are greeted warmly with "Hi, Love," as Ed stands behind the Dutch door taking money and dispensing tickets for the productions at The Acting Company, as the theatre company became officially known in more recent years. The vision of the pipe, so positioned in one hand or between that and the full white beard that trails down his chest, and the stories he tells as he stands at this doorway are as much a picture of the greeting, and little forgotten by all who visit the theatre. When the shows are finally up and running, with most of the frenetic preparatory activity completed, Ed is usually found napping on the couch to our left in this office, resting up before the hour's ride home to Emlenton at the end of the night.

He continues his thoughtful reflections, the utterance "heartbreaking" surfacing much throughout, intertwining as a transition from part to part.

The main struggle as an artist was to stay alive. Esther had given us a great deal of her work [to be stored at our four gallery spaces]. It was wonderfully vibrant. She was a true artist. A lot of people paint but Esther was a genuine American artist. She had some friend in Virginia, someone who seemingly had an art gallery, who'd occasionally send her a check. Esther was bitter. Her sister—seemingly very willingly—would not help her, and times were getting so desperate for her. Esther stayed with friends for a while. She [usually] had no place. Later, her sister was sending her a little money—for rent and a little sustenance. But the crime was that someone . . . [Ed, though wistful throughout, fully chokes up only here, and takes a moment before continuing] . . . couldn't have helped her sooner. It was heartbreaking and Glen and I helped as much as we could but it was desperate times for all of us . . . and here we have the wealthiest city and it pushes our artists to the streets.

Tall and thin, with long white hair and delicate features almost obscured by this and the matching beard, Ed sits back just a moment, now being filled in on the details of Esther's life before he ever knew her, before she ever left this, her city of Pittsburgh, for New York. He listens, puffing slowly on the pipe that is ever with him and leaves a lingering aromatic presence on the air. He absorbs the information with weighted measure, and then continues, weaving topic to topic, providing information on all that he remembers of Esther, memories both of his times with her, and information on the rest of her life that she shared with him.

I did know that Esther went to school with Gladys Schmitt and that her novel *The Gates of Aulis* is about Esther. I never read it, but according to Esther . . . The fact that we [as artists] could do whatever we wanted to do . . . [meant so much to him, Esther and the others]. She had a wonderful sense of humor—a real nice human being. We had opened a small shop on Patchen Place, it was a little courtyard of studio apartments. The tenants were Djuna Barnes, e.e. cummings, writers from the '20s, Steichen. The people of those days weren't as impressed with themselves as the people today tend to promote themselves. They were much more accessible to talk to and be around. It was a very accessible time. **Nobody had any money**, but it was a really wonderful time to be in New York. . . .

Esther and I—we'd get annoyed with Glen. Because invariably we three'd be painting a scene and somebody would come along and buy his, and Esther and I would be left still holding our canvasses. It used to tick the both of us off because we could have used the money as well as Glen!

I don't know—it seems like we live in so many different worlds . . . but during that period if you were an artist, that's what you were. You didn't sell shoes, you just painted, and if you didn't make a living at it, that's because people bought more shoes than they did paintings. . . .

Esther was always fanatically clean, her clothes, her body. Her painting things, her canvasses and such, she never took too great a care of. I had Ralph Mayer as one of my art teachers at Columbia, and he said that your work is only as good as your materials. I was always a little amazed at Esther 'cause she didn't care what she painted on, just as long as she painted and got it down.

Eddie has now picked up the same articles and accompanying photos that Van Trump saw, written during that time a posthumous show of her work was held in 1991 in Pittsburgh.[3] Details of her later years are verbally shared with him, as he begins to dive into the material he holds, but a ringing phone now interrupts our conversation. He excuses himself to rise and answer the brief call, as clamor from the hall makes its way in the office. Glen and actors are on break. After thirty seconds, an invigorated-looking Glen walks in to enjoy a cup of coffee and share some memories, while Ed takes his seat once again, still interested in the article and gazing at photos of Esther. Though he certainly enjoyed seeing shots of Esther as a young woman artist in Pittsburgh, photos of the New York years, of images of his dear friend that he better recognized most gladdened Ed. "Oh—oh, yes, there's Esther," says a pleased

Ed with a lilt to his voice. While it's being mentioned to Ed at this point that some of this material can remain for both he and Glen to read and look at later, Ed becomes transfixed on something. Completely oblivious to all conversation in the room, Ed murmurs first to himself, "Ha," then in a delighted, more vocal exclamation to Glen, who's now over his shoulder—"That's you and I, and Esther, in this photo."

A disbelieving Glen utters, "Where?"—and then, with three times the volume—"Oh it is!" Only now does Eddie definitively state, for all to hear, "That's me and there's Glen," as he points, with the glee of a child, his two fingers at the two men photographed on the Village street corner with Esther. (Fig. 25) "And look at this"—Glen begins to get further excited, laughing, while glancing down at words describing a Village ceramic shop and Esther Phillips, this woman he knew so well, yet hadn't thought about

FIG. 25   Ed Evans, Glen Gress, and Esther Phillips, circa 1955.

for years. He looks up and utters solely, "She was an absolutely fascinating woman." Still leafing through photos of her art, Ed, overwhelmed, murmurs again and again to himself, "Well I'll be damned. . . ."

Glen and Ed, though knowing Esther very well in the 1950s, would lose touch with her after the late 1960s. They had not heard word of her again until now, as they both sat rapt by the details of her life both before and after knowing them—ironically enough, in the city that is their adopted home only now, but the city of her birthplace. They provide some mutual remembrance before Glen has to return to rehearsal, including one that Eddie begins, about "two dear sisters who owned an art supply store and let her swipe stuff." "All the time," amusingly adds Glen, to Ed's statement. He prepares to exit as Ed continues to talk of this period 40 years long behind him. "It seems we spent all of our time together. It was much like a family." It was fast becoming obvious that Glen and Ed, come the mid 1950s, had provided for Esther what Eugenia's circle had in the 1930s. What all her close friends provided at various times in her life, even if they were not in close proximity—but what had been lacking from her real family.

Ed continues, "The three of us would trek over very early on Sunday morning [to the Staten Island's Ship's Graveyard]. Our main problem was getting ten cents to get over and back on the ferry, and then we'd get a donut and coffee. We'd try to gather 50 cents every day. Occasionally we'd sell a painting for $10 each. I remember once when someone traded a painting with one of us for one of those paintings of the rusted hulks. (Color Plate 26) Glen, who had by now left but was back again in the office to retrieve something from the desk, adds to this, "she was moving so constantly at the time. We would run into her and make plans to go painting or something. . . . We'd plan a day or two at a time and we'd meet somewhere. We'd have no way of getting in touch with her to cancel. We didn't know quite where she was and she didn't have a phone." Says Ed, "Esther was never in one location too long. She moved and camped out—sometimes with friends."

"There was an elderly man we'd meet on Coney Island, a primitive [painter]," states Ed. "His name was Besty Davis." He then explains, "A big uptown gallery spotted him and then immediately took him under wing." Memories of the Staten Island trips especially seemed to be happy ones for Ed as he recalled that activity that seemed to so bond the friendship between himself, Glen and Esther, whom he continuously referred to as "a wonderful free spirit, very loving, a lovely woman." Ed faintly recalls "Jerry," as Glen would, too, later—"the woman friend whom Esther stayed with occasionally off and on for several weeks 'til she'd find another place." As they understood it, Esther could stay with her "for only a couple weeks at a time." Concludes Eddie, "Artists are very hard to live with. They're just a breed apart. And Esther was a bit of a maverick even in that [artist's] world." Both Glen and Ed had thought Esther "too proud for welfare" as a solution to her housing problem, though of course she reluctantly went on relief several times in her life.

Esther frequented the automats in the 1950s with Glen and Ed, just as she had, and likely still did from time to time, with Eugenia and some of the older circle of friends. Ed describes, "A lot of us would go— they had slot machines where you paid . . . there were rows and rows of cubicles. And an island in the middle that dispensed change. Ten cents or 25 cents for a pot pie or cheese sandwich. The food was actually good and very cheap. They were open all night—and warm. A lot of writers, artists, musicians . . ." and again he adds, "like family." He especially remembers the one at 6th Avenue between 41st and 42nd Street. "Often, we'd wait 'til someone came in with money—everyone shared. . . . When an artist had money, he was buying art supplies. It's hard for those with a 9 to 5 lifestyle to understand that concept."

Ed, who says Esther "turned out a lot of stuff," remembers her work as "very bold, very rich. European—in the school of Andre Derain." (One of Esther's youthful favorites). Ed, and later Glen as well, even recall Esther's touting around with her some review from supposedly a national arts magazine of years earlier that also compared her work to the French painter. She always had it with her, almost as substantiation of her artistic worth (Or perhaps it was a local review, though no longer preserved to this day, of her 1947 Pittsburgh Arts and Craft Center show). Ed and Esther continued to show their work at the Washington Square Outdoor show, while Glen, though involved with his and Ed's gallery spaces, was doing acting work about the city. Of those shows of the mid 1950s, Ed recalls, "so many people came. Some very bad artists." In addition to the realization that less-fine work was selling better, Ed confirms that the very logistics of having a show outdoors also prompted artists to sometimes bring less quality work. "Because of inclement weather, it was much easier to break out a card table with ceramics than to bring a dozen paintings and hang them . . . [and] because you'd have to find a house with a fence." (Fence spikes seemed to serve much creative purpose in the Village.) Eddie continues, "It was a much safer investment [to display plaques and jewelry]." Ed further stresses that the artists always had one or two paintings along with them, anyway, their 'real art' to show to others like themselves that knew the difference—the other fine artists, collectors and dealers going by.

Ed laments that Greenwich Village in general was "a wonderful place for artists to live, but only tourists visited." By the mid 1950s, not only the Abstract Expressionists were popular, but also the Beat Poet movement was taking off. There indeed was tremendous interest from the mainstream public in witnessing all these odd artists—the famed in the taverns and the starving in the streets, but there just wasn't genuine understanding of the *work* of artists, most of whom were still "starving." Confirms Ed, "It wasn't until back in the late '40s that average Americans were even aware of art. . . ." He details, "From Boise, Idaho, people would now come to buy art. They wanted it to be from Greenwich Village but wanted to be sure it had the Woolworth stamp of approval."

Though artists like Esther and Ed put out some commercial work at the outdoor shows in order to pay the rent, they and their peers would never mistake that for one's best work. Ed offers that he, Glen and Esther had a friend named Margaret Leighton, whom Ed describes as "one of the first to paint what I call 'American French' scenes—little houses with little window boxes, etc. And sure enough, she got commissions from hotels and all because the works started being lithographed. Margaret was always trying to get Esther and I to be a little bit more commercial in our art but it wasn't our way. . . ." It was nearing 9:30 P.M.; Eddie had been talking almost two hours now. The conversation wrapped up, to be continued at another time. . . .

Glen was receptive to the idea of a meeting to discuss any specific memories he alone held of Esther, to elaborate, if possible, on Ed's recollections. Conversation was scheduled before an evening's rehearsal, again at the theatre, this time in the performing space, which was the converted old church hall itself. Not a hall, really, but a small, sacred space, now theatre-in-the-round. The pews remained, set up with little pillows for the comfort of patrons, and arranged in three sections that looked toward an interior once occupied by minister, now filled with set pieces. Glen sat down to talk, cigarette in hand, with other arm draped over the back of the hardback bench. He was relaxed, comfortable, before the night's work with the company was to begin in about an hour's time.

> Ed knew her before I met him . . . I knew her from about 1954 on . . . I wouldn't have known her on Bedford Street. . . . At one point we had about one hundred of her paintings . . . and then she'd come and take them. We stored work for her all the time and I'm sure we weren't the only ones! . . . Some landlords would let her stay awhile—some on the basis of painting an apartment, fix[ing] up a place and they'd give her free rent for three months, and she'd never paint the place and disappear. The people she stayed with I assumed were gentleman friends—that she had short-term things with. And there was some woman friend she'd stay with occasionally off and on for several weeks 'til she'd find another place. I'm sure Esther probably would have been difficult as a house mate. Her hours were extremely irregular.
>
> She was quite feisty, had a temper on her. She read me the book once—when we opened our gallery. Esther had been painting for years and I had no formal training. . . . I started painting—both she and Ed got pissed—the first paintings that sold were mine. Esther expressed 'how dare you put your paintings up for sale. You had no training. No experience.' For an hour

and a half she was angry at me. She didn't speak to me for about six months. She was really pissed mine sold rather than hers.

Glen remembers Esther's paintings as extremely interesting—"over the edge, just a bit . . . as if there were not a real cool rationale behind them. Instead a different vision was behind the paintings. They were somehow just 'off.'" Glen also comments on the difference between the work, and philosophy of art, of Esther and Margaret Leighton. "Esther and Margaret had a strange relationship. Esther really resented Margaret because she was very successful. Yet Esther was still a friend of both Margaret and her husband. Margaret would buy some of Esther's paintings and they would get into these horrendous discussions because Margaret would say, 'Esther, if you'd paint what people wanted to buy . . . but instead you insist on painting using these garish colors, etc.' Margaret and Esther were very close, and they were in contact a lot."

Glen continues describing at length what he remembers of this woman friend whom, it was evident, he loved as dearly as Ed did. As Ed, Glen strung together memories of both significant qualities of her character and interesting anecdotes, to conveniently provide a rather full picture of Esther's life around this time in the mid 1950s.

> She was quite erratic. Basically happy-go-lucky. If she had ten dollars, within ten minutes it'd be gone. She'd go to a coffee shop and buy herself and others coffee. Esther made most of her money on the [Washington Square] Outdoor shows, and would then try to eke it out, but she was not very successful.
>
> In attempting to sell her work, she could be quite aggressive. It probably hurt her because sometimes she would say too much—be a little too pushy. It'd scare people off. She'd say [to us] 'Well, I just saw so-and-so, I've been there and they said they'll come see my studio. . . .' And she did that. But the problem was, by the time the people came, she had moved.

Glen confirmed that Hans Hoffman indeed knew Esther and her work. Esther had even told her niece that an agent of Hoffman had been sent, by him, to purchase one of her works at the Outdoor show. Of that, Glen says, "It's quite possible. A lot of the dealers *would* go scouting there." With Glenn's company now slowly, a bit at a time, starting to file in the performance space, as it was close to their rehearsal's starting time, Gress concludes his exclusive memories of Esther by relaying the following anecdote of Esther and Hans Hofmann:

> Hofmann she did know. I remember he came into evans studio at one point. Even though that was not an art gallery, to try and help Esther out we'd try to have some of her paintings in there. Occasionally, we'd sell some; also, that's how we [came to have some of her work]. She'd need money and we'd give $25 or so to help her out.
>
> Hans Hofmann came in and was looking. I was surprised he knew the work. I didn't know who [he] was at the time and he said, "Oh, that's Esther Phillips work—do you carry her work regularly?' And I said, 'Well, we usually have several of her things in—she's a friend. She's a Village person.' He said, 'Well, when you see her next, tell her that Hans Hofmann stopped in and saw her painting.'
>
> Esther was, as a lot of artists tend to be, somewhat antagonistic toward successful artists. So, I have to say that in her comments to me about him, when I told her that, she was not too gracious. Kind of sarcastic. 'Well, that's real nice of him. Why didn't he buy the damn thing?'. . .

"Sometimes artists create their own history," spoke Glen. There were definitely aspects of Esther's life that she retold to others only after flowering them up a bit. Perhaps this was simply to add spice, or in some cases, to protect some measure of dignity (But, likely with Esther, more the former). This certainly goes for some of what she shared with Glen and Ed, of course, and only in their now discovering the truths behind bits and pieces of her life, as this dear friend had surfaced again for them, did the two men begin to realize this as well. Though Glen and Ed had always been aware of Esther's jocular way, and certainly kept this in mind when receiving information from her, little details that she told them remained the truth for them until this spring of 1993, decades later, as they mused, during the course of three interviews, over her, and their, life.

Smaller details first. Esther had prevalently remarked about one sister, in particular, to Glen and Ed. This would be Dorothy, still the "treasurer of the family," and, Esther knew, the main source of help if any were to come to her in New York City come the mid 1950s. (A change in Esther had evolved over time. She had slowly shed any former misgivings about accepting some forms of help. In this case—money from the family who not only disagreed with her life choices but whom never had visited her while institutionalized.) Glen and Ed definitely recall, without a doubt, Esther's saying that this one sister, who "just would not help," resided in Philadelphia, not Pittsburgh. (So they never associated their new home, Pittsburgh, with their old New York friend, until now.) This sister, they were also led to believe, was apparently rather wealthy, "but seemingly very disapproving of Esther's lifestyle." Perhaps because at the time Pittsburgh still retained its "smoky city" image, and because she may have wanted to strengthen her bitterness, Esther stretched the truth as to where her sister resided and exactly how much money she actually had. "Esther," remarks Glen, with a smile, of this situation, "was just glossing the lily."

"The friend from Virginia, who owned an art gallery," was Merle Hoyleman, or so Glen and Ed thought. For when asked of her name, both recalled it and attached it to this person. They remember Esther bringing it up from time to time, but she never revealed all that much of any of her other circle of friends. Glen and Ed even assumed that Merle was a man. The truth that does remain, of course, is that this person *did* send her a check occasionally.

Esther had also been, amusingly, a little less than honest about some incidents in her love life. She certainly mentioned Gladys Schmitt to Glen and Ed, playing up that *The Gates of Aulis* was about herself. Though John O'Connor again comes to mind, Esther's first mentor in

Pittsburgh, the interior decorator Harold Schwartz, especially fits the bill of the older, influential gentleman moving within Pittsburgh art circles and somehow connected with the young artist Esther—or Ellie, that is. Though of course there was no intimacy between Esther and Harold, it is clear that Schwartz nevertheless became the model of a lover in the tallest tale that she told to Glen and Ed—which had its beginnings in her early love life and ended with her institutionalization.

Though both men felt that Esther wasn't involved in any major love relationship the period that they knew her, she "gave every indication that she at least once did. That part of her life was always very secret. She was a very lusty lady," says Glen. "She did constantly have men after her." Ed would add that Esther was "tremendously sensual, very earthy in her sexuality . . . it just oozed, naturally, from her." He'd also recall flirtation, her at times "blinking those eyes" at men. Though hospital records suggest that Esther had strong homosexual tendencies, Glen and Ed didn't see that in her. "I don't think she was a lesbian at all—she didn't give any indication," recalls Glen. "She resented men because they had all the power, but that didn't stop her from lusting after them. She was a very lusty old lady."

Now, to others that perhaps knew her in the days of the earlier Village, Esther may have been more truthful about what led to her institutionalization. However, to Glen and Ed, the composition of this segment of her life was painted a little differently. According to what Esther confided in Ed, and he related to Glen, Esther was married at a time, to an interior decorator, who became very wealthy and moved to Washington, D.C. (Turns out, Schwartz did later leave Pittsburgh and became a very wealthy and renowned decorator out of New York City, according to Van Trump and Sybil Grucci, who read mention of him in the New York Times. Esther would no doubt have known of this success, though she didn't ever seem to connect with him again. But charmingly, she made out that the success really was had in Washington.) Glen even got the impression that Esther lived in D.C. for a time with her impressive husband. And, adds Eddie, due to this marriage, of course, Esther was very wealthy at this one point in her life. Just a desire, surely, on Esther's part, to have lived such a life of ease.

Esther's "husband," too, while in Pittsburgh, was also associated with the Carnegie Museum, as they understood. All an exotic blend of details straight out of *Aulis* and her very real association with Schwartz. And perhaps some hinting at her intriguing connection with Edward Duff Balkan and John O'Connor, both of the Carnegie. Though really either of these two married men could have played the part as lover, there has been nothing factually to indicate any more intimate a relationship by them with Esther other than that interest in her painting, and care for her well-being.

Well, Esther's story followed along the lines that, once married, she found out that her husband was a homosexual, and they divorced. "Esther told us that the news of the husband "tipped the scales" and she ended up in an institution," said Ed. "It wasn't an acceptance thing [about homosexuality]," for Esther, adds Glen, "it was just based on her own emotional needs." A juicy story, all mythologized by Esther, but including hints to the fact that her institutionalization did come on the heels of a less-than-stable intimate relationship. For all in all, there was indeed no marriage in Esther's life—only many loves.

Because Ernie Wright, her homosexual friend, became suspicious and vengeful of Esther's other homosexual friends, as she detailed in that engaging letter to Merle, she may have been inspired to weave a tale around this theme. Of course, Schwartz's being homosexual makes him the old stand-by. Nevertheless, Esther created a more compelling context in which to reflect her institution stay—not, of course, that the truthful context of mitigating factors surrounding her breakdown were any less interesting. She just likely considered her constructed events more glamorous, however, to tell her two friends, than the very real bottom line that life as an artist had gotten to her and brought her down temporarily. Perhaps, too, Esther couldn't quite pinpoint what her inward struggle of those years was over. Glen had actually offered:

She never talked to me about [her institution experience] at all—talked to Ed more. The only thing I knew about it was some of her paintings. Women in the showers . . . I remember . . . One done from recollection of when she was in the institution. [This actually was done in the institution, little did Glen realize.]

Glen remarks that "it bothered Esther a great deal [that some] were making names for themselves and [she wasn't]." Esther mingled aplenty with those who would hit success, but "ultimately, because her work was not in line with their vision, her work would not have been shown [at the major galleries opening up]." Ed remembers that Esther had taken her work to artists Milton Avery and Robert Motherwell, both who were becoming famous. She was furious at them for dismissing her paintings. "She ripped for two hours about these two men afterward." Come the success of a handful, literally, of the thousands of New York City artists in the 1950s, Esther surely questioned why, come then, even within the artistic circles, she may not have been taken as seriously as an artist as before. (Of course, other artists were stuck with this question as well.) Her work was still uniquely her own style—with a pseudo-primitive quality at a time when others were delving en masse into a different abstract. "Poor Esther, says Ed, "because of her style of painting, and the way she worked . . . [she was overlooked]. But she was wonderfully vibrant, a true artist." He repeats himself from an earlier meeting, "A lot of people paint but Esther was a genuine American artist. She was truly led by what she saw and felt. In her work she responded totally to her own emotions, without the concept of whether that was marketable."

Both Glen and Ed fondly remember Esther as having enjoyed her life, despite difficulties. They had both known that it had been a struggle for her. Ed explains that all creative people exulted in being able to do whatever they wanted to do, yet there seemed a realization by all that such a life might age you beyond your years. When asked if Esther might have been "crazy," Ed answers, "Oh no . . . She was a true . . . [pause] . . . just a normal artist. Really a genuinely free-spirited woman. Unfortunately, after a while the pangs of reality finally brought her down." Ed concludes, "Esther knew who she was an artist and somehow couldn't understand why the mass public couldn't receive her as such."

Everybody knew everybody else in the Village and it was a very comfortable place to be . . . and it was a very safe city. There was no crime, you were not bothered on the streets—even in the late hours of the night. This was before the dope scene. But with the new coffeehouses springing up, later came the flower children. Until that time, all liquor stores and bars in New York were controlled by the mafia and they suddenly found that the young crowd was going to coffeehouses instead of bars. So they tried several unsuccessful ways to shut the coffeehouses down; but then marijuana came in. That was their clue—they started introducing dope into the coffeehouses. At that point on, New York went belly up.

—Ed Evans

Chapter Nineteen

"A LITTLE TIRED OF IT ALL"[1]

Once, while drinking our beers in a booth of the San Remo . . .
our privacy was suddenly invaded by a wild man who looked
like a bum, waving sheets of paper at us with poems he had
written. He wanted to sell them, for either a dime or a quarter
apiece (the price was negotiable). We got rid of him as quickly
as possible and laughed as he left. A long-haired woman on her
way back from the bar saw us laughing and said reproachfully,
"That's Bodenheim."

"Bodenheim? . . . Who the hell's Bodenheim?" [we said] as the
poor man went to other tables and booths . . . I later learned, to
my shame, that the man we were mocking had been a well-
known poet in the twenties. I liked to think justice triumphed . . .
that serious artists who didn't sell out would somehow be rewarded or saved.

—Dan Wakefield, *New York in the Fifties*[2]

*M*ax Bodenheim was actually described in more than a couple
books that tell of the Village of the first half of this century, he as
infamous in later decades for roaming the bars and selling once-valu-
able poems on thin paper as when he recited poetry in a more self-
respecting fashion in earlier times. Gress and Evans recall being out
with Esther in the 1950s and seeing the very incident that Wakefield
recounted being tragicomically replayed over and over. Only when

Esther "regaled" them of the '30s and '40s did they, for the first time, happen to learn of this man's past—he ever-bedecked with suit and feathered hat, the beau of many flappers, with the audience and critics of his writings (and needless to say the content matter as well) being a genuinely interested coterie about him.[3] "Max Bodenheim had been a very chic poet [back then in earlier decades] but by the time we knew him," says Ed, "he was reduced to what we call a street person and he'd mimeograph his little poems—there was no xerox back then—on cheap paper and sell them at ten cents each."

Equally memorable to all Villagers as to what his life once was and had become, was the death of Max Bodenheim, and Esther was sure to provide her niece with the accurate, ugly details. Further unique specifics of the death come together through both Glen and Ed's account and that of Lenore Monleon. Max's unfortunate end came when he was murdered in the 1950s by a drug addict who was fooling around with his girlfriend. This man knifed both the woman and Max, killing them both. Glen and Ed indeed remember Esther as the bearer of that tragic news. She came into their studio, having just learned it from Lenore Monleon, who had been called upon to identify the bodies.[4]

⑥ ⑥ ⑥

Art dealer Leo Castelli soon caused a stir with the opening of his new gallery in Manhattan. Early on, he gave a solo show to Jasper Johns, from which the New York's Museum of Modern Art bought some works. The big-time New York galleries had begun to focus only on the few artists who floated to the top and were thus able to leave behind the less-than-desirable living conditions of the typical artist in the Village. So left behind were genuinely talented artists overlooked by society, by the established connoisseurs of art (galleries, museums, and collectors), and even, at times, by some of the newly-famed, be it inadvertent or deliberate. Since the 1920s the morale of the mass of Village artists might have been extremely low, save for the fact that, despite problems, some old and some new, the Village was still the most free and colorful place to be in this country. The artists knew it. But even the first-famed saw their possible imminent demise, as the public assiduously next focused on Jasper Johns and Robert Rauschenberg, then others. . . . Eventually come the mid fifties, some of the dis-affected famed and those around them "declared their independence from all institutionalized concepts of the artist's role in society. By becoming models of self-motivated individuals, who were well able to sustain their creative course over long periods of time, even without affirmation from society at large, the artists were better able to resist the blandishments of a benign and neutralizing cultural establishment. . . . In the downtown gatherings the representatives of the old bohemian tradition still called the tune," despite the youthful new arrivals.[5]

In the late 1940s and early 1950s average Americans gained their awareness of art from the *Life* articles and subsequent media stories. The magazine had endorsed a select few American artists and the so-called school they represented. America devoured them as it would any pop frenzy, and then spit them back out again. Jackson Pollock commented, "They put you up so that they can cut you down."[6] By the late 1950s, "when success began to make its inroads," according to art critic John Gruen, "the atmosphere became wild, ebullient, and circus-like. Liquor drowned the participants at a heady round of parties, exhibition openings and gatherings in East Hampton during the summer"[7] (where the more successful artist retreated). Jackson Pollock died in 1956, at the age of 44, from a car crash. His life had become increasingly chaotic and he increasingly self-destructive. Franz Kline, too, died fairly young, by the late 1960s.

Without truly realizing what art, or good art, might be, and certainly uninformed and disinterested in the artistic life process, America had looked to what was offered on a platter to them. They didn't want to have to think about creativity, or worse yet, critically examine the conditions and constraints under which creative people usually live. Americans hadn't really thought about fine art at all, until it had recently become hip to recognize the few famous names out of New York City. The inherent irony is that some forms of culture mass society consumes readily, and steadily, as "entertainment," with no thought as to what constitutes quality and worthiness, genuine fine art. Americans devour Hollywood movies, yet few know of the "art films" out there, created by extremely hardworking, independent filmmakers whose work is dedicated to fine craft. It's a sad fact that the less daring creative work gets the public's attention because it easily fits in with the dining room color scheme, or is heard on MTV. Truly, the work of the artist, especially the fine artist, is disregarded in this society. Those few duly recognized for some quality work, such as the Abstract Expressionists, were processed through a thinly disguised "artworld-friendly" media mill that parallels the bourgeois mentality of any corporate beaurocracy.

Society dissuades people from distinguishing the good from the bad, the quality from the quantity of consumerism. Society pressures any artist, musician, or otherwise creative individual to not dare to be different in any way from the mainstream norm—whatever that be at the time. Society instead wants only what is easily understandable, what fits popular conceptions of what is "pretty" or pleasing or "pop." Unique voices of millions of creative souls are squelched early, or dismissed later, if ever personally cultivated and nurtured along by an interested teacher, mentor, or family member. If fate and talent should have it that one or a few individuals stay with their art, then rise to the top, if the timing is socially right, those individuals usually become media darlings, flightily picked up by the mainstream, and, beaten to death, "made hip." The Abstract Expressionist movement was a worthy one. Like most movements, an extreme response by society to it, in addition to artists reveling in once-unfamiliar celebrity and money, tainted the harvest. Many artists, Esther certainly included, felt frustration and disgust at the ridiculous ability of the mass public to gobble up mass-produced doctor's office art, yet to not even consider, or worse yet deride out of their own simple-mindedness, original creativity. This frustration tugged at Esther, causing her the same self-doubt that plagues even the most confident, radical, "screw the establishment" artist to this day.

⑥ ⑥ ⑥

Esther kept busy with the Outdoor Shows in both spring and fall of 1956. According to archive records, at least in the spring, she was still exhibiting crafts, ceramics, and jewelry. Back in Pittsburgh, Merle had arranged, just the previous winter, a show of Esther's work at the Guild Theatre in Pittsburgh's Squirrel Hill. (Merle had noted in her journal in March that there were "many comments and inquiries of the work," and that she'd later like to see new works of Esther's hung there as well.) As in the last letter and numerous preceding, Esther amusingly writes, "if you have any sales will be happy to receive $." She again asks that Merle tell more of what is going on in her life.[8]

Around this time, Esther also took to displaying her wares on the street when the Outdoor Show wasn't going on. As a street vendor, she'd set up an aluminum folding table and have a shopping cart by her side, filled with ceramic figures, jewelry, and belts, often in front of Our Lady of Pompeii Church on Bleecker Street. At times, Ed's young daughter would be by her side, assisting. Milton Salamon fondly recalled this scene. "She did quick studies—figures in ceramics—She'd bring them out and have them all lined up." Sold off of her table for 25 cents, perhaps $1, "these small figures were her bread and butter, not her paintings."[9]

FIG. 26

FIG. 27

But Esther of course always had, as Ed mentioned, a few paintings with her, less now of the institution works than more recent ones. Megan Shay later described Esther's art at this time. "Some time after she returned to New York, a sort of explosion occurred in her work. She briefly began using a very watery method of painting, so that a loose, scattered effect was achieved; this is especially evident in some paintings that survive from the late 1950s." Shay added, "Right on the tails of this body of work, Phillips went back to sketching her environment, only this time the paintings were crowded, frenetic, color-packed cityscapes fraught with myriad lines suggesting New York's industrial lower East Side. Materials ranged from bright, pure-pigmented watercolors to murky impastos. But the work was always busy, intense and uncomfortable."[10]

The glimpse of Esther as street vendor, and of Esther in the automats with friends, stood out vividly in Milton Salamon's memory. He recalled the very "strange" activity in the automats and cafeterias, the precariousness surrounding the friends' ordering food and then having to pay for it. He observed their creative use of the condiments available, eating ketchup on crackers, and using tea bags over and over again. They'd sit there for hours talking—and waiting until one of their friends came in to bail them out, often after selling a painting outside on the sidewalk. Said Milton, "They semi-starved together."[11]

The antics here described by Milton, also echoing Ed's memories, were age-old, common to most artists of the Village. Elaine deKooning commented on such tricks to stay fed before success came to her and her close circle. "Sugar bowls from the automats began to appear in artists' studios . . . a major source of energy in diets that were skimpy."[12] Joe Gould had made tomato soup out of the ketchup and hot water ordered for tea. Said Gould at the time, apt spokesman for all bohemians, "I make a practice to eat all I can get. It's the only grub I know of that's free of charge." He added, "When I'm hungry, I don't have any self-respect."[13] He frankly articulated what the other artists, including Esther, would certainly have felt, if not said. She surely continually found herself trying to feel better about her position as artist only to be minimized by the degrading, yet equally hilarious, situations she and her friends found themselves in.

It was at this time that the two sisters Glen and Ed referred to allowed Esther to steal art supplies from their store. Esther's own sense of self-respect had long evaporated as she was competing with the forces of nature more and more just to conduct her artistic affairs. At least within the Village community, empathy for the struggling creative artists set an atmosphere of acceptance of their antics as they tried to stay alive. For, as Wakefield related in *New York in the Fifties*, "There's a family feeling [within the Village] . . . a sense of closeness with neighbors and friends and even business people that comes from the feeling you are part of a common enterprise, a shared vision of the value of art and literature, of music and drama, of individuality and personal freedom."[14]

Esther had been enjoying the past seven years on her own since being released from the institution. She had experienced, in fact, many happy times in the 1950s, especially those spent with Glen and Ed. With these two good friends, she lived the bohemian life of a middle-aged artist. Even though she was no longer young, she associated with those decades younger than she was, and kept a wide circle about her who shared a similar artistically focused life. But the torment felt inside because her life as an artist took her down such a twisted path, full of obstacles that seemed not to have to be there, never entirely left Esther.

"We were much like family . . ." echoed Ed over and over, "and then the times started to change. . . ."

Perhaps Esther was now coming to the conclusion that the world can be a cruel and heartless place, as Harold Winters had long ago hinted to Merle. For Esther had always wanted to work, and she did work constantly on her paintings. She was extremely talented, like many others around her. But she hardly saw compensation for this, her vocation. She always had to scrape by in order to survive. It's hard to keep up self-respect when not respected by others. So her mental health continued, understandably, to suffer.

Esther's eyes had slowly begun to bother her, according to little references in letters to Merle. Sometime in the fall of 1956, she moved to 222 16th Street. These were to be the last six months or so of the relatively good period she had since leaving the institution. With her sight failing her, she would soon go downhill—and she was only 55 years old. Ed had mournfully noted that, by 1957,

> Times had gotten so desperate for her. . . . She couldn't pay the rent on her little flat anymore. No one was buying her work . . . and the only out for her. . . . She couldn't cope. . . . I think she made her eyes bleed—mentally, emotionally. . . . I think it was a self-inflicted sorrow wound.

Come May of 1957, Esther still participated in the Washington Square Outdoor Show. She gave 222 W. 16th St. as her address, but according to a letter to Merle,[15] in April she had actually moved into a welfare hotel, the St. George, located at 49 E.12th Street. In Pittsburgh during that very spring, Merle was still "taking Esther's drawings along as [she] went to town."[16]

"When Esther went to the St. George, we saw very little of her after that, except from time to time we'd run into her at a coffee shop. She sort of became a bit of a recluse, due to the eyesight problem," stated Ed. He added, "At that point, she hardly went beyond the immediate area of the St. George. We were in the West Village and the St. George was the East Village. Glen offered that he and Eddie "had three businesses at the time—we were busy. . . . She couldn't do what she had been able to do and I think that bothered her." Though they didn't realize it, Esther was still going on some painting excursions about the city, according to the date 1957 on these existing paintings: *Rudy's Luncheonette, Still Hockey, Wylie Farms, Ruggieri's, Bridge on Gowanus Canal, Under Manhattan Bridge, Newtown Creek, Long Island,* and *Century Old House.* Around this time, Esther started to write on the backs of her paintings, "By Esther Phillips." Once again her works were of various playground and other street scenes and business districts. Esther was still drawn to water and bridges, surely fostered early by the three rivers and the abundance of bridges comprising the city of Pittsburgh. (Color Plates 27–28)

In the winter of 1957–58, still before Merle had received word from Esther of her move to the St. George, Merle writes to Sybil Barsky and husband Joe Grucci in response to a letter from them. "Thank you for the information. Am trying to get in touch with Esther Phillips. Don't know if rumour you heard is true. For some time I have not heard from her, but that has happened before. Will get in touch with you at Christmas so you can see drawings. . . ."[17] Another rumor of death, like fifteen years earlier, or just news of failing eyesight and being checked into a welfare hotel? Obviously many in Pittsburgh had continued to speculate on Esther's fate throughout the years. The last letter Merle had received from Esther thus far was in August 1956. She had tried to locate her, of course—this time with a string of registered letters again to her Cornelia Street address, but to no avail.[18] By 1958, though, Esther had been long gone from Cornelia Street.

Esther finally wrote Merle at the beginning of February, spelling out her latest predicament, and for the first time, referring to family.

Dear Merle,

I am living in a hotel temporarily (ten months now). Hope by late spring to get apt— which requires a lump sum of about $200 at least. I hope you are well—Merle—& what are you doing? Let me know—I suppose you have some of my watercolors left. Could you bring the rest of them to my sister who lives at 20 Forbes Terrace. Her name is Dorothy Rosenthal. If you have sold any, the $ could be sent here—to me.

love Esther

So it was in 1957, after her eyes began failing her, that Esther broke down and personally asked for help from the family. Though she had wanted only distance from them years ago, around this time she "sent a letter asking if [her brother] Joe could send $," according to Dorothy. "She heard he had a good job." After this, Dorothy and her husband Pete began helping Esther. "We sent her rent plus a couple hundred a month for expenses. Pete's bookkeeper said to send the rent money directly to the landlord."[19]

On the 14th of February, just six days from the last letter sent, Esther writes again:

> Dear Merle-
>
> In case you didn't get my letter—I simply want to ask you to please hand over the rest of my paintings to Mrs. Dorothy Rosenthal, 20 Forbes Terrace, unless you have sold some and in that case you could send me the $ as I'm desperately in need.
>
> love Esther

Times were surely desperate for Esther to issue such a message to her confidante and comrade, the only woman in Pittsburgh who truly did work solely on Esther's behalf during the institution years. Merle had been handling Esther's work for years, and successfully at that. It is easily imaginable the disbelief, anger, sadness and even fear that Merle must have felt at Esther's request that her sister, from a family long estranged, now handle the paintings. But Esther of course was focusing solely on the assistance from Dorothy—money to provide some minimal security.

Another letter came on the 21st of the month, and again a little over a month later, on April 7. Merle noted these in her journal but actual copies are missing. The only surviving bit of correspondence, what appears to be the last between Esther and Merle after two and a half decades of friendship, is one more letter from Esther on May 5, 1958. She does not mention her sister. Merle obviously had written Esther back in April, and Esther was responding to this. It appears the tension and the strained affairs between them had lessened, according to the tone of this last letter. (Merle had noted in her journal that her April letter to Esther included a comment on how much she—Merle—had "enjoyed the recent drawings.") Esther wrote, in this, the last letter:

> ... *Was happy to hear from you—also that you liked my new things. Am very busy painting and ekeing out an existence thereby. Have sold to lots of collectors around here—and depend a great deal on the Outdoor Show ... twice a year for good part of money—am looking for apartment...*

Back in Pittsburgh, trying to make sense of the changes wrought by time and experience, Merle learned a few months later, but apparently not by Esther, that Ernie Wright had died, according to a journal notation that does not detail the cause. And in that year, as well, came news of the death of Homer St. Gaudens, formerly of the Carnegie Museum. In a few years, both Gladys Schmitt and husband Simon Goldfield would have emotional breakdowns, Gladys' due in part to the fact that she at times ate very poorly. But toward the end of her life, Gladys Schmitt suffered with depression and despair over not making a larger name for herself through her writing, despite much success as a teacher at Carnegie Tech in later years.[20] As Anita Brostoff noted about Glady's writing, in her Introduction to *I Could Be Mute*, "Her Gestalt surely reflects the experience of other talented women who have missed a full measure of recognition and who are unable to fulfill themselves as women or as artists."[21]

Merle likely didn't hand over Esther's work to Dorothy, nor at least much of it, for many of Esther's paintings were found in Merle's effects after her death many years later. Though Esther had requested that she give them to Dorothy, she and Merle probably made peace over the situation. It is uncertain how much communication there was between Merle and Dorothy after Esther attempted to acquaint them. Dorothy said that her younger sister Betty did introduce her to Merle, whom they'd spot from time to time on the first floor of Webster Hall, a hotel at the north end of the Bellefield District, where Betty lived and Merle went for coffee. Dorothy said of Merle, "She'd have a bag beside her and the bag had papers. She spread the papers on the table. . . . She must have weighed 250 lbs."[22]

Esther stayed at the St. George much beyond what she thought she would. In 1959, she would still be there. Though Glen and Ed didn't see much of her, the details of her existence then seemed very plain to them. They saw her sitting on the stoop of the St. George, sometimes waiting for a bus. They could tell that her eyes were bothering her. When recalling this enduring memory, Ed had trouble expressing his emotionally laden thoughts about Esther's state of being at that time. He had murmured, "Her eyes . . . her body . . . she was . . . punishing oneself because the world punishes you. . . . I think she knew she was doing it."

Like Glen and Ed, Eugenia saw little of Esther anymore as well. Only a couple of notations in her journal of later years mention her long-time friend. The few there are not only depict sorry conditions of the St. George, but also provide matter-of-fact, almost wry commentary on Esther's increasingly disturbing somatic complaints. In early 1959, Eugenia notes, "Esther has thrombosis and God knows what else." Later in May of that year: "Saw Esther—moldy carpets disturbed me. We sat and talked of death as we usually do."[23]

Dorothy recalled Esther's mentioning her "good friend Hughes. Dorothy and Jerry may have even corresponded at one point. "She had a wonderful friend by the name of Hughes [who said], 'If there's a doctor, anything she needs—we'll take care of it.'" Dorothy had actually been urging Esther to use some of the money sent to see a doctor, but Esther wouldn't go.[24] She surely had a bit of a fear of physicians ever since being institutionalized. But she also likely saw the money better put to use for what still provided her comfort in her horrible living situation—painting supplies. Esther somehow still painted over these years, despite her apparently failing eyesight. Titles from 1958 and 1959 include *Pretzel Woman* (of a woman street vendor), and *Family Chicken*. She was also painting cats and single figures again. (Color Plates 29–32)

Esther's life in 1960 is noted through one small, yet poignant journal entry of Eugenia's: "Esther was reminiscing about her years at Carnegie Tech, where life seemed good and she had dreams and hopes. . . ." In

September 1961 came Eugenia's last notation about her friend. It again shows Jerry's sarcastic wit, yet doesn't deny the love and strength of friendship between these two women, despite their difficulties. "Esther calls—in her plaintive voice, sighs and wishes for death—and she knows what she's got (cancer) and she can't eat (she's alone all the time and she can't see—but enough to still dial my number)."

These sad years seemed to fly by for Esther, who was caught in a downward spiral. Come 1963, Glen and Ed made a final visit. "My life at this time was falling apart," says Ed, whose family was breaking up. He and wife Carol had just lost an infant child to crib death, and they were going through divorce. "Over the years," explained Ed, "Esther had given me a great deal of her works, but [at this time] I didn't know what to do with them." Glen added that "at one point, we had one hundred of her paintings and then she'd come and take some." Ed was now having to move, as he no longer had studios and galleries with Glen, and he had to make a decision about what to do with all of Esther's work. Carol Evans ended up retaining a few, including paintings and a "marvelous wooden cat."[25] But Glen and Ed decided that they should take the remaining paintings back to Esther. They didn't keep any, much to their later dismay.

Dorothy knew of such constant storing of her sister's paintings in other places. She recalled Esther telling of the dire fate of many works due to this very fact. The owner of one building, where Esther had stored works in the basement, told her that she could not have them back. "[Esther] just said she walked away—left I don't know how many in this one guy's basement," said Dorothy. "I asked her why she didn't fight. And Esther said she didn't have the energy. She needed to paint."[26] Niece Millie also told of other related mishaps, from her aunt's testimony, including a group of paintings of Victorian houses stored in a building that burned down.[27]

Describing the relinquishing of the works that they so cared for, Ed stated, "When we took the paintings back to her, the whole hotel was stinking of urine. It was heartbreaking." By this time, he and Glen had learned that "the sister was sending a little money—just for the St.

George rent and a little sustenance." Ed reiterated, "It was heartbreaking and we helped her as much as we could but it was desperate times for all of us. . . ." Broken-spirited himself, when he recalled his last memories of Esther and the image of the St. George, and what it represented to him, he summoned enough anger amid the remembered misery to state: "I wish [Jesse] Helms, [George] Bush . . . and the bunch of other infants that we have running government . . . that we could take them to the Hotel St. George and make them see an artist's dying. Smell the dingy, dirty, God-awful hotel room. . . . It still makes me cry. . . ."

"It was the last time we spoke with her," says Ed, his voice falling, of the visit to return her work. Despite her then sorry state, his reflections moved him to comment that, then as always, "The one thing that she held onto was that she was an artist." He continues, "When we took the paintings back to her . . . we knew she couldn't last much longer. We felt that she would have died by now." Both he and Glen had always thought of the St. George as "where Esther ended up." But it was actually only where their time with her came to an end. They just so strongly felt that the deplorable conditions there would have killed her.

Throughout the 1960s, however, until approximately 1970, Esther lived at the St. George Hotel. Little else is known of her life at that time. Of Esther's latter years there, Dorothy would be able to offer only one anecdote. She recalled having received a strange letter that read, "You don't know me, but I want to tell you some people are coming into Esther's room and stealing her paintings. And I think you should do something about it." Dorothy stated, "I didn't reply to the letter. There was nothing that I could do. Esther was a mature lady; but I wrote Esther asking her to be more careful with her paintings."[28]

Before ending their talk about Esther, Ed Evans said that he and Glen never forgot their time with their dear friend. He pulled out of the office file cabinet a play entitled *Phantom's Dance*, and had handed it across the table. Ed would write it about a decade after they had said goodbye to her. It was a one-act play for three characters, one of whom was Esther. According to Ed, it recalls Esther's latter years, and even recounts the death of Max Bodenheim.[29]

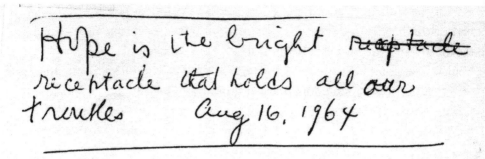

FIG. 28

"Hope is the bright receptacle that holds all our troubles."
August 16, 1964

—Merle Hoyleman[30]

Eugenia Hughes would die an untimely death at the young age of fifty-five in 1964. She died a single, independent woman, as she had been all her life, despite numerous love attachments. Found among the varied ephemera of her effects was an article caption that must have caught her eye: "Single Women Happier." Where Eugenia's effects are to be found is a bit unusual. At some point, she came up with the whimsical idea of donating her journals and letters to the New York Public Library. Apparently she did just that during a sickness the year before she died. In December 1963 and January 1964, the library acquired her donated effects and organized and classified them within its Special Collections.

Here Eugenia echoes Joe Gould's bequeathing two-thirds of his infamous manuscript to the Harvard Library, his alma mater, and one-third to the Smithsonian Institution.[31] (But in his case, of course, no manuscripts were found upon his death.) Eugenia had a collection that contained, according to library listings, "correspondence, diaries, art work [sketching and watercolor studies], writings, family papers, photographs, memorabilia of Eugenia and her family, and printed matter."

The statement describing the vast collection, this description made available to the general public, of the "Eugenia Hughes Papers" continues that, among other family-related matter, the information contains letters from friends, and includes many love letters . . . and photographs of friends.[32] The Accession Sheet then states that "[Eugenia's] father was an artist and newspaper illustrator . . . who moved to Greenwich Village, New York City, to find work as an artist. Eugenia joined him in the mid 1930s and both remained long-time Village residents (with frequent returns to Pennsylvania for financial and health reasons) . . . [The contents of her donated material] document the life of a single woman and a widower from the 1930s to the 1960s, their social and romantic involvements with the artistic community in Greenwich Village and Pennsylvania. . . . The letters between Roy and Eugenia are rich in detail about the life of a struggling artist, the social life of New York City, and the relationship between father and daughter."[33]

The collection provides a wealth of documentation available of Esther's life as well, alongside Eugenia. Esther indeed recalled to her niece Millie that Eugenia was going to send her journals to the library, expressing, "The curators loved it!"[34] Beyond the fancy of it, Jerry and Esther little knew how well the voluminous material would provide illustrious content matter about not only the Village but their unique friendship.

I'm One

I do not have.
I do not expect.
I do not owe.

I'm one,
the only one,
free in my life.

Each day perfect,
each day a thousand years.
Time is in me.

I swallow the sun.
I'm the one, the only
one in my life.

Oh, windless day
within me,
Oh, silence and sun.

May Swenson[35]

Chapter Twenty

"HER ENERGY MYSTERIOUSLY SOURCED"[1]

Phyllis Chesler's *Women and Madness* reveals the story of "Carole," one among many women Chesler interviewed in her research. She was a mental institution "graduate," living in a New York City welfare hotel, much like the St. George that Esther found as her horrible home in the 1960s. There Carole lived "behind a locked door in a small room." She had been an actress. Her family was very strict with her, and very disappointed that she never got engaged. They sent her to a psychiatrist; after assessing her he told the family that she wouldn't be able to deal with the "rat race" of Hollywood, or New York City. However, she moved to the latter and met her business manager, a man who got things going sexually for her. She wound up with two prescription drugs, her eyes blurred, and she ended up in an institution. She didn't want the family contacted. Carole was aggressive, uncooperative. She herself said, "That's the big one. If you're uncooperative, you're crazy."

Chesler stated of her interviewee, "She has spent ten years in New York mental asylums. Her smile is dazzling, her energy mysteriously sourced."

ⓑ ⓑ ⓑ

Dorothy stated that around 1970, "A good friend named Regis helped Esther find a place to move to when the St. George was torn down." This of course was Reggie Masson, still a dear friend to Esther after three decades, and six years after the death of Jerry, who had introduced the two all those years ago. According to Dorothy, who spoke with him on the phone, "He raved about her spirit and her sense of humor." So Esther lived at the St. George Hotel about twelve years, longer than any other place she stayed at in New York.[2]

With money sent from Dorothy, Regis Masson helped Esther move out of the Village—about as far socio/economically as you can get—to the Upper West Side. Her new home was one of the Lincoln Square Apartments (actually rooms in a hotel) on West 75th Street. It was around this time, 1971, that, according to Dorothy, Esther actually did develop a full-blown embolism in her eye. Understandably, Esther was "very distressed" when this happened, and started to curtail her art even more, but did not stop painting altogether. Any painting was likely done from her hotel room or close by on the premises outside. Dorothy added, "That's when we started supporting her completely—I got the sisters, the relatives—together. It was a project. We got a fund for her—kept her head above water."

At Lincoln Square, Esther lived until January 1980, approximately ten more years. Even less is known about her life during this period at Lincoln Square. The family still had not yet made any trips to New York to see Esther. While at her new residence, living in what Dorothy only later saw and called "a dumpy, neglected" room, it can be surmised that Esther still painted. Likely she enjoyed the new surroundings as different content material if nothing else. Dorothy's one recollection of this period for Esther involves an unknown woman, whom Dorothy would vaguely remember, who wanted to help Esther get on Medicaid at some point in the 1970s. So Dorothy sent some paperwork to her. Nothing else other than this small bit of information is known of Esther's life for yet another decade, for she lived at Lincoln Square until January 1980.

It was likely the very same lady friend, supposedly a next-door neighbor, who called Dorothy at the beginning of 1980. Dorothy and her husband finally made the trip to New York City—the very next day.

Esther had apparently collapsed; the paramedics had tried to take her to the hospital the day before but she wouldn't go. When Dorothy and Pete arrived, Esther wasn't able to get out of bed. They called an ambulance to the Lincoln Square Apartments.

Dorothy recalled Esther's room as "a disaster—paintings strewn all over . . . in drawers, on walls, in closets everywhere. . . . We looked through her drawers. There was clothing. She had a little food in the refrigerator. We gave the food to the woman who had helped us out." Pete Rosenthal called the manager about the neglected condition of the apartment. He told Pete that they "tried a couple of times to come in and paint Esther's apartment, but she wouldn't let [them] in."

In recalling when she first saw her sister again after 44 years, Dorothy added, "When we came for her, her purse had no cards, or other identification! There were just seven or eight envelopes that I had sent her—the letters had been taken out. It had our return address. The only reason I can think that she had these there was that this was how she wanted to be identified." Dorothy went on, "Later we sent the paintings back [to Pittsburgh] UPS. There were approximately 300—400." Dorothy believed that most of the works were from 1957 to 1958, early on in Esther's time at the St. George. "We put all [of them] into storage. Pete had them sign a lot of forms so that nothing would disappear. . . . We [then] closed the door to her apartment."

Dorothy and her husband helped Esther into Roosevelt Hospital. "She didn't want to go. [But] she wasn't well. She said she couldn't walk." At the hospital, she was diagnosed with acute diabetes, a condition often resulting from poor dietary habits over years, and one that certainly sometimes does affect the health of the eyes. Esther got her strength back after a few months' stay at Roosevelt. During the time she was there, Dorothy and Esther talked much. Describing the sister that she hadn't seen since the age of thirty-four, Dorothy observed that Esther, at the age of seventy-eight, had "long, white, flowing hair. She swore a lot. And she was so tough and feisty in her vocabulary." Esther immediately asked Dorothy which of her nieces or nephews played the piano; she remembered that "Esther had played the piano very nicely" during childhood. Esther at this time described to her sister the many hats she wore throughout her life. "She liked hats. She would describe the hats she used to buy. . . . You can see hats in her paintings." Esther's sister and her husband asked about the people that Esther met and knew over the years. Esther's response was that "they were not in the same league as she. . . ."

"[Esther] never talked about her blindness. . . ." She told her sister that "malnutrition and depression drove [her] into the asylum." Dorothy said family "believed [the asylum] was in upstate New York. . . . She had what she called a little breakdown." After Esther felt a bit better come a few months later, Dorothy and Pete had her transferred to Thomas Jefferson Residence for the Elderly in Brooklyn. (Apparently, she had by then developed embolisms in both eyes and was declared legally blind.) Despite very little sight, she was ambulatory enough to go downstairs to the dining hall. In her room, she happily played the radio given to her at this time, recalled Dorothy.

Dorothy and Pete tried to help Esther utilize what little sight she had left. "I don't know how many stores we went to in Pittsburgh, buying different magnifying glasses for her, but they weren't enough." They made three or four trips to visit her over a three-month period. It was then that Dorothy's daughter Millie came up to meet her aunt for the very first time, beginning the short series of visits that provided Millie with all the vivid details of Esther's interesting life—Esther's Oral History, of sorts. The paintings that had been shipped back to Pittsburgh were first stored in closets in Dorothy and Pete's house. No doubt they provided Millie a visual connection to the aunt who had broken ties with the family over forty years ago. "Esther was a mythical figure to me—the aunt who ran away from home and never was found.[3] She broke away from the family at a time when women didn't do that sort of thing."[4]

Millie spent "several hours on several days with [Esther]." Esther was able to share feelings with her that might have been difficult to express directly to Dorothy. Esther acknowledged to Millie that although she left Pittsburgh without saying goodbye, she insisted that she was not mad at the family. Upon reflecting on some of the thoughts Esther shared with her daughter, Dorothy added, "Maybe she felt we were all hurt when she left Pittsburgh. . . . She told us she couldn't say goodbye to anyone." She also offered, "She had moved away from the family and I think she felt she wasn't entitled to much from them. It was always a heartache for the family, not knowing about her."

Esther no doubt appreciated the attention and devotion that her niece was paying her. Like she did with Glen and Ed, she "regaled" Millie with stories about living the life of an artist through the 1930s and 1950s in Greenwich Village. Esther apparently conversed in a rambling fashion. She hinted to Millie about an unhappy love affair, [bohemian] men having "toenails like prehistoric animals," and selling to millionaires on Fifth Avenue but not being let in because she was beneath them. Esther provided Millie with a myriad of details, most very factual. Esther even mentioned the Fourth St. Studios of Glen and Ed. Millie did not transcribe their last names accurately, though. She wrote everything down quickly so she could remember all that her aunt was telling her.[5]

According to what Esther told Millie, which was verified by the available paintings themselves, "[Esther] painted street scenes, boat scenes, a series of abstract musicians, Third St. nightclubs in the Village, a series of people in the street, and a cat series." Dorothy said that the family didn't realize that Esther had traveled around the city as much as she did. "She got out to Coney Island. She didn't even tell us about that." Seeing the familiar water and bridge scenes over and over, Dorothy remarked, "She painted the bays, rivers, canals, she knew the types of boats, but she didn't like painting people that much." Esther apparently told Millie that she did some portraits, but didn't like it. She did so only for money.

Millie offered that "Esther described her style as 'semi-abstract,' and color was very important to her—She used color to create mood." Esther discussed with Millie her painting on cheap cardboards most of her life, even shirt cardboards when necessary. She described her working lots in casein, a professional watercolor medium with a cheese base. Esther preferred it "because it was fast-drying and looked like oil." (And it was dictated by her economic means.) Millie readily discussed her aunt's paintings, which she obviously had taken to, and studied with fascination, saying that all the work "seems to be very active, congested and vibrant." She noticed that the series of approximately ten paintings of children playing at a playground was done in "an abstract and geometric style." She saw, too, her aunt's varying signatures (usually *Esther Phillips*, but also *E Phillips*, and *EP*).

While Esther lived at the Thomas Jefferson Home, Millie attempted to contact some galleries close by her home of Chicago about her aunt's work: "I am writing to you with hope that you might help me resolve an artistic dilemma. . . . My aunt . . . lived and painted in Greenwich Village for 45 years. . . . I recently met her in New York for the first time. She grew up in Pittsburgh in a home with immigrant parents and 6 brothers and sisters who couldn't understand her artistic temperament. . . . When my parents went to New York last January to get her into a hospital, they found approximately 400 paintings in her one room apartment." Millie's exploratory letters continued, "This was the body of work from 1957–58 that she was unable to sell. . . On my last visit to Pittsburgh, I took whatever I could carry with me (about 125 paintings: half of them small 11" x 14" and the other half are approximately 20" x 36"). . . . I need help in assessing the quality and value of her work—whether it is worthy of exhibition—and in general, what options are available." Ten were done in oil, the rest were casein. Most were on some type of paper or cardboard, a few on masonite.[6]

In the spring of 1982, Millie was successful at arranging a presentation of Esther's work at a luncheon gathering at the Noyes Cultural Art Center in Evanston, Illinois. She was invited to speak, to share her discoveries about her aunt's life, drawing, of course, on the extensive notes she took while Esther was getting settled into the Thomas Jefferson Home for Adults. Esther was still there when this presentation took place.[7] Dorothy and Pete, as well, were beginning to think about organizing a show of Esther's work in Pittsburgh about this time. "The idea that Pete had," said Dorothy, "was that getting recognition in Pittsburgh and selling some of her work would give her a lift." Dorothy recalled that, "We felt that we should ask Esther's permission before going ahead with the show." Pete offered, "Esther was reluctant. She said the paintings we had were not her best stuff." Esther hadn't lost her critical judgment despite age. She would have known that she did her finest work prior to living at the St. George. (And these paintings would have been with Merle.)

According to Virginia Roman, a social worker at the Thomas Jefferson Home in 1983, Esther still retained her wit and a good deal of her spirit, as well. Roman remembers the staff as being encouraging to Esther, who was "happy, not depressed." She recalled that Esther was blind, but able to roam about to get her meals and such. "She was a very nice lady, very funny." The social worker remembered Esther's remarks about a good-looking male nurse (apparently she had a bit of sight still left in her). Esther joked with Virginia "to bring her a black negligee—she'd like to have him as her boyfriend." Though she often made Virginia laugh, there still seemed a "very private" side to Esther Phillips.[8]

Throughout 1983 Dorothy and Pete worked on securing a Pittsburgh exhibition. A show was scheduled at the Pittsburgh National Bank on Craig Street in Oakland for the fall of the following year, 1984. However, Esther would die before that date. On May 6, 1983, she was hospitalized at Astoria General Hospital in Queens. She died on the 17th of May. She was cremated and her ashes brought back to Pittsburgh, to the B'Nai Israel Cemetery in the east end of the city. Her death certificate does not list cause of death, but does list her "usual occupation" as "Artist," and "kind of business"—"Fine Arts."[9] Esther had lived at the Thomas Jefferson, her last of many residences in New York, about three years. Finding out later that the last years of her life were in such a good home with attendant attendant care comforted Glen and Ed. For years they thought of the horrendous St. George as the place where she would perish.

◎ ◎ ◎

"I felt very sad that she struggled, that we weren't in the position to make things a little easier for her while she had that crying need for expression." In recalling her sister's death, and her last years, especially the time at the Roosevelt Hospital, where Esther confided a lot in both Millie and herself, Dorothy related the lasting impression that her sister left on both her and the rest of the family. Dorothy remembered one particular visit to the Roosevelt, where "[Esther] was reciting poetry. Edna St. Vincent Millay's 'My Candle Burns At Both Ends.' She said, 'Dorothy, I think of Edna St. Vincent Millay' . . . [and] I said, 'Esther, you didn't live that kind of life.' She said, 'Maybe I [did], maybe I ran too hard. Maybe I didn't realize I was running down my health.'" That was the closest Esther came to expressing reservation about her life choices, for, as Ed Evans had noted at the St. George, "the one thing that she held onto was that she was an artist." Immediately after bringing up Millay and that comment on her health—and throughout her stay at the Roosevelt, up until her death—Esther said over and over again something that Dorothy and Millie could not forget.

I consider myself very lucky. I did exactly what I wanted to do in my life and I was happy doing it. . . . I lived the best life. When I got up in the morning I looked forward to the day. I was happy I could paint.

```
=+=+=+=+=+=+=+=+=+=+=+=+=+=+=+=+=+=+=+=+=+=+=+=+=+=+=+=+=+=+=+=+=+=+=+=+=+=+=+=+=+=+=
:::::::::::::::::::::::::::::::::::::::::::::::::::::::::::::::::::::::::::::::::::::::
```

in search of stories, impressions, memories of

ESTHER PHILLIPS
painter and ceramic artist

WORK: *only job Esther had outside of art, that of a bookkeeper, briefly. Fired for doodling in the margins of the ledger. As a child doodled and drew on nearly any availa piece of paper. Her father fed stray cats out in the yard and the cats sometimes reappe in Esther's work as a meditative presence.*

EXHIBITED: *in the 50's at the Washington Square Outdoor Show. Tried to make ends meet on income from that show and from making and selling ceramic figures, jewelry, belts. She had a folding aluminum table and a shopping cart and could be seen on Bleecker Stre near Our Lady of Pompeii Church. A young girl helped her.*

ADDRESSES: *1936-38: 7 Morton St., Apt. 7, 107 West 3rd St., 426 Hudson St.*
1950's: 159 W. 23rd St., 68 Bedford St., 24 Cornelia St., Saint George Hotel

FRIENDS INCLUDING: *Harold J. Winters who wrote under the name "B. M. Lawn" for the "Hand Writing Magazine and the Satiricon"*

SIGNATURE: *usually Esther Phillips but sometimes E. Phillips, Phillips, or EP. Esther worked in watercolors, oils, and casein. Often didn't have the money for oils. Short on materials. On the back of one wonderous work might be a second wonderous work.*

DESCRIPTION OF ESTHER'S ART: *in her paintings the roads might vanish to a distance and a house begin; land with contours like the sides of a whale and clouds like flying sauc A road passes behind a tree but can yet be seen. Esther did a series of watercolors ana oils from the inside of a mental hospital: a women's ward at night, a phonograph on wheels reappearing in several paintings. In her best work the paint and the feeling are all together: strong composition through color invigorated by rhythm.*

Please send any information on Esther to Ken Chute, 1143 Jackson St., Pittsburgh, Pa. 15221. Thanks!

```
:::::::::::::::::::::::::::::::::::::::::::::::::::::::::::::::::::::::::::::::::::::::
=+=+=+=+=+=+=+=+=+=+=+=+=+=+=+=+=+=+=+=+=+=+=+=+=+=+=+=+=+=+=+=+=+=+=+=+=+=+=+=+=+=+
```

"Esther is one of my heroes."[10] Though she had many champions throughout her life and after, a kind and gentle man by the name of Ken Chute perhaps became Esther Phillips' biggest fan. As her arduous life was drawing to a close, he was beginning to hear of bits and pieces of Esther's story. Eventually he became as intrigued as anyone else who had heard of her life. He never met Esther, though, only Merle Hoyleman, who befriended him in the mid 1970s.

To Ken, Esther Phillips at first was an artist-figure as oblique and mysterious as his new friend Merle was eccentric. Little by little her story filtered through to him via Merle, who detailed the depth of their friendship over decades. Because she trusted him completely, Merle told Ken about Esther's being institutionalized, subsequent creations made while there, and how, with the help of administrators, she was able to ship out work for sale. Merle's explanation for the hospitalization was that Esther was so hungry, she "lost her sense of balance."[11] As Ken understood it, "in the hospital, she was able to eat. . . ." Though Merle's anecdotes about her friend in New York were interesting, Ken never paid more attention than what the moment warranted. "Merle had told some stories off and on about Esther, but [until later] I hadn't seen her work, hadn't known what it looked like. . . ."

Though no correspondence survives after 1958 between them, Merle perhaps was in some contact with Esther while she resided at the St. George. Ken remembered Merle referring to knowing Esther even about 1970. (Since Merle had the St. George as an address for Esther, likely she did write her there.) Merle apparently conveyed to Ken the sorry state that her dear friend was in at least until that time, with failing eyesight, no money, and looming depression. Perhaps like Glen and Ed, Merle assumed that Esther would not last much longer. Ken got the impression, at least indirectly from Merle, that Esther was no longer living at that very time he and Merle talked about her.

Ironically, while Ken Chute was developing a friendship with Merle, Esther was still alive in New York City, living in the Lincoln Square Apartments. Ken believed that by 1970 Merle and Esther "had fallen out of touch, and given how close at times they were," according to all the stories told of their travails, "I never thought that'd happen. . . ." (He did not realize how often Esther and Merle had lost communication with each other from time to time.)

Ken had met Merle when she was living at the corner of South Craig and Forbes, above what is now a busy Uni-Mart that sits catty-corner to the entrance to the Carnegie Museum of Art. From the outside it is a very beautiful apartment building with stained glass windows. It sat in the 1970s as it does now, still on the corner of that very artsy, bohemian street. As far back as the 1920s, creative souls galore have tread its sidewalks, and still today artists, writers, musicians and punks frequent Craig Street's used bookstores, art supply, record graveyard, coffeehouses and beloved Macondo, the eclectic import store. Just east on Forbes Avenue falls Carnegie Mellon University, to the west, past Bellefield and Dithridge Streets, the University of Pittsburgh. The nonconformist feel of this corridor to the Richard Serra sculpture and fountains that beckon one down the long, shallow outdoor steps into the northern, main entrance to the art museum hasn't changed since Esther lived there—the time of Van Trump, Gladys Schmitt, Sybil Barsky and Harold Schwartz, when the Bellefield Y and Carnegie Museum beckoned young creative types.

Ken was introduced to Merle through "Chuck," an artist and musician who played saxophone and flute. Apparently Chuck introduced Ken to art and was the embodiment, to him, of "an artist as a person," one who fully lived his life from the core of his being. "Chuck used to play the flute walking down Craig Street. Merle would have her window open. We all considered Chuck to be serenading the street, if you will, the folks. . . . so maybe Merle and I met through Chuck's music." Ken had the sense that Chuck would have understood Esther, if he had met her.

Merle Hoyleman, thought Ken, was a "fine poet, who should receive much more recognition in times to come. In the kind of world that doesn't value art, Merle sort of put a lot of value in art. She believed something like 'a few well-written words of poetry are worth a couple of libraries'. . . ." He also substantiated the crazier notions that Merle entertained. "Among other things, Merle believed she could smell radiation and she'd call people in the county to check it out. During WWII, she and a friend lived not far from Mellon Institute, which bridged the Pitt and Carnegie Tech campuses. She lived with a lady pianist and the two could hear rats screaming as they were being tortured in research tests there." (Indeed rats were, and still are tested there. Whether she heard them or not is another story. But Merle's convictions led her to protest, not unlike the protests held to this day on the neighboring steps of CMU's Software Engineering Institute, which is generously funded through Westinghouse's nuclear division.) "Merle believed a lot of things that most would not. She believed that great artists were followed around by secret agents from various countries—Russia and this country. She thought she was followed around."

There came a time when Merle and other residents were asked to leave their apartments in the corner building at the end of Craig Street. Though beautiful once again today, the building was in bad need of rehab during the 1970s. Merle was the last to go, and she certainly didn't go voluntarily. The whole place was infested with cockroaches." Towards the end of her time there, "someone had broken in and all kinds of stuff was littered on the floor." But Merle clung to the apartment as she did her convictions.

After Ken met the elderly yet spirited writer who, like Esther at that time in life, also had long, white, flowing hair, Merle began to hibernate more and more. Ken guessed she was in her late seventies or early eighties at the time. He expressed that "Merle had two secrets. One was where her income came from and the other was her age." Her weariness about a life that seemed to her too unfair and arduous had worn her down. Her suspicions about people insincere and close-minded enlarged to include the circle of like-minded souls around her. "Merle's heart just grew increasingly out of touch and so she drove away her friends and just isolated herself." Merle, too, spent the day in bed. Struggling to fully explain the complexities of the scenario, Ken could only offer, "it's a complicated story"—a script he'd often add to the story of how he stumbled across Esther Phillips' life, and when overwhelmed by the nuance and nostalgia of remembering Merle Hoyleman.

Merle grew increasingly worse mentally. "During one stretch, she was put in Western Psychiatric for awhile. . . . Mentally, I think Esther and Merle were very different. Esther I picture as being very emotional . . . but as thinking relatively clearly. Merle had an intense streak of paranoia, where she thought people were trying to steal her manuscripts." Ken and other friends tried to encourage Merle to send those out to potential publishers, "but there was just paranoia that became worse and worse over the years." Ken acknowledges that he knew about Merle's shock treatment in the early 1950s.

Merle was finally placed, likely by the state, in Shadyside Nursing and Rehabilitation in Pittsburgh around 1982. A social worker, Mrs. Helen Bonn of Vintage Adult Services, assigned to sort through Merle's possessions, of which there were many, called upon Ken and a man by the name of Mike Vargo (considered her closest friends) in order to make a decision as to what to do with them. Both Mike and Ken were of enormous help to Mrs. Bonn. Though officially Mrs. Bonn held the right, unusually so, to the possessions, because Merle became deathly ill and there was no family nearby (it is not known what became of Merle's Oklahoma brother), Ken and Mike were seen as the two who should ultimately get that guardianship. Upon Merle's death, which shortly came, they decided to clear away and take to a storage facility in north Oakland Merle's manuscripts galore, tons of letters and journals, and also Esther's paintings.

When Ken first saw Esther's works, Merle's stories about her came vividly to life. "The social worker called, Esther's paintings surfaced, and I responded [to them] immediately." Merle had apparently kept Esther's paintings hidden away somewhere in her apartment. Probably she realized that if Dorothy had found out the surviving paintings, Merle would have had to relinquish them. But paintings there were many, and respond to them Ken indeed did. The stories he found fascinating came back to him in fuller depth, now that a visual connection was made with this woman painter. Esther's style truly spoke to Ken;

the paintings showed for him that she "had her own language, a personal vocabulary of forms."

And so Ken Chute, who knew not much about art, but who was constantly taking self-enrichment courses across the broad spectrum of the arts and humanities, began to define for himself a way to speak about Esther's art so that he might bring her work to the attention of appropriate people. Little did Ken know that Esther was still alive, in the last year of her life in a New York City nursing home not unlike where resided Merle (who also had no idea that Esther was alive). If he had known that, Ken certainly would have tracked her down and paid her a visit.

In becoming better acquainted with the creative world through friends like Chuck and Merle, Ken enthusiastically embraced that world as his own. He understood that "the way one looks at everything determines the way one looks at a painting and the way one looks at paintings may alter the way one looks at the world."

> Esther gave us ways of seeing the world about us. [She] contributed unique visual perspectives: she simplified forms to reveal rhythm and feeling. In terms of perspective, the unexpected happens. [Her] best work is first-rate. Her simplifications of form have rhythms that reveal more than [what] is. Her paintings have an intangible quality coming from her emotional integrity.

In August of 1982, Ken took photographs of most of the paintings that had made their way into Merle's hands, and now his own. Like Millie, he was immediately compelled to attempt to attract attention to Esther's work. And like Merle, he wrote and visited the appropriate people, and his main focus indeed was Pittsburgh's Carnegie Museum of Art. Little did he know that many of Esther's earlier works, bought by former museum staff, were likely still there, hidden away in storage. But Ken had simply to concern himself with the works left in Merle's possession. He initially wrote the Museum in the spring of 1982, but got no reply. He then wrote again and dropped off the correspondence along with photos of the work that had been in Merle's possession, all addressed to Oswaldo Rodriguez, who was the Curator of Fine Arts at the time.[12]

[I] would like to see the paintings in a safe home. They deserve a better fate than to sit in storage, with the risk of being lost, should they come under the control of people who don't appreciate or understand art. Many people find it easy to ignore work when the primary focus is not technique.

The hope is for the museum to accept these paintings as a donation and for an art historian to try to follow Esther Phillips' trail.

The work has passion; it is work that if Esther Phillips had not done these paintings, no one would know the world could look this way. . . . I know, from all my experience and all my feelings . . . that very exciting things are happening in the simplification of forms, in the feeling for color, in the sense of composition. An intangible quality exists within the work the way an intangible quality exists within the work of Henri Rousseau and the quality runs very deep.

If you find the work very moving, please do contact me. I could bring in the originals. . . . Basically I feel the museum has a duty to save what is actually art and Esther Phillips has Pittsburgh roots.

Sincerely,

Ken Chute

Oswaldo Rodriguez called Ken in, with a request to see the original works themselves. With the help of his elderly father, Ken carried in a group that included some of those that Will Barnet had selected as the best from the institution (the ones not bought up by Esther's Pittsburgh "public"). Rodriguez was very interested, "very enthusiastic," remembered Ken, who was so pleased to have someone knowledgeable and in position of authority to substantiate what he already believed. John Lane, director of the Museum of Art at the time, came in to view the originals, and also liked the work. "A portfolio of watercolors for gift and loan consideration" was thus taken in by the Carnegie Museum of Art on May 17, 1982, under Rodriguez and Lane's service there.[13] These were works that Esther had sent Merle over the years, that had never sold. (Interestingly, the better ones that did sell probably went to O'Connor and are likely hiding somewhere in the bowels of the museum.) How very satisfied Esther would have been to know that current-day administrators at the Carnegie museum felt as strongly about her work as John O'Connor and Edward Duff Balkan had. But of course she had no way of knowing, even though she was still alive, because museum actions were not made public, and Esther's family was disconnected from any course of events transpiring, essentially, due to Merle's efforts over the years.

Unfortunately the celebratory relief Ken felt didn't last long, for Rodriguez soon left the Carnegie and so did Lane, for the San Francisco Museum of Art. Ken was left trying to pursue permanent placement of the works the museum had taken in. Rodriguez stored the paintings in the flat files of the administrative offices of the art museum. They were actually quite accessible, located in the conference room/library right off the main hall in the offices.[14] Here they would sit for some eventual consideration of putting them out for public view. But administrators after Rodriguez and Lane "didn't have the same level of enthusiasm" they did, and Ken has been trying ever since to get the Museum to reconsider the works it still has. When Henry Adams came on board as curator of Fine Arts in the fall of 1982, with Rodriguez and Lane now gone, he wrote to Ken, trying to ascertain the owner of the works and "their status vis-a-vis our collection." He added, "Basically, I think we are not interested in *purchasing* [author's italicization] any of these watercolors, but would be interested in receiving some or all of them as a gift to the museum."[15] Good news, that the Carnegie at least wanted to keep the works and perhaps put them out for future public view, so Ken immediately wrote, with not too quick a reply back. Like Merle, Ken persisted in writing when he did not receive a timely response. So he wrote again, his feeling for Esther's art apparent, as always.[16]

Henry Adams:

Weeks and weeks have passed and there's been no reply to
my reply to your letter! I don't know if my letter got lost
in the mail or what happened!

Mrs. Helen Bonn's phone number at the New Tradition Senior Citizens
center is 771-0303. She is a social worker andiis Merle Hoyleman's
legal guardian. Merle is in a nursing home. Mrs. Bonn wouldbe
gladdhotbalklkiwhityou and she has the legal authority to lend
the works to the museum. Ideally, the works would be donated
to the museum but we do not know Merle's position on this and
that is why the idea of a loan has been suggested. Esther Phillips,
I feel certain, would have wantegldidefworkoto be in the museum.
In the museum, the work is safe and there is the possibility of
people seeing the work and being moved by it.

If you are free sometime during the afternoon of Wednesday,
December 8th, I could bring in additional work by Esther,
including one of pepple in a station, a watercolor I believe to
be first rate and both humble and visually stunning. If that is
not a good time I am free most any Saturday. If that is not possible
I could probably get approval for time off from work (I work as a
typesetter in Office Services at Duquesne University.)

Ken Chute

It seems no positive response came from Adams. But Ken did not give up. He kept trying whenever the museum had new administrators. He also wrote to a variety of others about Esther, to find out further information and to have her work receive the respect he felt it deserved. Sometimes a flurry of writing activity took place.[17] But in the meantime, Merle died—as Esther had by then—and Ken stumbled across Dorothy and her family for the first time.

> So here is my identity, Christopher . . . perhaps if life retain us
> until fame finds us, mortality will but greet us.
> —Merle Hoyleman, *Letters to Christopher*[18]

In October 1984 was the Pittsburgh National Bank show of Esther's works that Dorothy and Pete Rosenthal had put together. As a community arts service, the bank allowed paintings to hang in the lobby. The practice continues widely to this day. The works were for sale; anyone interested in purchasing one simply gave money to one of the bank tellers and it would then be passed along to the artist—in this case, Esther's family.

Ken Chute happened to be passing by the busy intersection of Craig Street and Fifth Avenue one day that fall on his way toward the University of Pittsburgh. "I was taking a course at Pitt's Informal Studies Program . . . I was just heading toward my class and I saw in front of me these art works at Pittsburgh National Bank and I got closer and closer and when I saw one of the figures . . . well, there's a certain way that Esther draws women that's unmistakable. . . ." Ken realized it was the same woman artist whose works he had been thoroughly taken with (and in the process of vigorously marketing to the Museum just up the street). "The next day at lunch time I hastened from work." Ken immediately purchased three paintings for himself, handing the teller $400.

Ken set out to talk to the family, to learn all he could about Esther. Ken's hope was that "Esther's art might be where many people who love art can see it and visually grow through Esther's vision." As he soon wrote in a letter to Millie,[19] all he had seen were paintings from the late 1940s or early-to-mid 1950s, as Esther stopped sending Merle works around 1957. These new works were from about 1957 on. Ken spoke to Dorothy and Pete in Pittsburgh, then wrote to those out of town. He took vacation, using his Greyhound travel miles to venture to Chicago and Florida to visit Millie and Milton Salamon, respectively. Ken learned upon meeting Esther's family that he had just missed meeting Esther herself by a short year and a half, a fact that dismays him still to this day. Regarding his researching the life of Esther Phillips, Ken humbly says, "I'm basically pretty shoddy. I'm not a researcher. . . ." Yet research he did. He began with colorful letters showing enthusiasm for the works, and a dedication to finding out more about the artist.

Milton Salamon,

Greetings! Merle Hopleman and I had many cups of tea together at her apartment on Craig Street in the 1970's. The conversation might range from geiger counters to Mrs. Collins turning up the heat before it rains! She felt a few good words could be worth all the words in a number of libraries. She felt secret agents follow around the revolutionary writers and she felt followed. I felt refreshed by her belief in art. In later years she became more and more distrustful and chased away friends, meals on wheels, visiting nurse, the person who delivered her groceries. She needed help, she could walk only a little. The building was sold. Merle was sent to a mental hospital and later one nursing home and then another. She picked up, was talking with people and reading the newspaper. A sudden kidney infection set in and rapidly spread. She died in July of last year.

After Merle left the building it sat vacant. Merle's apartment was broken into. A friend contacted the social worker Helen Bonn and we made arrangements for the storage of Merle's papers. Papers, some important, some the opposite (catalogs), were scattered about an inch thick across the bedroom and the kitchen and it was a case of being areful to try one's best to save everything personal. Helen had found aintings and asked what did I think. It was the first time I had seen sther's work, and my feeling then, as now, is one of enormous xcitement. Esther brings integrity and passion and a fine sense of olor and composition to painting. She is very inventive with perspecti hen she simplifies forms, exciting things are happening, visual evelations. Esther paints in a way no one else paints and there s an intangible quality that runs very deep in the way it is present n the work of Henri Rosseau. One can see the world through her eyes nd visually grow. The work needs to be where it is safe, where people ho love art can study it, where the art can do good.

Through Oswaldo Rodreiquez, I was able to bring a number of Esther's best watercolors in for consideration by Carnegie Museum. He felt very enthsiastic about Esther's work. He really enjoyed looking at them. He left for a very prestigious position at I think the Metropolitan Museum in New York City and the person who took his place did not share his enthusiasms. Luckily this person in recent times found another job.

The Rosenthals are eager to donate works to Carnegie Museum, Helen Bonn is hoping the works by Esther that Merle had find a good home. My biggest fear is if the museum were to return what it has of Esther's work. Our hope is that they might accept many more. I'd lik to send the museum good photos and a cover letter with a biographical sketch of Esther.

From September 7 to September 28th I have a vacation and I hope to buy a 15 day Ameripass, good for anywhere Greyhound goes. Greyhoun goes to Cocoa Beach. I wondered if there is a chance we might be ab to meet for a couple hours and talk extremely eager to hear what you have to say about Esther and there are many questions I have.

Sincerely,

Ken Chute

(412-241-2778)

Just as Millie took notes on what her aunt told her, Ken began to do the same. Both Millie and Milton provided Ken with knowledge about their aunt's life, and showed Ken paintings. Ken organized his information into files, and diligently photographed the works. He learned more about Esther's life from pouring through Merle's effects, where he found the journals and letters that give so much detail about Esther's life.

Since Esther's death, other nieces and nephews had started to acquire some of her paintings through Dorothy. Richard Goldman, Molly's son, "line[d] the hallways of three [of his] Florida childcare centers"[20] with them. He owns the Another Generation Preschool franchise; in 1986, reporters for the *Miami Herald* spotlighted the centers' showcasing of the paintings. "Bright colored merry-go-round horses, absent of riders, are suspended in midair and frozen in a surrealistic dance."[21] As well, paintings depicting "bridges, factories, shops and street life" all helped the teachers to present city life to the children, and to hopefully implant an awareness and appreciation of modern art.[22]

Ken Chute also traveled to New York City, the place where he believes Esther basically got lost as an artist, to look up the addresses where she lived. He took photos of the buildings on the the front sidewalks of which Esther set up to paint. He persisted, throughout all of the 1980s, in his writing about Esther to any and all respected in the art field in Pittsburgh. To a modern-day Carnegie Tech professor, he inquired of Esther's time there: "Any information you could pass along about Esther is . . . a contribution toward the hope that Esther's work might be where it is safe (major art museums) and where people who love art might study it and grow from it. The art needs to be where it can do good."[23] He tried again with the Carnegie Museum of Art in 1986, writing Barbara Phillips, assistant director for administration.[24]

One of the great twentieth century American artists is Esther Phillips. . . . I feel this with all my heart and I can not, and will not, unsee what I see. . . . If you look her name up in an art history book you will notice her name is not yet there. Pictures of her paintings are not yet there . . . A number of great works by

Esther are already at the museum, in storage. You can imagine how I feel, realizing folks at the museum are travelling around the world and I have immense difficulty encouraging them to look at art that is right there. . . .

In 1987, Ken wrote Annagreth Nill, also on staff at the Carnegie, all still to no avail.[25]

As early as 1985, there had been a push on the part of the family to try to get Esther's work shown at a major art gallery in Pittsburgh. At some point in the late 1980s or early 1990s, Patrick J. McArdle, a rock music promoter and independent collector of art in Pittsburgh (including much primitive or primitive-like work), found out about and became interested in Esther's art. He caught the interest of Barb McClure at the now-defunct Carson Street Gallery in Pittsburgh's Southside. "Pat and [writer friend] Megan Shay put the gallery show together, with Dorothy's approval." (For her article, Megan interviewed a few individuals who had known Esther, including Milton Weiss. She even bought the portrait that Weiss had been compelled to paint of Esther that day long ago in Sybil's apartment.

Dorothy had retained a great number of the works that Esther had given her and her husband. She still maintained a small interest in doing what seemed appropriate with the large number of paintings that she held—putting on a show. "They should be in people's homes where people can enjoy them."[26] Pat McArdle wanted to do the exhibit on Esther, in part, because "he wanted to see justice served for the support Phillips showed the struggling John Kane in the 1930s," stated Nicole Buchlmayer, who also wrote an article accompanying the Carson Street Show.[27] "[Kane] was a common man with great vision." McArdle also said, "I knew I could bring her work to a wider public because the art was nice and strong. . . ."[28] With Pat's influence, Dorothy consented to the show. Ken was involved in the preparation for the show in that he retained in his possession many, many works that Merle had. Ken, totally self-effacing, explained his connection with the work—that he did not really own them but was simply representing them on an ongoing basis (But at that time, talk of proceedings had started which would enable him and Mike Vargo to hold title to Merle's possessions, including these paintings.)

The October 1–16, 1991 Carson Street Gallery show, entitled "Esther Phillips: A Life in Paint," was a success. Approximately 60 percent of the show was provided for by Ken Chute's submissions. In other words, mostly figurative watercolors from the institution—the women series—and paintings of the institution grounds comprised the show, plus works from the early-to-mid 1950s. Also included in the show were a couple of early Pittsburgh paintings, a few New York pre-institution works, and what would be her later New York work, which Dorothy and Pete sent from her Lincoln Square apartment. Perhaps some of the better works of the institution period, the ones that Will Barnett had selected to hold on to for a short while, which never made their way into a major New York show, might have been included in the Pittsburgh show, considering that Ken could only bring in so many to the art museum. Definitively not included were the works in storage in the vertical files at the Carnegie Museum of Art's administrative offices, and "lost" works somewhere in museum storage, bought by John O'Connor and Edward Duff Balkan.

Carson Street Gallery proprietor Barb McClure said of Esther's work that it was "very vital, like it almost doesn't want to stay within the confines of the canvas." She was taken with the wide variety in Esther's work; to her, changing styles shows an artist's integrity and stature. What interested McClure especially in the work was its "emotional intensity." She felt it was "definitely modern art . . . of the world now—but more accessible than most of what I see today." She added, "You don't have to know the artist to appreciate the work."[29] Nicole Buchlmayer, in her article written for the Pittsburgh entertainment weekly *Standing Room Only*, was the only person to quote from interviews with Ken Chute. "Esther Phillips paints a mental hospital from the inside out. She had a rare form of integrity. All she did was paint. She committed herself to art without compromise. . . . I believe in Esther's work totally. This (showing) is a step forward."[30] It pleased Ken that people were seeing and buying her work, but he later expressed that he didn't want people to scoop up her paintings. He desires to have her work on view at museums, her life as artist given due recognition. In her article, Buchlmayer provided some insight into Ken's art collecting philosophy: "He has several pieces of 'endangered art,' most bought cheaply at thrift stores and flea markets."[31]

Many people in Pittsburgh saw Esther's works, and several sold, with prices ranging from $250 to $1300. Dorothy felt that Esther "would have been pleased to know that she's getting a real gallery show and all this attention now." [34] Attending the show's opening would be an elderly Milton Weiss, who saw for the first time the full range of Esther's work. Of her work done in the 1950s, he commented, "These paintings are colorful ones—very pseudo-primitive. The perspective is way off. Intentionally. [Some] are more sophisticated [than others]. That's interesting. Shows how far ahead she was. Charming. Very contemporary."[33]

Megan Shay's article concluded by saying, "There are large gaps in what is known about Esther Phillips that further research and study may someday piece together. In the lace work of what is known, the pattern of dedication, persistence and passion for paint is rare and radiant." After the run was over, all the paintings, wrongly, went back to Dorothy, who put them under the supervision of Pat McArdle. Included were the works that were under Ken's guardianship and even those he personally purchased at the Pittsburgh National Bank. (Ken modestly and regrettably chose not to speak up.)

Later the following year, Esther's works went to the Johnstown and the Blair Art Museums, a couple of hours outside of Pittsburgh, in a show entitled "Another World: Esther Phillips." A small passage of writing by this author, who had already begun her research on *This Fantastic Struggle*, was included in the accompanying show catalog which described Esther's life and art.[34] Curator Madelon Sheedy added to Barb McClure's comment about Esther's paintings not staying within the confines of the canvas: "Neither did Esther Phillips. She lived and painted in another world, a world without confines."[35]

Chapter Twenty-One

"THE INNER LIFE OF THE ARTIST"[1]

"*S*he was by no means naive"—the words of director emeritus of the Carnegie Museum of Art, Dr. Leon Arkus, of Esther Phillips as artist. Arkus had been appointed director in 1968, and guided the museum through a period of physical growth and impressive acquisition of impressionist, post-impressionist, and European decorative art. He saw Esther's work for the first time only after retirement, in the winter of 1992, when the author approached him for feedback on Esther's art. He affirmed her talent and validated the researching and writing of her life.[2]

It was evident to Leon Arkus that Esther had training and that she was choosing her approach to the landscapes and women-shapes before him. Arkus knew the difference between her work and that of true primitives like John Kane, of whom Arkus wrote a biography. Arkus certainly saw Esther's appreciation for primitive style, which her work at times emulated. But he stressed a second time that she was "not a naive person," the same thing Milton Weiss and other knowledgeable artists said of Esther's art.

As for influences and tendencies apparent in her work, Leon Arkus felt that Esther must have seen a show of German expressionism. He also noted her similarity to Milton Avery, not in content matter (where Esther used a "stylistically female form") but surely, according to a contemporary Pittsburgh artist also stricken with the similarity, in her color fields.[3] (Likely this is why Esther took her work to Avery in the

1950s, as Glen and Ed had mentioned.) Arkus even saw a bit of the traditional Flemish artist Peter Bruegel in Esther's painting and a bit of a distillation of modern artist Stuart Davis, as well. (The Bruegel similarity is likely in the "voluptuous women-forms" that even Ed Evans had commented upon as being "European," Rubenesque, he felt.)

Leon Arkus respectfully found "amusing" some of Esther's works in the women series. He sensed an intended wit amid the nevertheless poignant depictions of institution life, and the playful, lighthearted take on all the surrounding scapes to be found about her throughout life. Like early twentieth century experimentor Florine Stettheimer, some of Esther's "deliberately naive compositions" were perhaps as wry and witty as was her verbal commentary, and as charming as her demeanor. According to Charlotte Streifer Rubinstein in *American Women Artists*, Stettheimer and peer Romaine Brooks "forged [an] independant and unique style" at the beginning of the modern movement. Esther, too, like these women, could be considered a "maverick, [a] deeply rebellious personalit[y] who created [her] own forms from [her] personal visions."[4]

"Esther was composing." She'd obviously take what was in her field of given view and fit what she wanted to on canvas or board, contemporary Pittsburgh artist Evan Knauer said upon viewing Esther's work. "The important thing was to get the image [any barns, cows, washbasin that she wanted in the picture] across." Similar to what Will Barnet had remarked of Esther's work, Knauer stated, "She played with space. She would make [content matter] large or small not according reality, but to her feelings." In this toying with the perceived field of vision, Esther was not unlike like artist Doris Lee, who in "convincing manner . . . replaced the obvious requirements of physical reality with her own peculiar juxtapositions of figures that charm the viewer. The presence of birds, which frequently adds very little to the composition, adds to the personal pleasure of the artist."[5]

Knauer was impressed with Esther's field of colors, both in the women series and the landscapes, and was especially taken with her "Milton Avery dark blue" that shows up in a "towel-draped woman" painting owned by Dorothy Steinberg and the "Avery pinks" of the institution landscapes. He noted that she was a "colorist"—mixing her paints first, off the board or canvas, and then applying them. "Her colors are not chosen lightly." He suggested that it was to her credit that she so concerned herself with and succeeded at the application of her colors, a difficult matter when it comes to watercolor painting.

Significant to Knauer was Esther's painting the air around a figure, something Matisse was known for, and her attention to where one color touches another. He also found interesting that she really had her nurse whites pop off the canvas. "She was going for effect," desiring to lighten up the area. It seems she did this through oil. "Where the paint is applied thin in some of her paintings, the texture behind is visible . . . her paint strokes are textured, her brush strokes unifying."

Artist Doris Lee was noted for her primitive-like landscapes (farms and orchards); Robert Henkes, in *American Women Painters of the '30s & '40s*, suggests that her "primitive approach succeeds because of the sophistication of the artist." It was not happenstance nor due to lack of training.[6] Indeed, it was "sophisticated stylization . . . the result of training," suggests even Rubinstein of Lee. "The primitive quality that critics found in her work in the mid-thirties was deceptive."[7] This would be the very concept that Arkus pointedly made about Esther and her work, as had Milton Weiss, Knauer, and other contemporary Pittsburgh artists.

Lee's feigned primitivism permitted some critics to dismiss her work. Esther surely encountered a bit of the same, at least from any who wrongly categorized her work as primitive, childish, or "outsider." (The Outsider Art/Art Brut genre includes artists without schooled instruction, who are outside of artistic movements but especially alienated in some major capacity from society. It usually involves a mental health connection; this framework even includes "Schizophrenic Art.")

Like Esther, the men around her in the 1930s, who later were able to make a name for themselves as Abstract Expressionists, set their training to the side. They did not abandon it, but broke from established patterns in order to find an individual artistic way. She and they employed the artistic sensitivity that comes with training, matching it with a strong, unique voice. Together, this is the marking of any avant-garde artist of some proportion. They all experimented, getting "in touch with the 'chaos of ecstasy,'"[8] finding one's own primitive artistic flow, and then using technique gained from training when it could best serve the individual voice.

Knowledgeable people in the arts understood that Esther's work did not fit neatly within any particular genre, though it definitely is *not* primitive or outsider. Esther was most a self-made independant artist of the modern movement. Though she never really took on the abstract completely in her work, she definitely flirted with it small-scale. Interestingly, Knauer had suggested that Esther—unlike the Abstract Expressionists, who made the abstract a viewable object by using an expressionist style—actually came to abstractionism from her expressionist point of view. That is, she didn't take nothingness and capture that essence expressionistically, turning it into something glorious. "She'd instead take a subject and then dismantle it mentally," gloriously abstracting the reality before her. "The abstraction was in her, so she didn't need to go any further."

Milton Weiss had stated, "I don't know if [Esther] was aware of the modern movement at all." (Of course, she was very aware of it, and set out to stake some place of her own within it.) But he knew the movement "was just in her. . . ."

⑥ ⑥ ⑥

"Esther had a compulsion. She wanted to paint. Nothing else mattered," spoke Dorothy, recollecting her sister's life of painting via phone interview, about a year after the close of the Carson Street show.[9] Hers was an accurate statement, relevant to the understanding of an artist's life. But any insight Dorothy gleaned of the artistic existence never quite approached acceptance. Typical of most outsiders to the artist's world, Dorothy continually appended to her commentary expressions less positive, ones that belied a judging, a belittling of the way of life of the artist, rather than lending any hopeful sign that an artist's life had now become any less obscure.

> · Esther was not interested in anything except her art, her painting. She could never make a living at it, though . . . [She] said many times [toward the end of her life] that she loved me—but

she didn't concern herself with me, or my family. She was not interested in family or anybody else's problems. She didn't give a damn about anyone else. She did nothing for anybody—just herself.

But Esther Phillips' true family was her circle of various friends, her peers, the whole Greenwich Village community of creative artists and other displaced individuals there, such as homosexuals, all in a similar struggle to her own, and all who appreciated each other's creative work and passionate identification with unique lifestyles. Esther had plenty of friends who helped her and whose lives she equally touched. Dorothy, who only knew Esther at the end of her life, cannot surmise that she did nothing for anyone. Likewise no one can rashly comment with any knowledgeable authority on the lives of a group of people deeply, meaningfully different from one's own, yet Dorothy's comments echo what has been said by many, since the beginning of time, about all artists—that they are selfish and lazy.

Esther helped and concerned herself with the problems of fellow artists. If she didn't concern herself with her birth family, it was because they didn't think enough to allow her to become the person her spirit intended. They shied away from visiting her while she was most troubled, when institutionalized. They didn't think to ever concern themselves with her circle of humanity. Their only thought, like much of society, was to attempt, consciously or not, to scold or convert the artist. As Dorothy expressed, "[My family] couldn't change her attitudes about life"—as if Esther's attitudes needed to be changed. Indeed, the old sense of righteousness was still strong within the family, like the message sent early on that she must give back financially to the family, though Esther and her friends had long given up expecting that they would find an economic place within and emotional support from parent society. Certainly they were suffering, to various degrees, because of it.

Though Dorothy admitted that Esther was "tremendously talented, very gifted," she simultaneously added that "there were elements in her character that were obviously nonexistent—because she only believed in herself and her painting. Esther had absolutely no practicality." This is a statement also often uttered and familiar to many; aware of a bit of its legitimacy, some creative artists even say it of themselves. But a deeper apprehension is warranted. Of course Esther believed most in herself and her painting, but also of her community, one far removed from Dorothy's world, the world of mainstream society. The reality of existence for Esther and those other artists was very different from most. How the mainstream definition of "practicality" factors in is extraneous.

"There were no restrictions on her life," spoke Dorothy, with a touch of resentment well evident across the phone line. Perhaps this is what most bothered her, as it does others outside the artistic circle. The creative artist seems free to choose and appears to exercise that freedom sometimes with reckless abandon, exulting in it even. But the artist is simply making use of a choice granted all of us in this life—the ability to decide to go forth with what one does best, to try to find and follow the natural intended course of one's life, one's inclinations and abilities as they slowly present themselves over time and consequence and through the exercising of individual choice and free will. Artists rightfully and healthily will not accept others' projections of identity upon them. And yes, with that liberty often comes exultation, revelry.

Esther and her friends did celebrate their freedom, their attention to the self and their collective human joys. To be able to live tending to the expression of the self is glorious. However, like anything else in life, any reveling in freedoms requires measure, a steadying balance. "Nothing else mattered" as much as painting to Esther, however, a fact that even Dorothy stumbled upon. No partying was as important to her as the creative work itself. With the liberating lifestyle must come a self-discipline that allows genuine, working artists, like Esther and others, to bring their focus to their talent, their work, defining their art and their life.

Dorothy Rosenthal grew tired of talking about her sister's life and abruptly drew to a close her comments about Esther. That was the last time she granted a conversation about Esther. It seems that, with the articles accompanying the Carson Street show, Dorothy felt that enough had been written about Esther. "I don't understand why anyone would want to further write about the life of my sister. Her life was not that significant. She added, in her closing, "Yes, I'm proud of her. But also her life left much to be desired."

Now, questioning the desirability of complete freedom, to work and live without restriction, but without security, without assurance of the basics of life being available to you, is valid. But only the person making the choices affecting his own self, his own life, can answer that query. Esther, of course, did so, not simply at the close of her life, but throughout. The spiritedness with which she conducted her affairs certainly confirmed her end vocalization, that she "lived the best life one could possibly lead." She certainly felt that her struggle was worth it, for she persisted lifelong in identifying with being an artist, though at times downtrodden by it. Esther embraced what she was good at, and she went after a life that tended to that very thing wholeheartedly. She followed the wise suggestions that Carnegie Tech put forth concerning a career in art. And the sacrifices such as they laid forth unfortunately proved all too true.

Though she surely hoped that some of her early challenges as an artist in Pittsburgh would dissolve once in New York City, Esther of course found differently early on in New York. But though she didn't become a "known" artist, it certainly wasn't because she didn't try. She worked hard at her craft because she enjoyed her work, and was freely choosing the course of her life. She willfully chose those risks that naturally come with being an artist and an artist only, that come to any who decide only to paint or to make music and minimally survive at that, because it is what one does best, where one wants to focus his time, as opposed to perhaps "selling shoes" on the side. Esther made that difficult choice and came to her own terms with it, which is what is required. There is so little regard and reward given, though, to those like Esther who willfully choose an artistic existence, whether it be accepting only creative work or squeezing creative work in after a day laboring at odd jobs (as did John Kane). Though it is a necessity that the person choosing a certain way of life comes to his own terms with that, any society that wants to consider itself enlightened must aim for an acceptance, if not understanding, and certainly an accommodation of, different ways of life. This can come about only through a thorough, intelligent, nonjudgmental insight into that which is unfamiliar and preliminarily uncomfortable.

Why do we try to prejudge what is unfamiliar to us? Why the desire to remark upon it, criticize it from afar, but not to acquaint oneself with it—in an attempt to see, to look upon, and better get to know? Can we not accept that some things foreign, which we can not completely understand or embrace for ourselves, might speak to others? Can we not at least find some identification with another's struggle, perhaps different than our own, but a struggle nevertheless? With such an identification could come finally an understanding, and perhaps even incorporation of some attributes that the lifestyle of the other holds for all of us. Society should ultimately aspire to this.

Genuine, committed creative artists work so very hard. Does society realize? Many work one job all day, only to come home and devote oneself to one's true work at a certain point in the evening. Unlike many people, with a defined work-week, after which, each day and weekend, they have time off, to spend with family, with hobby, time to simply relax, the artist often gets to his real work only after returning from some job that simply pays the bills. True work for many artists begins here—and goes often into the night. Then, perhaps, a release, maybe meeting with other like-minded souls over a beer or to hear a band late-night. A generalization, but often legitimate. The artist gets a bad rap for all of the above—he's considered not to have a profession, be wasting time, be off in his own world. He's a partier, a bum, running with a rough crowd. . . .

The true artist's work is certainly not a hobby, done to occupy time outside of whatever work activity pays the bills. If only he had more time. There is first the artist's work, his art, and then there is secondarily the task of making a living—whether it be waitressing, playing music someone else wrote, or scrambling to sell your less-than-fine art (as Esther did with her ceramics). An artist must find the time and energy for both. For truly inspired and talented artists can not choose to *not* be creative. Their art is usually not something they simply want to spend aimless time at. They have projects they want to see through, images they want to translate into paint, words to write, and meanings to convey. The genuine artist's work *does* compel him. He feels within a drive to create, singularly and collaboratively—music, visual art, written and interdisciplinary work, theatre, and movement art.

Significantly, unlike most holding "regular jobs," the sincere creative artist is defined by his work. It means everything to him. His identity is tied up in living creatively. But not pretentiously, to put on a show for the outside world, but because he is driven to do such for himself, with or without money. He cares about his work, pours forth everything in it. Because he enjoys it so, he endures the toil of energy spent. But he receives little if any financial reward, and little respect—in fact, ridicule. Not all of society can say this, save for the rare individuals who really like their jobs and thus enjoy working hard at those jobs. Surely no one is as wrapped up in work as someone self-employed, because of the investment and discipline needed to make it. The self-employed creative artist, by both necessity and nature, usually tops such a list. Like any small business owner, the amount of work really needed to survive overwhelms the artist, but he is proud of his connection to his creative work, which really is his life. However, there is simply no money or respect attached to the artist's attempts to carve out his niche in society.

If he spends too much time on his art, and the food doesn't appear on the table, society laughingly questions the artist's intent (or intensity), and ultimately condemns his activities as frivolous. So is the artist's energy dismissed. To be on the receiving end of the desultory comments, or to just pick up the non-verbal vibes, is amazingly frustrating. Esther, Eugenia, Van Trump, and many others have felt it. If there is no financial reward for an artist's efforts in clear sight, the interrogation that sometimes occurs by family, friends, and others will focus on the vast amount of time spent producing, compiling, playing an instrument. At the same time, when asked what he has been doing with his time, the artist can't seem to talk of the day's events in context of it having been work because he's aware that he won't be understood or taken seriously within that context. Suddenly it will be declared, ironically defined by others, that the artist is doing nothing. Without money, the vast amount of creative activity is amazingly rendered suddenly invisible.

"You're spending so much time painting, rehearsing, getting resources and supplies together." A statement surely aimed at Esther, as well as at many creative artists—writers, actors, musicians. And yet indeed within this incredulous declaration does lie the acknowledgment of the time and energy expended. So how is it that the artist who so often has these words posed to him will from the same mouths hear uttered, "You're lazy. You don't want to work. You don't know how to work. You're not doing anything"? Of course the artist knows how to work. Perhaps more than most, who must have direction from a supervisor to stay to task. Any musician who's ever practiced alone in his room, a painter or sculptor who rigorously experiments with different mediums and techniques, an actor tediously learning lines—they all know that discipline and dedication for creative work come from within or don't come at all. All of the aforementioned do the above activities without pay 90 percent of the time, in order to hone their craft, but still with the hope of some "break," some paid work interspersed throughout, some success to come to them, for a somewhat easier life, at least at times, if nothing else. In fact, in order to conduct their artistic work and then to market it appropriately, artists must pour, albeit apprehensively, what little money they have into their work—with independent filmmakers likely suffering the hardest financial squeeze.

One need only witness, for example, an independent theatre artist who, night after night, goes into rehearsal for hours and weeks on end, putting together with others a unique creation that they toiled over, with great joy but no pay, to begin to understand how very hard genuinely creative people do work, and how much they believe in their unique voice, as opposed to that simply dictated by watered-down Broadway standards. To open to almost nonexistent houses in cities where "standard art fare"—rehashed musicals, nonchallenging art, touring MTV bands with absolutely no unique musicality about them—is attended and paid for regularly. Beside the fact that they are receiving no pay, what an insult, then, not to be taken seriously, to not be admired at least for drive and dedication and vision, but to instead have these activities that make up their time written off as worthless. Thankfully, some corporations, independent business sponsors, and private individuals do recognize dedication and vision and support even the independent arts through advertising in playbills and the like.

Actually, any of the various utterings by outsiders that so madden creative artists ironically make the best sense when coupled with the factor of money. "Why are you spending so much time playing your guitar, drawing, writing, participating in theatre, etc., when you are not getting paid for it?" Here, the value system is exposed at its ugly best, and it has not so much to do with effort expended as it has to do with money. Though working probably harder than many who take home a fat paycheck, with all the benefits and perks that go with it, Esther's activities and those of other artists are at best skeptically queried and at worst insultingly degraded. It is as if money were the only sought-after outcome for what one does, for how one spends time, how one expends energy in this life. Indeed, the work dilemma of creative individuals is a dilemma of values—a serious difference in values from most of society. Genuine creative artists do their work without care or concern as to whether they are given money for it and, for the most part, without much reflection on others' no-win judgments against them, as best they are able. Why the righteousness from society? If only a wider scope of people could come around at least to an understanding, and ideally an embracing of the values inherent in the artistic lifestyle. For the values of the serious creative artist, the way he goes about the world, his way of being, are all so different from those of the consumerist mainstream.

By the time he has made it to adulthood, the artist usually has gotten very hardened to the mass-marketed pop world. At the same time he has refined his own creativity, knows who he himself is, and accepts himself for what he does. But this doesn't mean that these same artists occasionally don't question why society just cannot purchase their creative products or output. Thus they sometimes furiously try to find buyers of their work, patrons of their art. Believing strongly in what they have created, there is still a striving for self-preservation amidst that sacrifice of bodily needs that occurs while expending energy to make art. There is certainly often a hope that some means of living can be earned by one's talent. Because they are working anyway, because they want to, some artists will thus try ever-hard, as Esther and Eugenia did, to seek out supporters, believers in the creators of fine art.

Members of bands that try to get by just with their music are so grateful for the little bit of food and perhaps a dent in the rent money that comes from a weekend of playing. Usually, this minimal life is the norm for a creative person. But to hope, to strive for more than a minimal life, is natural. Artists' primary concern is to create what speaks to themselves and feel blessed when it also speaks strongly to a peer. Musicians hope to have their music heard by getting it out there—not necessarily to huge audience, just heard at a club or by selling some recordings. But there is of course a strong hope for opportunity, a desire to rise above poverty-level living. In that journey to thus market one's work, there is still constant concern for retention of originality and integrity of one's creation, especially as buyers might look for more. Supporters must be as sincere as the artist, not about to ask him to produce less-than original work to please the public, and/or, once successful, to go along with hype, momentary only, that their work is somehow greater and larger than anyone else's.

It seems, unfortunately, that always at the not-too-distant other end of the spectrum of poverty for an artist looms the danger of "selling out." Money dangled before a band or any artist is so tempting. But, with the commitment to a record label or a dealer often comes the sacrificing of an original, unique vision (if ever there was one to begin with, as certainly there are "artists" who don't even know what that means). So the corporate world of art—in the form of dealers, record companies, major public theatres that only produce mass hits—when it occasionally gets its jaws on a uniquely vibrant creative artist, churns and spits him out not very differently than were Pollock, Kline, and the Abstract Expressionists dis-affected by the phenomena of success in the 1950s. Perhaps it is a mixed blessing that the corporate art world doesn't often come knocking on the doors of genuinely talented creative individuals with unique voice. Most artists never have to deal with the disingenuous agent from the gallery or record label, though, because opportunity to get their product seen, heard, purchased, and treated with respect never comes in a large way. The appreciative audience is the fellow artist most of the time, perhaps sipping a beer while hearing their friends' original compositions played in a dive club, or seeing truly original painting and film in an underground gallery space like Mary Shaw's Number 8 Center Court.

The reality that this unfortunate demon exists at the other end of the spectrum of artistic success must not overshadow the need for viable work opportunity for all creative artists, opportunity that somehow affords the retention of the original voice, the unique vision that each artist holds within, and has the potential to share with others. But there is little such opportunity in American cities today, for our current mainstream culture values art far less than the high esteem it holds for sport, for example. "Having artists helps the general energy of a town,"[10] spoke Mary Shaw. Milton Weiss, too, when reflecting on Esther's and his own artistic life, had said that Pittsburghers don't really appreciate art, but do sport. Very true, but Pittsburghers are no different from the people of most American cities.

Esther herself said decades ago that Pittsburghers who buy art do not buy Pittsburgh art.[11] John O'Connor, too, in his 1936 letter to Mrs. John Bowman, wrote, "I know the fact that [Clarence McWilliams'] painting has been purchased is going to be great encouragement to [him]. I am wishing that more Pittsburghers would take a little interest in Pittsburgh artists."[12] What both are saying is still said today in Pittsburgh (and by artists in other cities). Mainstream society enjoys existing within a framework of mass-produced entertainment and wall-coverings. If visual art receives attention, it is usually an easily-palatable style or content with the backing of current trend. If music by a city's local bands is paid attention to, it is in the form of a city's mayoral office sponsoring public square gatherings where musicians are supposed to be grateful for being given "exposure," but no pay, and the same brand of artists playing derivative, run-of-the-mill music are usually employed over and over again. Most people don't know or care about the thriving but overlooked underground art scene of their community. If at all, it takes a long time for unique individual voices in the arts to be noticed and respected. If only the cultural aesthetic could be changed so that inde-

pendent artists, musicians, and thinkers are, if not understood completely, at least esteemed.

Exceptions certainly exist, with some few artists, certainly possessing talent, managing with skill but also luck to make a name for themselves locally. But it's rare for an underground artist to break through
with his or her truly innovative, fresh approaches. It's usually easily
palatable art, period. For the most part, too, creative work commands
attention if it comes out of New York, San Francisco, or Los Angeles.
There is little glamour attached to a working hometown artist, unless of
course he spits out formulaic music that sounds like the latest that
MTV endorses. If only an adequate examination were to take place, a
teeming underbelly scene, like Esther and Mary Shaw's would be found.
Today's Carnegie Museum in Pittsburgh certainly sponsors no such
search for local visual artists. Even within the three mentioned cities,
whose artists' work is noticed *outside* those parameters, artists tend to
scramble within, as they really started to en masse in the 1950', to the
top of a huge pile, clamoring over what little scraps are out there for a
working artist. Thus the well-known fact (at least among artists) that
artists "get lost" in New York City, San Francisco, or Los Angeles.

It is no hidden fact among an art community who is especially intent
on their work. Though Esther's fame, too, was "not what it should be,"[13]
her work was not lost, did not go undiscovered. For she had an effect
on those artists she came into contact with. Her work was known by
her peers, and she realized that their judgement was the most significant. It is they who well knew the self-design and integrity of her life
and art, the strict personal honesty that characterized her behaviors.
For essentially it is our peers that know our work best, and despite in-
fighting that occurs within any subgroup of society, they will always
give their fullest measure of attention and, when warranted, appreciation and congratulation.

Most artists do try to find some appreciative audience outside the
close circle, despite the near futility of such effort. Like Eugenia and
Esther, they do so with a spiritedness that keeps them semi-sane amid
rejection. Esther certainly proved this, ever hopeful for a sale, even

when, to the reader of her life circumstance, such seemed almost impossible at times. There is always the hope for a "break" to come about in one's career, as well as the strong feeling that one can't possibly be consistently working, with conviction, to no profitable and estimable end. "Not if, but when"—is the attitude that keeps many artists maintaining their drive toward perfecting their work. Esther herself felt this way, as she remarked to Merle in the summer of 1952, "The sooner things break for me the better." Are artists crazy, then, working ever hard on their craft, disregarding convention, commerce, and marketing savvy that would doom the sales forecast of the unique products they have to offer? Are kids who are into art "unworldly and unbalanced," as parents view them? How ironic to consider them not of this world when it is actually the young artist who realizes that he must fend for himself by being worldly—going out into the world, often traveling, scraping to get by through all sorts of odd jobs, often working twice as hard as most—just to make ends meet. Too, they usually don't settle down to family life due to their tough struggle to stay alive—the doing of their real work, and their work to make a living.[14]

Are artists "out of touch" by not only holding different values, but also by steadfastly maintaining diligence and hope, projecting confidence in their abilities, despite vast rejection, as Esther did, evidenced by commentary in her letters to Merle? Or profoundly the opposite? Maybe amazingly strong individuals? Trying to weather a storm that defines their life almost as much as their urge for creativity—with poverty looming around every corner of artistic choice. A storm, a fantastic struggle to contend valiantly, one that surely holds great potential to fell them—breaking spirit, bank account, determination to make a name, or, usually, all of the above.

Certainly outside society does not hold sole title to the questioning of the way of life of the artist. While living this existence devoted to their creativity, an existence honoring the inherent choice available to us all in this life, artists themselves battle thoughts questioning the benefits of such a free life. Due to the sorry physical conditions that many well know—lack of enough food to eat or a secure roof over head—many artists, like Esther, sometimes find themselves in a severe internal battle, despite their strength. For Esther, and unfortunately far too many other creative people, psych/physiologic manifestations of the frustrations of an artistic life can lead to the institution. For others attempting to cope in a world that doesn't embrace the creative or other alternative lifestyle, the consequences may seem less severe, but are still commonly identifiable as emotional or psychological troubles.

There is a disconnection that takes place with many artists, as with any people seen as too different from the mainstream to take viable part in it. The disconnection can take the form of outward creative rage, as found in part of the punk music movement that so epitomized rebellion, defiance, frustration at alienation and various forms of oppression throughout the world—a movement made up, for the most part, of well-intended youth, creative figures striving for true progressive social change. Or the distancing can take the form of the more archetypal artist figure who, with degrees of reclusivity, becomes so far removed from the world of commerce as to have absolutely no business sense. Sometimes manifestations of this disconnection take the form of unusual, very original behaviors that are just too odd not to be labelled off-base. In each and all of these scenarios, the individuals involved are more or less directly stigmatized for all or some of their actions, which feed their sense of being dispossessed.

An artist finds ways to cope, to adjust to the fact that his value system is different from the main. Sometimes the adjustments are healthy, such as with the punk "do it yourself" aesthetic, but just "different" enough to be labeled crazy. Sometimes they are less healthy adjustments, as in Esther's case, with hypochondriacal symptoms surfacing, true signs, of course, of dis-ease, symbols of her internal battling of the stigma associated with and tribulations of being an artist. Then having to accept the fact that she got ill, Esther faced further stigmatization as a woman once institutionalized. For sure, the adjustments that any marginalized group of society make are epitomized by some form of disconnection, a movement away from the world at large. To be in a world whose rules don't make sense to your genuine self is very disquieting. It surely placed Esther, and places other artists, elsewhere, bringing them to a psychic space that instead nurtures their creativity, a respite, a cove holding the "encroaching world at bay." She, and many creative individuals, sometimes walk a fine line between the two spaces—the boundaries of their own strong senses of self, the strong sense of self-identity that sees themselves and their friends through, and what emerges onto them from the world. Because artists like Esther do strive, healthily, to disengage in some way from the painful knowledge that creativity is not all that nurtured and affirmed in this society, there is somewhat a buffer from experiencing the real pain of alienation. So there is an underground fight, an anarchist rebellion, perhaps, and a strange acceptance that those who care about art— theatre, music, dance, painting—must live in a strange underworld, a community of like-minded souls, an underground peopled by tremendously intelligent, perceptive and sensitive, at times jaded, remarkably *feeling* individuals.

Though there is an uncanny community resolve to not go toward those values embraced by the mainstream, a creed so present one can almost touch it as it floats mist-like above the heads of everyone attending an underground art opening or in a crowded dive-bar with independent musicians both on stage and in the audience, the reality is often that this creative otherworld has its birth in the pain and anger of misunderstanding and unacceptance. The strength, the resolve, the spirit, the compelling connection between everyone, the sassiness and spunk and downright defiance present, have usually developed for a reason. To have the intelligence and wisdom and perceptiveness to see the world as it is, and the sensitivity, creativity to offer ideas different, to have such a strong inner voice that is listened to and respected by those within a surrounding "scene," but not heard or understood by those outside it, makes for what Esther's sister Dorothy rightly labeled "a crying need for expression," with an accompanying way of survival askew from other models of self-actualization.

Not all of the fury and sadness at being stripped of economic opportunity in the "real world" come out creatively or in camaraderie, for some. As with Esther, a good many artists repress the strong feelings of resentment at being disenfranchised from society. Perhaps they manifest them in other ways. For her, the balance that she was able to maintain for the most part, the steadying of herself enough that she could get up daily to paint, the ecstasy of a new creation outweighing the despair of no new buyers and no additional money for food, was tipped twice in a major way. First, right before being institutionalized and second, toward the time she was forced to move into the St. George. Of course the latter never saw her fully recover. During these two times in particular, Esther was truly off balance. Anxiety had sufficiently worn her away to the point where she became very unwell, distanced from reality, out of touch with herself. This showed as she curtailed her painting, only at these two times. All throughout the rest of her life, even though her existence was difficult and she was troubled from time to time, she'd paint and paint as much as possible. Of course in the institution, the change in Esther's initial dark outlook only came about due to her simply painting once again, this being her balm, as she got back to herself.

When the affirmation Esther received from herself and her community of friends was enough to ground her, she could hold sway over the hounding anxiety, she still had a place in this world. When such affirmation wasn't enough, when she was still looking for more and agonized over that, her discomfort, her dis-ease being in a world so foreign to her, showed through. James Van Trump had remarked that Esther was the type of person "with not a very strong hold on the life she had." Actually her grounding was not so slippery as some may have feared, but indeed it had given way in 1942. Esther likely began doubting her decision to be an artist the first time she thought her eyes were strained from painting, at the end of the year in 1941. Rather than acknowledge that, she may have taken her insecurity out on her eyes, it manifesting itself there. They did at times show weakness, but when she willed herself to feel better, she could still paint. Toward the very end of her life, her will lessened and indeed she developed an embolism, with no doctor discounting that. In general, the eyes became weak, as opposed to Esther acknowledging her despair at times, and trying, with help, to address it. Perhaps if she could have done this, her eyes might not have failed her.

During his recollections, Ed Evans had remarked that Esther was "not of this world." And James Van Trump remarked that Esther was "under the surface." They, and others, sensed it about her. Her retreat to a place outside the common world, her withdrawal to a place within herself, was likely at times a bit more visible than is seen in most artists. Essentially all artists living minimally, however, show some signs of the effects of the valiant effort, the fantastic struggle it takes to wrest a place in this life as a creative artist. Though she desired and needed to have adequate housing and enough food to survive just like anyone else in other professions, she worked hard but saw no recompense. Esther always tried to "get a hold of life," make sense of the crazy world about her as much as she could—wandering around quite proficiently, actually, marketing to leaders in business, and the like. But despite the urgings of an enlightened few, like Edgar Kaufmann, there has been no place for paintings in the world of commerce.

Esther was not able to "openly fight" the "kind and benevolent"[15] state that kept her kind struggling, that world that would not acknowledge her and other artists, so hers was a slow and painful inward battle to blot out that world. Surely at least part of her mental illness was "a reflection of the inequalities and conflicts within society."[16] Out of desire the artist seeks out and revels in an exclusionary inner life that brings more joy than the outer world has been able to offer, that renders a life more meaningful, and that best allows the perception, reception, and conveyance of "the spirit and significance of things."[17] But arguably, as much out of *necessity* the artist indeed creates "a self which . . . embodies her in the world and marks her out as distinct . . . unlike any other being."[18] Truly, Esther and other artists are spectres under the surface of life. They embody different spirit-forms as they attempt to stay afloat in a world that is terrified of the possibility they represent, and thus just does not see them.

> Perhaps for a while, waiting for more knowledge, one must content himself with watching the monstrous figures of Miss Hoyleman's visions pass and repass in their own world. . . . For the figures are well-drawn and meaningful; in watching them one apprehends, without explicitly understanding, their reality in the world of the imagination—that world in which, perhaps, one comes nearer to the truth than elsewhere."[19]

The artist has the age-old stigma of being an outsider to a society that scorns a creative life as frivolous, a society that rewards only the scientists and architects of objects of necessity and mainstream desires. All dispossessed people can identify with the wall Esther found herself constantly up against. And especially artists—to this day, in any city—can identify not only with the resistance she encountered, but the tough spirit she had to possess in order to survive. Valiant though the efforts for an original life might be, powerlessness in a money-equals-power society, and the pain that this position brings, takes its toll. Madness can be seen, after all, as "the desperate communication of the powerless."[20] Most artists lucky enough to be in the boundless freedom of creative life still find themselves straitjacketed in this desired role, which ironically keeps them and the mass of society distant from each other.

Ironically within the shade of mental dis-ease society perhaps gets a glimpse of the stigma of disenfranchisement that a societal outsider such as an artist feels. For depression and the like befall almost all of us at some point in our life, though few are willing to thus admit. The reasons are varied—we are indelibly altered by death, divorce, unemployment, or simply nagging dissatisfaction with the course of our lives. In being even temporarily without our healthy emotional faculties, we experience an isolation of self and an isolation from community. To utter to oneself, let alone to another, that one is feeling off-balance, insecure, depressed, or manic is one of the terrible trials of life, though a necessary beginning for transformation to take place. But denial of course rules with a strength unmatched by little else. There is an awful connotation associated with feeling unwell, or different from the rest of functioning society. And this connotation, like all the wrongheaded conceptions about those who are different from the rest of society, must be abolished for people to find wellness.[21] Feeling mentally uncomfortable is not something to be ashamed of. If Esther could have sensed her own nagging dissatisfaction that crept up periodically throughout her life, plaguing her otherwise wondrously joyful existence, if she could have sought out help at those times, and if there were structures well built into the community to provide such help, her life story might have been different.

Certainly like the life of artists, there is much to be learned, understood, and accepted about mental illness and the mentally ill in this society. Many misconceptions and misrepresentations must be fought for us as a society to accept the fact that many of us have or will at least temporarily encounter such dis-ease as Esther did, and to understand the contributions that some of those unfortunately plagued with mental illness might have been able to make to society despite their illness. Even such individuals, who might exhibit what seems ridiculous personal behaviors, indeed have a lot to offer—often intelligence, creativity, unique perspectives. (Interestingly artists, often familiar with mental illness and certainly familiar with dispossession, are much more accepting of these "characters" than the rest of society.) Not all people in institutions are artists, but many an Esther Phillips surely has passed through institutions and clinics unnoticed due to an unwillingness to believe that people off-balance have anything to offer. They pass through this life without consideration or advocacy made on behalf of their capabilities and potential. Perhaps it should be examined why they are ill in the first place—the answers to which may be found in examining just how healthy the society is from which they came.

It is interesting to ponder what might have been had Mrs. Sheldon, Harlem Valley's librarian, not noticed and then advocated for Esther, and what might have been for others if they were given the consideration that Esther was given at Harlem Valley. What this society could be like if—the opposite of stigmatization—all were *encouraged* to seek out mental health care. (Certainly if any one type of health care needs to be available for everyone in this country, with lack of money as no barrier, it should begin with mental health care.) What might have been for Esther and scores of other artists, as well as other generally dispossessed people, had there been more consideration and respect by society for their lives? Surely society needs to address the fact that women still rebelling from traditional roles, men trying to break from the stereotypical role model, artists, the poor, and homosexuals still encounter dis-ease at an alarming rate. Their lives need to be understood, attitudes and policies need to be changed, stigma must be abolished and quality treatment affordably offered. For Esther's family was not uniquely cruel. The problems they had with accepting, understanding, and ultimately valuing Esther's contributions to this life are problems of society. All persons have pain, as the prevalence of mental illness in our society attests, and each person's pain does have "its own history, its own roots—and its own solution. We must listen to our own—and each other's **voices**."[22] We must pause to try to acknowledge and understand what is going on with each of our own lives. We must make it a point to understand the diversity of all lives on this planet.

Some of us are born into more opportunity than others. Each of us is certainly equipped with different faculties. But regardless of our upbringing and our genetic makeup, we must strive to have lives where we are always vicariously examining, readjusting, and choosing the criteria by which we not only create our own life, but accept others'. Exposure to people different from the main is critical—to see that others unlike ourselves actually exist. To see how others live and make bonds of relationship, how they work, what joys and freedoms make up their life, and what struggles particularly haunt they as a people. For, as Harold Winters wrote Merle now long ago, seeing another's suffering puts one's own in perspective.[23]

> They say we live on the fringe but it's not by choice
> The main stream world a dollar a voice[24]
>
> —Evan Knauer, from "Louise"

"The grinding poverty is very real. No society . . . has been as cruel and as viciously indifferent to its best artists as ours," wrote the McDarraghs in *The Artist's World In Pictures*.[25] "The stark tragedy of trying to exist on nothing"[26] unfortunately defines far too many artists in existence in any city to this day. Poverty was certainly a factor in Esther's becoming unwell; that cannot be underplayed. If it is disputed that Esther got sick because she was looking for an acceptance that wasn't out there, it cannot be denied that the tribulations of living the artistic life greatly contributed to making her ill. If you don't have your basic needs met, if you are hungry, there is not any way that spirit alone can carry you. As psychologist Abraham Maslow defined the hierarchy of self-esteem, in the 1960s, self-actualization is first built upon a foundation of food and shelter. Wholeness of person is created only upon that foundation. But artists are never on firm ground. Some are able to be strong despite. But constant living minimally will wear on a person.

"A maverick first to his family, an artist has to work twice as hard merely to remain alive in the world outside, a world in which his aspirations are almost always subject to harsh criticism and ridicule. Keeping body and soul together is a daily victory,"[27] wrote Gloria McDarragh. Esther and many artists really are not looking for much. Not necessarily success and recognition, fame. As artist Andree Ruellan stated about artists from the 1920s, "We wanted society to improve and we felt injustices deeply. Our aim wasn't to get rich. We wanted freedom in our work and in our careers. We wished it for everyone and we expected to find it in Paris. We did."[28] What Esther and many of the artists in the 1940s and 1950s wanted—when all went a little crazy in the art world and they trampled on each other, scrambling to get something massive, yet elusive, dangling before them—was simple recognition from the mass public, respect and dignity for their work. Along with this comes genuine opportunity for work, the elimination of stigma about their lifestyle, and the removal of all forms of oppression affecting them—economic, political, and otherwise. The support that Esther really wanted all along from her parents, unbeknownst to family, was more emotional than financial. (And it is for lack of emotional support that financial support does not come in this country for artists.) The "something" that Esther "wanted intensely but . . . wasn't getting"[29] was not fame and success—though she surely longed for a taste of this as well, especially when some of her comrades were getting it in the '50s—but instead general esteem and respect. This could come, slowly, but likely, if society is really exposed to, and comes to better understand, the life of an artist.

Certain skills bring money, but creative talent does not. But creative artists, like all people, need work in order to survive. It is a terrible predicament to be good at something, to know you have a unique ability to do something that not everyone can, to see its value not just for yourself but universally, and to believe strongly, to know that it should have a place in this society, but to see little prospect for work of that nature. All artists "deserve a better fate"[30]; they need opportunity to earn money using their talent, doing what they do best—whether the opportunity be in the form of public schools and institutions hiring artists en masse for residencies, communities buying original works of art from local painters, people hiring musicians who play original music, not just cover tunes of top-40 crap, or grants and fellowships being awarded to creative individuals so that they can develop their craft and expose ordinary citizens to the vast expressions of beauty and sometimes harsh, vivid, diverse realities within this life—all through art. There should be work for artists; for that to take place, some of it may have to be subsidized. Just as there is money for education, so should there be money for the arts. In this "land of plenty,"[31] it is certainly a shame that a society supposedly as advanced as ours treats its artistic and intellectual property so shabbily as to not only *not* put forth some new means of federal support—creative approaches to viable employment for artists—but to have decreased funding for agencies like the NEA and NEH, which our country has done en masse throughout the 1980s and beyond. As Claudine Brown, director of arts programs at The Nathan Cummings Foundation, so aptly writes,

> Those of us who fund arts programs are often reminded that the arts are spiritually and intrinsically essential, touching every aspect of the human experience. . . . To view them as something separate and apart from the rest of society is short-sighted. . . .
>
> Few members of our society are as widely misunderstood as [artists]. . . . Artists with strong visions have a unique ability to show us a mirror, so that we may better face ourselves. Our need to embrace and employ artists is no different than our need to employ lawyers, teachers, ministers and doctors. . . .
>
> We have few or no awards for artists who are national treasures. Some of our nation's greatest cultural contributors live in poverty, have no health plans, and have no ability to protect

their cultural property. . . . We have an obligation to nurture young artists, to sustain and create opportunities for adult artists, and we must respect, honor and protect older artists.[32]

To do what the artist does, to choose to be an artist despite wide adversity, takes tremendous guts, conviction in the highest sense, an integrity that most people lack. Yet these intense, strong individuals are predominantly regarded as crazy. These very individuals have a highly defined sense of self, a noble trait in a world awry with people who don't know who they are, leading lives with numerous missteps but no reflection upon such, having children before their own life has a sense of purpose, working jobs without even attempting to understand what they'd really like to do, in relationships without significant relationship to self first, essentially living lives without significant meaning. So crucial is it to come to a self-knowledge, an understanding and appreciation of one's talents and weaknesses, of ways of being that are inappropriate for us and of strengths best put to use, in order to render this life meaningful. It is only healthy to attend first to the self, before the other—be it child or love partner. In getting to know the self, one then finds one's work, one's life, one's love and familial relationships. Artists rightfully and *healthily* will not accept others' projections of identity upon them. Perhaps it is that very reason that led artist Louise Bourgeois to comment (and entitle a show), "Art is a guarantee of sanity."[33]

Esther sacrificed having what others see as a comfortable life in order to do what she loved. Unlike Ellie, supposedly her prototype in Gladys Schmitt's *The Gates of Aulis*, who struggles "between self-abnegation and self-fulfillment" and then essentially goes toward the former, Esther chose a life of self-fulfillment. "Ellie [was] the sort of woman who finds peace only in giving of herself to another."[34] This was not Esther. She did not accept the martyred role that so many women choose, often unknowingly, as society still so encourages it—to service so many others without care for self first. Esther, like many liberated women, realized that there was no necessary place for self-denial in a full, meaningful life, even one with love relationships and children. A woman or man can still nurture without complete self-sacrifice, in fact can best nurture by providing an image of a healthy adult, one who is content with his place in life. Such an adult can nurture all the better those he has chosen to with a full degree of meaning and measure. Esther's fulfillment, and what she and other artists are criticized for, was that she cared for her self in a glorious fashion. She fed her soul with her painting activities and through cohorting with others enlightened to the fact that true beauty and meaning can come out of an artist's brush or a musician's notes. It was these very things that spoke to Esther and her peers of the uniqueness and the universality of the human spirit. Esther and her friends realized that relationship and family life are not the sole bearers of that title. And what a family they were for each other!

Surely Esther would agree with noted artist Alma Thomas: "I have remained free. I paint when I feel like it. I didn't have to come home . . . there was nobody to interfere with what I wanted, to stop and discuss what they wanted . . . It was what I wanted, and no argument. That is what allowed me to develop." And Elaine deKooning had described her feeling of satisfaction at living such a life surrounded by art and people who cared about art. "Now, at last, every minute of my life was chosen by me. I was free of constraints. . . ."[35] Henke wrote in *American Women Painters of the '30s & '40s* of the profiled women artists possessing "a selfishness, a personal responsibility to oneself rather than to society as a whole,"[36] a trait of course that Esther and these other women shared and vocalized. Like Alma Thomas, Elaine deKooning, Lee Krasner, and Doris Lee, just to name a few, Esther insisted on this personal freedom. And each of these vibrant women artists was striking out for her personal creative vision when the odds were very against anything but motherhood and housekeeping.

Esther had always strived for a personal freedom, as her many friends and fellow Villagers had. The freedom to express and convey one's own way of looking at life through the chosen medium of art, music, writing, dance—a personal, unique voice. Unlike Harold Winters, whose own life was sadly "not what it should be," Esther felt quite the opposite. Though certainly she felt that there were elements that could, and should, have been different, she still felt that she "lived the best possible life." She made the choices that rang true for her, and the rest was out of her control. She ultimately had to accept the circumstances of choice and action wrought by others that affected her own life. She grievously viewed society's not changing, and it did affect her emotionally. But even though she got sick, she never gave up her vital attitude, her sassiness about the challenge that was her life as artist.

A contemporary of Esther's who later met fame, artist Alice Neel, stated that "[being a] good artist takes being sensitive and having tremendous willpower . . . to 'react intensely,'" . . . and to have "a very strong adamant self." Very much like Esther, she "never followed any school, never imitated any artist." She explained that "the way I see the world . . . that is what I paint,"[37] Like an even young Esther, as depicted in the early Pittsburgh reviews, Neel was gutsy, determined, courageous; she credits this as helping her to survive. (Neel was the artist told by a psychiatrist that her bohemian lifestyle had gotten her nowhere.) It was quite evident that even the young Esther had this very will, an energy, a wildness about fighting for her terrain as an artist. The spunk and sassiness that kept Neel creating likewise fed Esther's ability to continue painting, despite personal hardship. Even as she was just being released from the institution, Esther was sane enough and had enough will in her at that moment to realize that she didn't dare allow herself to be discouraged.

Like most artists, Esther indeed refused to let others define her and her existence. Her life typified the genuine creative artist, a person totally committed to a singular vision, totally invested in what was a life's work. Esther's suffering was not because she made this choice, but because the fact of being an artist brought the ills of society about her. She knew from early on that the choice was hers, to be an artist and likely struggle, or to fit the mainstream mold, live with a lot more security, but essentially give up her art, that which most spoke to her in this life. By the end of her life she surely saw that her choice, though it had brought hardship, was something that had to take place. She could not have lived any differently. For though it was a challenged existence, though it was a struggle, it was still fantastic, wildly magnificent.

Many people saw the articles written and the attention being brought to Esther's life and art after the Carson Street show. Of course, one had been James Van Trump. Actually the first comment uttered by him that day in Wightman Nursing Home in 1991 was, "I knew that she had died. I was kind of amazed when I saw her story coming back. She was under the surface. . . . Somehow or other I never thought that she'd surface again, but this shows you. . . ."

APPENDIX

PHANTOM'S DANCE

by

Edward Kinchley Evans

ABOUT THE AUTHOR OF PHANTOM'S DANCE:
Edward Kinchley Evans was born in Sylvania, Georgia. He holds a B.A. and M.A. from Columbia University in Fine Art. He has two children, a son and a daughter. He was an original member of Edward Albee's Playwright's Unit at the Village South Theatre in New York City, where his one-act play A ROOM IN HOTEL BABYLON was given it's premiere performance with Maria Karnilova in the lead role. He was playwright-in-residence with the Carriage House Experimental Theatre in Huntingdon, Pennsylvania for the years 1974, 1975, and 1976. His recent play MAUSOLEUM was produced by this theatre in May 1977.
PHANTOM'S DANCE was given it's premiere performance November 21, 1975 at Carriage House Theatre and was subsequently performed at Pittsburgh Laboratory Theatre and at Cafe La Mama in New York City as part of their New Playwright's Series.

CHARACTERS:

Gorde
Bird
Lydia

PHANTOM'S DANCE

a play in one act for three characters

by Edward Kinchley Evans

SCENE: *The stage is bare except for three platforms. The platform to stage right is empty. The center platform holds a single iron cot with white sheets and two pillows, one on top of the other. To stage left is a platform on which there is placed a tall stool painted black. As the scene opens, the stage is in semi-darkness. There is heard music. (Preferably the Kouros section of Tragoedia by Andrew Rubin [Nonesuch Records H-71198-A electronic music synthesizer].) Slowly coming onto stage is seen GORDE, a boy-man in his mid-forties. He is costumed in a voluminous white clown's costume as PIERROT. His face is clown white except that he is made very pretty, with the hugeness of his eyes emphasized. However, there are blood stains at the corners of his eyes, running down his cheeks and soiling the front of the costume. On his head is a white skullcap, on his feet, white ballet slippers, but his hands are bare and covered with long black animal hair.*

GORDE is leading before him, LYDIA. She is a woman in her mid-sixties, in a white hospital shift and confined in a straight-jacket with her arms tied. Her hair is loose and uncombed. Her face is without make-up except for a ruby-red smear of lipstick across her mouth that is more like a blister of blood than make-up. GORDE leads her to the iron cot and sits her on it, with her back resting against the pillows and her feet covered by the sheets. GORDE then goes back offstage and leads BIRD on and places him on the platform stage right, facing the audience. BIRD is a man without age. He should be thin and preferably tall. He should be filthy, his clothes an accumulation of rags, his hair matted and covered with a cap of sorts. His feet, however, should be shoed in new leather and highly polished, as if his feet were his one vanity. There should also be about him an air of tidiness and style. He is without hands and the arm stumps should be bandaged in blood-stained gauze strips. GORDE should start back offstage and then slowly turn and go seat himself on the high black stool. There should also be a backdrop of a torn white membrane splotched with pink stains. The lights fade to blackout and the music ceases.

A dim spot comes up on LYDIA.

LYDIA: Hurt. *(A dim spot comes up on BIRD.)*

BIRD: Hurt. *(A dim spot comes up on GORDE.)*

GORDE: Hurt.

LYDIA: *(Starts to laugh maniacally then quiets to a remembrance.)* Hurt.

BIRD: Hurt.

GORDE: Hurt.

LYDIA: I'm blind!

GORDE: Blind?

LYDIA: I'm blind and I can't see anymore.

BIRD: *(Looking at his arm stumps)* Blind?

GORDE: Lydia? Is that you Lydia?

BIRD: Lydia isn't her real name. It was something..Biblical.. as I recall.

LYDIA: Gorde? I can't see anymore. They say my eyes hemorrhaged..or..something.

BIRD: She used to be a great painter..claimed to have had a novel written about her.."Gates of Aulis"..said she knew the authoress..had gone to school with her.

LYDIA: Oh God! Oh my God! Oh my good God!! They've tied my hands. I can't move my hands!

GORDE: Lydia..I don't really remember when I first met her.. a poet named Bodenheim..Maxwell Bodenheim..one of those fugitive figures from the Twenties..had fallen on hard times and would stand on the corner of Thompson and West 4th Street by the Judson Memorial Church and sell his poems.. mimeographed on cheap paper..for ten cents a poem. A scarecrow of a man..I never bought one of his poems..but he was a friend of Lydia's from better days..and the first memory I have of her is the two of them arguing over something..then her laughing..she was dressed in an assortment of skirts and sweaters, all dowdy washed-out colors..a gypsy moth..Lydia turned from Bodenheim and saw me. She waved a hello..I waved back..She came over to the Park where I was standing.

LYDIA: I hear you paint.

GORDE: She was dressed in rags..but very clean..Her eyes always reflected mischief.

LYDIA: When we first met, you didn't tell me you painted.

GORDE: Did you buy a poem from your friend?

LYDIA: Max? Do you know Max? He and I go way back. He used to be quite a ladies' man..and..a fashionable poet..those were the days!..now, he's just a poet..and what say, we go painting sometimes together?

GORDE: I loved you Lydia.

LYDIA: 6 A.M. Sunday morning! I'll meet you at the Subway entrance, we'll have donuts and coffee on the Ferry going over.

GORDE: A.M.? 6 A.M.?

BIRD: Maxwell Bodenheim doesn't stand on the corner across from the Park anymore. Not too long after..Bodenheim..just a poet..and a ladyfriend with whom he was sharing his somewhat devalued affections..were butchered in an East Village basement where they had taken up temporary refuge for the night..a marvelously pointless death..violent end for a gentle poet..reminds me of how little Death cares..about who we are..or who we were..

GORDE: Where are you staying now, Lydia?

LYDIA: In a friend's apartment..23rd Street. He's hardly ever home and the light is good..but he says I've soon got to find a place of my own. He can't stand the paint odor.

BIRD: She has a wealthy sister living in Philadelphia..but Lydia was an embarrassment to her.

GORDE: I was with a friend..we were out sketching..we had wandered down to Fifth Avenue and around 26th Street. I had wanted to paint the Flatiron Building for some reason I've now forgotten. My friend asked if I had ever been to Staten Island? I said..no..he said..'Let's go this Sunday morning.. we can sketch all day..there are some great old estates over there..'....'Why don't you sleep over at my place,' I asked, 'that way we can get an early start'...

BIRD: The city was cheap in those days. Five cents on the Subway to South Ferry..five cents for the trip over..past the Statue of Liberty..past the tugboats..sea gulls patrolling the air..then we caught a bus and just rode until we came to a desolate area ..then we got off and walked..some beautiful old homes as promised..but long since deserted..abandoned to the Joads of the world. They stood eyeing us with great despair..Caution! Time passing! Caution! Time passing!

LYDIA: My eyes! I can't see to paint anymore. I can't see my beautiful world. Gone..gone..gone from me.

GORDE: We turned from the main road and walked towards the river. By the road was an old store with a gas pump in front of it and a Hires Root Beer sign on the screen door. Across from it was a narrow dirt road leading to the river's edge. We passed a house with a small dog tied to a tree. It barked at us until a woman came to the door and told it to shut up. She looked at us with our canvases and paint boxes and asked us what we wanted. We told her we were going to paint the river. "Don't come too near the house," she said and then went back inside. In back of the house was the river and a dozen or so half-sunken hulks of old rotting and rusting ships. It was a ship's graveyard and a painter's paradise.

LYDIA: Caution! Time passing!

GORDE: We painted until the sun went down and we had to leave. I asked my friend...would he stay another night?

LYDIA: Gorde knew of this marvelous place over on Staten Island. It was summertime...and we all met at some God-awful early hour..had coffee and a donut on the Ferry over..and then we went to the ship's graveyard to paint..we started back about three in the afternoon. While we waited on the bus to come by, we stopped in this old store and had cokes, some cheese and ginger snaps..We each took a separate seat on the bus guarding our wet canvas from the other riders. At one stop, two middle-aged women got on, each holding a small child and helping two or three other children up the steps. They all went to the back of the bus. They had been to a small Circus that afternoon and were heading home, I suppose. Two of the small boys, I guess they were five or six years old, sat together on the side seat and were sticking their heads and arms out the window yelling at the countryside. The women were paying them no attention. Suddenly, from behind came a motorcyclist and as he whipped by the side of the bus next to their open window, one of the little boys hit his head trying to get himself back into safety. In a loud, hurt, happy voice, he shouted to the passengers in the bus,'Shit! Look at him go!!' We all turned,electrified, to stare at the small boy with the loud observation. One of the women, obviously his mother, embarrassed, cautioned him,'Johnny, one shouldn't say that word..one should say..' and she looked around approvingly at us..'Holy Cow!..or something like that.' The little boy thought for a moment..then as another motorcyclist raced by in an effort to catch his friend..the little boy, his eyes glazed with joy, turned to the passengers on the bus and in his loudest voice piped,'Holy Cowshit! Did you see him go!!'

BIRD: Those were happy days..and not so happy days. The last time I saw him, I was having an exhibit in a small gallery on Tenth Street. It was a co-op affair and each artist had to baby-sit his own work. We hadn't seen each other for several years. I spent my summers in Maine with an elderly artist for whom I had an attachment..my winters teaching at a private school on the upper East Side. He came in with his son, a boy of six and a daughter, I would guess around four..beautiful children.. very quiet..very sober..His wife stayed outside the Gallery with another child in a carriage. We spoke..acknowledging the passing of time..

LYDIA: Caution! Time passing!

BIRD: He introduced his children..then..he left in order that his wife might see the exhibit. She eyed me coldly, looked at the work without interest and left. We had met before..when they had first married. Her mouth was a little too thin for my taste.

LYDIA: I was married. When I was very young. A handsome man.. he's very wealthy now..an interior decorator..lives in Washington. After the divorce, I had my first nervous breakdown. He told me I might could paint..but that I was stupid..and he couldn't stand stupidity. I told him, I never had loved him.. but that I had married him just for the hell of it!

FORDE: Stuck in the middle of the block on one of those cross streets in lower Manhatten..is a seedy, rundown Hotel called the St. George. One Autumn night when my world was narrowing, I gathered up all of Lydia's work that I had collected and stored for her..vibrant canvases with bold, rich strokes of color outlining the heavy scented world she knew and captured with oils she stole from the handful of little artist supply stores in the Village whose owners quietly busied themselves elsewhere when Lydia came to browse. There were small gouaches of naive girls, wide-eyed and secretive, dressed in white shifts and roaming Institution halls and bathing in cavernous shower stalls..Child-women..purple with controlled rage at a world less than innocent....I took a cab to the St. George. I asked the night clerk Lydia's room. The place smelled of urinal cleaner. It was dark in the room. She was propped up against the bed pillows..a small light burning above her head. A smell of Death, clammy, sweaty, hung in the air like thick mucous.

LYDIA: I can hardly see anymore, Gorde. Both eyes have hemorrhaged. I can see a little, just enough to get around.

GORDE: How are you?

LYDIA: Oh..fine, Gorde. My sister..you remember my sister? She lives in Philadelphia...She sends me so much a month now.. pays my hotel room and a little left over to eat. My teeth are about all gone anyway..and soup is cheap.

GORDE: I've brought you all your work back.

LYDIA: Nothing sold?

GORDE: Nothing. But I don't know what's happening at my place and I thought I should bring them to you.

LYDIA: I'll never paint anymore. I can't see you know. I can't see my beautiful colors, Gorde! I can't see!

GORDE: I'm sorry, Lydia. I'm sorry I couldn't help more.

LYDIA: So who cares about art anyway, eh Gorde?

GORDE: I loved you Lydia.

LYDIA: Oh God! Oh my God! Oh my good God! Gorde! They've tied my hands. I can't move my hands.

BIRD: I don't know if she's alive or dead now. The last time I saw her it was Spring. The air was beginning to warm a little and I was riding past the St. George on the bus. She was sitting on the front stairs in a little patch of sunshine eating a cruller and sipping out of a container. A dumpy little wad of human flesh...blinking at the sun with gypsy moth eyes..all by herself.. warming in the Springtime sun.

GORDE: It doesn't matter who you love in this world, it seems you can't protect them.

LYDIA: I never loved anyone..I loved the whole world..but I
never hurt anyone.
BIRD: Hurt.
GORDE: Hurt?
LYDIA: Caution! Time passing!
GORDE: My heart broke. You never told me that you had quit
loving me.
BIRD: What is love? Each has his own definition. His own rules
that others must live by. When I love..it is because someone
else needs that love. If it gives them comfort and their heart
ease..I will make love with them but not to them.
GORDE: Comfort? It was a fourth floor walkup on a side street
near the Hudson River in lower Manhattan. The candy place
that makes JuJubes scented the Sunday morning air. There was
no heat, no hot water, and a corroded john in the hall I shared
with an old artist in the back apartment who spent his nights
roaming the docks. An Irish family lived downstairs and there
was an Irish bar on the first floor. Across the street was a
Spanish bar and over it a whorehouse. One could watch the
river or the whores at pleasure...or cars disappearing into the
caverns of Holland Tunnel. I would sit up in bed and watch
you sleep. My whole world was ahead of me. I was young..
the mere touch of your flesh blistered my hands.
LYDIA: You were in love.
BIRD: You were infatuated. Nothing more..nothing less..
GORDE: Hurt.
LYDIA: Hurt.
BIRD: Nothing more..nothing less.
GORDE: Caution. Time passing.
LYDIA: Gorde! Come look at the baby...
GORDE: Hurt!
BIRD: The child had been born perfect. Not a blemish. A perfect
child.
GORDE: Hurt!
BIRD: Mr. Davis, you have two children, a boy and a girl.
GORDE: No! I have three.
LYDIA: Gorde..come look at the baby!
BIRD: You have only two indicated by your chart..a boy and a
girl..
GORDE: No..I have three!

LYDIA: Gorde..come look at the baby!

BIRD: If you have a third child, it is a gift from God.

GORDE: A gift? From God?

BIRD: A gift of love.

LYDIA: I had put the children to bed as usual. They all slep in the same room.

GORDE: Will this take long?

BIRD: The ah.....they should have brought the body in by tw o'clock.

GORDE: But they took her this morning.

BIRD: They have others to pick up..it will only take a few minutes.

GORDE: I don't want them to touch the body!

BIRD: They will have to make an autopsy.

GORDE: I don't want them to touch the body. The child wa born perfect..

BIRD: It will only take a few minutes.

LYDIA: Mr. Davis? Will you step this way please.

GORDE: Miss? Miss? I don't want them to touch the body

LYDIA: You are the father? A relative has to identify the body

BIRD: In the city..when someone dies..you have to call a Docto to certify that death has occurred..then the police come..an then they stay with you until a vehicle from Bellevue arrive to remove the body and determine the cause of death..an someone in the family has to go identify the body..all in th same day..all in a few hours..and the vehicle that picks u the body is making only one of several stops before unloadin its sad cargo at Bellevue morgue.

GORDE: I don't want the body touched. The child was bor perfect. I don't want them to cut her. I don't want her body touched!

LYDIA: Is the child yours?

GORDE: The child was a gift from God.

BIRD: It was a crib death..cause unknown..after the autopsy the body was released to the Funeral Home for preparation for burial.

LYDIA: Gorde..come look at the baby..

BIRD: Mr. Davis, the child was born under a bad water sign. Fluid rose up in her lungs and in a sense the child drowned.

GORDE: You knew?

BIRD: I told you the child was a gift of God. The child gave you and your wife this gift..but it was the child's choice.

LYDIA: Gorde! Something's happened to the baby!

GORDE: What honey? What did you say? What time is it?

LYDIA: Hurt!

BIRD: Hurt?

GORDE: Hurt..

BIRD: You knew I loved her.

GORDE: It wasn't love, remember. It was infatuation.

BIRD: You said that. I never did.

LYDIA: I never loved anyone.

BIRD: But you let me make love to you.

LYDIA: I felt sorry for you. You seemed to need me.

BIRD: Need? You?

GORDE: You're confusing need with love.

LYDIA: I never needed anyone..and I loved the world..but if
     sleeping with me gave you comfort, what's a few hours warmth?

BIRD: I loathe myself.

LYDIA: You were much too proud, much too proud.

GORDE: We had to bring you down.

LYDIA: You seemed to need no one. You were careless with your
     freedom.

GORDE: You even told me that you loved her.

BIRD: I thought you would be happy for me.

GORDE: Happy! For you? When you took our friendship and drug
     it through the mud of desire like some kid playing in a rain
     puddle?

LYDIA: (Whispering) You ate me alive. I couldn't breathe. You
     smothered my mouth with kisses as you tore the flesh from my
     body.

BIRD: I loved you.

GORDE: That kind of love is very selfish. You eat at a table
     for one.

LYDIA: (Whispering) You became gluttonous. You stuffed your-
     self with my flesh..my warmth..

BIRD: I thought you loved me.

GORDE: He was innocent, Lydia. Innocence born of hunger..
     his talons tearing us apart..his mouth dripping blood from
     our flesh..gorging his child-like hunger for love...

LYDIA: (Whispering) I couldn't breathe..it was like living with
     some giant prehistoric winged creature who came daily to tear

at the flesh..then went soaring back off..out into the wilderness of the world..

BIRD: I don't understand you two. One of you I loved with all my heart and mind and body..the mere touch of your flesh sent me into a raging fire of desire..I would touch with my lips that tender spot by your eyes..and think..my God!..but I am favored above all men for my beloved is by my side and her dreams are of me.

LYDIA: My head was empty of dreams. The weight of your body oppressed me. I couldn't breathe.

BIRD: ...and you...I loved as a brother. I wanted to share all my happiness with you.

GORDE: You are a fool. I shared all your happiness.

LYDIA: I went to him. I told him I couldn't breathe..you were smothering me to death.

BIRD: He was a comfort to you?

LYDIA: He set me free! I could unbend your talons..one by one..and free myself. No one owns me!

BIRD: I never said I owned you. I said I loved you.

LYDIA: Your claws around my heart. I peeled them back..one by one..and escaped you.

BIRD: You were never that gentle..*(He holds the stumps of his arms up and looks sadly at them.)* ..You didn't peel my claws back. You chopped off the hands at the wrists. There are nights when I wonder if one or two of my..fingernails..still fester in your heart.

GORDE: We were desperate. We took the great silver bow of our hurt..dipped the golden arrow of your trust into the semen of opportunity..and shot Bird down.

BIRD: You almost killed me.

GORDE: We only meant to wound..to hurt you as you hurt us.

LYDIA: I wanted to be free.

BIRD: Are you free..now? Free to whore your way through life?

LYDIA: I can breathe.

BIRD: I fell into a great sickness. My heart cracked and a terrible emptiness overtook me.

GORDE: I told you, she wasn't a good influence in your life. She kept you from doing what you need to do. It was for your own good.

BIRD: How many murders are committed for the victim's own

good?

LYDIA: I live now with an elderly artist. A very famous one. We go to Maine during our Summers. He seems very happy. When we sleep together, he never says he loves me. And quite often when I'm shopping in the Village, I meet some young boy who is just passing through and needs comforting. Ever so often, one of the young boys will kiss me by the side of my eyes..sometimes..to kiss a tear..away..

GORDE: The last time I saw you, you were at a movie..you were sitting in front of me. You seemed happy.

BIRD: Happy! What is happiness? What is love? What is this great need we have for each other and in our desperation to get it, we kill, mutilate, hurt, wound...and we settle for what we can hold onto with both hands...and then in frustration, we hide the rest of our lives behind eyes of hurt..accusing the world for our misery..for not winning the prize..love re-quited..But then..what is love?

LYDIA: Caution! Time passing!

GORDE: Caution! Time passing!

BIRD: Caution! Time passing!

LYDIA: Hurt.

GORDE: Hurt.

BIRD: Hurt.

LYDIA: Gorde! Something's happened to the baby!

GORDE: It wasn't love, remember..it was infatuation.

BIRD: But then..what is love?

LYDIA: Hurt! *(Spot fades on LYDIA.)*

GORDE: Caution! Time passing! *(Spot fades on GORDE.)*

BIRD: But then...what is love? *(Spot fades on BIRD.)*

Lights dim up as in the beginning and the Kouros of Tragoedia begins as GORDE helps LYDIA out of bed and leads her off stage and then returns for BIRD..He returns to the stage... looks carefully around and then he exits. Lights fade to black-out..music stops..

THE END

AFTERWORD

Until one is committed
there is hesitancy, the chance to draw back,
always ineffectiveness.
Concerning all acts of initiative (and creation),
there is one elementary truth,
the ignorance of which kills countless ideas
and splendid plans:
that the moment one definitely commits oneself,
then Providence moves too.
All sorts of things occur to help one
that would never otherwise have occurred.
A whole stream of events issues from the decision,
raising in one's favour all manner
of unforseen incidents and meetings
and material assistance
which no man could have dreamt
would have come his way.

—W. H. Murray

*I*ronically enough, on the last leg of researching the life of Esther
Phillips, I came across the journals of Eugenia Hughes. The project
had brought me once again to New York City in May of 1995. Late on a
Friday afternoon I ascended the steps of the New York Public Library,

after having exhausted avenues (and myself, more from the walking than anything) at the Archives of American Art and various other New York art museum libraries the preceding few days. Back in Pittsburgh, I had gotten anxious to get the writing finally under way, after reviewing the three and a half years' worth of interviews, notes, and other research done since first becoming acquainted with Esther's life. So I had specifically made this trip looking for any last bits of information, little pieces to flesh out my story of her, the Village, and its characters—in order to close the research segment of my project.

But it seems I had found as much as I was to find. I toted around with me little scribbles of half-thoughts that I had, about places to look for info. I also carried Ken's scribbles, and Millie's, her notes. All of these would taunt me from time to time as I strained to decipher them, again and again till my eyes ached, as I asked myself what the hell they meant within the context of Esther's life—if anything. But, after all, I would write my book from words and dialogue arising out of age-old pages, and I was determined to follow any lead to its even silly death. Finally, the only notation left staring up at me from the page (unscathed by the blue marker that, once used, brought relief from looming tangential dead ends) was the funny one about "Jerry Hughes wanting to donate diaries to the New York Public Library—the curator loved it!"

Well, I had not been able to find out who this guy Jerry was, and it had always appeared to me that the curator simply loved the *idea*. But I stood in the grand reference room of that beautiful building and of course contemplated that maybe it went beyond that. I knew I'd pack it in after this, enjoy the weekend in New York and head back to Pittsburgh at peace with the decision to start writing. Thus I mustered some energy, albeit half-heartedly, and tried to figure out where to look in the huge archive for a donated personal item. I discovered, to my happiness, though, that there actually was a whole section devoted to this very thing—bound indices with scores of names of others who apparently pleased the curator. I was proud to find the indices directory, but I sure couldn't find the donor I was looking for.

Not trusting my faculties come this point of the rather hot May day, I lugged to the reference desk area the weighty volumes that I felt should provide my coveted name. Disappointment and a wearied disgust hung over me, number eight in a line of ten people trying to figure out where the answers to their unique stories, as well, were. All around me were various accents that one could only hear in New York. Finally, to the front. I wanted so badly to plop the volumes down, but a buxom middle-aged woman addressing me actually reached over for them quite aggressively, lessening their fall. I told her my concern. That it was *notated*, after all, that this person donated diaries.

Clarifying the name from me, the clerk went to a computer terminal, her back turned to me. She started punching keys . . . there soon was the sound of a page printing. (I was numbly watching.) I distinctly remember seeing her rip two finished pages upward into her hands. Nothing victorious, just routine work on her part. She turned and walked back toward me and I must have come alive a bit. "Ah-huh. She's here. . . . You have no patience," she brusquely said, in heavy Brooklyn accent. She handed me the papers and waved me aside.

Perhaps no patience, but luck. In utter disbelief I looked down at the find, and felt that in the course of the last half-hour the trip had changed irrevocably. I was holding two pages identifying fourteen large boxes of effects donated by *Eugenia* Hughes, aka "Jerry," all clearly delineated and residing, since 1964, in the library's Special Collections Room, just one archway over, as my dear Brooklyn friend had motioned. I read on the Accession Sheet that the contents of her donated material "document the life of a single woman and a widower from the 1930s to the 1960s, their social and romantic involvements with the artistic community in Greenwich Village and Pennsylvania. . . . The letters between Roy and Eugenia are rich in detail about the life of a struggling artist, the social life of New York City, and the relationship between father and daughter."

I had no doubt I had found a friend of Esther's. "The Eugenia Hughes Papers" contained "correspondence, diaries, art work [sketching and watercolor studies], writings, family papers, photographs, memorabilia of Eugenia and her family, and printed matter," and had, among other family-related matter, letters from friends, photographs of friends, and many love letters.

My new acquaintance already seemed real to me. I sensed Jerry Hughes becoming a factor in this story—perhaps another woman Esther confided in and corresponded with. And thus another person I could rely on to tell a truer story of Esther's life. I looked up and gushed thanks to the clerk, by this point butting in on another's time with her, and went through those sacred heavy doors of the Special Collection room. Being that it was 4:30, with little time left to dive into the works, I applied for my Pass to review the materials and reserved them for Saturday morning. I left the library stunned that my already full story of this interesting woman's life was likely about to be made ever fuller with diaries and letters of a New York friend about to surface. I had no idea just what the boxes would hold, but for some reason I strongly felt closer to Esther than ever. I took the subway down to St. Mark's Place in the Lower East Side to join two New York friends for dinner. We celebrated the find together, they having been with me since I first embarked on this journey, when they had known me in Pittsburgh.

۞ ۞ ۞

What began for the author as a plan to write a biography—or one-time ideally-conceived catalog resume of Esther's work—transformed into a piece of writing that, at times, I don't know that I consciously directed! In undertaking the writing of the life of this artist, there were too damn many fateful events, remarkable coincidences—and even oddly identical phrasings by various friends of Esther—that surfaced in tracking down information relevant to her art and the way she made it.

In fact, as the story of Esther's life unfolded before me, a story yearning to be told, so did my essential purpose in writing about her. (All works of creation tend to present themselves to their makers I have found.) I had indeed found more and more along those paths twisted, and times tremendously not so, that everything that was surfacing about her was deeply reflective of not only one struggling artist's life sixty-some years ago, but of many, through the ages and up to the present day. Though her tale, as each of ours, is unique, it is nevertheless essentially the tale of my community of friends, and other communities, that try to create in a world not too attuned to creativity, nor desirous to know of people too different from the mainstream.

What I strived to do at Peoples Oakland, especially towards the last half of my working there, was fight the stigma the mentally ill face. It would stare at them in the form of the potential employer I would try to win over on their behalf, and could be seen behind the eyes of most in the community, even though Oakland certainly has its share of colorful students, punks, goth-rockers and other characters equally as interesting-looking and acting as the mentally ill carousing the streets. I desired to use the new space being offered with the National Institute of Mental Health grant as a forum for educators, business people and other professionals to come in and hear the concerns, the realities of coping in the larger world, from Peoples' clients—some of whom indeed had too-debilitating forms of schizophrenia and bizarre personality disorders to keep gainful employment, but many of whom were quite able-bodied, slightly-eccentric good souls who might be strongly debilitated with depression or mania if not on medication and therapy. I wanted family and friends to come in to find support and learn the advocacy I was successfully putting into practice in the field (finding jobs at Carnegie Mellon University and not McDonald's). I wanted all of the community to be present—to see what those diagnosed with any of the myriad forms of mental illness indeed have to offer, and to hear mental health professionals talk of the limitations within all of us, limitations that surely will surface at some point in our lives, and how, when they do, we can face them strongly and without shame.

It occurred to me throughout my work that the only real way to help the mentally ill deal with society's misconceptions (for that seemed part of my many tasks) was to abolish the misconceptions. Why continue fostering the coping mechanisms, thus enabling society to not change? So whenever I represented a client to an employer, I didn't lie. They knew where I was coming from and what people I was offering to them as viable employees. And many of my clients went out there into the larger world, into the workforce, with inner strength and encouragement from us at Peoples—to be fearless enough to represent themselves truthfully, as potential good employees, good people, who just also happened to have an ongoing mental health challenge.

۞ ۞ ۞

I left Peoples Oakland, dissatisfied with the looming presence of the University of Pittsburgh over the agency's shoulder, which came about due to the interconnection with the National Institute of Mental Health grant. I've never been much for beaurocracy, especially at its inefficient worst. I wrote the above passage of words, credo for the mentally ill, to myself in August of 1991, upon quitting. I discovered Esther in October. A friend and I bumped into Mary Shaw on a street in South Oakland, shortly after I had visited the library and committed to writing about Esther. She was living by herself after all those marriages, in a house full of art, which she gladly showed off to two appreciative young creative souls. "I never made a big issue of any of this stuff," Mary said of the paintings and the content of conversation, as guided by my questions about her artistic life. The next time I tried to speak with her, her lovely Oakland sanctuary, literally on the precipice of Panther Hollow, was being sold, as she, with help from her daughter, was being placed in the nursing home.

"Ken sort of rescued Esther's work from the brink of . . . whatever . . ." spoke Ken Chute's lovely mother, as she hustled from the dining room, retrieving cups and saucers for tea and cookies. I was making the first of many visits to Chute's home, outlaying my plans for a book, talking of research. Ken would disappear, too, not quite as swift of foot as his mother, and return with manila files stacked high. Here were his own archives of Esther, though he kept insisting he was a "shoddy researcher." He actually allowed me to leave with his ordered assemblage of Esther's life—notes galore, some readable, some not—and a binder full of photos of Esther's work. This entrusted material became the foundation for me to build my search. Without it, surely this would have been too daunting a task. I was relieved to be able to call him up in November of 1997 and tell him I finally had something to show for all those years I had been holding on to the loaned items.

Ken had allowed me to go to the storage area and borrow Merle's diaries, those that he hadn't already fully pored over and notated anytime Esther's name had come up. Much of the work of reviewing these, as with any research, was very tedious, but worth it whenever "Esther," "EP," or "E Phillips" surfaced. I had brought the material, many dusty journals and diary books, up to an attic room in my house to review— less for cleanliness than ambience, nostalgic as I am. I was sleuthing to find what no one else had yet found. The institution. After many diary books tossed aside, finally a lead when I saw a notation about a "Dr." from "Wingdale, NY" writing Merle. Nothing but the three abbreviations/words.

I utilized a map and directory assistance, and called the most central, generic location of this foreign place, the Post Office. With a trace of embarrassment, but professionalism, I inquired if perchance there was an institution in the town, and the response was that the institution essentially *was* the town. I had a name as important to my manuscript as Esther Phillips, Harlem Valley. No less exciting to me in my attic search was perhaps Esther's most significant letter to Merle, January 23, 1938, somehow overlooked by Ken. I knew immediately I had a title—"this fantastic struggle."

I had been glancing down at Millie's Notes, among the many papers forwarded by Ken Chute, as I spoke with my dear, now-departed friend, Susan Spier via phone. We were confirming an upcoming Well gathering, a women's cross-disciplinary creative group I was in. Susan, like many of my friends, was associated with a wonderful avant-garde theatre group, The Acting Company, and I had been down to see a couple productions thus far, in the old church considered The Laurel Highlands Regional Theatre. I well remembered the two dear men who ran it, though I hardly knew them save for my arrivals at productions. What was staring up at me from the page of Millie's Notes was interrupting my thoughts with Susan because one of the decipherable proper names was Ed Evans. (Another paired with it, equally decipherable but likely wrongly heard by Millie from Esther's mouth, was Glenn Coest. And "4th St. Gallery" was boldly spelled out.) Remembering that "Glen and Ed from the theatre" had lived in New York, I interrupted Susan to ask when her mentors lived there, and if they were from the Village. Being artists, Susan certainly suspected the latter and urged me to call and directly ask if they ever knew someone named Esther Phillips.

That I did. I got Ed at the other end of the line. I spoke her name, and there was a pause from him. "Oh, my dear child . . . Esther Phillips. Why, we were like family. I haven't heard her name or thought about her in some time." I asked if the woman he knew was a painter? And Eddie, as I, too, would soon affectionately call him) began one of many warm, long recollections of the Staten Island ferry and Ship's Graveyard excursions. I was in shock at having so simply found this unusual connection to the story, thought it too good to be true. I didn't even quite realize at the time that Glen and Ed had absolutely no previous connection to Pittsburgh. It was just a weird crossing of fate that they had settled artistically in the city from which their 1950s painting comrade had hailed from. (Of course, they had thought that Philadelphia. . . .)

Well, I had found the institution but didn't quite know what to do with it at first. Of course, I was going to call and inquire, but I had family concerns nagging me. Esther's family. For my last phone call to Dorothy was to be the last. She had actually told me to do something more important with my life than write about her sister, so I sent her my resume just to let her know that I had much going on besides this book in the works, and I swore to myself not to bother with her. I was worried the institution might not grant me information because of some formality related to family. I was partially right, but I was so pleasantly surprised at how very nice the institution administrators were to me.

I believe my call first went to Wendy Acrish, top administrator at Hudson River Psychiatric Center, which had taken Harlem Valley under wing. She very kindly directed my inquiries to Susan Hartman, whom I could never thank or credit enough for her considerate, direct assistance—totally unbeaurocractic. She was pleasant and helpful from beginning to end. She understood my desire to want nothing more to do with a family that indeed never visited their patient. (She affirmed and confirmed certain things for me as she'd consult the file that she was unable to share with me at the time.) She expressed both her and Ms. Acrish's sincere wish that they could just forward Esther's records to me, but because of a formality, they could not do that so simply. I'd either have to ask Dorothy, the closest sister, if I might request the records (I knew this would not only *not* be granted, but that the family then would ask for the records themselves, though it was my sleuthing that had found Harlem Valley.) I opted for a second choice that Harlem Valley's Sue Hartman put before me, which was that I could plead my case before a judge and ask to receive and use the records for my book. She carefully explained that I'd have to get a Court Order that forces, essentially, her as hospital representative to release the documents that they were more than willing to release to me!

I am as grateful to my Volunteer Lawyer for the Arts, Lisa Eastwood, as I am Sue Hartman, for making the legal treading I had to do for my manuscript very within reach. First I found her through contacting Philadelphia's Volunteer Lawyers for the Arts, because Pittsburgh had no branch at the time. They competently put me in touch with Ms. Eastwood, of New York City. She consulted with me weekly by letter and phone, prepared an excellent brief on my behalf (complete with color xeroxes of Esther's art), and fought my case without me needing to be in the court room, presenting it to a judge for the State of New York, all in about 5 months' time. She, like Ms. Hartman, had an enthusiasm for my projected work, and presented my case as a reasonable scholarly request. She won for me, on a January day in 1994, as I sat in Pittsburgh thinking of the goings-on in New York State. Eastwood and Sue Hartman both projected such confidence that I didn't fret as I might have, and I'm indebted to them for their steadfast support.

While I had been receiving correspondence from Eastwood the preceding fall, as she assembled documents for my case, Hartman extended the invitation for me to visit the institution, as I had said I wanted to. I travelled to Wingdale on a dreary day in early November because I would have no access to the buildings come the new year. Even though Harlem Valley Hospital proper had been closed for several years, the big change-over was about to come, with Hudson River Psychiatric relinqueshing many of the buildings in order for them to be transformed into a state correctional facility. So I went without institution documents reviewed, hoping that I would indeed later secure them for my book. Sue Hartman realized the process in motion to receive a court order for the documents; she assured me she could give a thorough tour independant of those records, yet that would highlight the records should I receive them. Thus Susan Hartman and her assistant that day unlocked buildings and walked me through many of those that Esther likely spent time in, including Building 28 (according to Esther's file, which Hartman consulted.) Hartman answered questions as best she could without revealing anything specific that would have to wait for court permission. It felt very odd seeing the basketball court and the basement bowling alley where Esther painted. Nothing was as chilling, though, as setting foot in a dayroom and sleeping room of Building 28, with baths visible along the walls of both. It was as if the air captured and locked away inside, that rushed out upon the turn of Hartman's keys, belonged in part to each and every woman that had ever been secured within that building over time, including dear Esther. I was also able to go by car and then foot to the exact locations where Esther must have set up easel to catch odd perspectives on the barns, which still stood.

Over the month that passed between my receiving word from Lisa Eastwood that "our" case was won, and the institution file could be xeroxed, packed up and sent to me, I remember pondering this *life* I was writing about. I had sensed early on that Esther's tale was a bit of an unusual one, but it really began to hit me that this piece of writing about her should surely make for a true, and very interesting, *story*. What had started out square biography had turned into something different due to the carrier of the facts of her life—interviews with aging bohemians and Village artists, crumbling journal pages, and now institution documents. When the 5-lb. package arrived certified mail for me in February 1994, I felt very fortunate, and that my work, my piece of writing, with continued hard work, might be something powerful. I again went up to third floor space and opened the box of material. Everything about Harlem Valley was before me, and I smiled, then teared up when, amidst the xeroxed pages, I fingered a small photo of Esther, which had been attached to her Abstract of Commitment. Sue Hartman had chosen to send me the original of apparently the only institution photo taken of her.

❦ ❦ ❦

I suppose the only real tangent I got on and stayed on awhile in this journey was the temporary search for husband. It kept eluding me, the trying to substantiate what the rumours pointed toward. Millie's Notes (apparently Esther as the source) speaking of an "unhappy love affair," Milton Salamon believing she was close to someone from Carnegie Tech, Glen and Ed's surprise story that left me reeling, and more, including even Mary Shaw's obtuse comment about whom Esther's lovers might have been, that any love affair "certainly would be nothing to write about at this point." (I couldn't get a straight answer from Mary— part of the fun of interviewing her.)

While passing through Philadelphia around 1993, which I did often back then, returning from New York and eastern Pennsylvania, I came across the work of another "Esther"—an Esther "G," in an antique gallery. I thought perhaps she might have been my Esther, married. The content of the painting—a ship's graveyard. The style was not too dissimilar. I came home to Pittsburgh and made many calls, searching state artist directories, to no avail. I searched the east coast, particularly Washington, D.C. because Glen and Ed thought the husband had moved there and because Shay's article had a notation about one of Esther's paintings showing up in a restaurant there. They all seemed like hot leads, I was quite excited for awhile. But it just didn't seem to add up. Though enticing, I decided against writing Esther as possibly once married. Then the institution records arrived, seeming to substantiate my decision. Finally, some document checks from my lawyer, Lisa Eastwood, arrived. The Death Certificate, listing no husband and more importantly, marriage license checks from the five New York Boroughs coming back negative. It seemed I had my answer, but it still took forever to sort out just where those tangled rumors came from, and how they intertwined. Esther was behind it, I realized (during her life, of course) to my amusement, and exasperation. She simply liked to tell tales.

She wasn't alone at this, I suspect. Some of my interviewees liked to stretch things a bit. I began to learn where Mary Shaw was poking fun at friends, herself, and even me. And Jamie Van Trump would speak in such a flowery fashion at times that I wasn't sure if he was declaring something, telling a story, or asking me a question. I began to realize over time that you have to learn the idiosynchrasies of each of your sources. Most importantly, you have to figure out who of the people you are interviewing are most reliable. I began to notice that Esther was labelled different even from fellow artists in Pittsburgh who didn't quite share her drive to make a go of it in New York City. To Glen and Ed, very sane and reasonable, but also very creative artists who like a true metropolitan creative energy, Esther wasn't crazy, wasn't very different, really, than the typical artist. So there in a sense became a spectrum for me to judge my sources, and to weigh the merit of certain comments. Some just shone a little purer than others. Certainly Milton Weiss had nothing but praise to bestow on Esther. Likewise, Will Barnet and Carole Evans, she an artist in her own right. The latter two, among many others, including Dr. Arkus, stressed to me the importance of my work, *the value in writing of her struggle*, encouraging me. Said Barnet, after his comment that the family just didn't understand her, "It would be a bit of justice to write about her."

๑ ๑ ๑

What I had suspected from the very beginning became realized with my research, that Esther was ever young and fresh in thought, unafraid to defy convention, full of energy and spirit and genuine talent. What I would discover only after some time was that she remained connected enough to that spirit throughout all of her life to fully realize her creativity, and yet detached enough at times to retreat from a harsh world. Long hidden from view, her paintings and her life, her story, invoke hope as they depict a gutsy woman trying to get by in this life of adversity. Discovering her, writing about her, has been quite gratifying, and of course a tale in itself, which I've only touched upon in this Afterword.

Now that her story has become familiar, I would like, as Ken Chute has always hoped, for her art to become truly familiar. It is a shame that her work has sat so long at the Carnegie, but it is now time for the paintings that John O'Connor, Edward Duff Balkan, Oswaldo Rodriguez and John Lane saw value in to be exhibited. And if Esther Phillips' work would come to reside on the walls of the Carnegie, and other art museums, the viewer shall see the uniqueness of her work, yet be reminded that her tale brought attention to the many equally deserving that likely will never be shown, her friends, all artists.

With this writing, I was attempting to make the general public view an artist's life. To see that it is a hard one, but very fulfilling, as Esther points out. We don't choose it as much as it chooses us. If you do not feel yourself creative, do know that everyone has creativity in them. It is a part of all of our lives that must be nurtured to some degree in order to feel balanced and whole. If you are not a practicing artist, do look at the differences of our lives from yours. There are plusses in such a life of self-design, which everyone can have to a certain extent, and certainly minuses in the artistic lifestyle, much of which can be corrected. Society can change, I surely not too idealistically believe.

It is certainly not this writer's intent to suggest that solely the artistic way of life is *the* only hard way of life, nor that all artists are good people. Surely by focusing on the troubles befalling artists, ridicule and criticism will come, as it does to anyone attempting to highlight wrongs, inadequacies, inappropriatenesses that befall members of a certain group of people. But I will allow Eugenia Hughes to offer her word here, one simple fact that should not be forgotten. Oddly identical to verbal offerings by Van Trump and Milton Weiss, both who never knew Eugenia, was a scribble of hers on the back of one of Esther's small paintings found in her effects: "She was a Painter and She Starved."

It does not have to be this way. Artists have much to offer. Respect what they do, sponsor and commission their performances, buy from and offer them work. Provide an opportunity for their original, very unique, **needed** visions to surface, make an impression, and stay.

NOTES

Note for Introductory Correspondence: Harold J. Winters to Merle Hoyleman, November 21, 1937, New York, NY. From the collected papers of Merle Hoyleman, housed at A-1 Self-Storage, North Oakland, Pittsburgh, PA.

Chapter 1. "SHE NEEDED TO PAINT"

1. Esther Phillips' sister Dorothy Rosenthal, conversations with Ken Chute, fall 1984, Pittsburgh, PA. (Hereafter cited as Rosenthal conversations.)
2. Megan Shay, "Passion for Paint: The Life of Esther Phillips," *Pittsburgh History*, vol. 74, no. 3 (Fall 1991): 119.
3. Ibid.
4. Irene Kaufmann Settlement Art School informational pamphlet, December 1933: 4. Jewish Archives of the Historical Society of Western Pennsylvania, Pittsburgh, PA. (Hereafter cited as IKS pamphlet.)
5. Rosenthal conversations.
6. Esther Phillips, series of meetings with niece Millie Silverstein, 1980, New York, NY. Millie took extensive notes of the visits with her aunt; at times it appears she quoted Esther directly. These were forwarded to Ken Chute, who enhanced them with notations of his own conversations with Millie; all was then forwarded to author in 1991 (Hereafter cited as Millie's notes.)
7. IKS pamphlet, 1.
8. Esther's father David Phillips, as quoted by Dorothy Rosenthal in conversations with Chute.
9. Rosenthal conversations.
10. Millie's notes.
11. Charlotte Streifer Rubinstein, *American Women Artists from Early Indian Times to the Present* (Boston: G. K. Hall & Co. and NY.: Avon Books, 1982), 40.
12. Ibid., 157.
13. Ibid.
14. Ibid., 165.
15. Rosenthal conversations.
16. Ibid.

17. Shay, "Passion for Paint," 119.

18. "Permanent Record of Student Esther Phillips," Carnegie Institute of Technology College of Fine Arts, date of entrance September 29, 1919. Stored in the Registrar's Office of present-day Carnegie Mellon University, Pittsburgh, PA.

19. "Division of the Arts, School of Painting and Decoration," informational publication of the Carnegie Institute of Technology College of Fine Arts, academic year 1919–20. Records Office archives of the College of Fine Arts, Carnegie Mellon University, Pittsburgh, PA.

20. E. R. Bossange, "Suggestions Concerning the Choice of a Course in Art," publication of the Carnegie Institute of Technology College of Fine Arts, academic year 1919–1920. Records Office archives of the College of Fine Arts, Carnegie Mellon University, Pittsburgh, PA.

21. Streifer Rubinstein, *American Women Artists* , 40.

22. Dr. J. Barasch, "Abstract of Commitment," October 28, 1942, in the psychiatric records of Esther Phillips, patient at Harlem Valley State Hospital, Wingdale, NY. Record depository now at Hudson River Psychiatric Center, Poughkeepsie, NY. (Hereafter depository for this and other records cited simply as Institution Records.)

23. Marohnic's remembrances and Dorothy Rosenthal quoted, both in Shay, 119.

24. Mary Shaw Marohnic interview with author, June 1993, at the Marian Manor Nursing Home, Pittsburgh, PA. (Hereafter cited as Shaw Marohnic interview.)

25. Or, Esther could have been referring to the cafeteria on campus at the college, Carnegie Institute of Technology. This was in Langley Laboratory, erected in 1918, a space actually used throughout the years, before being demolished in 1959, as an art studio. Historical information from Phillip Rothsted, janitor at Carnegie Tech, phone interview with author, spring 1992, Pittsburgh, PA. Also Ann Curran, "Not Heaven On Earth: A Short History Of Skibo." *Carnegie Mellon Magazine*, vol. 17, no. 2 (Winter 1998), 29.

Chapter 2.   "THE WHOLE TOWN WAS ON A PARTY"

1. Shaw Marohnic interview.

2. Rosenthal conversations.

3. Wendy Slatkin, *Women Artists in History, From Antiquity to the 20th Century,* 2nd. ed. (Englewood Cliffs, NJ.: Prentice-Hall, 1990), 2.

4. Barasch, "Abstract of Commitment."

5. Shay, "Passion for Paint," 119.

6. Sybil Barsky-Grucci, State College, PA., phone interview with author, spring 1992.

7. Sybil Barsky-Grucci as paraphrased in Shay, 119.

8. Shay, 119.

9. Rosenthal conversations.

10. Sybil Barsky-Grucci as paraphrased in Shay, 119.

11. Barsky-Grucci phone interview.

12. Rosenthal conversations.

13. *Pittsburgh Associated Artists Catalog 1923*

14. Shaw Marohnic interview.

15. *The Associated Artists of Pittsburgh: 1910–1985. The First Seventy-Five Years*, compiled, written, and designed by Teresa DallaPiccola Wood, Mary Brignano and Richard Brown for The Associated Artists of Pittsburgh, publisher. Pittsburgh, PA., 1985, 26. (Hereafter cited as AAP publication.)

16. Unless otherwise noted, all of the information in the following passage is taken from Shaw Marohnic interview.

17. Fred W. McDarrah, with text by Gloria S. McDarrah, *The Artist's World in Pictures—The Photo Classic that Documents The New York School Action Painters*. (New York: Shapolsky Publishers, 1988), 11.

18. There are several references for this note. Author's interview with an acquaintance of Esther, James Van Trump, revealed Esther's connection with the interior decorator and his connection with a major department store. Barsky-Grucci phone interview confirmed the connection and identified both the last name of the "Harold" in question and the name of the store. The author's research at the Historical Society of Western Pennsylvania, Pittsburgh, PA., substantiated the details provided by both sources. (James Van Trump interview with author, February 1992, at the Wightman Health Center, Pittsburgh, PA.)

19. Barsky-Grucci phone interview.

20. Ibid.

21. Barasch, "Abstract of Commitment."

22. Rosenthal conversations.

23. Though her "Permanent Record" does not show it, a name search conducted in the Registrar's office of Carnegie Mellon University has Esther actually taking classes again throughout this time.

24. From a small news clipping in the *IKS Neighbors*, February 13, 1927, that detailed an Associated Artists of Pittsburgh exhibit that opened February 11, 1927. Esther exhibited only one painting according to this article, though the title is not known, for the Associated Artists of Pittsburgh catalog of this year does not list her.

25. From records listing "Submissions for the Internationals," Carnegie Museum of Fine Art administrative library, Pittsburgh, PA.

26. Shaw Marohnic interview.

27. Just this quote, from an undated article, was found in the Biography Files (under John O'Connor) of the Historical Society of Western Pennsylvania.

28. John O'Connor to Mrs. John Bowman, June 1936, Pittsburgh, PA. "1927–1936 Correspondence on Microfilm." (Carnegie Museum of Fine Art administrative library; Pittsburgh, PA., text-fiche).

29. Unless otherwise noted, all of the information in the following passage is taken from Milton Weiss interview with author, March 1993, Pittsburgh, PA.

30. From a program for an "Irene Kaufmann Settlement Neighborhood Art School Exhibit," May 1928, at the Neighborhood Art School, 1835 Center Avenue, Pittsburgh, PA. Jewish Archives of the Historical Society of Western Pennsylvania.

Chapter 3. THE REVIEWS

1. *Pittsburgh Associated Artists Catalogs,* Years 1928–1930.

2. Two sources pointed the way to find early information on Esther as a "listed artist." One, her "Pittsburgh Artist" file, which, in addition to having copies of her reviews, referenced the Pittsburgh Associated Artists Catalogs, and the *Supplement* to *Mallett's Index of Artists* , an international biographical index, which simply cross-referenced her AAP records and some independent Pittsburgh exhibitions she took part in. (Mallett, Daniel Trowbridge. New York: R. R. Bowker Co., 1940).

3. Weiss interview.

4. Edgar J. Kaufmann, Foreword to a pamphlet detailing the "Art In Industry Contests," sponsored by Kaufmann's Department Store in collaboration with *The Pittsburgh Press*, 1930.

5. Marie McSwigan, "Bold and Original Designs Replace Pretty Pictures," *Pittsburgh Press* , May 1932.

6. AAP publication.

7. McSwigan, "Bold and Original Designs Replace Pretty Pictures."
8. Joseph J. Cloud, "Art Exhibit Awards Seem Satisfactory," *Pittsburgh Press*, February 12, 1932.
9. Joseph J. Cloud, "Pittsburgh Artists Show Good Work in 21st Exhibit," *Pittsburgh Press*, 13 Feb. 1931.
10. Penelope Redd, Foreword to "Esther Phillips: Exhibition of Water Colors, Starting March 31, Warner Theatre," March 1933.
11. This information is according to the last paragraph of Naylor's "Can't Find Any Fun Going Along with Mob in Life," of Esther's involvement in the AAP show of the year prior. (Douglas Naylor, *Pittsburgh Press*, August 20, 1933)
12. Art Editor, "Associated Art Show Opens With Full House," *Pittsburgh Sun-Telegraph Times*, November 2, 1933.
13. AAP publication, 31–32.
14. Art Editor, "Associated Art Show Opens With Full House."
15. *Pittsburgh Associated Artists Catalogs,* Years 1933–1936.
16. *Exhibition of Paintings by Pittsburgh Artists* , Years 1932–1936. Four individual bulletins that accompanied the shows. 1932 publication, only, found stored at Carnegie Library, other years at Carnegie Mellon University's Hunt Library.
17. "1927–1936 Correspondence on Microfilm." (Carnegie Museum of Fine Art administrative library; Pittsburgh, PA., text-fiche).
18. Dorothy Steinberg interview with author, May 1995, New York, NY.
19. Millie's notes.
20. Unless otherwise noted, all of the information in the following passage is taken from "Records of the Works Progress Administration," Carnegie Museum of Fine Art administrative library (Hereafter cited as WPA records.)
21. From a notation in the journals of Merle Hoyleman, August 13, 1952. From the collected papers of Merle Hoyleman.
22. WPA records.
23. Homer Saint-Gaudens, *The American Artist and His Times* (New York: Dodd, Mead and Co., 1941), 252.

Chapter 4. "FLIPPY"

1. Walter Kidney, "The Author," preface to James Van Trump's *Life and Architecture in Pittsburgh* (Pittsburgh: Pittsburgh History and Landmarks Foundation, 1983), xiv.

2. Unless otherwise noted, all of the information in the following passage is taken from James Van Trump interview with author, February 1992, at the Wightman Health Center, Pittsburgh, PA.

3. Barsky-Grucci phone interview.

4. Lois J. Fowler, "The Marriage," in *I Could Be Mute: The Life and Work of Gladys Schmitt*, ed. Anita Brostoff (Pittsburgh: Carnegie-Mellon University Press, 1978), 67.

5. Kidney, "The Author," xiii.

6. James Van Trump, "An Antiphon of Stones: Some Random Native Notes in Reply to a Visiting Architectural Critic in Pittsburgh," in *Life and Architecture in Pittsburgh*, 17. This essay was originally published in *The Charette*, July 1963.

7. Arthur P. Ziegler, Introduction to Van Trump's *Life and Architecture in Pittsburgh*, xix.

8. Written for the flap copy of Gladys Schmitt's *The Gates of Aulis* (Garden City, NJ: Sun Dial Press, 1942).

9. Barsky-Grucci phone interview.

10. George Marion O'Donnell, Introduction to Merle Hoyleman's *Asp of the Age*. Self-published. "Printed from the author's manuscript in an edition of 326." 1966, Wood Printing, Toronto. The piece "Asp of the Age" originally published in *Hound and Horn*, fall 1931.

11. Ibid.

12. From notations in "1927–1936 Correspondence on Microfilm." (Carn. Mus. of Fine Art admin. library; Pittsburgh, PA., text-fiche).

13. *Exhibition of Paintings by Pittsburgh Artists*, 1936.

14. Merle Hoyleman to "Sara and Ted," 29 Oct. 1952, Pittsburgh, PA. The draft of this letter, on which Merle then printed "NOT SENT," was found among her collected papers.

15. Steinberg interview.

16. Van Trump interview.

17. Rosenthal conversations.

18. Ibid.

19. Shaw Marohnic interview.

20. Sara Via Pais, "Shapes of the Feminine Experience in Art," in *Women, the Arts & the 1920s in Paris and New York*, ed. Kenneth W. Wheeler and Virginia Lee Lussier (New Brunswick, NJ.: Transaction Books, 1982), 52.

21. All of the journal entries come from the collected papers of Merle Hoyleman.

Chapter 5. "SHE WAS AN ARTIST & SHE STARVED"

1. Van Trump interview.
2. Millie's notes.
3. Joseph Mitchell, "Joe Gould's Secret," in *Up In The Old Hotel, And Other Stories* (New York: Pantheon Books, 1992), 660.
4. Both the names Goody's and Minetta's show up in Millie's notes; they also appear frequently in published accounts of happenings about the Village of this era.
5. Though not the case here, often Merle's notations about correspondence, that she would log in her journals, can be cross-referenced with actual documents received (originals) or drafts of letters sent out. According to the timeline of reflections in the journals (in that a date was not actually attached to all thoughts put down), Merle indeed logged that she wrote Esther around early January.
6. Hereafter text dates set in brackets from any letter sent by Esther to another party reflect that either author is viewing the postmark on attached envelope, or that the receiving party placed the date atop the correspondence noticeably in their own hand.
7. Hereafter journal entries and correspondence of Merle's that require no other clarification than what text presents will not be additionally cited in these Notes.
8. Eugenia's journals are stored among The Eugenia Hughes Papers, Manuscripts and Archives Section of the New York Public Library, New York, NY.
9. Dan Wakefield, *New York in the '50s* (Boston: Houghton Mifflin, 1992), 116. Description of Wakefield's personal impression of Village in 1952.
10. Calvin Trillin, a report for *The Nation*, quoted in Wakefield, 118.
11. William H. Hemp, "Washington Mews" (General Publishing Co., Limited, 1975). This article was found among the records of the Washington Square Outdoor Show, which are housed at the Archives of American Art, New York Regional Center, New York, NY.
12. Wakefield, *New York in the '50s*, 116.
13. Lenore Monleon interview with author, May 1995 at her Chelsea Antique Center, New York, NY.
14. The same treatment that applied to assessing the exactness of some dates of Merle's journal entries applies to Eugenia's, in that she, too, did not attach a specific date to all her entries. Also as was the case with Merle, hereafter

journal entries of Eugenia's that require no other clarification than what text presents will not be additionally cited in these Notes.

15. Bossange, "Suggestions Concerning the Choice of a Course in Art."
16. Esther as quoted in Millie's notes.
17. Rosenthal conversations.
18. This journal entry appeared approximately in early 1939.
19. (Book's Introductory Letter—See beginning of Notes)
20. Harold J. Winters to Merle Hoyleman, October 6, 1936, New York, NY. and September 29, 1936, New York, NY.
21. Van Trump interview.
22. These words show up in numerous places throughout years of Merle's journals and letters.
23. Merle Hoyleman to Harold J. Winters, December 1, 1937, Pittsburgh, PA.
24. Harold J. Winters to Merle Hoyleman, December 20, 1937, New York., NY.
25. Harold J. Winters to Merle Hoyleman, January 2, 1938, New York, NY.

Chapter 6. "THE A.M. AFTER THE NIGHT BEFORE"

1. This journal caption of Eugenia Hughes appeared in the late 1930s, according to the timeline of reflections in the journals.
2. Esther Phillips to Eugenia Hughes, November 21, 1942, Wingdale, New York. Eugenia retained the correspondence and it is stored among her papers. Eugenia would specifically put the date of Esther's letters in brackets herself, it can be surmised, according to postmarks that were on once-attached envelopes (no longer existing, as is the case with Merle's effects).
3. Exact substantiation of Esther's addresses came about only due to a variety of research, beginning with Merle's journals—she scribbled the changing addresses of friends from year to year inside the front and back covers. Also information was provided by Eugenia's papers, Millie's notes, and records of participating artists in the Washington Square Outdoor Show. (Archives of American Art, New York Regional Center, New York, NY. Lent for microfilming by Vernon C. Porter. Reels NWS1) Also helpful to author was the careful ordering of facts done by Ken Chute.
4. Esther Phillips to Merle Hoyleman, August 16, 1938. New York, NY.
5. Dore Ashton, *The New York School: A Cultural Reckoning* (New York: The Viking Press, 1972), 48.
6. Ashton, *The New York School,* 48.

7. The love letters, like the journals, are among the Eugenia Hughes Papers.

8. Edward Kinchley Evans and Glen Z. Gress interviews with author, summer 1993, at the Laurel Highlands Regional Theatre, Pittsburgh, PA. First quote is Gress.

9. Eleanor Munro, *Originals: American Women Artists* (New York: Simon and Schuster, 1979), 252.

10. Snapshots of friends and family are among the Eugenia Hughes Papers.

11. Notations of Esther's knowing the specific artists mentioned, as well as the soap incident, come from Millie's notes.

12. Ibid. Quotes appear to be Esther's.

13. The Eugenia Hughes Papers. Save for the few additional notes to be referenced throughout, source documentation for any referring to Eugenia, family, and friends is from the variety of material in this collection, including the collection's Accession Sheet and Summary Description Sheet. The numerous and various details of Eugenia's actions, and her friends, as the text suggests, come from Eugenia's journal reflections and other supporting material found among her papers, unless otherwise or further noted in cases of material of special significance.

14. Catharine R. Stimpson, Introduction to *Women, the Arts & the 1920s in Paris and New York*, ed. Kenneth W. Wheeler and Virginia Lee Lussier (New Brunswick, NJ.: Transaction Books, 1982), 4 and 39.

15. Via Pais, "Shapes of the Feminine Experience in Art," 51.

16. Ibid.

17. Editors Kenneth W. Wheeler and Virginia Lee Lussier, Preface to *Women, the Arts & the 1920s in Paris and New York*, xi.

18. This journal entry appeared in mid-1941.

19. This journal entry appeared around February 1938.

20. Millie's notes. Last quote appears to be Esther's.

21. William H. Hemp, "Washington Mews."

22. "The Washington Square Outdoor Art Exhibit Records & 74 Posters of the Washington Square Outdoor Art Exhibit." Archives of American Art, New York Regional Center. Lent for microfilming by Vernon C. Porter. Reels NWS1 (Hereafter cited as Washington Square Show records.)

23. Esther Phillips to Eugenia Hughes, winter 1942. New York, NY.

24. Washington Square Show records.

25. Ibid.

26. Robert Henkes, *American Women Painters of the '30s & '40s: The Lives and Work of Ten Artists* (Jefferson, NC: McFarland and Co. Publ., 1991), 93.

27. Ashton, *The New York School*, 44.

28. Ibid, 49.

29. Holger Cahill, quoted in Ashton, 47.

30. Ashton, *The New York School*, 45.

31. Ibid., 48–49.

32. Jeffrey L. Geller and Maxine Harris, *Women of the Asylum: Voices From Behind The Walls, 1840–1945* (New York: Anchor Books, Doubleday, 1994), 252–253.

33. Ashton, *The New York School*, 49–50.

34. Harold J. Winters to Merle Hoyleman, October 6, 1936, New York, NY.

35. Lewis Mumford, from December 30, 1936 issue of *The New Republic* , as quoted in Ashton, 49.

Chapter 7. "HAVING DRIFTED"

1. Dr. E. Kaufmann, Doctor Visit Note, June 9, 1947, in the Institution Records.

2. Rozanne R. Knudsen, Sea Cliff, New York, phone interviews with author, 1994–98. Ms. Knudsen was the last partner of May Swenson and wrote *The Magic Pen of May Swenson*. She holds the collected papers of May and spoke of reading diary notations about Esther (quote in text is Knudsen's), and that those notations also had May in 1938 taking art classes in Queens along with May's partner Anca.

3. The Eugenia Hughes Papers.

4. Millie's notes.

5. Mitchell, "Professor," and "Joe Gould's Secret," in *Up In The Old Hotel, And Other Stories*, 52–70 and 623–716.

6. Ibid., 54–68.

7. Ibid., 629.

8. Ibid., 58–59.

9. Ibid., 649–697.

10. Robert Mattison, "Franz Kline's Vision—Pennsylvania's Coal Region in B&W," *New Arts Program Text(s): A Literary Journal* , vol. 3, no.1 : 1.

11. Donald S. Howard, *The WPA and Federal Relief Policy* (New York: Russell Sage Foundation, 1943), 239.

12. Regis Masson to Eugenia Hughes, March 1940, received in Williamsport, PA. (Exact place of departure unknown.) The Eugenia Hughes Papers.

13. Millie's notes.

14. Stefan Lorant, *Pittsburgh: The Story Of An American City.* Authors Edition (Lenox, MA: Published by Stefan Lorant, 1975), 347.

15. Ashton, *The New York School,* 117.

16. Artist Adolph Gottlieb quoted in Ashton, 118.

17. (Unpublished) From the collection of papers of May Swenson, held by the executor of her estate, Rozanne R. Knudsen.

18. Regis Masson to Eugenia Hughes, March 1940.

19. Reference to Via Pais, "Shapes of the Feminine Experience in Art," 52.

20. Dr. J. Barasch, "Abstract of Commitment."

21. George Knight to Eugenia Hughes, June 1942, New York, New York. Not all of the summer 1942 letters are well dated or organized in The Eugenia Hughes Papers. Author best judged the context presented and accordingly ordered them in the chronological fashion that the text presents. Remaining letters presented in this chapter, from Esther to Eugenia; George Knight to Eugenia; and Roy Hughes to Eugenia all come from the Eugenia Hughes Papers.

22. Dr. E. Kaufmann, Doctor Visit Note, June 9, 1947.

23. Dr. J. Barasch, "Abstract of Commitment."

24. Esther as quoted in a Doctor Visit Note, Dr. A.F. Rizzolo, April 13, 1943.

Chapter 8. "IN A HELL OF A MESS"

1. Esther as quoted in Dr. J. Barasch, "Abstract of Commitment."

2. The actual notice from The Eugenia Hughes Papers. (Eugenia saved originals of correspondence sent to her. Unlike Merle, she did not save drafts of letters she sent out.)

3. Dr. Sidney Rubin, "Petition, Certificate and Orders in the Case of Esther Phillips," October 16, 1942, within the Institution Records.

4. All indications are that Harlem Valley State Hospital kept meticulous records; they would have retained a responding letter from Eugenia, but none such appears in Esther's institution file.

5. "Ward Notes," October 23, 1942, and the "Ward Admission Record." Institution Records.

6. Information comes from Susan K. Hartman, Supervising Medical Record Administrator, interviews with author, fall 1993, Poughkeepsie and Wingdale, New York. Author corresponded with Hartman via phone throughout the fall, as well as visited institution, which had been since shut down, and spoke with Hartman in person there. Hartman accompanied author on tour of buildings; author also went about the grounds. Hartman's office is at the Hudson River Psychiatric Center in Poughkeepsie, which oversaw operations at Harlem Valley in latter years.

7. Information taken from Ward Notes, October 23, 1942, the Statistical Data Sheet, and a Physical Summary Sheet, detailing a physical given by a Dr. Gourdin, October 24, 1942. Institution Records.

8. Merle Hoyleman to George Marion O'Donnell, November 26, 1937, Pittsburgh, PA.

9. Barsky-Grucci phone interview with author.

10. H. A. LaBurt, M.D., Superintendent of Harlem Valley State Hospital, to Eugenia Hughes, October 23, 1942, Wingdale, NY. The Eugenia Hughes Papers.

11. Copies of this correspondence exist within the Institution Records and the actual documents themselves show up in The Eugenia Hughes Papers.

12. Michael Duner to Eugenia Hughes, October 1942, New York, New York.

13. "Anamnesis," recorded by Dr. Barasch. "Informant: Annino Mariano, friend." Institution Records. Mariano's address was listed as 44 Washington Square, the same as Eugenia and Esther's.

Chapter 9. "GREETINGS FROM WINGDALE, NY."

1. Esther Phillips to Eugenia Hughes, Wingdale, NY, December 7, 1942,

2. City Directory (Pennsylvania Room Archives, Carnegie Library of Pittsburgh; text-fiche), p.1219, P-202, no. 65.

3. H. A. LaBurt, M.D., Superintendent of Harlem Valley State Hospital, to Barney Phillips, June 30, 1943, Wingdale, NY, within the Institution Records.

Chapter 10. DIAGNOSIS

1. H. A. LaBurt, M.D., Superintendent of Harlem Valley State Hospital, "A Christmas Thought." Brief statement issued to relatives and friends of Harlem Valley State Hospital patients. The Eugenia Hughes Papers, Manuscripts and Archives Section of the New York Public Library, New York, NY.

2. Within institution records.

3. Dr. J. Barasch, "Clinical Summary," February 22, 1943. Institution Records.

4. O. Spurgeon English and Stuart M. Finch, *Introduction to Psychiatry* (New York: W. W. Norton and Company, 1954), 332.

5. Geller and Harris,Women of the Asylum, 98.

6. Ibid., 180.

7. English and Finch, 139 and 146.

8. Ibid., 391.

9. Dr. Gourdin, "Physical Summary Sheet," October 24, 1942. Institution Records.

10. D. Rowe, "A Gene For Depression? Who Are We Kidding?" *Changes* 891 (1990): 15. Author gathered this information from Jane Ussher, *Women's Madness: Misogyny or Mental Illness?* (Amherst: University of Massachusetts Press, 1992), 133.

11. English and Finch, 44.

12. Esther Phillips to Eugenia Hughes, Wingdale, NY, Dec. 1942.

13. Roger J. Williams et al., *The Biochemistry of B Vitamins*, University of Texas, Austin (New York: Reinhold Publishing Company, 1950), 410.

14. English and Finch, 332.

15. Found within the Institution Records and the Eugenia Hughes Papers, respectively.

16. I. M. Rossman to Michael Duner, December 14, 1943, Wingdale, NY. Institution Records.

17. Margaret Starr, quoted in Geller and Harris, 215. Starr's account is from her *Sane or Insane? Or How I Regained My Liberty*, 1904.

18. Hoyleman, *Asp of the Age*, 4–5.

Chapter 11. THE VIEW FROM BEHIND BARS

1. Jane Ussher, *Women's Madness*, 6.

3. Ibid., 130.

4. Ibid., 148.

5. Thomas S. Szasz, *The Myth of Mental Illness: Foundations of a Theory of Personal Conduct* (London: Secker Publishing, 1961). Author gathered this information from Ussher.

6. R. D. Laing, *The Politics of Experience* (Harmondsworth: Penguin, 1967). Author gathered this information from Ussher.

7. Reference to Via Pais, "Shapes of the Feminine Experience in Art," 52.

8. Thomas S. Szasz, *The Manufacture of Madness—A Comparative Study of the Inquisition and The Mental Health Movement* (New York: Harper and Row, 1970), xxiii-xxiv.

9. Ussher, 149.

10. Elaine Showalter, *The Female Malady: Women, Madness, and English Culture, 1830–1980* (New York: Pantheon Books, 1985), 5.

11. Phyllis Chesler, *Women and Madness* (Garden City: Doubleday, 1972); Kate Millett, *The Loony-Bin Trip* (New York: Simon and Schuster, 1992); Shere Hite, *The Hite Report: Women and Love—A Cultural Revolution* in Progress (New York: Knopf, 1987).

12. Chesler, 16.

13. Adeline T. P. Lunt, quoted in Geller and Harris' *Women of the Asylum*, 117. Lunt's account is an excerpt from her *Behind Bars*, 1871.

14. Margaret Aikins McGarr, quoted in Geller and Harris, 306.

15. Geller and Harris, 99.

16. Charlotte Perkins Gilman, *The Yellow Wallpaper*, 1892 (London: Virago, 1988 reprint).

17. Via Pais, "Shapes of the Feminine Experience in Art," 51.

18. Phyllis Chesler, Foreward to Geller and Harris, xix.

19. Showalter, 136.

20. Eleanor Munro, *Originals: American Women Artists* (New York: Simon and Schuster, 1979), 123–127. Quote is Neel's, describing doctor's comment to her.

21. Ussher, 7.

22. Ibid., 167.

23. Szasz, *The Manufacture of Madness*, 168.

24. Showalter, 198–199.

25. Surmised by the author after careful examination of what Esther wrote of when she corresponded with her friend ("Haven't heard from you since...."), of the sequencing of Esther's letters **to** Eugenia (some are inquiries one right after another), and examination of Institution Records that revealed external sleuthing on Eugenia and Roy's part, urging hospital reply. There is no docu-

mentation of Eugenia's writing to Esther in the institution records. These letters, after likely getting first gaze by administrators, went directly to Esther and there is thus no surviving copy. (As she would deal with her life really only in paintings, Esther would leave only these, and not papers, upon her death.)

26. Dan Wakefield, *Island in the City* (New York: Corinth Books, 1959), 261.

27. Dr. Alfred M. Stanley, Director, Harlem Valley State Hospital, to Vito Marcantonio, May 25, 1945, Wingdale, NY. Institution Records.

28. Edward Adamson, *Art as Healing* (London: Coventure, Ltd., 1990), 7–8.

29. Observed from author's visit to the institution, which had since been shut down, in Wingdale, NY, the fall of 1993 and interviews with Susan K. Hartman, Supervising Medical Record Administrator, there at that time.

30. Margaret Isabel Wilson, quoted in Geller and Harris'*Women of the Asylum*, 277. Institutionalized from 1931 to 1937 at her pseudonymous "Blackmoor."

31. "Joyce" (pseudonym), quoted in Phyllis Chesler's *Women and Madness*, 172. As in *Women of the Asylum*, Chesler interviewed 24 women hospitalized for psychiatric reasons between 1950 and 1970 in a section of her 1972 book.

32. Hartman interviews.

33. Mary Jane Ward, quoted in Geller and Harris, 295. Institutionalized in 1941 in a New York City psychiatric hospital. Ward's account is an excerpt from her *The Snake Pit* (New York: Random House, 1946).

34. Wilson, quoted in Geller and Harris, 278.

35. Ward, quoted in Geller and Harris, 298–299.

36. Shay, "Passion for Paint, 123.

37. Henkes, *American Women Painters of the '30s & '40s*, 93.

38. McSwigan, "Bold and Original Designs Replace Pretty Pictures."

39. Adamson, *Art As Healing*, 31.

40. Sophie Olsen, quoted in Geller and Harris, 71–72. Institutionalized from 1862 to 1864 at Illinois State Hospital for the Insane. Olsen's account is an excerpt from her *Mrs. Olsen's Narrative of Her One Year at Jacksonville Insane Asylum*, 1868.

41. Information about term usage at Harlem Valley came from Hartman interviews with author.

42. Margaret Starr, quoted in Geller and Harris, 217.

43. Kate Lee, quoted in Geller and Harris, 203. Institutionalized from 1899 to 1900 at Elgin Insane Asylum. Lee's account is an excerpt from her *A Year At Elgin Insane Asylum*, 1902.

Chapter 12. THE LIBRARIAN

1. Vito Marcantonio to Alfred M. Stanley, Senior Director of Harlem Valley State Hospital, June 28, 1946, New York, NY. Within the Institution Records.
2. Jane Hillyer, quoted in Geller and Harris, *Women of the Asylum*, 240. Hillyer's account is an excerpt from her *Reluctantly Told*, 1927.
3. William Barnet, New York, NY., phone interview with author, May 1995.
4. Robert Doty, *Will Barnet* (New York: Harry N. Abrams, Inc., 1984), 12.
5. Dore Ashton quoted in Doty, 49.
6. Information in the following passage is from Barnet phone interview with author.

Chapter 13. "ABOUT ESTHER PHILLIPS"

1. Scrawled across the front of an envelope, containing correspondence from City of New York Department of Hospitals, Bellevue Hospital, to Merle Hoyleman, postmarked November 13, 1946, New York, NY.
2. Though no journal notation or letter exists to this effect, it can be surmised when taken into consideration with the content and tone of the ad Merle was about to place in the Bulletin Index, and considering the saved envelope from Bellevue Hospital on November 13, 1946.
3. The Bulletin Index, October 26, 1946, Classifieds, Box 301–M.
4. City of New York Department of Hospitals, Bellevue Hospital, to Merle Hoyleman, postmarked November 13, 1946, New York, NY.
5. Merle Hoyleman to "Sara & Ted," October 29, 1952, Pittsburgh, PA. The draft of this letter, on which Merle then printed "NOT SENT," was found among her papers.
6. Hartman interviews.
7. This correspondence is missing from the institution file.
8. Rosenthal conversations.
9. Dr. Alfred M. Stanley to Merle Hoyleman, March 18, 1947, Wingdale, New York.
10. Steinberg interview.
11. Merle's journal entry dated March 16, 1947.
12. Merle's journal entry dated 28 March 1947.
13. Merle's journal entry dated April 18, 1947. Author's telephone interview with Lois Monahan (the former Lois Naylor), Grove City, PA, fall 1991, confirms that she still has this work.
14. Merle's journal entry dated March 22, 1947 confirms Merle's relaying to

Gladys Schmitt that Esther would like to see her and Merle's journal entry of April 21 of that year has reference to Esther receiving correspondence from Gladys.

15. Merle's journal entry dated August 21, 1947.

16. Elizabeth Schmitt Culley, Gladys Schmitt's adopted daughter, "Lasting Impressions," in *I Could Be Mute: The Life and Work of Gladys Schmitt*, ed. Anita Brostoff (Pittsburgh: Carnegie-Mellon University Press, 1978), 28.

17. Van Trump interview.

18. Culley, "Lasting Impressions."

19. Van Trump interview.

20. Merle Hoyleman to Earl E. Moore, September 2, 1952, Pittsburgh, PA.

21. Merle Hoyleman to George Marion O'Donnell, November 26, 1937, Pittsburgh, PA.

22. Merle's journal entry dated October 29, 1952.

23. Merle Hoyleman to Dr. Alfred M. Stanley, June 6, 1947, Pittsburgh, PA.

24. Dr. Alfred M. Stanley to Merle Hoyleman, June 9, 1947, Wingdale, NY. In this letter Dr. Stanley states that "a package of paintings was mailed from here on June 5 to Mr. John O'Connor, Jr., Asst. Art Director, Carnegie Museum, Pittsburgh, PA."

25. John O'Connor, Jr., Assistant Director to Dr. Alfred M. Stanley, June 10, 1947, Pittsburgh, PA.

26. Dr. Stanley writes Merle on May 21st that he has written Will Barnet, asking him to send along 10 of the best watercolors, and in a June 9th letter he informs Merle that Barnet "promised to send 10 from New York City."

27. Merle's journal entry dated June 9, 1948: "wc's arrived from Will Barnet, 50 W. 106 St. NYC."

28. Geller and Harris, *Women of the Asylum*, 262.

29. Jane Hillyer, quoted in Geller and Harris, 244–245.

30. Geller and Harris, 4.

31. Author is drawing on her previous experience within the Mental Health profession as a counselor and vocational development coordinator for a psychosocial community rehabilitation center—Peoples Oakland in Pittsburgh, PA, in 1990–1991. Peoples Oakland served a clientele from the "catchman areas"

where St. Francis Medical Center, Allegheny East Mental Health, Western Psychiatric and Northern Southwest drew from and staff worked extensively with contacts of each, as well as the Vocational Rehabilitation Center.

32. Ussher, *Women's Madness*, 289.

Chapter 14. "THAT MAD SCAMPERING ABOUT"

1. Esther Phillips to Eugenia Hughes, early winter 1948, Wingdale, NY.
2. Steinberg interview and Barsky-Grucci phone interview.
3. Steinberg interview.
4. Barsky-Grucci phone interview, and Merle's journal entries dated June 17, 1947 and October 22, 1947.
5. Merle's journal entries dated August 30, 1947 and September 2, 1947.
6. From a *Pittsburgh Press* "Who's Who" column tucked inside a 1946 letter to Merle. Date of column and sender of letter unknown.
7. Merle's journal entry dated September 30, 1947.
8. Merle's journal entry dated February 27, 1948. "Mrs. Naylor bought a watercolor—a snowscape for friends at Bradford, PA."
9. From information found within Anais Nin's *Delta of Venus* (New York: Quality Paperback Books, 1993).
10. Byron G. Wales, "Adjustment to the Total Institution," in *The Age of Madness: The History of Involuntary Mental Hospitalization*, ed. Thomas S. Szasz (New York: Jason Aronson, Publ., 1974), 267.
11. Author is drawing on her previous experience within the Mental Health profession.
12. Geller and Harris, *Women of the Asylum*, 262.
13. Wales, "Adjustment to the Total Institution," 268.
14. Ibid.
15. Chesler, Foreword to Geller and Harris, xvii.
16. Lunt, quoted in Geller and Harris, 120.
17. Geller and Harris, 262.
18. Ussher, *Women's Madness*, 297.
19. Dr. Alfred M. Stanley to Merle Hoyleman, August 5, 1948, Wingdale, NY, within the Institution Records.

Chapter 15. "LOOKING FORWARD . . . WITH MUCH ENTHUSIASM"

1. "LB," of the Psychiatric Institute, New York, NY, Convalescent Care Note, June 16, 1949, within the Institution Records.
2. Ashton, *The New York School*, 14.
3. Ibid, 6.
4. Ibid., 6 & 13.
5. Ibid., 13–14.
6. Auden quoted in Ashton, 136.
7. McDarrah, *The Artist's World in Pictures*, 11.
8. Taken from Wakefield, *New York in the '50s*, 135–136. Wakefield is quoting Seymour Krim, a writer for the *Village Voice*. Krim's reflections on psychiatrists first appeared in Krim's *Voice* essay "The Insanity Bit."
9. McDarrah, *The Artist's World in Pictures*, 71.
10. Nell Blaine quoted in Eleanor Munro, *Originals*, 266.
11. Rubinstein, *American Women Artists from Early Indian Times to the Present*, 240. Author also studied and compiled information from a variety of other sources for this and following related passages, namely Ashton, Munro, McDarragh, Wakefield, Slatkin, and Alice Goldfarb Marquis, *The Art Biz: The Covert World of Collectors, Dealers, Auction Houses, Museums and Critics* (Chicago: Contemporary Books Inc., 1991).
12. Rubinstein, *American Women Artists from Early Indian Times to the Present*, 267.
13. Ashton, *The New York School*, 121.
14. Millie's notes.
15. Munro, *Originals*, 108.
16. The deKoonings quoted in Munro, 252.
17. McDarrah, *The Artist's World in Pictures*, 52.
18. Marquis, *The Art Biz*, 44.
19. Rubinstein, *American Women Artists from Early Indian Times to the Present*, 278.
20. Evans and Gress interviews. This is a reference to Evans' quote from Chapter 6, Note 13.
21. Rubinstein, *American Women Artists from Early Indian Times to the Present*, 278–279.
22. Munro, *Originals*, 27 and 275.

23. Rubinstein,*American Women Artists from Early Indian Times to the Present,* 265.

24. Slatkin,*Women Artists in History* , 115.

25. Rubinstein,*American Women Artists from Early Indian Times to the Present,* 268.

26. Ibid.

27. Ibid., 273.

28. Munro, *Originals,* 107.

29. Rubinstein quoted in Munro, 484.

30. Munro, *Originals,* 27.

31. McDarrah, *The Artist's World in Pictures,* 153.

32. Rubinstein, *American Women Artists from Early Indian Times to the Present,* 279.

33. See "Sept. 8 1948: CONVALESCENT CARE APPROVED," Dr. C. Greenberg, at end of Chapter 14 for how this figure was calculated.

34. Merle Hoyleman to Dr. Alfred M. Stanley, February 8, 1949, Pittsburgh, PA. Institution Records.

35. Dr. Alfred M. Stanley to Merle Hoyleman, March 9, 1949 Wingdale, NY. Actually the letter only refers to "one of the women with whom she had left some things when she went to New York City," but atop correspondence another hospital administrator had written "Mrs. Rizzolo will deliver."

36. Washington Square Show records.

37. Evans interview.

38. Shay, "Passion for Paint," 123.

39. Ashton, *The New York School,* 154.

40. Ed Evans and Glen Gress would comment of their circle of friends, including Esther, crossing paths with Milton Resnick. Author reached Resnick, in attempt for a phone interview, but an elderly Resnick did not grant that.

Chapter 16. "THE FLIGHT OF ESTHER PHILLIPS' FINGERTIPS"

1. Scribbled notation in a journal entry of Merle's, dated October 3, 1952.

2. Rubinstein, *American Women Artists from Early Indian Times to the Present,* 273. Author also studied and compiled information from a variety of other sources for this and related passages, namely Ashton, Munro, McDarragh, Wakefield, Slatkin, and Marquis.

3. Soyer quoted in Marquis, 51.

4. Munro, *Originals*, 107.

5. Rubinstein, *American Women Artists from Early Indian Times to the Present*, 279.

6. Mitchell, "Joe Gould's Secret," 635.

7. Ibid., 660.

8. Ibid.

9. Evans and Gress interviews. First quote is Gress, second is Evans.

10. Evans interview.

11. Millie's notes.

12. Evans interview.

13. Rubinstein, *American Women Artists from Early Indian Times to the Present*, 285. A summary of art critic John Gruen's description of the atmosphere in the '40s.

14. McDarrah, *The Artist's World in Pictures* , 10.

15. Shay, "Passion for Paint," 123.

16. Observed from author's visit to Greenwich Village.

17. Millie's notes. First quote appears directly to be Esther's.

18. Sidonie S. Bartok, Case Supervisor, City of New York, Department of Welfare to Director, Harlem Valley Hospital, May 7, 1951, New York, NY, within the Institution Records.

19. Leo P. O'Donnell, Director, Harlem Valley Hospital, to Sidonie S. Bartok, Case Supervisor, City of New York, Department of Welfare, May 16, 1951, Wingdale, NY. Institution Records.

20. Esther Phillips to Dr. Greenberg, spring 1951, New York, NY. Institution Records.

21. Elizabeth T. Stone, "A Sketch Of My Life," in Geller and Harris' *Women of the Asylum*, 32–41. Account is Stone's combination of excerpts taken from three of her previously published writings.

22. Chesler, Foreward to Geller and Harris, xvii.

23. Margaret Aikins McGarr's account in Geller and Harris, 306. Account is excerpts from *and lo, the STAR*, published in 1953.

24. Save for the few additional notes to be referenced throughout, source documentation for the following passage is as follows: Draft of letter Merle typewrote while still in Mayview, and kept in a file that contained addresses for

various personal and professional contacts. Heading reads "South Z-1A, Mayview State Hospital, Mayview, PA., July 10 to August 3, 1951

25. Shay, "Passion for Paint," 118.
26. Mention of Roy Hughes' death is made in the Eugenia Hughes Papers.
27. Esther Phillips to Merle Hoyleman, January 31, 1952, New York, NY.
28. Merle's journal entry dated February 19, 1952.
29. This appears to have happened for the first time on May 25,1952, as noted in Merle's journal.
30. Merle's journal entry dated August 13, 1952.
31. This phrase shows up in numerous journal entries of Merle's.
32. According to a journal entry dated this fall.
33. Merle's journal entry dated October 29, 1952.
34. Merle Hoyleman to "Sara and Ted," October 29, 1952, Pittsburgh, PA. Merle printed "NOT SENT" across the draft of this letter.
35. Scribbled notation in a journal entry of Merle's, dated October 3, 1952.

Chapter 17. "EVERY INCH OF STRENGTH AND STRATEGY TO CALL FORTH AID"

1. Merle Hoyleman to George Marion O'Donnell, November 26, 1937, Pittsburgh, PA.
2. Mitchell, "Professor Sea Gull," 54.
3. Millie's notes.
4. An undated scribbled notation references Gould, and an article Eugenia cut out and saved, among many others, tells of his death. Stored among The Eugenia Hughes Papers.
5. Mitchell, "Professor Sea Gull," 62 and 97–98.
6. Mitchell, "Joe Gould's Secret," 711–712.
7. Esther's letters to Merle are stored within the collected papers of Merle Hoyleman; the latter information came from Millie's notes.
8. Esther Phillips to Merle Hoyleman, March 25, 1953, New York, NY.
9. Esther Phillips to Merle Hoyleman, February 19, 1953, New York, NY.
10. According to various journal entries of Merle's around this time.
11. Rosenthal conversations.
12. Esther Phillips to Merle Hoyleman, June 22, 1953, New York, NY.
13. Merle's journal entry dated August 21, 1953.
14. Esther Phillips to Merle Hoyleman, August 26, 1953, New York, NY.

15. Bowman family phone interviews with author. Eva Bowman, Seattle, WA, and Polly Bowman, Santa Cruz, CA, both 1994.

16. Eugenia's journal entries dated August 15, 1937 and December 19, 1938.

17. Ziegler, Introduction to Van Trump's *Life and Architecture in Pittsburgh*, xix.

18. Written for the flap copy of Gladys Schmitt's *The Gates of Aulis* (Garden City, NJ: Sun Dial Press, 1942).

19. Merle's journal entry dated August 27, 1953.

20. Clara Eisner, Case Supervisor, City of New York , Department of Welfare to Merle Hoyleman, October 23, 1953.

21. Merle's journal entry dated December 1, 1953: "Picked up E's drawings from Balkan."

22. Esther Phillips to Merle Hoyleman, February 13, 1954, New York, NY. Shay, p. 124 has Henry Bursztynowicz, one-time Director at Pittsburgh's Arts and Crafts Center, attesting that American House was an elegant crafts shop. Shay, "Passion for Paint," 119.

23. Esther Phillips to Merle Hoyleman, March 1, 1954.

24. E. Cole, Medical Social Worker, City of New York, Department of Welfare to Director, Harlem Valley State Hospital, May 6, 1954, New York, NY, within the Institution Records.

25. Leo P. O'Donnell, Director, Harlem Valley State Hospital to City of New York, Department of Welfare, May 12, 1954. Institution Records.

26. Hemp, "Washington Mews."

27. Ashton, *The New York School*, 210–211.

28. Washington Square Show records and Monleon interview.

29. Milton Salamon, Cocoa Beach, FL, phone interview with author, 1993.

30. Rosenthal conversations. (Dorothy's recollection of Salamon's statement.)

31. Taken from Shay, "Passion for Paint," 124.

32. Ibid.

33. Ibid.

34. McDarrah, *The Artist's World in Pictures*, 10–11.

35. Merle's journal entry dated September 30, 1947.

36. Esther Phillips to Merle Hoyleman, August 6, 1955, New York, NY.

37. Esther Phillips to Merle Hoyleman, October 20, 1955, New York, NY.

38. This journal entry of Eugenia's appeared in September of 1955.

39. Wakefield, *New York in the '50s*, 117.

Chapter 18. "THAT SITUATION INDELIBLY IN OUR MEMORY"

1. Michael Duner to Eugenia and Roy Hughes, December 10, 1943, New York, NY. The Eugenia Hughes Papers.
2. Unless otherwise noted, all of the information in this chapter is taken from Evans and Gress interviews with author, summer 1993, at the Laurel Highlands Regional Theatre, Pittsburgh, PA, these interviews being the context of this chapter.
3. Shay, "Passion for Paint."
4. Ed Evans, Evans interview.

Chapter 19. "A LITTLE TIRED OF IT ALL"

1. Esther Phillips to Merle Hoyleman, November 1937, New York, NY.
2. Wakefield, *New York in the '50s*, 43.
3. Millie's notes.
4. Monleon interview with author.
5. Ashton, *The New York School*, 221 and 224.
6. Pollock as quoted in Ashton, 214.
7. Rubinstein, *American Women Artists from Early Indian Times to the Present*, 285.
8. Esther Phillips to Merle Hoyleman, August 30, 1956, New York, NY.
9. Ken Chute, of Pittsburgh, PA. visited and interviewed Milton Salamon in his home in Cocoa Beach. He took notes of this interview and forwarded them to author in 1991. The information that precedes this note in this paragraph comes from this source, from a picture that appears in Shay, "Passion for Paint," 125, from Chute's visual researching in New York City, pinpointing the church, and from Carole Evans, New York City, interview with author, May 1995. Direct quote in passage comes from Salamon phone interview, 1993.
10. Shay, "Passion for Paint," 123.
11. Salamon phone interview.
12. Rubinstein, *American Women Artists from Early Indian Times to the Present*, 284.
13. Mitchell, "Joe Gould's Secret," 640–641.
14. Wakefield, *New York in the '50s*, 157.
15. Esther Phillips to Merle Hoyleman, New York, NY, February 8, 1958.
16. Merle's journal entry dated May 16, 1957.

17. Merle Hoyleman to Sybil Barsky and husband Joe Grucci, December 7, 1957, Pittsburgh, PA.

18. Merle's journal entries dated 11 & 24 Dec. 1957.

19. Rosenthal conversations.

20. Brostoff, ed.,*I Could Be Mute*.

21. Brostoff, ed., Introduction to *I Could Be Mute,* 15.

22. Rosenthal conversations.

23. Eugenia's journal entries are not more specifically dated.

24. Rosenthal converations.

25. Carole Evans interview.

26. Rosenthal conversations.

27. Millie's notes.

28. Rosenthal conversations.

29. Evans and Gress interviews. *Phantom's Dance, a play in one act for three characters*, Edward Kinchley Evans, 1975. SEE APPENDIX

30. This scribbled notation appeared among Merle's journals.

31. Mitchell, "Professor Sea Gull," and "Joe Gould's Secret," 52–70 and 623–716.

32. Summary Page of The Eugenia Hughes Papers.

33. Accession Sheet of The Eugenia Hughes Papers.

34. Millie's notes.

35. May Swenson,"I'm One." Taken from Rozanne R. Knudsen's*The Magic Pen of May Swenson* (New York: MacMillan, 1993). Ms. Knudsen was the last partner of May Swenson and holds her collected papers, Sea Cliff, NY.

Chapter 20. "HER ENERGY MYSTERIOUSLY SOURCED"

1. Chesler, *Women and Madness,* 176–178.

2. Rosenthal conversations.

3. Shay, "Passion for Paint," 124.

4. Ken Chute, of Pittsburgh, PA. visited and interviewed Millie Silverstein in her home of Evanston, IL, in 1985. He took notes of this interview and forwarded them to author in 1991. Reflections by Millie in this chapter come from this interview unless otherwise noted.

5. Millie's notes.

6. A form letter, dated October 31, 1980, that Millie apparently sent out to a variety of places. Included among Millie's notes.
7. According to the "cover sheet" describing the agenda of the afternoon at the Center. Included among Millie's notes.
8. Virginia Roman, New York City, phone interview with author, May 1995.
9. Death Certificate of Esther Phillips, issued by The City of New York Department of Health, filed May 19, 1983, in the borough of Queens.
10. Quote that opens this paragraph is Ken Chute interview with author, fall and winter of 1991–92. A careful ordering of facts (based on the available information at the time) was done by Chute. Ken organized Merle's letters to Esther and vice versa and placed them in ordered files, just as he did with other information pertaining to Esther and his search for information about her life and art. The latter is a form letter composed around 1982 and that he sent out to a variety of places, was among such information, all forwarded to author in 1991. All other reflections by Ken in the following section come from this interview unless otherwise noted.
11. These were Merle's words to Ken. From Chute interview with author.
12. These two letters have exact date and heading missing, but are among the files of information Chute forwarded to author. Any other information in this chapter that originated with Chute were also forwarded to author and the latter will hereafter not be noted.
13. A notation in records held at the Carnegie Museum of Fine Art Administrative Library, Pittsburgh, PA.
14. Source is author's visit to museum in 1992 to view the works, chaperoned by Vicky Clark, Curator of Contemporary Art at the time.
15. Henry Adams, Curator of Fine Arts, Carnegie Museum of Art, to Ken Chute, September 10, 1982. Among the information forwarded to author in 1991.
16. Ken Chute to Henry Adams, Curator of Fine Arts, Carnegie Museum of Art. Exact date missing.
17. Included would be letters to Sybil Barsky-Grucci, October 9, 1985, to Henry Pisciotta of the University of Pittsburgh's Frick Fine Arts Department, January 26, 1986, and a Special Collections librarian at Carnegie-Mellon University's Hunt Library, February 1986.

18. Taken from Shay, "Passion for Paint," 116.

19. Ken Chute to Millie and Daniel Silverstein, August 1985, Pittsburgh, PA.

20. Nicole C. Buchlmayer, "Esther Phillips, the Reality of a Starving Artist," *Standing Room Only*, October 3, 1991: 7.

21. Ronald Dawkins, "Paintings Brighten Preschool,"*The Miami Herald*, September 9, 1986: 6BR.

22. Amy DePaul, Art Appreciation column, *The Miami Herald*, specific date unknown.

23. Ken Chute to Bruce Breland, January 27, 1985, Pittsburgh, PA.

24. Ken Chute to Barbara Phillips, February 5, 1986, Pittsburgh, PA.

25. Ken Chute to Annegreth Nill, November 30, 1987, Pittsburgh, PA.

26. Rosenthal conversations.

27. Buchlmayer, "Esther Phillips, the Reality of a Starving Artist," 7.

28. Patrick McArdle, as quoted in Buchlmayer, 7.

29. Barbara McClure, as quoted in Shay, 118.

30. Ken Chute, as quoted in Buchlmayer, 6–7.

31. Buchlmayer, "Esther Phillips, the Reality of a Starving Artist," 6.

32. Dorothy as quoted in Buchlmayer, 7.

33. Milton Weiss interview with author.

34. As well after this time, during her researching and preliminary writing, author would bring to the attention of Pittsburgh's Jewish Community Center (descendant of the Irene Kaufmann Settlement) the life and art of Esther Phillips. In the fall of 1994 they would hang a one-person show of her works, entitled "A Passion for Paint."

35. Madelon Sheedy, Curator, Johnstown Art Museum. From the catalog description of Esther's life and art, that accompanied that show.

Chapter 21. "THE INNER LIFE OF THE ARTIST"

1. Van Trump interview.

2. Dr. Leon Arkus interview with author, February 1992, Pittsburgh, PA.

3. Evan Knauer interview with author, January 1999, Pittsburgh, PA. Knauer is Pittsburgh, PA. artist, songwriter, musician, screenwriter, and filmmaker.

4. Rubinstein, *American Women Artists from Early Indian Times to the Present*, 57–158 and 193.

5. Henkes, *American Women Painters of the '30s & '40s*, 23.

6. Henkes, *American Women Painters of the '30s & '40s*, 22.

7. Rubinstein, *American Women Artists*, 233.

8. Rubinstein as quoted in Eleanor Munro, 484.

9. Esther Phillips' sister Dorothy Rosenthal, Pittsburgh, PA., phone interview with author, 1992. All quotes from Dorothy in the following passage come from this phone interview, that is, the context of this following section.

10. Shaw Marohnic interview.

11. Naylor, "Can't Find Any Fun Going Along with Mob in Life."

12. John O'Connor to Mrs. John Bowman, Pittsburgh, PA., June 1936.

13. Van Trump interview.

14. McDarrah, *The Artist's World in Pictures* , 39.

15. Gilman, *The Yellow Wallpaper.*

16. Ussher, *Women's Madness*, 148.

17. Bossange, "Suggestions Concerning the Choice of a Course in Art."

18. Reference to Via Pais, "Shapes of the Feminine Experience in Art," 52.

19. O'Donnell, Introduction to Hoyleman's *Asp of the Age.*

20. Showalter, *The Female Malady*, 5.

21. Author has been drawing on her previous experience within the mental health profession. Author found the issue of fighting stigma around mental health concerns the most significant with regard to her work as a vocational developer, as she went out to talk to potential employers of her mental health clients. This issue thus became a central force for her work within the mental health movement, one that she finds especially significant.

22. Ussher, *Women's Madness*, 297.

23. (Introductory letter) Harold J. Winters to Merle Hoyleman, November 21, 1937.

24. Evan Knauer, *Louise*, 1989. "Louise" was first performed by the band the Feral Family, in which the author is a violinist.

25. McDarrah, *The Artist's World in Pictures*, 10.

26. Harold J. Winters to Merle Hoyleman, November 21, 1937, New York, NY.

27. McDarrah, *The Artist's World in Pictures*, 39.

28. Andre Ruellan as quoted in Henkes, *American Women Painters of the '30s & '40s*, 90–91.

29. Van Trump interview.

30. Harold J. Winters to Merle Hoyleman, April 10, 1938. New York, NY.

31. Harold J. Winters to Merle Hoyleman, November 21, 1937. New York, NY.

32. Claudine K. Brown, Director of Arts Program, Nathan Cummings Foundation, "Funders' 21st-Century Focus: Community-Based Arts," *ARTSInk*, a publication of the Mid Atlantic Arts Foundation, vol. 9, no. 2 (Fall 1998): 2.

33. Louise Bourgeois, "Art Is a Guarantee of Sanity" Title of the octogenarian artist's show in Pittsburgh, Pennsylvania, fall 1998, at the Pittsburgh Cultural Trust's Wood Street Galleries.

34. Written for the flap copy of Gladys Schmitt's *The Gates of Aulis*.

35. Munro, *Originals*, 189 & 252.

36. Henkes, *American Women Painters of the '30s & '40s*, ix.

37. Munro, *Originals*, 121–128.

BIBLIOGRAPHY

Primary Source Collections, Correspondence & Documents

The Collected Papers of Merle Hoyleman. A-1 Self-Storage, North Oakland, Pittsburgh, Pa. Ken Chute, Executor. Items loaned to author for research purposes in 1991.

Esther Phillips to Merle Hoyleman. 1936–58.

The journals of Merle Hoyleman. 1936–58.

Harold J. Winters to Merle Hoyleman. 1936–38.

Merle Hoyleman to Harold J. Winters. 1936–38.

Merle Hoyleman to various other friends and professionals, including George Marion O'Donnell and Dr. Alfred M. Stanley. 1936–58.

Draft of letter Merle wrote to various friends and professionals while still in Mayview. "South Z-1A, Mayview State Hospital, Mayview, PA, July 10 to August 3, 1951."

Files that contained addresses for various personal and professional contacts, photos, and other miscellaneous information.

The Eugenia Hughes Papers. Manuscripts and Archives Section of the New York Public Library, New York, New York.

Esther Phillips to Eugenia Hughes. 1942–49. (Original letters)

The journals of Eugenia Hughes. 1937–61.

Various family, friends, and professionals to Eugenia Hughes, including Roy Hughes (her father), Regis Masson, George Knight, and H.A. LaBurt, M.D., Superintendent of Harlem Valley State Hospital.

The collection's Accession Sheet and Summary Description Sheet.

Love letters, snapshots of friends and family, and other miscellaneous information.

"Millie's Notes." Forwarded to Ken Chute, Pittsburgh, PA, 1991, and then to author in same year. Taken by Millie Silverstein of Chicago, IL, of the series of meetings with her Aunt Esther in 1980. NY, NY.

Files that include a variety of information Esther passed along about her life, her art, the Village, famed personalities, and other miscellaneous information, including direct quotations from Esther.

A form letter dated October 31, 1980, that Millie sent out to a variety of places to bring attention to Esther's art.

A "cover sheet" describing the agenda of the afternoon at the Noyes Cultural Art Center in Evanston, IL, where Millie spoke on Esther's life.

The Psychiatric Records of Esther Phillips, patient at Harlem Valley State Hospital, Wingdale, NY. Record depository now at Hudson River Psychiatric Center, Poughkeepsie, NY.

Dr. Barasch, J. "Abstract of Commitment." October 28, 1942.

Ward Notes

Doctor Visit Notes.

Various Correspondence, including Dr. Alfred M. Stanley to Merle Hoyleman and John O'Connor, Jr., Assistant Director, Carnegie Museum of Art, to Dr. Stanley. Also Vito Marcantonio, House of Representatives, 20th District, New York, to Dr. Murray Rossman, Acting Director, Harlem Valley State Hospital.

Other Collections & Documents

The Archives of American Art. New York Regional Center, New York, NY.

Records of the Washington Square Outdoor Show.

"The Washington Square Outdoor Art Exhibit Records & 74 Posters of the Washington Square Outdoor Art Exhibit." Microfilm, reel NWS1.

Hemp, William H. "Washington Mews." General Publishing Co., Limited, 1975.

Carnegie Institute of Technology College of Fine Arts and Carnegie Museum of Fine Art. *Exhibition of Paintings by Pittsburgh Artists* , Years 1932–1936. Four individual bulletins that accompanied the shows that were jointly sponsored by these two entities. 1932 publication, only, found stored at Carnegie Library, other years at Carnegie Mellon University's Hunt Library.

Carnegie Library of Pittsburgh, Music and Art Department. "Pittsburgh Artists" file. Esther Phillips.

Carnegie Mellon University (present day), Records Office archives of the College of Fine Arts. Pittsburgh, PA.

"Division of the Arts, School of Painting and Decoration." Informational publication of the Carnegie Institute of Technology, College of Fine Arts, academic year 1919–20.

Bossange, E. R. "Suggestions Concerning the Choice of a Course in Art." Publication of the Carnegie Institute of Technology, College of Fine Arts, academic year 1919–1920.

Carnegie Mellon University, Registrar's Office. Pittsburgh, PA.

"Permanent Record of Student Esther Phillips." Carnegie Institute of Technology College of Fine Arts. Date of entrance September 29, 1919.

Carnegie Museum of Fine Art administrative library. Pittsburgh, PA.

"Submissions for the Internationals."

John O'Connor to Mrs. John Bowman. June 1936. "1927–1936 Correspondence on Microfilm." Text-fiche.

Records of the Works Progress Administration Art Projects in Pittsburgh.

Death Certificate of Esther Phillips. Issued by The City of New York Department of Health. Filed May 19, 1983. Borough of Queens.

The Literary Estate of May Swenson. Sea Cliff, NY. Rozanne R. Knudsen, Executor. Holding published and unpublished writings, among other memorabilia.

Jewish Archives of the Western Pennsylvania Historical Society. Pittsburgh, PA.

Irene Kaufmann Settlement Art School informational pamphlet. December 1933.

I.K.S. Neighbors. February 13, 1927.

"Irene Kaufmann Settlement Neighborhood Art School Exhibit" handbill. May 1928.

A variety of press clippings detailing the history of Pittsburgh Jewish organizations. 1913–35.

The Pennsylvania Room Archives. Carnegie Library of Pittsburgh. City Directory. Text-fiche, p.1219, P-202, no. 65.

Historical Society of Western Pennsylvania. Biography Files. John O'Connor.

Interviews

Arkus, Leon. Director Emeritus, Carnegie Museum of Art. Consultation with author. February 1992. Pittsburgh, PA.

Barnet, William. Phone interview with author, May 1995. New York, NY.

Barsky-Grucci, Sybil. State College, PA. Phone interview with author. Spring 1992.

Bowman family. Phone interviews with author. 1994. Eva Bowman of Seattle, WA, and Polly Bowman of Santa Cruz, CA., 1994.

Chute, Ken. Interviews with author. Fall and winter of 1991–92. A careful ordering of facts about Esther (based on the available information at the time, and drawing from the Collected Papers of Merle Hoyleman) had been done by Ken since the early 1980s. This information was discussed in interviews and then forwarded to author.

Esther's letters to Merle.

Ken's interviews with Dorothy Rosenthal, Milton Salamon, Cocoa Beach, FL, and Millie Silverstein, Evanston, IL.

A form letter composed by Ken around 1982, which he sent out to a variety of places to bring attention to Esther's art.

Letters from Ken to various art professionals and Esther's family.

Evans, Carole. Interview with author, May 1995. New York, NY.

Evans, Edward Kinchley, and Glen Z. Gress. Interviews with author. Summer 1993. Laurel Highlands Regional Theatre, Pittsburgh, PA.

Hartman, Susan K. Supervising Medical Record Administrator, Hudson River Psychiatric Center, Poughkeepsie, NY. Phone interviews with author, fall 1993, and interview in Wingdale, New York, fall 1993.

Knauer, Evan. Interview with author. January 1999. Pittsburgh, PA.

Knudsen, Rozanne R. Phone interviews with author. 1994–98.

Monahan, Lois (the former Lois Naylor). Telephone interview with author. Fall 1991.

Monleon, Lenore. Interview with author. May 1995. Chelsea Antique Center, New York, NY.

Roman, Virginia. Phone interview with author. May 1995.

Rosenthal, Dorothy. Phone interview with author. 1992.

Rothsted, Phillip. Phone interview with author. Spring 1992. Pittsburgh, PA.

Salamon, Milton. Phone interview with author. 1993.

Shaw, Mary (Marohnic). Interview with author. June 1993. Marian Manor Nursing Home. Pittsburgh, PA.

Steinberg, Dorothy. Interview with author. May 1995. New York, NY.

Van Trump, James. Interview with author. February 1992. Wightman Health Center, Pittsburgh, PA.

Weiss, Milton. Interview with author. March 1993. Pittsburgh, PA.

Books/Periodicals/Other By Subject:

Esther Phillips

Buchlmayer, Nicole C. "Esther Phillips, the Reality of a Starving Artist." *Standing Room Only*, 3 Oct., 1991: 7.

Cloud, Joseph J. "Art Exhibit Awards Seem Satisfactory." *Pittsburgh Press,* 12 Feb. 1932.

——— "Pittsburgh Artists Show Good Work in 21st Exhibit." *Pittsburgh Press,* 13 Feb. 1931.

Dawkins, Ronald. "Paintings Brighten Preschool." *The Miami Herald,* 9 Sept. 1986: 6BR.

DePaul, Amy. Art Appreciation column, *The Miami Herald.* Specific date unknown. Included among Millie's Notes.

McSwigan, Marie. "Bold and Original Designs Replace Pretty Pictures." *Pittsburgh Press* , May 1932.

Naylor, Douglas. "Can't Find Any Fun Going Along with Mob in Life." *Pittsburgh Press,* 20 Aug. 1933.

Pittsburgh Sun-Telegraph Times . Art Editor.

"Associated Art Show Opens With Full House." 2 Nov. 1933. Redd, Penelope. Foreword to "Esther Phillips: Exhibition of Water Colors, Starting March 31, Warner Theatre." March 1933.

Shay, Megan. "Passion for Paint: The Life of Esther Phillips." *Pittsburgh History* 74, no. 3 (Fall 1991).

Sheedy, Madelon. Curator, Johnstown Art Museum. Catalog description accompanying a show of Esther's work. Summer 1992.

Arts

Ashton, Dore. *The New York School: A Cultural Reckoning.* New York: The Viking Press.

The Associated Artists of Pittsburgh. *The Associated Artists of Pittsburgh: 1910–1985. The First Seventy-Five Years* . Compiled, written, and designed by Teresa DallaPiccola Wood, Mary Brignano, and Richard Brown, 1985.

———*Pittsburgh Associated Artists Catalogs.* 1923, 1928–30, and 1932–36.

Brown, Claudine K., Dir. of Arts Programs. Nathan Cummings Foundation. "Funders' 21st-Century Focus: Community-Based Arts." *ARTSInk,* a publication of the Mid Atlantic Arts Foundation, 9, no. 2 (Fall 1998).

Doty, Robert. *Will Barnet* . New York: Harry N. Abrams, Inc., 1984.

Kaufmann, Edgar J. Foreword to a pamphlet detailing the "Art In Industry Contests," sponsored by Kaufmann's Department Store in collaboration with The Pittsburgh Press, 1930.

Mallett, Daniel Trowbridge. *Mallett's Index of Artists* , *Supplement.* NewYork: R. R. Bowker Co., 1940.

Marquis, Alice Goldfarb. *The Art Biz: The Covert World of Collectors, Dealers, Auction Houses, Museums and Critics*. Chicago: Contemporary Books Inc., 1991.

Mattison, Robert. "Franz Kline's Vision—Pennsylvania's Coal Region in B&W." *New Arts Program Text(s): A Literary Journal 3, no. 1.*

Saint-Gaudens, Homer. *The American Artist and His Times*. New York:Dodd, Mead and Co., 1941.

Arts/Women

Henkes, Robert. *American Women Painters of the '30s & '40s: The Lives and Work of Ten Artists*. Jefferson, NC: McFarland and Co. Publ., 1991.

Munro, Eleanor. *Originals: American Women Artists*. New York: Simon and Schuster, 1979.

Rubinstein, Charlotte Streifer. *American Women Artists from Early Indian Times to the Present*. Boston: G. K. Hall & Co. and New York: Avon Books, 1982.

Slatkin, Wendy. *Women Artists in History, From Antiquity to the 20th Century.* 2nd ed. Englewood Cliffs, NJ: Prentice-Hall, 1990.

Stimpson, Catharine R. Introduction to Kenneth W. Wheeler and Virginia Lee Lussier's *Women, the Arts & the 1920s in Paris and New York*. New Brunswick, NJ: Transaction Books, 1982.

Via Pais, Sara. "Shapes of the Feminine Experience in Art." In Kenneth W. Wheeler and Virginia Lee Lussier's *Women, the Arts & the 1920s in Paris and New York*. New Brunswick, NJ: Transaction Books, 1982.

Wheeler, Kenneth W., and Virginia Lee Lussier, eds. *Women, the Arts & the 1920s in Paris and New York*. New Brunswick, NJ: Transaction Books, 1982.

Arts/Village

Fred W. McDarrah, with text by Gloria S. McDarrah, *The Artist's World in Pictures—The Photo Classic that Documents The New York School Action Painters.* New York: Shapolsky Publishers, 1988.

Mitchell, Joseph. "Professor Sea Gull," and "Joe Gould's Secret." In *Up In The Old Hotel, And Other Stories.* New York: Pantheon Books, 1992: 52–70 and 623–716. The stories in this book were originally published in a somewhat different form in *The New Yorker*; 1951, 1964, 1979, 1992.

Wakefield, Dan. *New York in the '50s*. Boston: Houghton Mifflin, 1992.

Mental Illness

Adamson, Edward. *Art As Healing*. London: Coventure, Ltd., 1990.

English, O. Spurgeon, and Stuart M. Finch. *Introduction to Psychiatry*. New York: W. W. Norton and Company, 1954.

Laing, R. D. *The Politics of Experience* . Harmondsworth: Penguin, 1967. As quoted from Ussher's *Women's Madness: Misogyny or Mental Illness?* Amherst: University of Massachusetts Press, 1992.

Rowe, D. "A Gene For Depression? Who Are We Kidding?" *Changes* 8911990: 15. As quoted from Jane Ussher's *Women's Madness: Misogyny or Mental Illness?* Amherst: University of Massachusetts Press, 1992.

Szasz, Thomas S. *The Manufacture of Madness—A Comparative Study of the Inquisition and The Mental Health Movement* . New York: Harper and Row, 1970.

Szasz, Thomas S. *The Myth of Mental Illness: Foundations of a Theory of Personal Conduct* . London: Secker Publishing, 1961. As quoted from Jane Ussher's *Women's Madness: Misogyny or Mental Illness?*Amherst: University of Massachusetts Press, 1992.

Wales, Byron G. "Adjustment to the Total Institution." In *The Age ofMadness: The History of Involuntary Mental Hospitalization*, ed. Thomas S. Szasz. New York: Jason Aronson, Publ., 1974.

Williams, Roger J. et al. *The Biochemistry of B Vitamins*. University of Texas, Austin. New York: Reinhold Publishing Company, 1950.

Mental Illness/Women

Chesler, Phyllis *Women and Madness* . Garden City, NJ: Doubleday, 1972.

Chesler, Phyllis. Foreword to Jeffrey L. Geller and Maxine Harris *Women of the Asylum: Voices From Behind The Walls, 1840–1945*. New York: Anchor Books, Doubleday, 1994.

Geller, Jeffrey L., and Maxine Harris. *Women of the Asylum: Voices From Behind The Walls, 1840–1945*. New York: Anchor Books, Doubleday,1994. With first-hand accounts by Margaret Starr, Adeline T. P. Lunt, Margaret Aikins McGarr, Margaret Isabel Wilson, Mary Jane Ward, Sophie Olsen, Kate Lee, Jane Hillyer, and Elizabeth T. Stone.

Gilman, Charlotte Perkins. *The Yellow Wallpaper*, 1892. London: Virago. 1988 reprint.

Hite, Shere. *The Hite Report: Women and Love—A Cultural Revolution in Progress*. New York: Knopf, 1987.

Millett, Kate. *The Loony-Bin Trip* . New York: Simon and Schuster, 1992.

Showalter, Elaine. *The Female Malady: Women, Madness, and English Culture, 1830–1980* . New York: Pantheon Books, 1985.

Ussher, Jane. *Women's Madness: Misogyny or Mental Illness?* Amherst: University of Massachusetts Press, 1992.

Other

Brostoff, Anita, ed. *I Could Be Mute: The Life and Work of Gladys Schmitt*. Pittsburgh: Carnegie-Mellon University Press, 1978.

The Bulletin Index, 26 Oct. 1946, Classifieds, Box 301-M.

Culley, Elizabeth Schmitt. "Lasting Impressions." In Anita Brostoff's *I Could Be Mute: The Life and Work of Gladys Schmitt*. Pittsburgh:Carnegie-Mellon University Press, 1978.

Curran, Ann. "Not Heaven On Earth: A Short History Of Skibo." *Carnegie Mellon Magazine* 17, no. 2 (Winter 1998): 29.

Fowler, Lois J. "The Marriage." In Anita Brostoff's *I Could Be Mute: The Life and Work of Gladys Schmitt*. Pittsburgh: Carnegie-MellonUniversity Press, 1978.

Howard, Donald S. *The WPA and Federal Relief Policy*. New York: Russell Sage Foundation, 1943.

Hoyleman, Merle. *Asp of the Age*. Self-published. "Printed from the author's manuscript in an edition of 326." 1966, Wood Printing,Toronto. With Introduction by George Marion O'Donnell.

Knauer, Evan. "Louise", 1989. First performed by the band the **Feral Family**, Pgh., Pa.

Knudsen, Rozanne R. *The Magic Pen of May Swenson*. New York:MacMillan, 1993.

Lorant, Stefan. *Pittsburgh: The Story Of An American City*. Author'sEdition. Lenox, Massachusetts: Published by Stefan Lorant, 1975.

Nin, Anais. *Delta of Venus*. New York: Quality Paperback Books. 1993.

Schmitt, Gladys. *The Gates of Aulis* . Garden City, NJ: Sun Dial Press, 1942.

Swenson, May. "I'm One." Taken from Rozanne R. Knudsen's *The Magic Pen of May Swenson*. New York: MacMillan, 1993.

Van Trump, James. *Life and Architecture in Pittsburgh* . Pittsburgh: Pittsburgh History and Landmarks Foundation, 1983. With Preface by Walter Kidney and Introduction by Arthur P. Ziegler.

Wakefield, Dan. *Island In The City* . New York: Corinth Books, 1952.

Lisa A. Miles is a professional creative artist, a violinist based in Pittsburgh, Pa. who writes original music, collaborating with theatre, film, and movement artists. She has been awarded numerous grants for her creative work. She has published prose and poetry in *Unsilenced: The Spirit of Women* (Commune-A-Key).